HARDENING
Windows® Systems

Roberta Bragg

MCGRAW-HILL/OSBORNE

New York   Chicago   San Francisco
Lisbon   London   Madrid   Mexico City   Milan
New Delhi   San Juan   Seoul   Singapore   Sydney   Toronto

The *McGraw·Hill* Companies

McGraw-Hill/Osborne
2100 Powell Street, 10th Floor
Emeryville, California 94608
U.S.A.

To arrange bulk purchase discounts for sales promotions, premiums, or fund-raisers, please contact **McGraw-Hill/Osborne** at the above address. For information on translations or book distributors outside the U.S.A., please see the International Contact Information page immediately following the index of this book.

Hardening Windows® Systems

1234567890 CUS CUS 01987654

ISBN 0-07-225354-1

Publisher
Brandon A. Nordin
Vice President & Associate Publisher
Scott Rogers
Acquisitions Editor
Tracy Dunkelberger
Project Managers
Betsy Manini, Jody McKenzie,
Janet Walden
Project Editor
Emily Rader
Acquisitions Coordinator
Athena Honore
Technical Editor
Rodney R. Fournier

Copy Editor
Robert Campbell
Proofreader
Paul Medoff
Indexer
Rebecca Plunkett
Composition
Kelly Stanton-Scott
Illustrators
Melinda Lytle, Kathleen Edwards
Series Design
Kelly Stanton-Scott, Peter F. Hancik
Cover Series Design
Theresa Havener

This book was composed with Corel VENTURA™ Publisher.

For Dian, Shelley, and Christopher.
Your smiles, good words, and deeds have been
my constant companions.

About the Author

Roberta Bragg, CISSP, M.C.S.E: Security, Security+, is a 25-year survivor of IT. From mainframes to mobile systems, punch cards to .NET, dial-up to Internet, she's been there and lived to tell the tale. Current projects include high-level, short-term consulting engagements on Windows security, as well as security evangelism through monthly MCP Magazine Security Advisor columns, weekly 101 Communications Security Watch e-mail–based newsletters, and TechTarget Win2000 Security Expert Q & A columns. She is Series Editor of McGraw-Hill/Osborne's *Hardening* series—books that instruct you on how to secure your networks before you are hacked. Her company, Have Computer Will Travel, Inc., provides the medium whereby she can be your security therapist or security curmudgeon depending on her mood.

Contents

PART III   Once Is Never Enough!

Foreword

In the last three years, security has moved from being an afterthought in IT departments to being the primary priority. In this movement, not only has the need for qualified security professionals increased, but security has in fact become a core job requirement for nearly all IT administrators. Unfortunately, for most IT administrators, there are not enough hours in the day to accomplish their existing tasks, much less dig through piles of white papers, books, and web sites trying to find information on hardening Windows—especially if their organization's network uses multiple versions of Windows. If this description sounds familiar, you have picked up the right book.

In reading the manuscript, I was very impressed with how well Roberta covered hardening Windows NT 4.0, Windows XP, Window 2000, *and* Windows Server 2003. Most books only cover one or two versions of Windows, but very few cover all of them—and as a bonus, Roberta sprinkled in tips about Windows 95 and Windows 98. This, combined with her relaxed, entertaining writing style, makes for a truly unique and special security resource. (Having known Roberta for many years, I actually hear her voice come through the words as I read.)

One other area in which this book stands out is that it was written with the full realization that, while computer security is inherently about the computer, sometimes the biggest security vulnerabilities come from people. The good news is that once people are properly trained, they are the best security measure you can deploy; the bad news, of course, is that you cannot configure people through Group Policy. This book does an excellent job of illustrating the critical areas where the interaction among computers, users, administrators, and IT management can cause vulnerabilities to your network and what you can do about it now in addition to the technical aspects of configuring security.

I feel confident in saying that, by reading this book, you will be much better equipped to harden your organization's client and server computers running Windows.

Ben Smith
Security Strategist
Microsoft® Corporation

"An excellent security guide—I couldn't have written any better myself! A comprehensive, yet easily understandable reference to securing your Windows systems. A must-read for any systems administrator."

Eric Schultze,
Chief Security Architect, Shavlik Technologies
(and former member of Microsoft's Trustworthy Computing Team)

Acknowledgments

Thanks to Athena Honore, whose gentle reminders kept me on track;Tracy Dunkelberger, acquisitions editor extraordinaire and sparring partner; Bob Campbell, whose copy editing makes me sound better than I am; Emily Rader, project editor, keeper of all things; Rodney R. Fournier, technical editor and honesty keeper; and the rest of those whose names I will never know but who had some part in this production.

I'd also like to thank all of you who have sought to make the information systems of the world more secure, however you've done so. You've been a constant source of inspiration and other heartaches.

Introduction

If life as most of us knows it is to survive, we must solve the problem of securing our information systems. We must learn how to better defend those systems and how to aggressively fight those who, through careless curiosity, malicious intent, or ignorant meanderings, would work toward their destruction.

We have a big and almost incomprehensible job. We must not, however, let that deter us or prevent us from acting while we wait for some security experts to ride in and save the day. We cannot wait, we cannot hesitate—we need to act now. We have to work together and alone to engender a culture of security, harden all of the components of our networks, build more securable systems, train our people. If you have anything to do with IT, you must take responsibility. The *Hardening* series, of which this book is a member, can help. Each book takes a component of information systems and lays out the plan for it.

This book provides a master list of necessary steps for hardening Windows systems. It speaks to Windows 98, Windows 95, Windows NT 4.0, Windows 2000, Windows XP, and Windows

Server 2003. It is not meant to be a comprehensive guide to information security, nor even the only information you will ever need in order to understand and practice Windows security. It is, however, straightforward and detailed. Each hardening step is accompanied by step-by-step instructions. For some
of you, it provides a place to start; for others, a checklist against which you can judge your current program; and for still others, a sound foundation in Windows security.

Read it, absorb it, use it. If you like the book, tell others. If you don't, please tell me; but most of all, however you do it, go harden your Windows systems.

Part I

Do This Now!

Chapter 1

An Immediate Call to Action

- Strengthen the Password Policy
- Lock Down Remote Administration
- Lock Down Administrative Workstations
- Physically Secure All Systems
- Keep Secrets
- Disable EFS
- Ban Wireless Networks That Don't Meet Tough Security Policy Requirements
- Don't Allow Unprotected Laptops and Desktops to Connect to the LAN
- Use Runas or Su
- Disable Infrared File Transfer

We have a big problem. We aren't doing what we need to do to secure our Windows computers. We know what we need to do; we just don't do it. This is not to say that we have all the answers. Just as there is no way to keep a determined burglar out of your house, there is no way to ever make a Windows system, or any other operating system, 100 percent secure. But we do have a lot of answers. We know what to do to prevent most types of attacks from being successful.

But instead of systematically hardening the operating system; instead of physically securing systems; instead of instilling a culture of security that includes everyone—yes, I mean everyone—in the business of security; instead of doing any of these things, we frantically patch systems and complain about insecure products. Then, when our networks are broken into and credit card data or other sensitive data is stolen, or systems damaged, we blame the problems on someone else.

Stop. Stop right now. These actions are like 14-year-old boys and girls or the extras in a grade B movie when Godzilla attacks. You're either blindly reacting, or you're paralyzed into inaction. Stop reacting, stop sitting on the fence, and start acting. Take control of information security. Moreover, note that I said information security; computers are one small part of that. You need a comprehensive plan that secures information wherever it resides: on the mainframe; in the Linux web server; in the Active Directory; on a PDA; in or available through smart phones; and yes, in the hearts and minds of the employees, contractors, partners, and customers of your organization.

We know what to do, so let's do it.

Let's change our reactive model of information security to a more proactive one. "Hardened systems are secure systems." By hardened, we mean locked down, secured, and stripped of inessentials. By systems, we mean computers, networks, and people. So how do you do this? Write the policy. Engage management in the discussion. Dig out the reference works that tell you how to secure whatever it is you have to secure, and get busy. If you have to, harden one computer at a time. Harden one concept at a time. Harden one person at a time. If you don't have the authority to harden something, find out what you need to do to get the authority. If you don't know what to do, find out. If you're afraid that what you do may cause something to fail, test it. If you are overwhelmed with the sheer size of the project you have set before yourself, get help. Ultimately, you can't do it alone anyway. Security is everyone's business, and everyone must get involved. As an IT pro, though, it's up to you to start.

Above all, mount your hardening, securing campaign in at least two directions: the big picture, and the intimate reality of your day-to-day work. Much of the cultural change that we need to make will not come swiftly or easily. It requires planning and commitment. It requires evangelists and disciples, leaders and doers, talkers and strong, silent types. Making security as easy and as pervasive as breathing will not happen overnight. But you can effect significant changes in the security posture and actual security status of your networks right now by doing things that are under your control. What you can do will depend on your authority, but we can all do things that will have an enormous impact. Here are ten things that you can do right now, this minute, that will increase security on your Windows networks.

Strengthen the Password Policy

A strong password policy can go a long way. By a strong password policy, I mean a policy that

- Insists on frequent password changes
- Requires long passwords composed of random combinations of upper- and lowercase letters, numbers, and special characters
- Does not allow blank passwords
- Checks to ensure passwords are not repeated
- Prevents the use of any part of the user's name or user ID
- Does not allow the use of common dictionary words

You can provide technical controls that require most of this functionality by configuring the password policy of the default domain Group Policy Object (GPO) as shown in Figure 1-1.

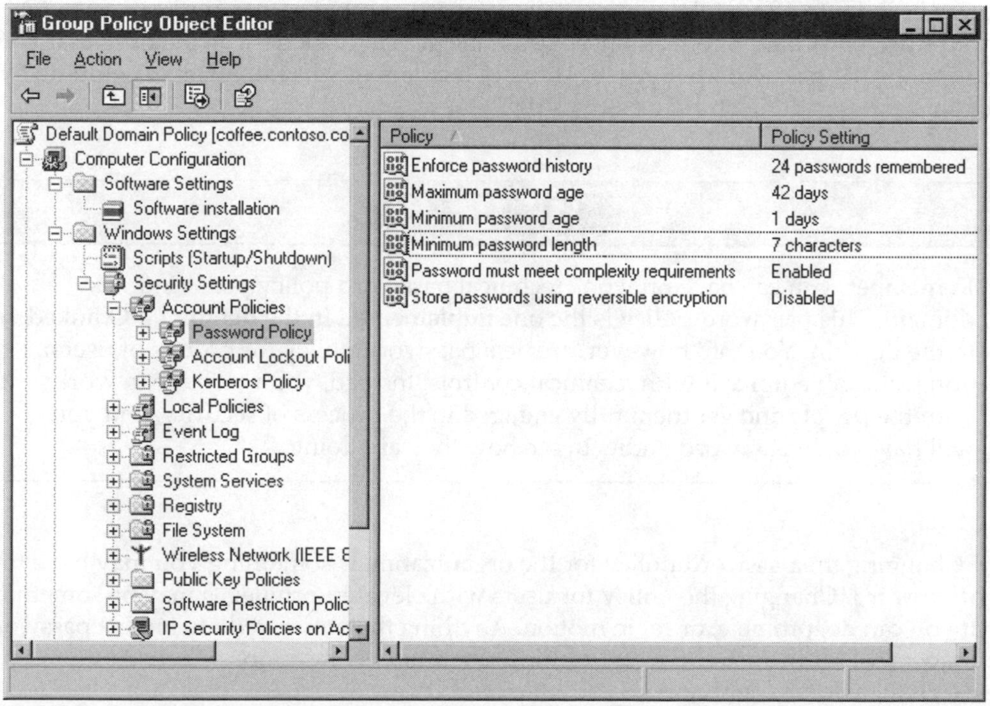

Figure 1-1.   Configure the password policy in the default domain policy.

A strong password policy is important because a weak policy makes it easier for intruders to guess or crack passwords. If passwords can be obtained, much of the security enforced by user rights, object permissions, and even file encryption falls by the wayside. Strengthening the password policy is probably the single most important blow you can strike for security.

Oh, I know that this may be something you cannot do for the whole organization. You can, of course, easily change the password policy of Windows domains. However, you may not have the authority to do so. Changing something that so broadly impacts every employee is never a move that can, or should, be undertaken lightly. Still, you should start work on it.

Meanwhile, you can, and do, have the authority to change the "logical" password policy. That is, the technical control of changes at the domain level may not be possible right away, but you can, depending on your authority, demand stronger passwords and password management by members of your own staff, by those who have local accounts on servers, and if nothing else, by yourself. While nothing may make you, or any other administrative staff member, use a 16-character password, or one composed entirely of symbols; while nothing will force you to change it every ten days; there is also nothing that says you cannot impose these restrictions by policy on IT administrators, or anyone who requires special access to servers. Examples of special access involve those who do backups, or anyone who must be an administrator on a server in order to effectively administer a database or other server application.

The accounts that, if compromised, pose the greatest risk may be the ones that you can change the password policy for. Think of the damage that an attacker could do by obtaining these administrative passwords!

HEADS UP!

Remember, you can have only one technical password policy per Windows domain. This password policy is the one implemented in the default GPO linked to the domain. You can, however, create a password policy for groups of users; you just can't enforce it with technical controls. Instead, you will have to work with the people and get them fully engaged in the process of security, and you will have to do password audits to see how they are doing.

Changing the password policy for the organization is something you may have to work toward. Changing the policy for users with elevated privileges may be something that you can do, promote, or set in motion. Anything that you can do to impact password management for the better makes your information systems more secure. At the very least, change yours, right now!

Create Logical Policies

Changing the password policy for an organization may be a rather large undertaking. If users can now use blank passwords or short ones, and if they do not have to meet complexity rules, making them comply with more restrictive rules may prove to be beyond your authority. This is something that you should evaluate, and it is really of the utmost importance. No single change can have as much impact on the security of your networks. Chapter 2 details many important issues surrounding the strengthening of password policy. Chapter 14 provides help in surmounting the political problems you may encounter.

You can, however, immediately improve the security of your networks by creating a logical password policy for a select group of individuals: those who have elevated privileges in the enterprise, in the domain, or on some systems. A prime target for such a policy are system and network administrators. IT admins and their management should be receptive to changes that will improve information security. Perhaps you can spearhead change by making the adoption of a strong password policy the result of working together to improve security. Working out ways to strengthen the policy without making it overly difficult to adhere to will make it easier to obtain and implement a stronger organization-wide password policy.

Change Policy for Local Accounts

Local accounts on servers and workstations cannot be entirely eliminated. Windows computers that are domain members retain their local account databases. Any accounts in these databases cannot be managed by the domain password policy. A password policy for these accounts should also be in place. This policy can be a very strong policy. In many organizations, local accounts are not used, with the exception of some administrative accounts on some servers. If accounts are not used, then password policies can be very restrictive; if accounts are used, then password policies should be very restrictive, and it should not be difficult to obtain approval, since many of these computers are controlled by IT.

Local password policies for NT 4.0 computers, and for those Windows computers joined in a Windows NT 4.0 domain, must be configured on the local system, or via custom scripts. Local password policies for computers joined in a Windows 2000 or Windows Server 2003 domain can be set and managed via Group Policy. Remember, password policies set at the OU level affect only the local user accounts of the computers in the OU. To use Group Policy to manage the password policy of local user accounts:

1. Place the accounts of servers for which the same password policy is required, in the same OU.
2. Create a GPO and link it to the OU.
3. Open the GPO for editing and modify the password policy.
4. Close the policy.

Change Policy for Individual Accounts

In addition to domain password policy and local password policy, changes can be made at the account level. That is, you can impact the password policy of an individual account. In many cases, changing policy at the account level is a way to prevent the weakening of password policy for the domain. Options may also strengthen policy.

For example, in some cases, it may be required to store a password using reversible encryption. This is not recommended; however, it is still better to do so for a couple of accounts, using the Store Password Using Reversible Encryption option, than it is for all accounts in the domain. Another questionable option is Password Never Expires. Expiring passwords is a way to make sure users change their passwords. Blocking this action weakens that technical control. However, if accounts are used by services, then passwords must be manually changed—the service program will not recognize or respond to reminders to change passwords and will simply be locked out when the password expires. Using the account level option allows the domain-level password policy to require periodic password changes. Incredibly, I still find domains where no user accounts are required to change passwords, because service accounts cannot.

While both of these options can weaken individual account protection, setting account level policy can strengthen protection for an individual account. For example, the option Smart Card Is Required for Interactive Logon can be set for an individual account. Long before smart cards can be installed as the primary authentication mechanism for an organization, it may be possible to require their use by administrators, or by other privileged users.

Finally, other options are temporary controls that can do much to prevent unauthorized account usage, the goal of a password policy in the first place. These options include

- User Must Change Password at Next Logon
- Account Is Disabled
- Account Is Sensitive and Cannot Be Delegated

Modify account password policy options on the Account tab of the Active Directory Users and Computers, user account property page as displayed in Figure 1-2.

Lock Down Remote Administration

If you have only a few computers to manage, you can insist on management from the local console. However, most organizations have more than a few computers to manage. You must have the ability to remotely administer systems. On the other hand, just

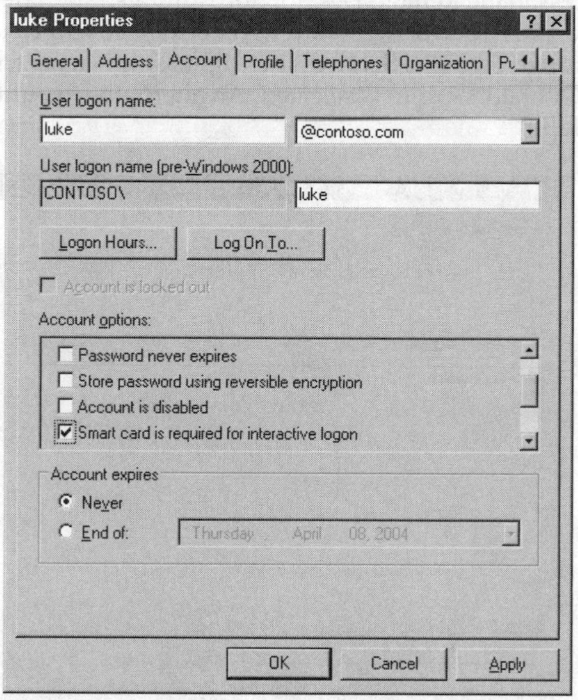

Figure 1-2. Modifications to account options impact the password policy for a single account.

because you need to remotely access a server to administer it, that doesn't mean you should leave that type of access open to anyone. Lock down remote administration.

1. Where possible, use IPSec or other protected communications. You can also use IPSec to block access to ports used by your administrative programs, and then allow appropriate administrator workstation access to the server. For example, block access to port 3389, which is used by terminal services, and then permit access to that port, but only from a limited number of computers. IPSec policies can be implemented for Windows 2000, Windows Server 2003, and Windows XP.

2. In many cases, only a few accounts need any access at all to a specific computer over the network. Lock the rest out. In Windows Server 2003 and Windows 2000 domains, use the user right to Access This Computer from the Network and the Allow and Deny Logon user rights to restrict logon.

3. Control access to the Remote Desktop for Administration (terminal services) using user rights. Control logon through Terminal Services using the Allow Log On Through Terminal Services user right as shown next. (In this illustration, the Server Operators group is selected. An alternative would be to create a custom group.)

4. Control remote access by disabling solicited Remote Assistance on servers and managing it for desktops. Remote Assistance for Windows XP and Windows Server 2003 is a tool that allows users to solicit Remote Assistance via e-mail, IM, and a file. An ordinary user can permit another user to remotely control her machine. This can be a boon to Help Desk assistance programs if properly managed. It can be a disaster if not controlled. Appropriate management includes restricting its use to authorized personnel, limiting the length of time the invitation remains open, and training all employees in the proper use of the service. To manage Remote Assistance, use the Computer Configuration, Administrative Templates, System, Remote Assistance, Solicited Remote Assistance Properties option as shown next. In the example, Remote Assistance has been disabled.

Solicited Remote Assistance Properties

Setting | Explain |

Solicited Remote Assistance

○ Not Configured
○ Enabled
◉ Disabled

Permit remote control of this computer:

Maximum ticket time (value):

Maximum ticket time (units):

Select the method for sending e-mail invitations:

Supported on: At least Microsoft Windows XP Professional or Windo...

Previous Setting   Next Setting

OK   Cancel   Apply

5. Control remote access by disabling the ability to offer Remote Assistance. This option does not require a user to solicit Remote Assistance; an offer to help can be made. (Assistance has to be approved by the user.) This option is located at the same place in Group Policy as solicited Remote Assistance.

6. Manage sensitive servers from the console. Just because the sheer number of computers to manage means you must do remote administration, that doesn't mean all servers must be managed that way. Require that computers with sensitive roles or data be administered from the console only, and enforce that by preventing administrative accounts from accessing the computer across the network.

Lock Down Administrative Workstations

Designate certain workstations as administrative workstations, computers that will be used to administer the network. Harden them. How much? Just as hard as you can. Start by putting them in a secured area and reinstalling the operating system and adding the latest service pack and security patches. Do this off the network. Use IPSec or a personal firewall to control ingress (what comes in) and egress (what goes out) and use software restriction policies to prevent the use of nonapproved software. Use the workstations only for administration—no playing of games, no e-mail.

Physically Secure All Systems

Start with your own system. If it's a laptop, do you cable-lock it at each place you use it? If you move about, even in your own buildings, do you take the time to secure it? When you travel, do you leave it unlocked in the hotel room? When you must leave the laptop in a hotel room, what data is on the hard drive? With most laptops, the hard drive can be removed even if the computer is cable-locked. The value of the data may be many times higher than the value of the computer. If data on the laptop is sensitive, perhaps you can remove the hard drive and carry it with you, or lock it in the hotel safe when you want to leave the laptop locked in the room.

What about your PDA? What's on it that would be damaging if lost? If your computer is a desktop, who can physically access it? Can it be stolen? The hard drive removed? From the data center to the traveling laptop, physical security is weak. Why would an attacker bother crafting code to break into your systems when all she has to do is steal them? Why penetrate your network defenses when she can walk by and insert a CD-ROM with malignant code on it? Or use her USB data-storing wristwatch to steal data?

Keep servers locked up. Remove CD-ROMs and floppies from computers in public areas. Provide traveling laptop users with cable locks. Make sure those with access to the data center don't allow others in. Don't prop open doors; don't allow "tailgating," the process where someone follows an authorized person into the data center. Teach security guards to look for contraband. (Picture-taking phones should be banned from many locations.)

Keep Secrets

Learn to shut your mouth. It's not rude, but a good practice, to refuse to talk about those things that might compromise security. It's one thing to share a security-hardening tip, or to alert someone to a bad practice that can be corrected. It's another thing to reveal your own systems' security weaknesses by talking about them to others. I know you would never intentionally do this, but I see and hear on a daily basis information that could be used to successfully attack other networks. You must become aware of what you are telling people or publishing to your web servers, where any one can find it by Googling on a few keywords. Think of the security of your information systems as if you were protecting your family or your country. Don't let your complaint, need to impress people with your knowledge, or request for help made to a public list reveal more than it should.

Disable EFS

Unless you have implemented a policy for the management of EFS that includes recovery procedures and key backup, disable EFS. EFS is enabled by default, but not turned on. Accordingly, it is easy for users to use the service to encrypt files without understanding how to protect themselves from data loss. EFS can be disabled in Group Policy. The local group policy, created by using the group policy snap-in and selecting the local computer, can be used to disable EFS on a single computer, while a domain-based Group Policy can be used to disable EFS for an entire domain.

To disable EFS:

1. Open the default domain GPO.

2. For a Windows Server 2003 domain:

   a. Right-click the Public Key Policies, Encryption File System policy.

   b. Right-click the Encrypting Files System folder and select Properties.

   c. Select to uncheck the Allow Users to Encrypt Files Using Encrypting File System (EFS).

3. For a Windows 2000 domain:

   a. Right-click the Public Key Policies, Encrypted Data Recovery node.

   b. In the details pane, right-click the certificate designated for File Recovery and select Delete.

   c. Right-click the Encrypting Data Recovery Agents folder and select Delete Policy.

More information on how best to manage EFS is included in Chapter 10.

Ban Wireless Networks That Don't Meet Tough Security Policy Requirements

Wireless networks can easily be implemented by users. Access points are available at low cost and can easily be plugged in to the network jack assigned to their desktop or laptop computer. Unfortunately, the default configuration on these networks has no security implemented and makes your wired network accessible to anyone in close proximity, not just authorized users. While it is possible to provide security for wireless networks, user-installed wireless access points are unlikely to have even minimal security applied.

The best policy is to ban wireless networks unless they meet the wireless access policy of your organization. Enforce this ban by including in the policy the statement that noncompliance is punishable by employment termination.

Your wireless security policy should require encryption and authentication. This can be implemented with newer wireless networks by using Protected EAP (PEAP) and 802.1x authentication. Older wireless networks should be segmented from the wired network and require the use of VPN connections to the wired network.

Don't Allow Unprotected Laptops and Desktops to Connect to the LAN

Even though network-wide patching and antivirus policies are enforced and stringently followed, an infection from some viruses and worms can be caused when users of laptop computers return them to the network. This is because these users may not have properly updated systems. If their systems become infected, they can infect others by simply connecting to the LAN. Likewise, desktop computers that have not been used for some time may lack proper patches and viral protection.

Users may bring systems from home, and contractors may also connect unmanaged, unprotected systems to the LAN. Your policies should ban these actions.

Instead of allowing these unsafe systems to connect to the LAN, establish a policy that requires their inspection and updating before their return. The policy may not be easy to enforce, as technical controls to manage connections are not widely deployed. Here are some options for managing network connections:

- **Use authenticating switches.** If a rogue computer (an unauthorized computer such as one that is brought in by an employee, a contractor, or an attacker) attempts to connect to the network, it can not authenticate and so is prevented from connecting. If you properly manage authentication, you can also disable computers taken off the network from being inadvertently connected without being updated.

- **Use network quarantines.** Segment a portion of the network to be used by mobile systems. Deny access to the rest of the network until systems are properly updated and any existing infections cleaned.

Use Runas or Su

If you have elevated privileges such as an administrative account, or user rights that extend your privileges on some or all systems, use a separate, nonprivileged account to do ordinary user activities such as e-mail, web browsing, and report writing. Many worms and viruses are spread because of simple actions such as opening an e-mail attachment. If the operating system is hardened, the malicious code may not do much harm if the user does not have elevated privileges.

The Windows NT 4.0 Resource Kit includes a tool called **su** that allows the use of a secondary logon. While logged on as an ordinary user, someone may use this tool to run applications using the security context of another user account.

Similarly, Windows XP, Windows 2000, and Windows Server 2003 provide the **runas** command. In these operating systems, the **runas** command requires the Secondary Logon service, or, for Windows 2000, the RunAs service.

Runas can be used by right-clicking the application and selecting runas (for Windows 2000, hold down the SHIFT key while right-clicking), and then selecting the alternative account and entering the password.

Disable Infrared File Transfer

By default, laptop computers and many others have infrared capability. This can be used to transfer photos from digital cameras, address books from PDAs, and files from other computers. All of these conveniences are enabled by default, and an attacker might be able to transfer malicious code to an unsuspecting user's computer by doing a file transfer.

If attempts at file transfer pop up a dialog that asks users if they want a file transfer, can you be sure that users will always answer No? You don't have to take the chance. File transfer can be disabled by selecting to disable the Allow Others to Send Files to Your Computer Using Infrared Communications check box on the Wireless Link applet in Control Panel, as shown in Figure 1-3. If users need to transfer files, they can be trained to check the box, and then uncheck it.

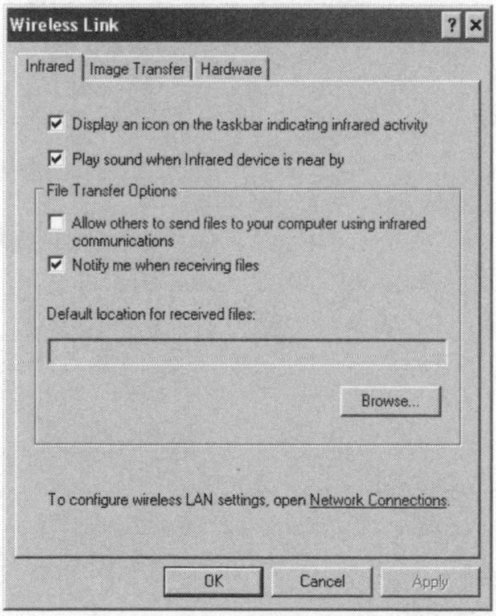

Figure 1-3.   Disable infrared file transfer.

Part II

Take It from the Top: Systematic Harden

Chapter 2

Harden Authentication—You Are Who You Can Prove You Are

- What Is Authentication?
- Authentication Credentials Choices
- Harden User Logon
- Harden Network Authentication
- Harden Computer and Services Authentication Processes

The very first control you have over your information systems is asking requesters for proof that they are who they say they are. This control, authentication, is basic to providing security. Windows systems from Windows NT up require authentication. However, without proper attention to authentication choices—without hardening—this requirement doesn't matter. To harden authentication:

- Eliminate or control anonymous access.

- Harden authentication credentials by using a strong password policy and/or smart cards, biometrics, or other two-factor authentication devices.

- Harden the attitude and practices of the people (the WetWare) who use your systems.

What Is Authentication?

Authentication is the process by which security identities prove they are who they say they are. In Windows, *security identities* may be users, groups, and computers. In addition, processes may run under the security context of special accounts, or operating system security identities. For example, prior to Windows XP, many services (background processes that run in the security context of an account) ran under the security context of the local system—a highly privileged account. Windows Server 2003 and Windows XP run many services under the security context of the Network Service or Local Service accounts, which are less privileged accounts.

When Is Authentication Required?

Anonymous access to all Windows systems is possible; however, most access to Windows NT 4.0 and above requires authentication. Both logon (the initial presentation of credentials) and access to network resources require authentication. The section "Web Server Authentication Choices" will briefly define the possible types of authentication credentials. The section "Harden User Logon" will provide instructions on how to harden the operating system by hardening all forms of logon, and how to restrict anonymous access. Windows 95, Windows 98, and Windows Millennium edition do not require authentication for access. However, their network authentication process, where they participate in providing credentials for access to network resources, can be hardened. Instructions in the section "Harden Network Authentication," in addition to providing instructions for hardening network authentication protocols, will tell you how.

NOTE   The authentication process also occurs when a user attempts to access a network resource such as a file on a file server. Any review of authentication processes for hardening purposes should consider network access as well as logon.

Authentication should guard every access to a computer, and to the resources on the network. Users are not the only security identities that touch computers and resources. Processes running on the computer and computers themselves may require access to resources and other computers. "Harden Computer and Services Authentication Processes" provides steps for hardening this authentication process.

Where Does Authentication Fit in the Windows Security Framework?

The process of authentication is, by definition, the ability to prove you are who you say you are. In Windows systems that require authentication, authentication is accomplished by providing an account name and the credentials that match those stored in an account database. Since accounts are used to define access rights and privileges on Windows systems, possession of the credentials necessary to authenticate can provide authorized or unauthorized individuals access and privileges on a system. Authorization, or what you can do once you have been authenticated, is often confused with authentication but is a separate component of the framework. It is possible to authenticate but have no ability, or authorization, to do anything. It is also possible to apply authorization controls that prevent authentication by legitimate accounts to specific computers. Authentication, or better still, the ability to authenticate, is the first component of the security framework. If a Windows system requires authentication, and if there is no way around it, then authentication is the linchpin that forms the first layer of defense. It protects and validates the authorization schemes defined on the systems. Hardening the authentication process, while not the only defensive measure necessary, is critical.

The protection provided by authentication is meaningless if other defenses are not in place. Systems can always be breached by other means. For example, a system might be booted to another operating system where the attacker can authenticate or is not required to, or the data drive or data might be moved to another computer and therefore become available. Authentication is only one component, which does rely on other security measures being in place, but it is also a key component, and one on which many other protective measures are dependent.

As you learn the lessons of hardening Windows systems, you must realize that every hardened component also depends on the hardening of the components around it. Lack of attention to physical security, for example, weakens the value of hardened authentication. Each hardened component is only as good as those around it. While this book presents instructions for hardening one component at a time, you must harden all components, in order to make the system itself more secure. Authentication sits on every edge and lives in the middle, but it is no good without the rest of the security infrastructure. Figure 2-1 illustrates the Windows security framework and authentication's place in it.

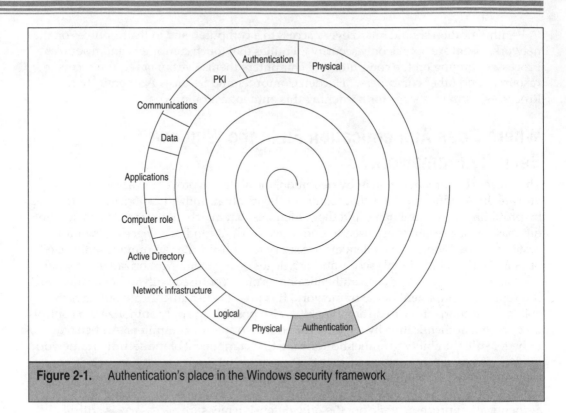

Figure 2-1. Authentication's place in the Windows security framework

Authentication Credentials Choices

The following types of credentials are available for use with the Windows operating system:

- **None** Windows systems such as Windows 3.1, Windows for Workgroups, Windows 95/98, and Window ME do not require authentication for access. Windows NT, Windows 2000, Windows XP, and Windows Server 2003 can be configured to autologon. If autologon is configured during installation, then the user of the system never need enter credentials.

- **Account and password** If autologon is not configured on Windows NT, Windows 2000, Windows XP, or Windows Server 2003, a user account name and alphanumeric password are required. (Blank passwords may be allowed.)

- **Account smart card and PINs** Some versions of Windows systems may be configured to use a smart card and PIN. Windows 2000 and later versions have built-in support for smart cards. However, this requires the implementation of

Windows certificate services in a Windows domain and third-party hardware, software, and smart cards.

- **Tokens**   Several third-party systems use tokens, hardware-based devices, or various combinations of information for authentication. An example of this type of authentication is the RSA ID.

- **Biometrics**   Third-party systems that support various types of biometric products are available for Windows.

- **Certificates**   Smart cards utilize a certificate and a related private key that reside on the smart card. However, certificates that reside in the certificate store of the computer may also be used for authentication. Examples include the use of machine certificates for IPSec, and Secure Sockets Layer (SSL) certificates for web server and web client authentication. Chapter 12 provides information on hardening Windows using certificates, and on how to harden the Windows public key infrastructure (PKI).

HEADS UP!

Windows, to many people, is Windows 98. When they think Windows, they think no authentication, no access control, everyone is an administrator, anything goes. While this attitude gets in the way of their management of Windows systems in their enterprise, or of their ability to think of Windows as securable, the opposite attitude is also a hindrance to the advancement of security.

Many Windows zealots think of Windows only as the more modern Windows systems that require authentication, provide granular access control, and include other built-in qualities that make it a securable operating system. Their attitude can get them in more serious trouble, since they may block out information that runs contrary to their prejudices, and instead of spending time learning how to best secure the entire range of Windows systems that may be on their network, they may fall into complacency and so weaken security.

Don't let your Windows tunnel vision get in the way of your security efforts.

Experts consider that the use of any system other than passwords is more secure. However, experts also agree that proper hardening of the password-using authentication process greatly strengthens it, and improper implementation of other authentication processes provides a weaker authentication system than passwords.

Harden User Logon

The first step in hardening authentication might be, "Use something other than passwords." However, if you do not understand how to harden the password authentication system, you may find the implementation of some other authentication system to be a challenge, and you may find that the result weakens, not strengthens, authentication.

HEADS UP!

One of the replacements for password-based authentication systems is biometrics. The theory is that a biometric is unique to us, and is not something that anyone can take from us. Our fingerprint, retinal blood vessel pattern, even the rhythm and pattern of how we type, can all be used as proof that we are the individual we say we are. It's only natural to assume that these unique physical characteristics are better than passwords. It is certainly hard to imagine easy ways to share or steal these things in a way in which the owner wouldn't know. However, just that type of attack has been demonstrated—a fake finger, complete with someone's fingerprint, can be manufactured from common ingredients and used to gain access to a biometrically protected system.

There are two more things to look out for when evaluating biometric products. First, look for intentional "workarounds." Workarounds may be built into systems so that owners of systems won't be accidentally and permanent locked out when the "users" are quit or fired. The workarounds are provided because "customers demand them." Unfortunately, like the knowledge of default passwords, knowledge of these workarounds gradually becomes public knowledge.

Second, look for things the producers of the biometric system forgot. For example, if the biometric product relies on keystroke analysis (in these systems, it doesn't matter if you know an administrator's password; you can't duplicate the way he types), then test the system by examining everywhere the password is entered and not just at logon. I tested a system once that appeared to work well; however, once logged on as an ordinary user, I could use someone else's password successfully when using the **runas** command. The product did keystroke analysis only at logon, not at secondary logon.

Taking the time to harden the password authentication system provides you with the opportunity to understand not only how password authentication works, but how authentication works in Windows. This information will help you harden any authentication system for Windows. Hardening user logon requires configuration of a strong password policy, hardening the people (WetWare) that create and use passwords, preventing the use of autologon, and restricting anonymous access.

Logon Types

In order to harden logon, you have to know where users are logging on and by what method. For Windows users, several possibilities exist.

- **Logon locally**   Each Windows NT, Windows 2000, Windows XP, and Windows Server 2003 or later system that is not a domain controller has its own local account database, the Security Account Manager (SAM), which resides in the Windows registry. By default, in all post–Windows NT versions of Windows, two default user accounts exist, Guest and Administrator. The Administrator and members of the Administrators and Power Users groups can add additional accounts to the local database. (Power Users cannot add users to the Administrators group, nor can they manage users who are administrators.) Users sitting at the console may use their local account and password to log on locally to the Windows computer.

- **Domain logon**   Windows NT domain controllers are Windows NT server computers installed as primary or backup domain controllers (PDCs and BDCs respectively). Windows 2000 Server and Windows Server 2003 domain controllers are servers that have been "promoted" to domain controller status. A Windows domain controller hosts a central account database. Users and computers with domain accounts use them to log on from their computer console to the domain. To do so, the user's credentials are used for network authentication. By default, Administrators and Account Operators can add user accounts to this database. (Account Operators cannot add to or manage users in the Administrators group.) In Windows 2000 and Windows Server 2003 domains, additional users or groups can be delegated the permission to add user accounts to the database.

- **Remote logon**   In addition to the logon performed when a user first attempts access to a computer or network, each network resource access request also requires authentication. If the account and password used for initial logon are valid, then the user is not prompted to enter anything additional. However, if they are invalid, either access is denied or the user is presented with a request for new credentials.

- **Anonymous logon**   Several types of connection to Windows resources may not require credentials.

Harden Accounts

Each account has rights and permissions on each Windows NT or later computer in the network based on the rights and permissions assigned to his account, or to groups that he is a member of. Take the steps that follow to harden accounts.

Disable the Guest Account

The guest account on a Windows NT 4.0 server or a Windows 2000, Windows Server 2003, or Windows XP Professional computer joined to a domain is disabled. However, the Windows XP stand-alone computer's guest account is enabled. This is because, also by default, all network-based access to the Windows XP stand-alone computer is given guest access only. Even a user with knowledge of the Administrator account and password will find that she has only guest privileges on the computer when accessing the computer remotely.

Windows NT 4.0   To check the status of the Guest account in Windows NT 4.0, follow these steps:

1. Start User Manager, or User Manager for Domains.
2. Select the Guest Account.
3. From the User menu, select Properties.
4. Check the Account Disabled button.
5. Click OK to close the property pages.

Windows 2000, Windows Server 2003, or Windows XP Professional Joined in a Domain   To check the status of the local Guest account in Windows 2000, Windows Server 2003, or Windows XP Professional joined in a domain, follow these steps:

1. From the Start menu, select Administrative Tools.
2. Click Computer Management.
3. Expand Local Users and Groups, and then select Users.
4. Double-click the Guest account to open the Guest Properties pages.
5. View the Account is Disabled check box. When checked, the account is disabled.

Windows 2000 or Windows 2003 Domain   To check the status of the Guest account for the Windows 2000 or Windows Server 2003 domain, follow these steps:

1. Click Active Directory Users and Computers.
2. Select the Users folder.
3. Double-click the Guest account to open the Guest Properties pages.
4. Select the Account tab.
5. In the Account Options box, view the Account is Disabled box. If checked, the account is disabled.
6. Click OK to close.

Restrict Group Membership

Default groups are granted privileges and permissions. Custom windows groups can also be granted privileges and permissions. Do not allow arbitrary membership in groups. Develop or follow written policies and procedures that specify how a user is granted membership in a group, how groups are granted privileges and permissions, and when users should be removed from group memberships.

Windows 2000 and Windows Server 2003 domains also provide the ability to restrict group membership via Group Policy by using the Restricted Groups policy. More information on restricting group membership is provided in Chapters 4 and 6.

Harden the Account Policy

An account/password policy is both the rules of the organization and a technical control. The technical controls available for Windows are located in the several Windows NT administrative tools and as part of Group Policy in Windows 2000 and above. Controls consist of

- **Account Policy** Password and account lockout policies.
- **Account properties** The account properties of the individual account.
- **User rights** These are broken into logon rights and user rights (what users can do once they have logged on to the system). Appropriate hardening of logon rights can enforce your written account/password policy.
- **Security options/registry entries** Some registry entries that can affect authentication/security are made directly in the registry for Windows NT 4.0. Many may be configured in the Group Policy Object (GPO).

Account Policy

To harden the account policy, use the recommendations in Tables 2-1 and 2-2. Screen shots of these policies are shown in Figures 2-2, 2-3, and 2-4.

Setting	Windows NT 4.0	Windows 2000 and Above	Comments
Maximum Password Age	Do *not* check Password Never Expires. Instead, set Expires in 42 days.	Set to 42 days.	Users must change password or will not be able to log on.
Minimum Password Age	Do *not* check Allow Changes Immediately. Instead, choose Allow Changes in 5 Days.	Set to 5 days.	Users cannot change password until the time has expired.
Minimum Password Length	Do *not* check Permit Blank Password. Instead, set the Minimum Password Length to At least 8 Characters.	Set to 8 characters.	Passwords equal to or over the assigned length are fine.

Table 2-1. Password Policy

Setting	Windows NT 4.0	Windows 2000 and Above	Comments
Password History/ Uniqueness	Do *not* check Do Not Keep Password History. Instead, set Password Uniqueness to Remember 18 Passwords.	Set Enforce Password History to 18 Passwords Remembered.	Users cannot reuse previous passwords.
Password must meet complexity requirements	N/A—there is no GUI selection for this; you must edit the registry. See the later section "Windows NT Registry Entries."	Enable.	Users must compose passwords with three of the following: uppercase characters, lowercase characters, numbers, or symbols. Passwords also cannot include any part of the user's account name.
Store password using reversible encryption	N/A	Disable.	Some third-party clients or protocols require this reduction in security.

Table 2-1. Password Policy *(continued)*

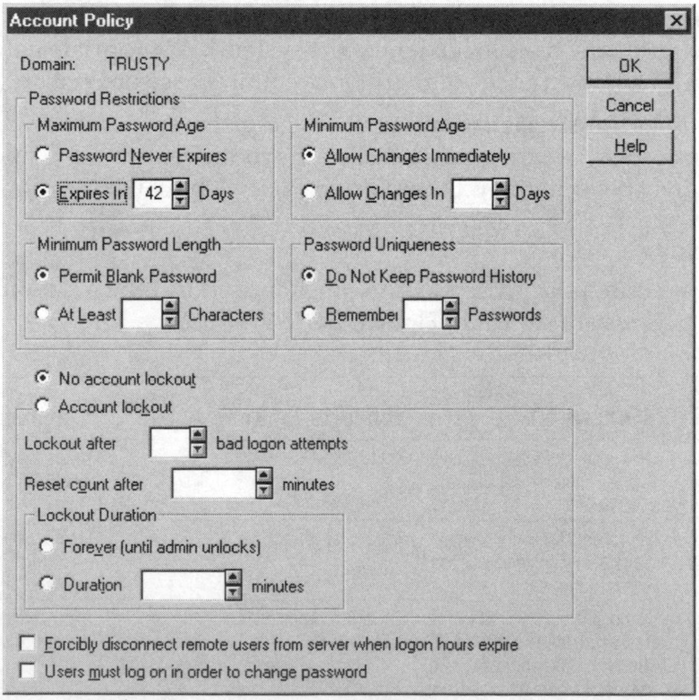

Figure 2-2. Windows NT 4.0 Account Policy dialog box

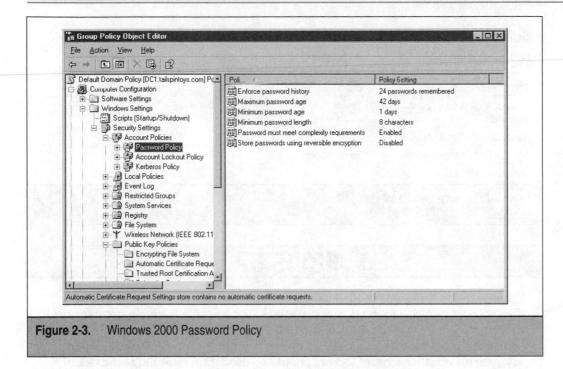

Figure 2-3.   Windows 2000 Password Policy

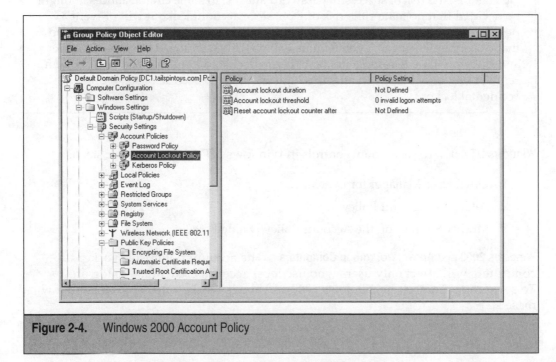

Figure 2-4.   Windows 2000 Account Policy

Setting	Windows NT 4.0	Windows 2000 and Above
No account lockout	Do not check, but see the upcoming HEADS UP! box.	
Account Lockout	Check.	
Lockout After X Bad Logon Attempts	25	25
Reset Count After X Minutes	5	5
Forever (until admin unlocks)	Do not check.	
Duration X Minutes	20	20

Table 2-2. Account Lockout Policy

HEADS UP!

When account lockout is used, it can backfire. An attacker might not be able to discover passwords using a dictionary attack, but he can effectively deny service to legitimate users as well. In addition, if the number of bad logon attempts is low, legitimate users may lock themselves out by fumbling a logon attempt. Experts disagree on whether account lockout should be used. You must judge the risk of DoS against the risk of successful password attacks. In some circumstances, it might be decided that no matter the risk of DoS, since account lockout will prevent a possible account compromise, the risk is acceptable. In others, it may be decided that closer monitoring of logon failures will provide warning of attempted attacks and therefore time to respond to them. If you decide to implement account lockout, set the number of bad logon attempts high enough, perhaps 30 or so, to prevent accidental lockout.

Windows NT 4.0   To set account controls in Windows NT 4.0, follow these steps:

1. Open User Manager for Domains.
2. Select the Account Policy.
3. Modify Settings on the Account Policy Dialog box.

Windows 2000 and Above, Workgroup Computers   The account policy for workgroup computers will affect only users who use local account credentials to log on. To set account controls in Windows 2000 and above workgroup computers, follow these steps:

1. From the Start menu, open Administrative Tools | Local Security Policy

2. Expand Account Policy.

3. Select Password Policy.

4. In the details pane, double-click the setting.

5. Enter the desired policy settings.

6. Click OK.

7. Repeat for every setting that needs to be changed.

8. Use the File menu and select Exit to close the console.

Windows 2000 and Above, Domain Policy   Configure the domain account policy in the default domain GPO. This is the GPO linked to the domain container. Only the account policies changed here will affect domain accounts. Although GPOs linked to organizational units (OUs) can contain account policies, these policies will affect only the local accounts in account databases of computers whose accounts are located in the OU. If you require different account policies for different groups of users within a domain, then no technical control can enforce these policies. Instead you must either create a domain for each unique account policy or enforce a separate policy by simply asking users to obey it and by monitoring its usage.

To set account controls in a Windows 2000 and above domain policy, follow these steps:

1. From the Start menu, open Administrative Tools | Default Domain Security Policy.

2. Expand Security Settings | Account Policy.

3. Select Password Policy to view the password policy settings in the details pane. Alternatively, select Account Lockout Policy to view the account lockout policy settings in the details pane.

4. In the details pane, double-click the policy setting you want to change.

5. Make the change and click OK to close the setting.

6. Repeat in order to change each setting.

Windows 2000 and Domain Member Computer Local Account Database   To set account controls in Windows 2000 in a domain member computer's local account database, follow these steps:

1. Place each computer account in OUs based on computer role (see Chapter 8).

2. Create a GPO for each OU:

   a. Right click on a site, domain, or OU.

   b. Select Properties | Group Policy and click New.

   c. Enter a name for the new policy and press ENTER.

3. Open the GPO in the Group Policy Editor by clicking Edit, and expand the Computer Configuration container.

4. Select Windows Settings | Security Settings | Account Policies.

5. Select Password policy to view the password policy settings in the details pane.

6. Alternatively, select Account Lockout policy to view the account lockout policy settings in the details pane.

7. In the details pane, double-click the policy setting you want to change.

8. Make the change and click OK to close the setting.

9. Repeat in order to change each setting.

10. When you are done, close the Group Policy Editor.

Harden User Logon Rights

User rights define what a user can do after authenticating to the system. User rights are granted by default to Windows built-in user groups but may also be assigned to custom groups. User rights in Windows 2000 and above may also be removed from built-in groups. User logon rights, a subset of these rights, are used to further constrain authentication. The following user logon rights exist on all computers running Windows NT and above and should be hardened:

■ **Access Computers from the Network**   Without this right, a user, even a user authenticated by the domain, cannot connect to or access the computer. Manage this right on each stand-alone computer running Windows NT 4.0 or Windows 2000 and above. To manage this right for computers running Windows 2000 and above in a domain, you may also use Group Policy. To properly use this right, consider each computer and the types of users that need to access it from the network. For example, resources on desktop computers should not be accessible over the network. To enforce this concept, removing the rights of users to access desktops over the network will prevent them from doing so, even if shares are configured on the computer. Another example of the use of this right is to restrict access to specific servers. A financial database server, for example, should not be accessible to all users; instead, a smaller group of users should be provided access. By default, Administrators, Backup Operators, Everyone, Power Users, and Users have this right. In addition to making selections based on computer use, restrict access, in general, to Administrators and Authenticated Users.

- **Log On Locally**   This right provides users the ability to log on from the computer console. Without this right, users will be prevented from logging on, even if they have valid local or domain accounts. Use this right to limit user access to computers. For example, ordinary users do not need to log on locally to servers and domain controllers.

- **Log On as a Batch Job**   This right allows logon when using a batch queue facility. Batch jobs are those that use batch files such as .bat files. In Windows XP and above, it also refers to jobs that are scheduled via the Task Scheduler. No user accounts needs to have this right assigned. It may be required by service accounts.

- **Log On as a Service**   Service accounts may be ordinary user accounts that provide the security context for background processes known as services. These accounts should be used only to run the services; no user account assigned to a person should have this right. By default, the Windows NT 4.0 group, Replicators, has this right, but no user account assigned to a person needs to be a member of that group.

In addition to these rights, Windows 2000 and above add additional user logon rights. Many of them are "Deny" rights. Users and groups are implicitly denied User Rights if the user and group accounts are not listed as having them. Use the Deny rights to explicitly deny users a right. These are additional user logon rights in Windows 2000 and above:

- **Allow Logon Through Terminal Services (XP and above)**   If Terminal Services is installed on the computer, or if the Remote Desktop Help Session (Windows XP) service is started, users may be able to use Terminal Services to log on and Remote Assistance to manage computers. (Chapters 7 and 8 explore Terminal Services and Remote Assistance.) By default, Administrators and Remote Desktop Users (Windows XP) are granted this right. Remove Remote Desktop Users unless this group is used in a managed environment to provide Help Desk employees access to desktop systems for servicing.

- **Deny Access to This Computer from the Network**   Adding user accounts and groups to this right explicitly denies them access via the network. Add the following accounts and groups: ANONYMOUS LOGON, Built-in Administrator, Guests, Support_388945a0 (Windows XP and Windows Server 2003), Guest, all non–operating system service accounts.

- **Deny Logon as a Batch Job**   Adding user accounts and groups to this right explicitly denies them the ability to log on as a batch job. Add Guests, Guest, and Support_388945a0.

- **Deny Logon as a Service**   Adding user and group accounts to this right explicitly denies them this right.

- **Deny Logon Locally**   Adding user and group account to this right explicitly denies them this right.

- **Deny Logon Through Terminal Services**   Adding user and group accounts to this right explicitly denies them the ability to use Terminal Services to log on. Add Built-in Administrator, Guests, Support_388945a0 (Windows XP and Windows Server 2003), Guest, all non–operating system service accounts.

Windows NT 4.0   To modify user rights for Windows NT 4.0, follow these steps:

1. Open the User Rights Policy dialog box, as shown here:

2. Use the Right drop-down box to select the user right.

3. To deny the selected right to a user or group, select the user or group in the Grant box and click Remove. (Users and groups that are not listed, with the exception of the Administrators group, are not present.)

4. To grant the right, click the Add button, browse to the user or group, and click OK.

5. Click OK to close the User Rights Policy dialog box.

Windows 2000 and Above   To modify user rights for Windows 2000 and above, follow these steps:

1. To grant or deny rights on the local computer, open the Local Security Policy and browse to Security Settings | Local Policy | User Rights, as shown here:

2. To grant or deny rights on domain controllers, open the Default Domain Controllers Security Policy and browse to Computer Configuration | Windows Settings | Security Settings | Local Policy | User Rights.

3. In the details pane, double-click the user right to open it.

4. To deny the right granted to a specific user or group, select the user or group and click Remove, then click OK to close the property page.

5. To grant the right, click Add User or Group and use the Object Picker to select the user or group, and then click OK to close the property page.

6. Click File | Exit to close the console.

Security Options

Security Options are registry entries that can be set through the GUI in Group Policy. Security Options therefore are generally available only for Windows 2000, Windows XP, and Windows Server 2003. Similar settings may be available through Windows NT 4.0 via registry settings. Security Options cover a large number of security settings. Windows XP and Windows Server 2003 provide more Security Options than Windows 2000. Security Options that pertain to authentication are shown in Table 2-3.

Security Option	Explanation	Recommendation
Accounts: Limit Local Account Use of Blank Passwords to Console Logon (Windows XP)	This setting recognizes that a strong password policy may not exist, especially on stand-alone computers. If it is Enabled, and a user account has a blank password, then the account can be used only for local logon. Any attempt to connect to the computer and use the account will be denied. This is important, because many computers are connected to hostile networks and this setting may prevent an attacker from connecting to the computer. This setting is enabled by default in Windows XP and should remain so, even if the password policy is set to prevent blank passwords. If the account is set to not allow blank passwords but is changed, the Security Option will prevent the account from being used for network logon.	Enable
Domain Controller: Refuse Machine Account Password Changes (Windows XP)	When a Windows NT or above computer is joined to a domain, it is given an account and password. The password is used to secure communications between the domain controller and the computer. The computer uses this account and password to authenticate to the domain when it is booted. The password is automatically and periodically changed. Computer account passwords can get out of synch if a computer is offline or the domain controller is unreachable. This can cause problems, for example, computer clocks will not be synchronized with the domain. This can cause problems for user authentication and for maintaining proper logs. However, this Security Option is a setting for domain controllers. If it is set, no domain member computer will be allowed to change its password. Enable this policy only if an entire domain cannot properly change computer passwords.	Disable
Domain Member: Disable Machine Account Password Changes (XP) Prevent System Maintenance of Computer Account Password (Windows 2000)	When a Windows NT or above computer is joined to a domain, it is given an account and password. The password is used to secure communications between the domain controller and the computer. The computer uses this account and password to authenticate to the domain when it is booted. The password is automatically and periodically changed. Computer account passwords can get out of synch if a computer is offline or the domain controller is unreachable. This can cause problems; for example, computers will not have their clocks synchronized with the domain, and this can cause problems for user authentication and for maintaining proper logs. However, this Security Option should be disabled or not configured for most network-present computers. Because the password is frequently changed, there is less chance that a rogue computer will be used to spoof a domain member computer. Computers that are offline, for example laptop computers that are carried from location to location, might need to have this parameter configured so that they do not lose connectivity with the domain.	Disable
Domain Member: Maximum Machine Account Password Age (XP)	You may be able to solve the problem of computer password changes by simply changing the frequency with which passwords are reset. If so, enable and use this policy.	

Table 2-3. Security Options That Impact Authentication

Security Option	Explanation	Recommendation
Interactive Logon: Do Not Display Last User Name (XP) Do Not Display Last User Name in Logon Screen (Windows 2000)	Enable this policy to prevent the account name of the last user that logged on , from being displayed when the next user enters CTRL-ALT-DEL. Enabling this policy prevents an attacker from discovering user names. Knowledge of a user name is important, as it is half of the information an attacker needs in order to masquerade as a legitimate user.	Enable
Interactive Logon: Number of Previous Logons to Cache (in Case Domain Controller Is Not Available)	When a user logs on, her logon credentials are cached. Cached credentials may be used to validate a user's entered password if a domain controller is not available. If cached credentials are used, domain user accounts that have been disabled may be used, since the domain controller is not accessed. Setting the number of previous logons reduces this possibility. However, if this option is set to zero and the DC is not available, no user will be able to log on. This may be desirable but is an impossible situation for traveling laptop users.	Set to 1
Interactive Logon: Require Domain Controller Authentication to Unlock Workstation	Making this setting will prevent the use of cached logons credentials in order to unlock a locked workstation.	Enable
Interactive Logon: Smart Card Removal Behavior	If smart cards are used, when enabled, this setting can be set to lock the workstation or force logoff when the user removes her smart card.	Force logoff
Microsoft Network Client: Send Unencrypted Network Password to Third-Party SMB Servers	Sends unencrypted password across the network. As far as I am able to determine, only very old third-party SMB servers require this setting.	Disable
Network Access: Do Not Allow Storage of Credentials or .NET Passports for Network Authentication	Storing network credentials removes a much needed protection. If an attacker can log on to the computer console, and network authentication is stored, he does not require knowledge of these different accounts and passwords in order to access a user's network resources.	Enable
Network Access: Sharing and Security Model for Local Accounts (Windows XP)	Two options are available. Either Classic: local users authenticate as themselves, or Guest only: local users authenticate as guest. The later option is not available on computers joined in a domain.	Classic
Recovery Console: Allow Automatic Administrative Logon	The Recovery console is used during the recovery process and requires administrative logon.	Disable

Table 2-3.   Security Options That Impact Authentication *(continued)*

To configure security options,

1. Expand the Computer Configuration | Windows Settings | Security Settings | Local Policies | Security Options node in the GPO, as shown here:

2. In the details pane, double-click to open the security option property page.

3. Enable, disable, and/or otherwise change the settings.

4. Click OK to close the property page.

Windows NT Registry Entries

Many Windows NT 4.0 registry entries can be used to add additional security. To modify the registry, run the **regedt32** command.

CAUTION In Windows NT 4.0 and Windows 2000, you must use the regedt32.exe tool when changing settings. The regedit.exe tool does provide superior searching capabilities but does not allow you to set security permissions and may not allow you to use the correct data type. Regedit.exe was developed for use with Windows 95 and does not support critical capabilities. Windows XP merges the features of regedt32.exe and regedit.exe. Using either command opens a common interface that provides all of the capabilities that you need.

Registry entries that harden authentication follow.

Password Complexity   Windows NT 4.0 service pack 3 introduced a new password complexity DLL, passfilt.dll. The use of passfilt requires password complexity, just as setting the password policy "Password must meet complexity requirements" for Windows 2000 and above does. Password complexity for Windows 2000 and above is enabled within the Password Policy and does not require a registry entry. Password complexity is enabled by default for Windows Server 2003.

CAUTION   Password complexity for Windows Small Business Server 2003 is configured after installation. An opportunity to configure a password policy is presented during the task Internet connectivity. This task adds a GPO to the domain, but a task to link the GPO to the domain container may be scheduled for a later time if selected. Be sure to enable password complexity for Windows Small Business Server 2003.

To use passfilt.dll in Windows NT 4.0, you must have at least installed service pack 3 and enter the following registry change:

1. Navigate to the following registry key:

   HKEY_LOCAL_MACHINE\CurrentControlSet\Control\LSA

2. Double-click the value Notification Packages.

3. Add the data value PASSFILT.DLL on its own line in the Multi-String Editor.

4. Click OK to exit the Multi-String Editor.

5. Close the registry editor.

Disable Caching of Logon Credential   To disable caching of the logon credential, follow these steps:

1. Navigate to the following registry key:

   HKLM\Microsoft\Windows NT\CurrentVersion\Winlogon\

2. Double-click the value CachedLogonsCount.

3. Set the value to the number of cached logons you wish to allow. A setting of 0 will prevent cached logons.

Do Not Display Last User to Log On   To avoid displaying the name of the last user to log on, follow these steps:

1. Navigate to the following registry key:

   HKLM\SOFTWARE\Microsoft\WindowsNT\CurrentVersion\Winlogon

2. Double-click the value DontDisplayLastUserName.

3. Set the value to 1 to prevent display of the name of the last user to log on.

Harden WetWare

People are the weakest link in security, but people can learn to be more sophisticated about it. The two biggest issues that concern authentication and people are the use of strong passwords and keeping the password secret. It may seem obvious that passwords should not be revealed, even to IT staff, but this is not intuitive to most users. Security awareness briefings and employee security policy documents should not only stress this concept but provide examples of the ways in which users might be tricked into revealing passwords. They should also describe the poor password management techniques that should not be used, such as writing the password down on a sticky note and posting it on the monitor or under the keyboard. Password construction should also be part of awareness training. There are techniques that can be used to create passwords that are harder to crack.

Some of these techniques may weaken security if they cause the user to write down the password where it can be easily accessed by others. They can also cause problems because using these techniques is harder. Many users have trouble with passwords, and using more complex passwords will cause them more problems. For this reason, the harder techniques to use have been separated and placed into the section "Password Techniques for Übergeeks." Users who are administrators, have other advanced privileges on the system, or have access to sensitive data should be required to use stronger passwords and can be required to use these more difficult techniques. Few of these techniques can be technically enforced by default; most will have to be enforced by making them policy and enforcing the policy.

Password Techniques for Mere Mortals

Enabling password complexity requirements will force users to compose passwords that contain three of these four options:

- Uppercase characters
- Lowercase characters
- Special characters (such as punctuation)
- Numbers

However, it is well known that users will typically take the easy way out. They will use uppercase letters at the beginning of the password and numbers at the end. Passwords such as Rbbbbbb3 are common. (What's also interesting is that the user will continue to use this strategy, changing the password only slightly each time. The preceding password becomes Rbbbbbb4, then Rbbbbbb5 and so on. An attacker who discovers the first password might easily guess the next iteration and still compromise the account.) No native technical control will prevent this type of password use. Developers of password cracking programs know this and attack these parts of the password first by testing for numbers, then capital letters. This shortens the time it takes to crack the password. To harden passwords, teach and require users to use the following techniques:

- Compose passwords that include uppercase letters and numbers or punctuation within the middle of the password. Doing so will decrease the likelihood that their password will be easily cracked.

- Compose passwords that contain all four of the options presented above. Doing so makes it harder and more time-consuming to crack the password.

- Compose passwords that use a special character somewhere in the middle of the password.

- Compose passwords based on the first character of well-known (to the user) phrases. Teach users not to use quotes that they use all the time, or that are commonly known to the user population. Company mottos, popular phrases, and statements attributed directly to the user are not good choices.

- Never use names of people, pets, sports teams, politicians, or other common information.

ONE STEP FURTHER

We all know that weak passwords weaken even the strongest security measures. Yet it is difficult to get users to compose strong passwords. Sometimes a good demonstration will help them understand why they must, and help them to create strong passwords that are not difficult to remember. One way to demonstrate this to users is to set up a dummy Windows domain controller on which you also install a password cracker. Then ask users to submit an example of a good password along with a fake user ID. Have them keep a copy of this information. Enter the user's fake ID and password in the domain controller. Then, explain to the users how a password cracker works, and run the password cracker against their fake IDs and passwords. Many of the passwords will be cracked quickly, and a lot of interest can be generated. Users will be curious to know if their password is cracked, and since you have explained how the cracker program works, they can understand why. Some users may have used strong passwords, and you might also enter some strong ones yourself. When these passwords are not cracked, find out or identify what they are and let users know.

When I have used this technique in presentations and in client meetings, it has always resulted in revised ideas about what constitutes a strong password and how users can contribute to security. When this method is used, it also provides a way of tracking how well users do in creating future strong passwords. Use the cracker program to audit passwords before the sessions on the real account database. Don't reveal the weak passwords, but do record the percentage of words cracked over time. Audit the account database a month after the demonstration to see how things have improved.

Password Techniques for Übergeeks

Those users with access and privileges beyond ordinary users should use password construction techniques to match. After all, the damage that can be done to systems and organizations if these users' passwords are cracked or discovered goes far beyond the damage that can be done by access to ordinary accounts. Here are techniques that can increase the security of password usage.

- **Use passwords 15 characters or longer.** Longer passwords are always harder to crack, but passwords 15 characters or longer have added value in an environment where the use of LM passwords (as described in the later section "LM, NTLM, NTLMv2") cannot be eliminated, or where there is any possibility that somewhere LM passwords have not been eliminated. LM passwords cannot be longer than 14 characters; using the longer password prevents the use of LM hashes for that account. No LM password hash will be stored, and no LM response can be issued to an authentication challenge. When no LM hash is available, password crackers cannot use their LM hash brute force techniques and must resort to NTLM brute-force techniques. This takes much, much longer.

- **Use certain Alt characters in the password.** Alt characters are those created by holding down the ALT key and entering a three- or four-digit number on the keyboard. Some Alt characters are translated into normal uppercase characters before being stored and therefore do not add to security. However, other Alt characters cannot be converted into normal characters. If this is the case, then these characters strengthen the password, since they cannot be stored using an LM hash. If an LM hash is not available for a password, it is much harder to crack. Examples of such Alt characters are 128 to 159. A table of other such characters is included in Chapter 3 of the Microsoft Windows 2000 Security Hardening Guide, available at www.microsoft.com/technet/treeview/default.asp?url=/technet/security/prodtech/win2000/win2khg/03osinstl.asp.

NOTE   If you use certain Alt characters in the local Administrator password, you will not be able to use the recovery console. A password that includes Alt characters also cannot be used with a DOS boot disk to install the operating system over the network.

Kill Autologon

Windows NT and later operating systems allow you to subvert the logon requirement by configuring autologon for local accounts. Autologon places a condition and a password in the registry. When the system is booted, the identified account uses the stored password to log on. The user may not be aware of the logon, as he never sees the logon screen, nor is he required to enter any credentials.

Autologon should not be configured. If it is, here's how to remove it:

1. Check the value, AutoAdminLogon at the following location:

    HKLM\SOFTWARE\Microsoft\Windows NT\CurrentVersion\Winlogon\

2. If the value is not set to 0, set it to 0 to disable automatic administrator logon.

Restrict Anonymous Access

Anonymous access is access allowed without the use of a user name and password, or other authentication credentials. Another name, used early on with Windows NT, is "Null Credentials Logon."

To log on and use anonymous access to test your restrictions, use the **net use** command.

```
net use \\servername\IPC$ ""/user:""
```

In Windows NT and Windows 2000, if this logon is used, the user becomes a de facto member of the group Everyone and can obtain access to any resource to which the group Everyone has access. Windows XP and Windows server 2003 do not include the null, or anonymous, logon in the Everyone group.

To restrict the use of anonymous or null logon in Windows NT, set the registry value RestrictAnonymous. It is located at the registry key

HKEY_LOCAL_MACHINE\SystemCurrentControlSet\Control\LSA

Set the value of RestrictAnonymous to 1 to disable anonymous access.

To restrict anonymous access for Windows 2000 and above, use the Security Options shown in Table 2-4.

Security Option	Meaning	Recommendation
Network Access: Allow Anonymous SID/Name Translation (XP)	Anyone who can connect, regardless of credentials, can submit a SID and receive a name or submit a name and receive a SID. This would allow enumeration of account names and discovery of the Administrator account.	Disable
Network Access: Do Not Allow Anonymous Enumeration of SAM Accounts (XP)	Anyone who can connect, regardless of credentials, can list the accounts in the local SAM. Knowing account names is half the information required to masquerade as a legitimate user.	Enable

Table 2-4.   Restrict Anonymous Access by Using Security Options

Security Option	Meaning	Recommendation
Network Access: Do Not Allow Anonymous Enumeration of SAM Accounts and Shares (XP)	In addition to SAM accounts, if an attacker can identify the names of shares, then he has specific resource that he can attack. This is not a good thing.	Enable
Network Access: Let Everyone Permissions Apply to Anonymous Users (Windows XP and Windows Server 2003)	The anonymous access token is not a member of the Everyone group in Windows Server 2003 and Windows XP. This prevents an anonymous user from taking advantage of the use of the group Everyone's access permissions. Enabling this setting would reverse this and weaken security.	Disable
Network Access: Named Pipes That Can Be Accessed Anonymously	Named pipes are communication portals that allow processes to communicate with other processes. Many of these pipes are used by server applications and their clients. Named pipes can be either authenticated or accessible anonymously. This list should be reviewed, as many named pipes are listed by default, and most of them are not even used by most systems.	Remove named pipes that are not used by this system. For example, the SQL\QUERY named pipe is needed only if SQL is installed on the computer. Likewise, CONMAP and COMNODE are named pipes used by the Host Integration server, a separately purchased server application that is not part of most networks.
Network Access: Shares That Can Be Accessed Anonymously	Shares are created to share resources over the network and should be protected by granting user access via share and folder permissions.	Remove COMCFG unless the host integration service is running; remove DFS$ if the distributed file system service is disabled.

Table 2-4. Restrict Anonymous Access by Using Security Options *(continued)*

CAUTION Watch out for double negatives in Security Options. For example, the Security Option may say "Do Not" and then the setting may be something you want to prevent. Enabling these settings is the correct answer. However, you might think that Disable would be correct and therefore be tricked into reducing security. For example, security experts agree that it should not be possible to anonymously enumerate SAM accounts, and you might therefore wish to disable this feature. However, the Security Option is stated as "Do not allow anonymous enumeration of SAM accounts" and should be Enabled.

Protect Passwords on Windows 2000

This additional process is necessary only if Windows 2000 computers were installed and used before the installation of any service packs. Windows 2000 computers installed and updated with service packs before use do not need to use this tool.

Use keymigrt.exe to increase security of the Windows 2000 protected store values. Windows 2000 uses the protected store, part of CryptoAPI, for Internet Explorer passwords (passwords saved by users that provide access to their accounts on web sites) and for storage of the private key. Later versions of the operating system use the Data Protection API (DPAPI). The Windows 2000 protected store default installation uses 40-bit encryption. Passwords and keys added to the store before the installation of a service pack will remain encrypted using the 40-bit keys. Passwords and keys added after the installation of a service pack will be encrypted using larger keys. To force the older values to be encrypted using larger keys, use the keymigrt.exe tool. The tool is provided with the service packs but must be extracted before use. (KB article 260219 provides more information; find it at http://support.microsoft.com/default.aspx?scid=kb;en-us;260219&sd=tech#appliesto.) Using **keymigrt** at the command line with the –**m** switch will upgrade the machine keys. Using **keymigrt** at the command line with the –**s** switch will show the current status.

Harden Network Authentication

Windows operating systems prior to Windows NT do offer logon screens and a place to store and configure user accounts for use in domain logon. However, when faced with a logon screen, any user can click the Cancel button and it will disappear, leaving the user in control of the local operating system. The password entry process is provided in order that users of the operating system can perform a domain logon that may be necessary in order to access network resources. The user who uses the Cancel button may have difficulty access network resources but will have no difficulty accessing local resources.

Windows NT and later versions do provide the ability to restrict access to local resources. Logon can be to the local computer, using a local account, or to a domain, using a domain account. Without an account and password, access to the system is denied.

Two network authentication protocols are available, depending on which Windows operating system is used, and how they are configured. The LAN Manager (LM) network authentication protocol is available in three versions. Table 2-5 lists the protocols and identifies the operating systems that use them.

The table indicates the protocols available to the operating system but only hints which protocol may be used. There are many reasons why a specific protocol may be chosen over another. Since some protocols are stronger than others (LM being the weakest and Kerberos the strongest), you should do what you can to bias selection toward the stronger protocols.

OS	LM	NTLM	NTLMv2	Kerberos
Windows 98	Yes	With AD client and configuration	With AD client and configuration	No
Windows NT 4.0	Yes	Yes	Server pack 4 and above and configuration	No
Windows 2000	Yes	Yes	If configured	Yes
Windows XP	Yes	Yes	If configured	Yes
Windows Server 2003	Yes but turned off by default	Yes	If configured	Yes

Table 2-5.   Network Authentication Protocols by Operating System

LM, NTLM, NTLMv2

The LM network authentication protocol, developed many years ago when Microsoft and IBM were co-creating an operating system, is weak, and attacks on it are often used in order to discover Windows passwords. LM is weak because

- LM does not distinguish between upper- and lowercase letters. All letters are changed to uppercase before the password hash is made. Passwords that are composed of many different types of characters are harder to crack.

- LM divides passwords longer than 7 characters into two chunks and processes each independently. An LM password can be attacked in two pieces— therefore, creating a password longer than 7 will not make the password stronger.

- LM passwords cannot be longer than 14 characters. Longer passwords are stronger passwords.

- The LM protocol uses DES. DES is a weaker encryption protocol than others.

- By default, Windows operating systems prior to Windows Server 2003 create and store an LM hash and an NTLM hash. In addition, during network authentication, LM and NTLM versions of the response to the challenge is sent. These factors make it possible to attack, and crack, account passwords by attacking the LM hash.

Much can be done to improve password security by eliminating the use and storage of LM hashes.

The NT LAN Manager authentication protocol was introduced with Windows NT. Unlike LM, NTLM does distinguish between upper- and lowercase letters. NTLM does an MD4 hash of the entire password (it does not chunk it into 7-character parts). While

NTLM can support longer passwords, the Windows NT user interface cannot accept more than 14 characters, so this is the de facto length for NT passwords. Windows versions beginning with Windows 2000 can accept longer passwords, up to 128 characters.

NTLMv2 supports the negotiation of message confidentiality and integrity. Using separate keys and an HMAC-MD5 algorithm, it can provide 128-bit encryption and NTLMv2 session security. When NTLMv2 is configured as the only allowed protocol, the LM version of the response is not sent.

Much can be done to harden authentication by requiring NTLMv2 authentication.

Mitigate Legacy Windows Lack of Authentication—Get Rid of LM

The first step in hardening network authentication is to stop the storage of LM passwords in the Windows account database. If the LM password hash is not stored, it cannot be attacked. To prevent its storage:

- On Windows 2000 post service pack 2, add the value NoLMHash to the following registry key:

  HKEY-LOCAL_MACHINE\System\CurrentControlSet\LSA

- On Windows XP and above, enable the Security Option, "Network security: Do not store LAN Manager hash value on next password change." This setting prevents new password hashes from being stored in the LM format.

- On Windows Server 2003, the LM password hash is not stored by default. Do not enable this setting.

Knowledge base article 299656 provides more information on the Windows 2000 registry setting, including the information that if you directly edit the NoLMHash value in the Windows server 2003 registry, you must enter a value of 1.

NOTE   Windows 98 users may have problems changing their password, and systems cannot be installed over the network using a DOS boot disk. (DOS does not support NTLM; LM must be used.)

Ensuring Use of NTLMv2

The second step toward hardened network authentication is to force the use of NTLMv2 where possible, and NTLM where it's not. This is important, even if you are able to prevent the storage of LM hashes, since Windows 98 will always, if unmodified, use LM in authentication attempts. If LM password hash storage has been eliminated in the network server's database, authentication will fail.

The use of LM, NTLM, or NTLMv2 is controlled by settings made in the Windows registry. The settings may be configured in Windows 2000 and above by using Security Options. The registry settings are available in Windows NT 4.0 post service pack 3 and Windows 98 after the addition of the Active Directory client. (The client is provided on the Windows 2000/2003 installation CD-ROM.) Windows 98 clients must also be using

Internet Explorer version 4.1 or above and have configured 128-bit support for IE. There are several options, and modifying these settings should not be done without testing, as it is easy to misconfigure clients and/or servers and block authentication. It is also possible that some applications on the network cannot tolerate NTLMv2, and therefore it is not acceptable to blindly configure all clients and domain controllers to use only NTLMv2. To harden authentication for Windows 98 (post AD client) and Windows NT 4.0 (post service pack 3),

1. Open regedt32.

2. Navigate to the following registry key:

   HKEY_LOCAL_MACHINE\system\CurrentControlSet\Control\LSA

3. If necessary, add the value LMCompatabilityLevel (use the REG_DWORD data type).

4. Set the value of LMCompatabilityLevel to 5 for Windows NT 4.0 domain controllers. The domain controllers will then refuse any attempts at authentication using LM or NTLM.

5. Set the value of LMCompatibilityLevel to 5 for Windows NT 4.0 servers and Workstations, and Windows 98 computers. As clients, these computers will use NTLMv2 only for authentication.

To restrict authentication to NTLMv2 in Windows 2000 and above, use the Security Option, LAN Manager authentication level. (The Windows XP and Windows Server 2003 setting is prefaced with Network Security; set it to "Send NTLMv2 response, only refuse LM and NTLM.")

Making this change is not without issues. For example, Windows NT RRAS servers cannot function when only NTLMv2 is required. If you cannot restrict all domains to use NTLMv2, at least prevent the use of LM. Table 2-6 lists the possible values for LMCompatibilityLevel.

Value	Action
0	LM and NTLM may be used, but not NTLMv2. Servers do not respond to NTLMv2. Domain controllers will respond to LM, NTLM, and NTMLv2.
1	NTLMv2 session security will be used if negotiated. Can use LM, NTLM, or NTLMv2.
2	Computers send NTLM only. NTLMv2 session security is used if supported. Servers won't use LM. Domain controllers will accept LM, NTLM, and NTLMv2.
3	Computers send NTLMv2 only and use NTLMv2 session security if supported. LM will not be used. Domain controllers accept LM, NTLM, NTLMv2.
4	Domain controllers refuse LM. Clients use NTLM and NTLMv2 session security if it is negotiated.
5	Domain controllers refuse LM and NTLM. Clients uses NTLMv2 if NTLMv2 session security is supported.

Table 2-6. LMCompatibilityLevel Values

Kerberos

Upgrade computers to Windows 2000 and above to allow the more frequent use of the Kerberos authentication protocol.

Kerberos is recognized by experts as a strong authentication protocol. Many components of the protocol were developed to specifically deal with known attacks on authentication systems. One way to think about the difference between Kerberos and NTLM is that NTLM was developed with its use on a trusted network in mind, but Kerberos was developed with its use on an untrusted network in mind. The Kerberos network authentication protocol was introduced with Windows 2000 and can be used by Windows 2000, Windows XP Professional, and Windows Server 2003 computers joined to a Windows 2000 or Windows Server 2003 domain. "Can" is the operative word. While Kerberos-capable Windows computers joined to a Windows Server 2003 or Windows 2000 domain will use Kerberos as the authentication protocol of choice, there are situations where it will not be used:

- If the Kerberos-capable Windows computer must authenticate to a Windows 98 or Windows NT 4.0 computer, Kerberos cannot be used and some version of LM or NTLM will be used.

- If the Kerberos-capable computer must authenticate to a Kerberos-capable Windows computer that is not joined in a Windows 2000 or Windows Server 2003 domain, Kerberos cannot be used and an attempt to use some version of LM or NTLM will be used.

- If a Kerberos-capable Windows computer must authenticate to a Kerberos-capable Windows computer that is joined in a domain in a different forest and there is no forest trust between the two forests, then Kerberos cannot be used and an attempt to use some version of LM or NTLM will be used.

- If a drive is mapped using the IP address of the server instead of the computer name, Kerberos is not used and some version of LM or NTLM will be used.

Other situations may exist. In addition, Windows 98 and Windows NT 4.0 are not capable of using Kerberos, so users who use them to authenticate to a Windows 2000 or Windows Server 2003 domain will not use Kerberos. While you cannot prevent the "fall-back" to LM or NTLM, you should reduce or eliminate the use of LM and require NTLMv2 wherever possible.

Remote Access Authentication Protocols

Allow only the highest level of protection by selecting only the most secure remote access protocols. For Windows 2000 and Windows Server 2003 Routing and Remote Access servers or Internet Authentication Services servers, select EAP and configure EAP-TLS if certificates or smart cards are deployed. Select EAP-MD5 if passwords must be used. Select Protected EAP (PEAP) to secure authentication for wireless clients. When access to the network is provided via a Windows Routing and Remote Access server, authentication can be hardened by reducing the number of authentication protocols that are allowed, and by requiring the use of L2TP/IPSec VPNs (L2TP/IPSec and VPNs are discussed in Chapter 11). IPSec hardens authentication because it provides for computer authentication in addition to user authentication. If the computer must also authenticate, the potential for man-in-the middle attacks is reduced, as is the use of authorized credentials (if the computer is not authorized, knowledge of an authorized user account and password is useless).

Authentication protocols are negotiated between the client and the server, so reducing the possible protocols on the server is the first step to hardening authentication. However, clients should also be configured to prevent the use of insecure protocols. This will prevent them from using a remote access server that is not hardened to these specifications. Possible protocols and their weaknesses are described in Table 2-7, which also lists some reasons you might not be able to eliminate a protocol.

Protocol	OS	Weakness	It Might Be Needed If:
PAP or SPAP	All	Clear text passwords. Messages cannot be encrypted using MPPE.	Older non-Microsoft clients need to remotely access the network.
CHAP	All	Decryptable passwords must be available. This would require Windows to store reversibly encrypted passwords in the password database. Messages cannot be encrypted using MPPE.	Older, non-Microsoft clients need to access the network.
MS-CHAP	All	Does not need to use reversibly encrypted passwords. Can encrypt messages using MPPE. Uses LM-encoded password changes and responses. Only one-way authentication (client to server). Same encryption key used for multiple connections (key based on user password).	Very old Windows clients (pre–Windows 95) or non-Microsoft clients are in use.
MS-CHAPv2	Windows 98 second edition and above	Corrects MS-CHAP issues. However, is subject to password cracking attacks.	Very old Windows clients or non-Microsoft clients are involved.
EAP	Windows 2000 and above. Some EAP types may not be available to Windows 2000 clients	Provides multiple choices for authentication known as EAP types. Use of these protocols can improve authentication. For example, EAP-TLS can be used with smart cards. Protected EAP (PEAP) can be used with wireless clients.	Pre–Windows 2000 clients are in use.

Table 2-7.   Remote Access Authentication Protocols

Remote access authentication protocols are selected from the property pages of the remote access server. If a Windows 2000 or Windows Server 2003 IAS (RADIUS) server is used, authentication may be managed from the property pages of the IAS server.

To secure authentication protocols for Windows 2000 or Windows Server 2003 Routing and Remote Access servers:

1. Open the RRAS console.

2. Right-click the server and select Properties.

3. Select the Security tab.

4. Click the Authentication Methods button.

5. Select and configure the protocols as shown here and click to deselect weaker protocols.

Web Server Authentication Choices

Web servers authentication is also hardened by configuring stronger authentication choices. The right choices for a particular web server will depend on the way the web server and its web sites are used as well as the version of Windows. There are, however, generic rules that should be followed:

■ If anonymous access is not required, eliminate this choice.

■ Eliminate any authentication method that is not required.

■ Configure SSL when sensitive information will be sent from clients to servers and vice versa.

■ Configure SSL to protect Outlook Web Access sites. The OWA site can be configured to use Basic authentication, since the entire communication will be encrypted.

■ Require SSL client certificates when application users are employees, customers, and/or partners.

■ Do not use Basic authentication unless it is protected by SSL. Basic authentication allows a plain text (non-encrypted) password to be passed over the network.

■ Do not use unprotected Integrated Windows authentication when communications will take place over an untrusted network such as the Internet. The challenge response can be captured and known password cracking attacks used to determine the password.

IIS authentication methods are shown in Figure 2-5 and described in Table 2-8.

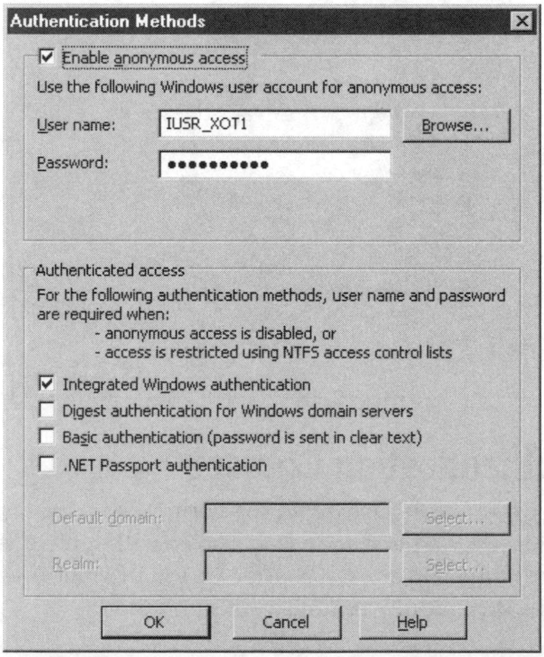

Figure 2-5. IIS authentication methods

Authentication	OS	Weakness	Required For
Anonymous	All	No accountability. Users are not identified; instead, a special account IUSR_*computername* is used. (*Computername* stands for the name of the computer on which IIS is installed.)	Web sites where public access is allowed
Basic	All	Plaintext password is used.	Non-Windows clients
Windows Integrated	All	Passwords are protected, but the response may be captured and attacked.	Protection of Windows authentication
Digest authentication	Windows 2000, Windows Server 2003	Passwords must be stored using reversible encryption. Only Windows clients can use.	N/A
Digest authentication for Windows domain controllers	Windows Server 2003 domains	Passwords must be stored using reversible encryption. Only Windows clients can use. Only users with domain passwords of the domain to which IIS belongs, or domains trusted by this domain, can be used.	N/A
.NET Passport	Windows Server 2003	A central, Internet-accessible passport server is used. If this method is selected, no other method is possible.	All web clients whose browser supports Microsoft .NET Passport can use this method
Certificates	All	SSL must be configured, and/or client certificates must be mapped to user accounts. SSL and certificate mapping are discussed in Chapters 11 and 12.	N/A

Table 2-8.   Web Server Authentication Choices

Harden Wireless Authentication

Wireless networks can introduce severe security risks to any network. Secure wireless networks by using 802.1x authentication. Wireless network security is detailed in Chapter 11.

Harden Computer and Services Authentication Processes

Computers and services also use authentication. Windows NT and later computers that are domain members have their own accounts and are subject to the authentication controls configured for the operating systems. Services require a Windows account; they use it to authenticate and use its security context when accessing resources.

Assign Strong Passwords for Service Accounts and Never Allow Users to Log On Using Service Accounts

When custom services accounts are required, they are created as ordinary user accounts and then given the privileges required. When creating these accounts, assign them strong passwords and then frequently change them. Service account passwords must be changed in two places:

- Reset them in the Active Directory Users and Computers or Computer Management dialog boxes for Windows 2000 and above, and in User Manager or User Manager for Domains for NT systems.

- Reset them in the Services logon property page, as shown here:

Service accounts should never be used by users to log on. Doing so provides the user with privileges they do not need; moreover, it makes it more likely that the account will be compromised, and an attacker may therefore obtain elevated privileges. In addition, do not use assigned user accounts as service accounts. You may find that the Administrator account or some account that is member of the Administrators group has been used as a service account password. The Administrators account should never be used. Check any account that is member of the Administrators group to ensure that it is used only by the service.

Use Local Service Accounts and Do Not Allow Service Accounts Access via the Network

If custom service accounts are required, they should be created in the local database of the computer on which they will operate wherever possible. For example, many services require only local machine access and therefore should not be created as domain accounts. Service account passwords are cached in the LSA secrets store and might be accessible to users who can physically access the computer and use cracking tools. If the service account has domain privileges, the attacker may be able to leverage his knowledge of credentials to compromise other servers in the domain.

Configure the User Right "Deny Access to this Computer from the Network" to deny service accounts network access to a computer.

Use Less Privileged Accounts for Service Accounts

Many components of the Windows operating system from Windows NT on, and of Microsoft server applications, are implemented as services. Custom services can also be written and distributed by software developers either commercially or by in-house development. Unfortunately, many of these services use the built-in local systems account as their logon account. This account is a highly privileged account. If the service is compromised, an attacker may have complete control over the operating system. The first step in hardening the services authentication process is to use less privileged accounts. This is possible when services are written to require only the privileges they need. In many cases, this may still mean that the use of the local systems account is necessary; in other cases, a less privileged account may be substituted. A good rule of thumb is to require services to be written to require only less privileged accounts.

Unfortunately, many built-in Windows services require the higher privileges, and changing the account they use for authentication will break the service. Do not arbitrarily change any service's logon account.

Windows XP and Windows Server 2003 have two new built-in accounts, Network Service and Local Service. These accounts are designed to be used in place of the local systems account. For example, the network service account is used by the DHCP client service. Insist that applications be designed to use these accounts where possible.

For all versions of Windows from NT on, ordinary user accounts can be created and provisioned for use as service accounts. These accounts should be granted only the privileges and permissions that they require.

Harden Computer Accounts

Computer accounts are assigned a complex password by the operating system, and by default, it is periodically and automatically changed. However, the change process can be modified and even disabled. It should not be, unless

- The computer is not able to participate in the change and therefore becomes disconnected from the domain. This might mean that time synchronization does not occur and that users will have trouble access network resources.

- The reason for the computer's participation problems cannot be eliminated.

Chapter 3

Harden Network Physical Infrastructure

- Segment Networks
- Provide Protection and Detection at Segment Boundaries
- Provide Protection for Critical Traffic
- Provide Protection for Critical Servers
- Secure Network Infrastructure
- Protect Access to Client Systems

ost Windows computers are connected to a network of some sort. The network under your control may only be the connection to the Internet, or it may be that of a large enterprise with thousands of networked Windows systems. No matter the size of the network, hardening the physical network infrastructure is an important part of the Windows hardening process. Four important steps to take are

1. Segment networks.
2. Provide protection and detection at segment boundaries.
3. Provide protection for critical traffic.
4. Provide protection for critical servers.

Segment Networks

Different network resources require different levels of protection. The best way to protect them is to segment the network into areas of trust. When networks are divided, two activities can increase protection for sensitive information and critical processes. First, at the boundaries between these networks you can utilize devices to filter the traffic that enters and leaves the network. Filtering can be simple blocking of traffic, or cleaning (removing attachments, for example). Second, because resources are located in a single area and partitioned, management and protection of the network can be more easily designed and accomplished.

Examples

In the simplest case, Figure 3-1, two areas of trust exist; the internal network and the rest of the world. The internal, private network becomes the trusted network, and the external, public network is untrusted. The border is protected by the addition of a firewall and other protective and detective devices. This simple, two-dimensional, trusted/untrusted network model of the world has existed for many years, and yet many small businesses and home networks today do not take advantage of it. Their networks are connected in many cases via a modem or DSL router. Their network is a distinct, separate network segment from the rest of the Internet. However, they do not use a firewall, nor otherwise restrict traffic in any way in any direction. While this is deplorable, it does provide an important lesson. It is not network segmentation alone that increases the security of your network; you must use additional mechanisms. Network segmentation is only an enabling process.

While every small, unprotected network should add a firewall, for all but the smallest of networks, the trusted/untrusted segmentation model is outdated. Two reasons for this are that today's networks do not have all of their resources located in one place, and today we recognize that network-based attacks do not all come from outside our network. Dividing internal and external components of the network into

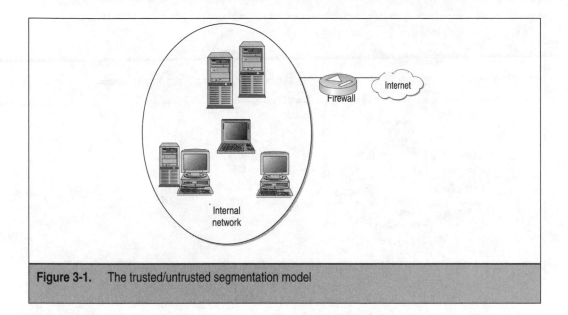

Figure 3-1.   The trusted/untrusted segmentation model

multiple areas of trust provides a better framework for protection. Possible areas of trust include

- External public networks such as the Internet
- Partner networks
- Perimeter network where servers such as web servers, that must offer connections to the outside world, exist
- Remote, organization-owned networks such as branch offices
- Remote networks such as hotels, homes, and other businesses where employees, contractors, and others with trusted access may connect from
- Internal areas of the network—financial, research, IT administration, test, development, and so forth

Figures 3-2 and 3-3 illustrate the second most common network segmentation model, the perimeter network model. This arrangement extends the trusted/untrusted model by adding a third area, or buffer zone, in which internal resources that must provide access to external, untrusted networks, are placed. The buffer area may be called a demilitarized zone (DMZ) when two firewalls segment the various networks (Figure 3-2). Another way of providing this three-network model is by providing three network interfaces on a single firewall. This model, the three-pronged model, shown in Figure 3-3, uses one interface for the external network, one for the internal, and the third for the perimeter network.

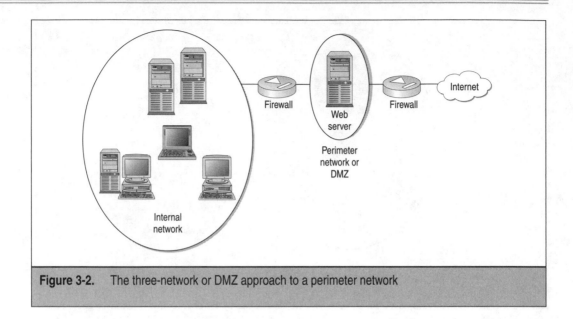

Figure 3-2. The three-network or DMZ approach to a perimeter network

While a perimeter network could also be constructed by using routers or switches instead of a firewall, the advantage of multiple segments is that gateways between the segments can provide protection by both preventing ingress (incoming) and egress (outgoing) of specific types of traffic and by filtering allowed traffic for malware.

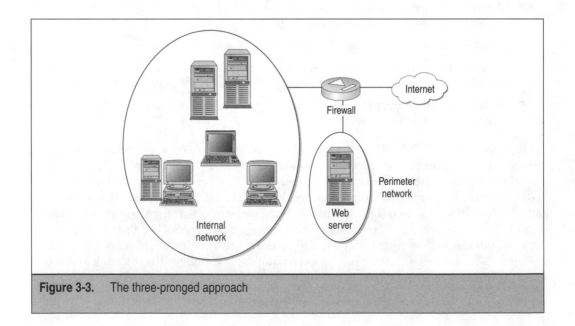

Figure 3-3. The three-pronged approach

All three of these models can be used to provide protection for the organization's assets and, if properly implemented, also protect the public network from attacks generated from within the private network. However, neither model acknowledges two simple truths:

- The connection with the public network is not the only connection with external networks that the organization's network has. There may be WAN-based or VPN-based network connections with partner networks, and with other locations that are part of the organization. Employees, contractors, and the general public may be linked via dial-up or additional network connections. Employees, contractors, and visitors may connect. Many of these connections may use additional access points to the internal network or, because they use a VPN connection, tunnel through the protection provided by the firewall. Wireless access points (wireless APs) may provide unrestricted entry points to internal networks.

- Not every trusted individual (employee, contractor, temporary worker, and so on) provided access to the internal network can be trusted to the same degree. Attacks on network infrastructure and resources can originate from within the trusted network.

For these reasons, it makes good sense to identify and control and protect all connection points to other networks and to provide additional segmentation of the internal network. Figure 3-4 provides an illustration of such a network. Note, however, that one aspect of controlling connection points is preventing them. A new connection path to another network should not be something anyone can establish. It is impossible to account for and protect all possible connection points between networks. Instead, develop and enforce a security policy that requires approval of new connections, prevents direct dial-up or Internet-based connections to and from desktops, and bans unauthorized wireless access points.

When you create clear borders between different areas of trust, border controls can be used.

Best Practices for Determining Appropriate Network Segments

The first step in hardening the physical network is determining how your network should be segmented. The following questions are designed to locate existing network segments and to provide information on which network segmentation decisions can be made.

- **Is there a connection to the Internet?**   The connection point to the Internet forms a natural choke point between the private and public networks. It's a segmentation that occurs simply by means of the connection. Create solid boundaries between the internal network and the external network. Do not allow unauthorized connections between the Internet and the internal network, but do provide protective and detective devices on the border.

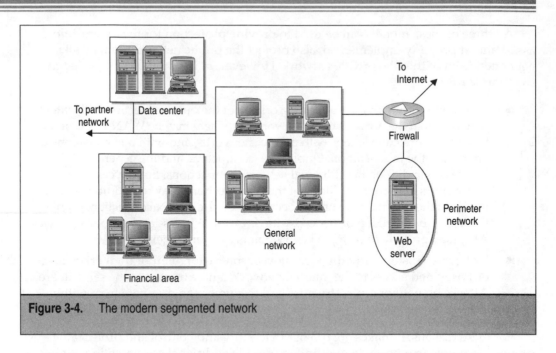

Figure 3-4. The modern segmented network

- **Are there multiple connection points to the Internet?** This can be a major source of problems. There is justification for multiple Internet connection points, such as separate connections for test networks, connections that provide increased access to bandwidth, or connections that provide redundancy in case of failure. There are also many improper possibilities. The use of modems from desktops for dial-up access to or from another computer, or the use of software intended to allow direct connections across the Internet to the desktop computer should not be allowed. Do not allow unauthorized connections between the Internet and the internal network, but do provide protective and detective devices on the border.

- **Do dial-up connections to the Internet exist?** In many organizations, additional connection points to the Internet are uncontrolled, such as desktop dial-up connections. Some of these connections not only provide the user with unregulated access to the network but may also provide external access to the desktop system. Ban casual dial-up access to and from the Internet to desktop systems. Approved remote access via dial-up remote access servers can be used if properly configured and secured.

- **What resources need connectivity from the public network?** Web servers, mail servers, and other application servers may be provided as resources to the public, or to employees, partners, and contractors who require access via the public network. These application servers are good candidates for placement in a perimeter network. Require separate perimeter networks for public, partner, and employee access. This approach recognizes the different risk levels engendered due to the different types of required access. Figure 3-5 illustrates a network with these types of perimeter networks.

- **Is there a varying level of risk dependent on the resources on the internal network?** Financial databases, employee records, customer information, and other resources may represent data that requires more protection than, say, the private intranet resources that announce company picnics or present information that is publicly available. Contain these resources in a distinct, segmented area of the network and screen access between the resource area and the rest of the internal network. Do not allow direct access from the Internet or from other public or partner networks. A separate network segment for financial resources is a good example. Employee information and test networks are others. If this model is extended, the entire internal network is divided into departmental or functional areas with appropriate border controls and rules of access. Each employee should be provided access to only the data and other resources necessary to do the job they are required to do. Where data must be available to all employees, a segment, much like the perimeter network, is provided.

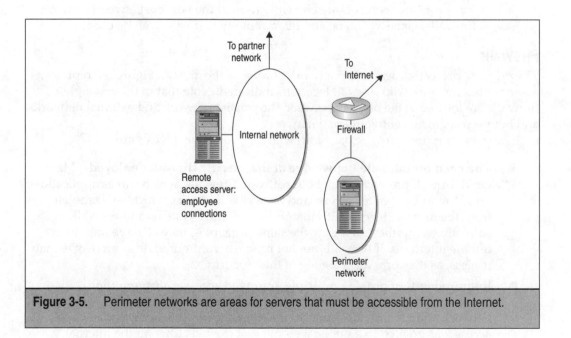

Figure 3-5.   Perimeter networks are areas for servers that must be accessible from the Internet.

Provide Protection and Detection at Segment Boundaries

It is often said today that we no longer have boundaries or perimeters to our networks. We no longer contain our digital resources at one location or even at organizationally owned physical locations. Our employees travel and must be able to connect back to headquarters. They also carry part of our information resources with them wherever they go. We must provide access for partners, contractors, and customers. We are part of a global network, the pundits say, and the old protective devices, such as firewalls, no longer have meaning because so much access must be granted. This new network, the boundaryless network, however, is not reality, unless we allow it to be.

Instead of bemoaning the status of a borderless and unprotected network, we can take control, creating hard boundaries where possible and fluid ones where it is not. We can limit connectivity to essential connectivity and to connectivity that can be protected. We can provide appropriate protection for each boundary, and we can recognize its imperfection and provide detective measures that warn of border breeches and responsive procedures that limit the losses of such breeches.

Protective Controls

Three types of protective controls are currently used at the borders between network segments: firewalls, gateway filters, and quarantine-type devices can be used.

Firewalls

The primary protective device for network borders is the *firewall*. Figure 3-6 represents a segmented network with firewall locations indicated. Note that in this example, firewalls are located at the borders between the private network and external networks, and between segments of the internal network.

Three major issues with the use of firewalls as protective devices are

- **The need for intimate knowledge of the specific firewall deployed**   Many good firewall products exist, both software firewalls, which run as applications on a Windows or other server, and firewall appliances, which are complete from the manufacturers, with their own operating systems and firewall software. While they all follow the same principles, they all have their own unique interfaces. If firewalls are not properly configured, they are worse than useless, as they provide a feeling of false security.

- **Requirements to provide multiple approved accesses through the firewall**   Originally, the firewall was used to block all access to the internal network and yet provide access to the external network from within. Next, access was granted to a public web site that existed either on the internal network or on a perimeter network. Over time, multiple applications joined the web server in requiring access from without. Since the most common (and

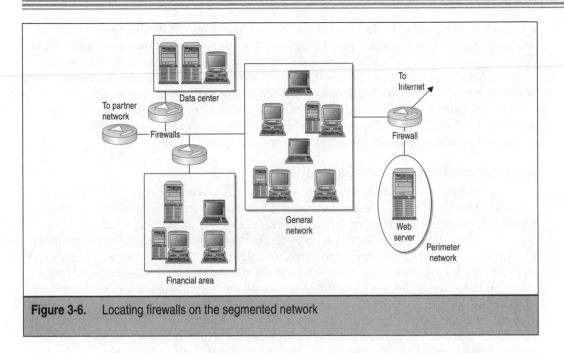

Figure 3-6.   Locating firewalls on the segmented network

correct) implementation of a firewall blocked all access, the most common way to provide access has been to simply allow access via the ports assigned to the application.

■   **The use of commonly open ports either to proxy unauthorized traffic or to provide "firewall friendly" applications and services**   The common denominator in firewall configuration has been the requirement for opening port 80 and hence allowing access to a web server on the other side of the firewall. On a simple network, only port 80 is open from the outside to provide access to the web site. Malicious individuals recognize this fact and have been successful in writing attacks that use port 80 to tunnel other protocols. Legitimate applications are written to detect what ports are open on the firewall, and then use them to obtain access. Legitimate development efforts, such as the development of web services, now utilize techniques that are built to require only port 80 access to work.

Still, firewalls can protect the network, or network segment, from many types of malicious access. Think of the use of firewalls as you do the use of locks on your house or offices. Even though a determined burglar is not deterred by door locks, you still use them to prevent many types of casual intruders from coming inside. In addition, you may select different types of locks such as dead bolts, biometrics, key cards, and other "lock" improvements. Many firewall features provide protection against common and more advanced types of attacks.

While the static firewall required acceptable ports to be open and nonacceptable ports to be closed, the *stateful* firewall maintains a database of ports that are opened only when used and remain closed at other times. By default, the responses to internal applications' requests are allowed access through the firewall. When stateful firewalls are used, a table is maintained so that legitimate responses are allowed to enter, while access requests using the same ports but originating on the external network can be denied. An *application* firewall takes inspection a step further. While basic firewall services inspect traffic and block or allow it according to the destination port, the application firewall inspects additional packet information. These firewalls contain knowledge of the format of specific application communications and can reject communications that do not meet these parameters.

Application Gateways and Gateway Filters

Application gateways are servers that block all access between networks by using two network interfaces and can be configured not to pass any traffic between networks. Instead, approved data arriving on one interface is stored on the server and is accessible from the other interface. Exceptions to this rule are the relaying capabilities of e-mail servers. Mail received at an interface might be relayed, or passed to other mail servers accessible on the other network. So, for example, e-mail sent from a mail client on the external network would be forwarded to servers on the external network. Mail arriving on the external interface might be forwarded to other internal mail servers, or relayed to other mail servers on the external network. The mail server, however, could be configured to accept only mail for which it had a mailbox, and to forward only mail it received that originated from clients with a mailbox on the server. In either case, traffic other than mail is rejected. Figure 3-7 illustrates an application gateway. Note that in this illustration, the gateway is also protected by a firewall.

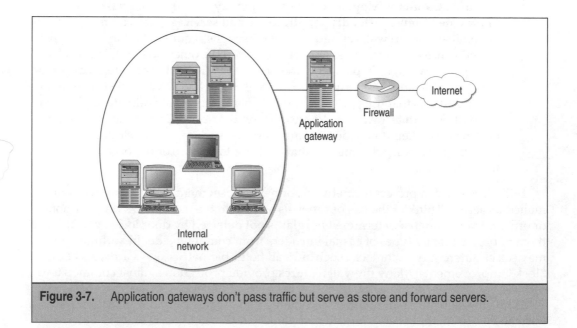

Figure 3-7. Application gateways don't pass traffic but serve as store and forward servers.

Gateway filters are devices that examine inbound or outbound traffic looking for specific types of unauthorized communications and either stripping the offending part of the communication or denying the traffic outright. Two notable examples of gateway filters are spam and virus filtering devices. Spam traffic can be dropped outright or quarantined. Intended recipients may or may not be notified. If notified, recipients can confirm the mail as spam or identify it is legitimate e-mail. In either case, typical spam filters can be configured to identify specific types of mail as spam or not spam. Virus filtering devices scan incoming traffic looking for known malware and preventing its access. They operate by comparing traffic to the known signatures, or contents of known viruses, worms, and other malware. The identified malware can be dropped, or quarantined. Some gateway filters use knowledge of normal traffic to quarantine suspected malware that is not yet identified by an explicit signature. Gateway filters should be deployed on mail servers and at other borders between external and internal networks. Figure 3-8 illustrates the use of gateway filters. In the figure, a spam gateway is located on a service provider's network. To use this type of service, all e-mail for the organization is directed to the service provider's network, where it is filtered for spam before being delivered to the organization's e-mail server. The e-mail server is shown with an on-board antivirus protection service installed.

Authentication Servers and Quarantine Devices

Public access to applications and web sites is often unauthenticated except for the possible use of a guest account. Microsoft Internet Information Server typically uses the IUSR_*nameofserver* account for this type of anonymous access. The IUSR_*nameofserver* account does authenticate to the server, but this occurs without user intervention.

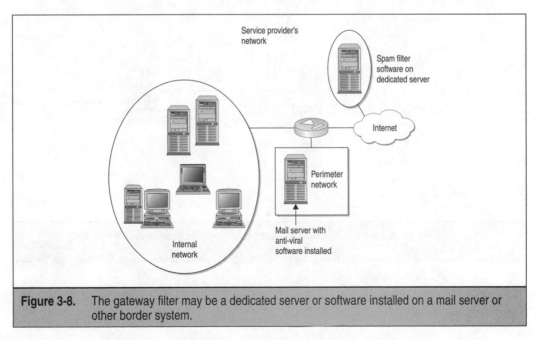

Figure 3-8.   The gateway filter may be a dedicated server or software installed on a mail server or other border system.

Access to restricted resources is controlled by some form of authentication. On the web server, authentication can take many forms; likewise, remote access via dial-up and remote access via the Internet through a remote access server have their own specific authentication protocols as defined in Chapter 11. Access to internal networks through wireless access points should also be managed through an authentication server. Wireless networks can also be protected by using wireless access points and clients that are compliant with 802.1x authentication, since this establishes a two-port–type access point. One port is used for initial connection to the AP. If authenticated and authorized, access to the internal network through the second port is allowed. Hence the network connection is quarantined until approved and properly and securely established. Additional control is possible when both mutual machine authentication and user authentication are used. Figures 3-9, 3-10, and 3-11 illustrate the use of remote access devices and authentication servers, the use of authentication servers for web access, and the use of 802.1x authentication for protecting wireless access. In Figure 3-9, several remote access servers use an IAS server for authentication and authorization; however, the IAS server uses the Active Directory as its authentication database. Without the IAS server, a member-server RRAS server will use AD for client authentication. More information on hardening remote access of these specific types can be found in Chapter 11.

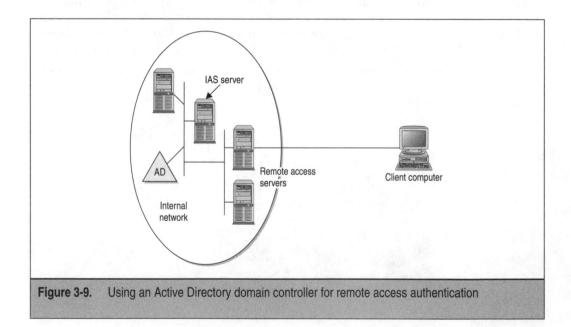

Figure 3-9. Using an Active Directory domain controller for remote access authentication

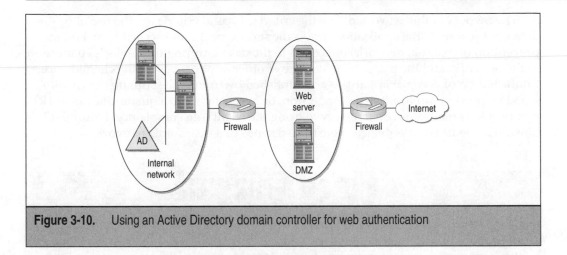

Figure 3-10.   Using an Active Directory domain controller for web authentication

A new type of border control, the network quarantine, is also available for Windows Server 2003 servers. While many network devices are now adding this capability, you can provide it through use of the native Microsoft Internet Authentication Service (IAS) by configuring network access quarantine control. Unlike traditional protective devices, which work by preventing access from or to specific networks or servers, dropping communications that use specific protocols, or filtering unwanted types of communications, the network quarantine protects networks by inspecting the device that is attempting a connection. Even if the type of communication is allowed, and even if the user and/or computer or device is authorized access, communication will be prevented, or allowed only with a special quarantined network, unless the device meets specific criteria.

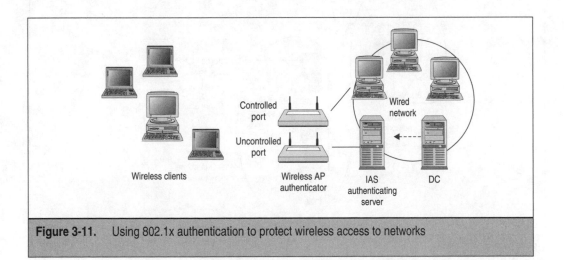

Figure 3-11.   Using 802.1x authentication to protect wireless access to networks

The owners of the network define the criteria. Typical criteria are the use of up-to-date viral scanners, the application of specific service packs and security patches, the prevention of external network connection to the device during the device's connection to the network, and the presence or absence of other applications on the client device. Confirmation of acceptable status is accomplished by running a script on the client. A failed inspection can result in disconnection, or in relegation to a quarantine network that provides the resources necessary to bring the client into compliance. Figure 3-12 illustrates the use of this device. Note the existence of a quarantine network.

ONE STEP FURTHER

Using network access quarantine control to protect the network from remote infestations by employee connections while on the road is a good idea. Take it one step further and use such a device on the internal network. When users return from trips and bring their laptop computers into the office, make them first authenticate to the network through the network access quarantine control process in order to assure laptops have all current service packs and security hotfixes, virus definitions are up to date, and so forth. This extra effort can also be used when computers are returned to active service, and before newly configured computers are allowed on the network.

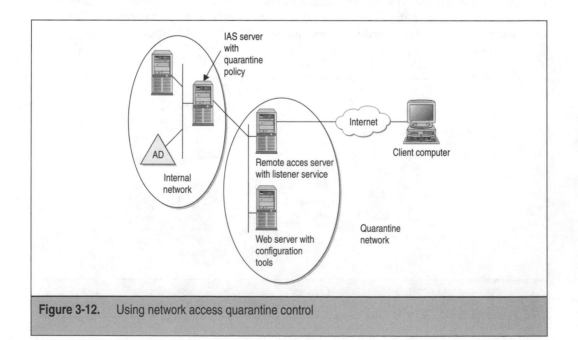

Figure 3-12. Using network access quarantine control

Use of this type of protective device can improve the overall security posture of the network by preventing the transmission of viruses and worms, as well as the possible use of a client to launch an attack from some other connection to the device. By improving the security of the clients that connect to the network, the security of the network is improved.

Detective Controls

It's not enough to provide protection at network and network segment boundaries. The detection of successful intrusions should be possible, and the response to these attacks well documented and followed. Intrusion detection can be accomplished by the use of special intrusion detection systems (IDSs) and by inspecting computer logs for records that indicate unauthorized access. Intrusion prevention and response is a natural continuation and is the basis for new intrusion protection systems (IPSs). These devices seek to detect attacks and block their access. Some can also be configured to respond by doing more.

The use of auditing and the review of logs to discover intrusion is outlined in Chapter 13. Hardening IDSs and IPSs is detailed in another book in this series, *Hardening Network Infrastructure* by Wes Noonan (McGraw-Hill/Osborne, 2004). However, some information on their location and use in the segmented network design follows.

Intrusion detection devices inspect traffic, looking for known signatures of attacks. If properly configured, and appropriately and strategically placed, they can both provide early warning of imminent attack and reveal attacks, both rebuffed and successful, while they are occurring. Two types of intrusion detection devices exist. The network IDS sits on the network, either outside the firewall or on the perimeter or internal network, and inspects all traffic as it passes from one network to the other. Figure 3-13 illustrates the

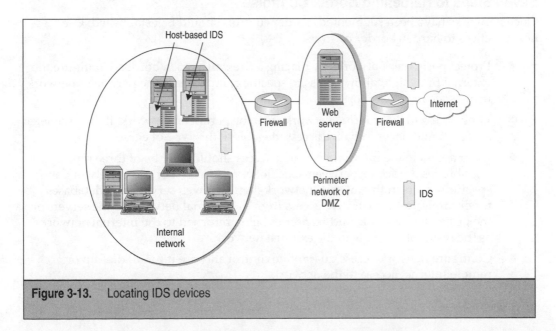

Figure 3-13.   Locating IDS devices

location of IDS devices. Host-based IDSs are installed on servers and respond only to traffic directed at the specific host. Management tools can also centrally configure and collect for analysis, traffic anomalies detected by the IDS. The main issue with IDSs is their high initial cost and the cost of keeping them correctly configured. An improperly configured IDS will have many false positives. False positives can inure responders to alerts. Without readjustment, the IDS alarms are ignored, and the system ceases to be useful.

Many IDSs, and most work done by IDSs, require the use of known attack signatures. Traffic patterns are matched against these signatures, and alerts are raised when a match is found. In many cases, this simply indicates an intrusion attempt, not a successful intrusion. An intrusion detection system can be tuned to record, but not alert on, attacks such as port scans over large ranges of ports. These types of scans occur with great frequency but typically mean little, since many automated and nondirected port scans are constantly being carried out across the Internet. Directed scans against specific ports, however, may be grounds for further investigation, and the IDS can be configured to alert on them.

Best Practices for Border Controls

Border controls are the devices and software that add protection and detection between areas of trust. A network that is not segmented offers a rich landscape for attack, since access to the network allows an attacker easier access to all of the network resources. Segmenting the network establishes borders between different areas of trust. However, without border controls, segmented networks provide little protection for the resources within them.

Seven Steps to Hardening Border Controls

Once networks have been segmented, border controls should be established. Use these best practices to harden border controls:

- Protect perimeter networks by placing a firewall at each border. Configure the external firewall to allow access to specific computers in the perimeter network using specific access ports.

- Limit access to the external network from the perimeter network. If the perimeter server should never initialize access, then block this type of egress.

- Limit access to the internal network. Access should only be of three types. Possibilities are access between specific servers in the perimeter network and specific servers in the internal network (between web servers and databases, for example), administrative access from the internal network to the servers on the perimeter network, and responses being returned to the internal network as the result of requests to the external network.

- Configure network access quarantine control and use it for all dial-up or remote Internet access to the network.

- Prevent the use of dial-up connections from or to the desktop. Ban the use of modems from inside your network unless required for specific server applications.

- Ban the use of services that connect directly to desktop systems from the Internet. This includes services that penetrate the firewall using port 80 traffic, such as "My PC" and unmanaged Internet messaging services.

- Provide border controls for segmented internal networks. Place a firewall, for example, between the finance network and the general network, and between human resources and the general network. Correctly configure the firewall to block specific types of traffic, and prevent normal access to critical and sensitive servers within the network.

Harden Internet Security and Acceleration (ISA) Server

This book is not a tutorial on hardening firewalls. However, especially since two Microsoft firewalls are available for use, some instruction in firewall hardening technique is useful whether you use these firewalls or third-party alternatives. Most important, when using application-based firewalls, particular attention must be paid to hardening the host computer on which the firewall will be run. The instructions that follow do not include all of the steps necessary to implement an ISA Server firewall; instead, they cover best practices for installation and configuration of a simple firewall host. Best practices for restricting access both to and from the Internet are given. For more explicit advice on firewall hardening, see the series book referenced earlier in this chapter, *Hardening Network Infrastructure*. For information on hardening the Microsoft personal firewall, the Internet Connection Firewall (ICF), see Chapter 8.

ISA Server is an application-based firewall that must be installed on a Windows 2000 or Windows Server 2003 server. Use the following steps to harden the ISA server:

1. Install Windows on a server that is not connected to any network. Apply all service packs and security patches and harden as per general hardening instructions provided in this book. Do not install IIS on the server.

2. Provide at least two network interfaces for the ISA server. This can be a combination of an internal network connection and a dial-up connection if the dial-up connection is the connection to the external network. It can also be a combination of internal and external network interfaces using network interface cards. Configure the network interfaces as described in the later section "Configure Network Interfaces."

3. Two versions of ISA Server are available: a Standard version that cannot be integrated with Active Directory and an Enterprise version that can. Use secure installation practices. If the standard version will be used, install ISA Server while the server is still unconnected to any network. Alternatively, if ISA Server will be integrated with Active Directory, make sure that the Windows server is connected via the internal interface to a network where it can connect

with a domain controller during installation. The external interface should not be connected at this time.

4. Install the ISA server as a stand-alone server, or as a server integrated with Active Directory. Integrating the server with Active Directory offers many advantages, including the ability to manage one firewall configuration profile over multiple firewalls, and the ability to use Active Directory accounts for authenticated access to the Internet and authenticated access to resources accessible through the ISA server. ISA servers integrated with Active Directory are installed into ISA server arrays. (Prior to ISA Server installation, support for integration must be provided by updating the Active Directory schema using software provided on the ISA Server installation CD-ROM.)

HEADS UP!

When you install ISA Server, all access to the Internet is blocked. This is by design. ISA Server follows the principle of making sure that all access is blocked by default, and only the access you define is allowed. This principle is followed by most firewalls; however, some do not block requests from the internal network to the Internet. ISA Server does. Do not implement practices that allow unfettered access in either direction. Do require specific definitions for what is allowed, and what is not, then implement it.

5. Select and install only the ISA Server services desired. ISA Server can be configured to be a proxy server or a firewall or both. It can also be configured to provide access to H.323 resources such as ILS servers and Net Meeting or to provide message-screening services for an internal Exchange server. Only the services that will be used should be installed.

6. When prompted, select the internal network interface and configure the local address table (LAT). The LAT is a list of the network subnets that exist on the internal network. By default, the private address ranges will be added, as will any subnets configured on the internal network interface. You can add or remove additional subnets. You should never add the subnets that exist externally to the ISA server. ISA Server uses the LAT to help determine which addresses are on the internal network and which are on the external network. An improperly configured LAT can allow unprotected access to the internal network. Apply ISA Server–specific service packs and security patches.

7. Configure ISA Server policy elements. *Policy elements* are items such as schedules, client sets, and destination sets. (Examples are described in the later section "Configure Policy Elements.") Policy elements are used to configure

site and content rules and protocol rules. Before a client can use ISA Server to access the Internet, site and content rules must be written. These rules use policy elements.

8. Configure protocol rules. By default, all access to the internal network from the Internet is blocked unless it is a response to a request from the internal network. A single, default protocol rule allows all protocols to be used to access the external network. Lock down this access by creating protocol access rules. See "Configure Protocol Rules."

9. Configure site and content rules. By default, no access to the external network is allowed from any computer on the internal network without at least one protocol rule and one site and content rule. Site and content rules specify which computers can access which sites when.

10. Configure clients. Computers do not need to run the ISA Server client software in order to access the Internet through the ISA server. Harden clients prior to configuring for access to the Internet. Internet access using ISA Server as a firewall presents three client options:

    ■ Install the Microsoft firewall client. This makes the use of some protocols easier, since client and server can negotiate the connection.

    ■ If the proxy service is used, configure the browser to use the proxy using the default port 8080.

    ■ Configure the client to use the internal IP address of the proxy server as the gateway, or configure routers the client may access as a gateway to direct Internet traffic to the ISA server.

11. Test connectivity by placing the ISA server and a single client on a test network and then connecting the ISA Server external network interface to the Internet. This test is merely to confirm that the system is working. All access from the external network should be blocked (the default), and then a test of the configuration for internal network access can be made.

12. After testing is complete, connect the ISA server's internal interface to the internal network.

13. If required, configure access from the Internet to services on the internal network. Built-in wizards can be used to configure secure access (publish) to an Exchange server, web server, VPN server, or other service. The wizards create any necessary packet filters.

14. Review the later section "Additional Best Practices for ISA Server."

Configure Network Interfaces   It is important to lock down the network interfaces. By default, Windows network interfaces assume an internal "trusted network." The first step is to use the Windows interface to make it easier to identify which network interface is the network card that is Internet facing and which one is connected to the internal network. You can do this by right-clicking an interface and selecting Rename, and then labeling the interface used to connect to the Internet "external" and the internal interface "internal," or use other names that will work for you. Make sure you correctly identify which network interface is which by checking the physical connections to each card. Next, modify the properties of each interface so that it has the minimal information and configuration necessary:

1. Right-click the internal interface and select Properties.

2. On the General page, if possible, deselect Client for Microsoft Networks, QoS Packet Scheduler, and File and Printer Sharing for Microsoft Networks, as shown in the following illustration. (If you need these services on the internal network, then keep them, but many installations will not need them.)

NOTE The MS Firewall client software is installed on the ISA server and can be downloaded from a share. However, if you are not using this client, then you do not need the share. In addition, it may be preferred to install the client via Group Policy, or place it on another server's share for download. It is critical to reduce the potential vulnerabilities on the firewall server.

3. Select Internet Protocol (TCP/IP) and click the Properties button.

4. In the IP Settings page, enter the internal network IP address for the server and the internal DNS servers and gateway.

5. Select the WINS page and, if no computers on the network require NetBIOS over TCP/IP, select Disable NetBIOS over TCP/IP, as shown in the following illustration. (Windows 98 and Windows NT computers require the use of NetBIOS over TCP/IP.)

6. Click OK three times to close the property pages.

7. Right-click the external network interface and select Properties.

8. Deselect network services, as shown in the illustration in step 2. (Make sure to deselect File and Printer Sharing for Microsoft Networks!)

9. Select Internet Protocol (TCP/IP) and click the Properties button.

10. In the IP Settings page, enter the external network IP address for the server and the DNS servers and gateway information provided by the ISP.

11. Select the WINS page and disable NetBIOS over TCP/IP, as shown in the preceding illustration.

12. Select the DNS page and deselect the setting Register This Connection's Addresses in DNS, as shown in the following illustration. (It is doubtful that

your ISP will appreciate your computer attempting to register its address in their DNS server.)

Advanced TCP/IP Settings ? X

IP Settings | DNS | WINS | Options |

DNS server addresses, in order of use:

> 151.164.1.1
> 151.164.1.7

[Add...] [Edit...] [Remove]

The following three settings are applied to all connections with TCP/IP enabled. For resolution of unqualified names:

◉ Append primary and connection specific DNS suffixes
  ☑ Append parent suffixes of the primary DNS suffix
○ Append these DNS suffixes (in order):

[Add...] [Edit...] [Remove]

DNS suffix for this connection: [   ]

☐ Register this connection's addresses in DNS
☐ Use this connection's DNS suffix in DNS registration

[OK] [Cancel]

13. Click OK three times to close the property pages.

Configure Policy Elements   *Policy elements* are used to define content and site rules and protocol rules; they should therefore be defined before those rules are. The major policy elements are schedules, destination sets, and client address sets. Policy elements are configured in the ISA Server Management console.

Schedules can be used to determine when ISA Server services may be used. To create a new schedule,

1. Expand the policy elements node, right-click the Schedules folder, and select New and then Schedule.

2. Enter a name.

3. Enter a description.

4. Select and drag across the grid spaces, and then select Active or Inactive to create the schedule hours. The following illustration shows a schedule for the hours 9 to 5.

5. Click OK to close the dialog box and save the schedule.

Destination sets are used to define web site locations. These sets can then be used to define site and content rules, either allowing or denying access to the web site locations. To create a destination set,

1. Expand the policy elements node, right-click the Destination Set folder, and click New and then Set.

2. Enter a name.

3. Click Add.

4. Enter a domain name, as shown in the following illustration, or enter an IP address of a server. A specific directory can also be entered.

5. Click OK to return to the New Destination Set dialog box shown in the following illustration. To add additional destinations, use the Add button.

6. Click OK to close and save the destination set.

Client address sets are the IP address ranges that identify clients on the internal network. Typical client address sets define desktop systems, servers, administrative workstations, and so forth.

1. Expand the policy elements node, right-click the Client Address Set folder, and click New and then Set.

2. Enter a name.

3. Click Add.

4. Enter a starting (From) IP address and ending (To) IP address to define a range of addresses.

5. Click OK.

6. Click Add to add additional address ranges in the Client Set dialog box shown in the following illustration. Click OK to close the dialog box and save the address set.

Client Set	? X

Name: desktop2

Description (optional):

Select the addresses of computers that belong to this client address set.

Members:

From	To
192.168.6.10	192.168.6.100

Add...   Edit...   Remove

OK   Cancel

Configure Protocol Rules   Protocol rules establish which protocols clients can use to access services on the Internet. By default, a rule exists that allows access using any protocol. To harden the firewall, best practices recommend deleting the rule and writing explicit rules that specify the protocols that are allowed.

HEADS UP!

Some may advise leaving the default rule in place but disabling it. It then can be enabled to use for testing. However, if the rule exists, I have found it quickly becomes the first thing anyone does when they cannot get a new rule to work correctly. This should not be the case. Delete the rule. If you find you need to test by opening all ports, you can always implement a "test" rule that opens all ports, and then delete it when you are through.

1. Expand the Access Policy node.
2. Right-click the Protocol Rules node, select New, and then select Rule.
3. Enter a name for the rule and then click Next.
4. Click Allow (or click Deny to write a rule that explicitly blocks a protocol) and then click Next.
5. On the Protocols page shown in the following illustration, select the Apply This Rule To drop-down box and then select the protocols to which this rule applies; then click Next.

6. Select the schedule to set the times and days that this rule will apply, and then click Next.

7. Select the client type, and then click Next. Client types are

   ■ Any request (all requests will be accepted)

   ■ Specific computer (specify the client address sets allowed)

   ■ Specific users and groups (select Windows users and/or groups)

8. Click Finish.

9. Select the default protocol rule and delete it.

Configure Site and Content Rules   Site and Content rules determine which clients can access the Internet.

1. Expand the Access Policy node.

2. Right-click the Site and Content Rules node, and select New and then Rule.

3. Enter a name for the rule and then click Next.

4. Click Allow (or click Deny to write a rule that explicitly blocks access) as shown in the following illustration, and then click Next.

5. Select which policy element types the rule will apply to (see the following illustration). You can select schedule, destination set, and client type.

6. Complete the entries, such as Client Type (see the following illustration), and then click Next.

7. View the summary of your choices and, if they are correct, click Finish.

Additional Best Practices for ISA Server   The following best practices should be followed to harden ISA Server:

- Write explicit protocol rules that specify which protocols can be used to access the Internet.

- Write site and content rules that limit specific clients by schedule, destination, and content.

- Use wizards, where available, to publish services on the internal network that may be accessed on the internal network.

- Do *not* disable packet filters. Packet filters may be written to allow access to services on the ISA server and on the internal network. It is possible to disable packet filters entirely. This defeats the purpose of having a firewall.

Control Internet Traffic

In the past, many organizations and security consultants believed that it was alright to allow access from the internal network to the Internet using any protocol, but that all access from the Internet to the internal network should be blocked, with the exception of protocols such as http that were required. Today we know that traffic in both directions should be carefully controlled. All protocols should be blocked by default, and only those protocols that are required should be allowed. Followers of this security best practice will be rewarded for the extra trouble. The blaster worm, for example, used port 135 and a Remote Procedure Call (RPC) vulnerability in Windows XP and Windows 2000 to compromise the computer and then required the infected computers to use TFTP (UDP port 69) to download code from the computer that originally infected it. Without this code, the spread of the infection could not continue. While port 135 should not be open from the Internet to the internal network, if for some reason it was, blocking port 69 from the internal network to the Internet could have halted the infection, or at least slowed its spread. (If a computer on the internal network was infected by another computer on the internal network, blocking TFTP on the firewall has no impact.)

Provide Protection for Critical Traffic

Communications between systems can be protected by encryption, and Chapter 11 will detail the use of protocols such as Secure Sockets Layer (SSL), IP Security (IPSec), PPTP, and L2TP/IPSec, as well as the use of VPNs. However, network infrastructure must be designed to support these practices.

When the physical infrastructure segments the network into areas of trust and uses border controls to filter and/or clean traffic that enters and leaves these areas, the risk to sensitive or critical traffic is reduced. Before an attacker can capture such traffic, she must gain access to a computer on the segment of the network on which the traffic exists. If, for example, all of the members of the finances area and the network resources that they use are located on the same network segment, then the traffic that represents their access to information, and their modifications to this information, are limited to the finance segment of the network. You may still want to encrypt sensitive communications within the area, but you have significantly reduced the risk that an outsider might obtain access to this information while it is on the network.

When it is not possible to limit all sensitive and critical communications to distinct segments of the network, then the physical infrastructure must accommodate and secure communications between segments. To continue the preceding example, imagine that senior executives must also have access to the financial information, but the executives' computers are not within the financial segment of the network. Secure communication can be configured, using either a VPN, or IPSec, or even SSL. However, if, for example, a firewall protects the financial resources, then appropriate configuration of the firewall must be done to allow the protected protocol through.

When choosing the border controls for network segments, you must keep in mind the types of communication that will need to traverse them. For example, if firewalls are using NAT, they may not be compliant with changes to IPSec that allow natting of IPSec. Another protocol may need to be used, or a different firewall must be selected. Some specific types of traffic that you may need to specifically protect are

- Active Directory and other domain controller traffic
- Web traffic
- E-mail

Protect Active Directory and Other Domain Traffic

The Active Directory serves as a repository for data of a critical and sensitive nature in Windows Server 2003 and Windows 2000 domains. This information is replicated between domain controllers in a domain, and some information is also replicated between domains in the forest. Domain controllers may exist at many different physical sites in an organization. In addition to Active Directory replication, clients may need to use domain controllers outside of their network segment, for authentication or DNS lookup (when the domain controller is a DNS server). Windows NT 4.0 domain controllers also communicate with other domain controllers. Domain controller traffic needs to be protected, as does the ability of domain controllers to communicate with other domain controllers located in different physical network segments. When planning the physical infrastructure of the network, including firewalls, accommodations need to be made for this traffic.

If full communication with a domain controller across a firewall is required, it is necessary to open many ports on the firewall. Opening some of these ports may expose the network to an unacceptable level of risk. In addition, password hashes and application data can be exposed in some of the protocols used.

There are three choices for firewall configuration to secure domain-related communications across the firewall:

- Establish VPN communications between computers and the network segment behind the firewall or create a gateway-to-gateway VPN between sites. Windows Routing and Remote Access Services can be used to create VPN servers.

- Establish IPSec policies between domain controllers and between domain controllers and domain member computers. IPSec policies can be created for Windows XP Professional, Windows 2000, and Windows Server 2003 computers. This has the advantage that both port and computer restrictions can be made. While VPN connections can be limited to authenticated users, and in some cases authenticated computers, IPSec policies can be written to allow or block connections and secure communications on the port level as well.

- Open the required ports, and only the required ports, on the firewall. Use the information in Tables 3-1 and 3-2 to determine which ports these are. See the later section "Determine Firewall Configuration" for example scenarios.

Best practices recommend that domain controller communications across firewalls be protected either by using IPSec policies (a good choice for interdomain traffic) or by establishing a gateway-to-gateway VPN between sites. The firewall(s) will only need to be configured to pass IPSec traffic or the protocols used for the VPN. Table 3-1 lists the ports necessary for IPSec traffic and for IPSec/L2TP and PPTP VPNs. If your VPNs use different protocols, you will need to obtain port information from the manufacturer. Securing communications using IPSec and VPNs is detailed in Chapter 11.

NOTE   When firewalls use NAT, or a NAT server is used, it may not be possible to use IPSec across the firewall. A newer version of NAT, NAT-T, will work, but both client and NAT server must be NAT-T compliant.

Protective Measure	Ports Required
IPSec policy	Three protocols are used: 500 UDP (ISAKMP traffic), protocol ID 50 (ESP), protocol ID 51 (AH).
PPTP VPN	TCP port 1723 for PPTP and IP protocol 47 for generic routing encapsulation (GRE).
L2TP/IPSec VPN	L2TP port 1701 UDP, IPSec ports, NAT-T port 4500 if NAT-T is required and available.
All Three	DNS and Kerberos ports may also be required.

Table 3-1.   Ports Required for Firewall Configuration

NOTE In addition to opening ports for IPSec traffic, the firewall must also permit or track fragments for ESP, ISAKMP, and AH traffic. IKE message fragmentation may be required when certificate authentication is used. Stateful filtering of IKE and IPSec communications should *not* be configured; instead, use static packet filters. Refer to your firewall documentation for additional configuration that may be necessary.

Alternatively, where risk may be less because firewalls are border controls for segments within a private network, instead of using IPSec, your organization may assume the risk and require that the necessary ports be opened. Table 3-2 lists the possible ports required for different Active Directory–related processes. Note that three possible problems exist with this method. Net Logon services, File Replication Services (FRS), and Active Directory replication do not use fixed ports. Instead, ports are assigned dynamically. In order to allow these services across firewalls, the entire range of dynamic port assignment must be opened. By definition, this range includes ports ranging from 49152 to 65535; however, services using RPC may also use ports in the Registered range—1024 to 49151. Opening such a large range of ports is too large of a risk. Methods to reduce the number of ports that may be required are identified in the table, and step-by-step procedures for doing so follow.

How RPC Works

To understand why domain communications require so many ports, you must understand a little bit about how RPC works. RPC is a network communication protocol that can be used to develop complex programs that operate over the network. When an RPC service starts, it obtains one of the dynamically assigned ports from the operating system. The port number is registered with the RPC endpoint mapper. Some RPC services attempt to use the same ports each time (if they are available), while others accept a random assignment. When a client needs to use the RPC-based service, it does not know which port the RPC service will have, but it can use the RPC endpoint mapper service in order to find out. If you attempt to open only the ports necessary for required services, you will still be required to open port 135 for TCP and UDP and all ports above port 1023. Opening this many ports on the firewall reduces the ability of the firewall to protect anything. To reduce this risk without establishing VPNs or IPSec policies, you can configure some RPC-based services to use a fixed port, and limit the number of ports that a computer will use for RPC-based services. Both solutions are detailed later in this section.

Service	Port	Related Processes and Notes
RPC endpoint mapper	135 TCP and UDP	Net Logon service (validate and authenticate trust between two domain controllers in different domains); replication.
RPC ports for Net Logon service	Dynamic	Net Logon. Can restrict number of ports used. (See the section "Limit the Dynamic RPC Ports.")
RPC ports for FRS replication	Dynamic	FRS replicates data between domain controllers from the same domain.
RPC ports for Active Directory replication	Dynamic	AD replication. Can demand the use of a static port. (See the section "Restrict Active Directory Replication to a Static Port.") Can restrict number of ports used. (See the section "Limit the Dynamic RPC Ports.")
Kerberos	88 TCP and UDP	AD replication; user and computer logon and authentication; establishing trust between domains; validating trust between DCs in different domains.
LDAP and LDAP ping	389 TCP	AD replication; user and computer logon and authentication; establishing trust between domains; validating trust between DCs in different domains.
LDAP over SSL	636 TCP	AD replication; user and computer logon and authentication; establishing trust between domains.
Global Catalog LDAP	3268 TCP	Data retrieval. Example: Exchange server.
Global Catalog LDAP over SSL	3269 TCP	Data retrieval if LDAP over SSL is configured.
SMB over IP (Microsoft DS)	445 TCP and UDP	AD replication; user and computer logon and authentication; establishing trust between domains; validating trust between DCs in different domains.
DNS	53 TCP and UDP	AD replication; user and computer logon and authentication; establishing trust between domains; validating trust between DCs in different domains.
Network Time Protocol (NTP) or Simple Network Time Protocol (SNTP)	123 UDP	Time synchronization. Necessary if time synchronization is performed with Active Directory domain controllers. See the section "Determine Where Time Synchronization Traffic Is Required" to identify where this is necessary.
NetBIOS name service	137 TCP and UDP	Replication if NetBIOS is required.
NetBIOS datagram service	138 UDP	Replication if NetBIOS is required
NetBIOS session service	139 TCP	Replication if NetBIOS is required

Table 3-2. Ports Required for Active Directory Replication, Mutual Authentication, and Domain Controller Location Mechanism

Table 3-3 lists and details the ports used by Windows NT services that might be used across the firewall.

Service	Port
Browsing	137, 138 UDP
Directory replication	138 UDP, TCP 139
DNS	53 UDP
File sharing	TCP 139
Logon, as well as pass-through validation, trusts, and WinNT secure channel	137, 138 UDP, 139 TCP
Net Logon service	138 UDP
WINS replication	42 UDP and TCP
WINS resolution	1512 UDP and TCP

Table 3-3. Windows NT 4.0 Domain Communications Ports

NOTE If HOST files are used on Windows NT, the use of DNS is not required. Likewise, LMHost files can be used to remove the need for WINS. DNS is required for Active Directory domains, and WINS can be eliminated if legacy systems such as Windows 98 and Windows NT are not used on the network.

For more information, download the document "Active Directory in Networks Segmented by Firewalls" (http://www.microsoft.com/downloads/details.aspx?familyid=c2ef3846-43f0-4caf-9767-a9166368434e&displaylang=en). It includes information on several scenarios, including internal segments and access over the Internet or WAN between different physical sites.

Restrict Active Directory Replication to a Static Port

The directory service and the file replication service (FRS) use dynamically allocated ports. To configure a firewall to allow these services to pass means opening up a large number of ports—often an unacceptable situation. FRS cannot be restricted to a fixed port. However, the directory service can be restricted to a single port by using a registry entry on the domain controller. Doing so will restrict replication of directory data to a single port. However, if FRS replication is also necessary, there is no net gain. The single port necessary for Active Directory replication can be opened on the firewall; however, a wide range of ports will be necessary in order to allow FRS replication to occur. Restricting AD replication to a single port is useful when FRS replication is not necessary, for example, when no intradomain replication is necessary across the firewall. To set a fixed port for AD replication,

1. Open the registry editor. (Type **regedit** at a command prompt.)

2. Select the HKEY_LOCAL_MACHINE hive and navigate to HKEY_LOCAL_
   MACHINE\SYSTEM\CurrentControlSet\Services\NTDS\Parameters.

3. Enter or select the DWORD value "TCP/IP Port" (quotes are not necessary, but
   the space is) and set it to the value of the port to be used.

4. Click OK.

5. Close the registry editor and reboot the domain controller.

6. Configure the firewall to allow access to the port you assigned. (You will still
   also need to allow the RPC endpoint mapper port, since clients will not know
   which port is assigned.

TIP   To make registry changes quickly, instead of manually using the registry editor, prepare a
text file with the .reg extension. Double-clicking on the file will modify the registry. For example, a
reg file to assign the static port 49152 for AD replication should include the following information:

[HKEY_LOCAL_MACHINE\SYSTEM\CurrentControlSet\Services\NTDS\Parameters]
"TCP/IP Port"=dword:0000c000

ONE STEP FURTHER

My friend Rodney Fournier recommends this additional step for firewall
configuration. It solves one of the problems that we all have: remembering what
port is used for what. Experienced IT pros know the common port assignments
for many protocols; however, ports are remapped by the network engineers, so
how can others identify them? What Rodney suggests, to make it easier to remember the
ports that are remapped and make it easier to monitor at the firewall, is to use the built-
in Windows calculator to find the hex equivalent of a word you want to use:

1. Start the calc.

2. View Scientific.

3. Select Hex.

4. Type **CAFE** (or any four-letter Hex word). (A hex word can use the letters
   A, B, C, D, E, and F.) What we are trying to do is to create an ASCII number
   between 10,000 and 65,535 that spells a word in Hex. Dead = 57005 ASCII.
   Other popular Hex words are ABBA (43962), DEAD (51966), DEAF (57007),
   and ACDC (44252). CAFÉ is a good choice for the FRS service, since FRS
   serves up files.

Assign a Single Fixed Port for FRS Replication

The File Replication Service is used to replicate system policy and login scripts. It can also be used to replicate files between Distributed File System (DFS) roots or child node replicas. After installation of Windows 2000 service pack 3, FRS replication can be restricted to a single fixed port by making a registry entry. (FRS replication is not a component of Windows Server NT 4.0.) To do so,

1. Open the registry editor. (Type **regedit** at a command prompt.)

2. Select the HKEY_LOCAL_MACHINE hive and navigate to HKEY_LOCAL_MACHINE\SYSTEM\CurrentControlSet\Services\NTFRS\Parameters.

3. Enter or select the REG_DWORD value "RPC TCP/IP Port Assignment" (quotes are not necessary, but the space is) and set it to the value of the port to be used.

4. Click OK.

5. Close the registry editor and reboot the domain controller.

6. Configure the firewall to allow access to the port you assigned. (You will still also need to allow the RPC endpoint mapper port since clients will not know which port is assigned.)

Limit the Dynamic RPC Ports

When both AD and FRS replication must occur across the firewall, another possibility is to restrict the dynamic RPC ports that the domain controller will use. (This can also assist when the Net Logon service must be available over a firewall for authenticating trusts between DCs in different domains.) This way, a smaller range of ports must be open on the firewall. You will have to carefully consider all services that do not use a fixed port, as you will want to adjust the number of ports according to these requirements. If FRS replication is the only requirement, Microsoft recommends a range of 20 ports that starts on or above port 5000. To limit the range of RPC ports available,

1. Open the registry editor. (Type **regedit** at a command prompt.)

2. Select the HKEY_LOCAL_MACHINE hive and navigate to HKEY_LOCAL_MACHINE\SOFTWARE\Microsoft\Rpc\Internet.

3. Enter or select the REG_MULTI_SZ value Ports and set it to the range of the port numbers to be used.

4. Click OK.

5. Close the registry editor and reboot the computer.

Determine Where Time Synchronization Traffic Is Required

Time synchronization is an essential element of security. It has two purposes: First, time stamping of log entries must be accurate if it is to be useful forensic evidence.

Second, network protocols such as Kerberos are time dependent. Authentication can fail if domain controllers and clients are not time synched. Windows 2000 computers use the Simple Network Time Protocol, while Windows XP and Windows Server 2003 use the Network Time Protocol for time synchronization. Synchronizing time by Windows NT 4.0 requires a third-party product or must be done manually. One way to do so is to add the net time command to a logon script.

The Windows time service is started by default for Windows XP, Windows 2000, and Window Server 2003 computers joined in a domain. By default, the first DC in the Windows 2000 forest root domain becomes the time synchronization source for the forest and must be synched with a valid time server. Additional domain controllers in the domain will synchronize with this server. As new domains are added, the domain controller with the PDC-emulator role synchronizes time with the forest root domain, and the other domain controllers and member servers and workstations can synchronize with a domain controller in their domain. Time service settings can be configured using the Windows 2000 service pack 4 registry. In a Windows Server 2003 domain, the time service can be configured using Group Policy. The time service can also be started manually on stand-alone Windows XP and Windows Server 2003 computers. Stand-alone computers can then be pointed to time servers either on the local network or on the Internet for time synchronization. For more information on the time service and synchronization, see these articles: for Windows Server 2003 and Windows XP— "Windows Time Service" (www.microsoft.com/technet/treeview/default.asp?url=/ technet/prodtechnol/windowsserver2003/maintain/security/ws03mngd/26_ s3wts.asp), and for Windows 2000—"Windows Time Service" (www.microsoft.com/ technet/treeview/default.asp?url=/technet/prodtechnol/windows2000pro/ maintain/w2kmngd/16_2kwts.asp). Windows NT 4.0 domains do not synchronize time between domain members.

Require SMB Signing

The Server Message Block (SMB) protocol is used during printer and file sharing as well as the administration process. The process of signing SMB packets can be implemented in most versions of Windows and protects this traffic because each packet is identified as originating from a specific Windows computer. This allows another Windows computer to validate that the information it is receiving is coming from the computer that claims to be sending it and that the packets have not been tampered with in transit. Using SMB signing can mitigate the risk of a man-in-the-middle attack. A man-in-the-middle attack is an attack in which an unauthorized computer intercepts communications from both client and server. To the client, the computer appears to be the server, and to the server, the computer appears to be the client. Anyone controlling the unauthorized computer has access to all communications between the client and the server and may even change them.

SMB signing is turned on by default on Windows Server 2003 computers. To require SMB signing for Windows 2000 and Windows NT 4.0 computers, use the instructions in Chapter 11.

Require Encryption or Digital Signing of Secure Channel Data

Secure channels are communications channels established through Net Logon to protect authentication data and pass-through authentication data. Secure channel connections are themselves authenticated, and sensitive information such as password hashes are encrypted, but the entire communication is not encrypted or signed by default on all Windows systems. Group Policy Security Options can be set to either require the encryption or signing of secure channel data or allow the server or client to respond if requested. When digital signing or encryption of secure channel data is required, no secure channel communication can take place unless the other computer is configured to either require it, or do so "when possible." A strong, Windows 2000 or later, session key can also be required. These settings are labeled slightly differently depending on the operating system. Windows XP and Windows Server 2003 options are

- Domain member: Digitally encrypt or sign secure channel data (always)
- Domain member: Digitally encrypt secure channel data (when possible)
- Domain member: Digitally sign secure channel data (when possible)
- Domain member: Require strong (Windows 2000 or later) session key

Windows 2000 options are

- Secure Channel: Digitally encrypt or sign secure channel data (always)
- Secure Channel: Digitally encrypt secure channel data (when possible)
- Secure Channel: Digitally sign secure channel data (when possible)
- Secure channel: Require strong (Windows 2000 or later) session key

If the "always" settings are used, all clients and domain controllers must be able to digitally sign or encrypt secure channel data. Windows NT 4.0 service pack 6a computers can be configured to digitally sign or encrypt secure channel data by using a registry setting. Windows 98 Second Edition clients can support the setting if they have the Active Directory service client installed.

1. Open the registry editor. (At a command prompt, type **regedt32** for Windows NT 4.0 or **regedit** for Windows 98.)
2. Select the HKEY_LOCAL_MACHINE hive and navigate to HKEY_LOCAL_ MACHINE\SYSTEM\CurrentControlSet\Services\NetLogon\Parameters.
3. Enter or select the REG_DWORD value SignSecureChannel and set it to 1.
4. Enter or select the REG_DWORD value SealSecureChannel and set it to 1. (If SealSecureChannel is set to 1, SignSecureChannel will also be set to 1.)
5. Click OK.
6. Close the registry editor and reboot the computer.

Use SSL for LDAP

LDAP communications are used in e-mail communications and directory inquiries and administrative processes. LDAP communications may contain sensitive information such as passwords. To ensure protection of LDAP communications, require the use of SSL. To implement this functionality, all domain controllers must obtain a certificate from a Windows Enterprise Certification Authority (CA) or a compatible third-party CA. Information on implementing and providing security for a Windows CA appears in Chapter 12.

Once domain controllers obtain certificates, you must configure applications to require the use of SSL. Domain controllers cannot enforce the requirement; they can only support it.

Require LDAP Packet Signing

When LDAP packets are signed, any tampering with the packets will be discovered and the packets can be rejected. Signing does not encrypt the traffic. LDAP packet signing is implemented in Windows Server 2000 by making the following registry settings.

Only require LDAP signing of clients that will be used for administration. To require the client to sign LDAP packets,

1. Open the registry editor. (Type **regedit** at a command prompt.)

2. Select the HKEY_LOCAL_MACHINE hive and navigate to HKEY_LOCAL_ MACHINE\SYSTEM\CurrentControlSet\Services\LDAP.

3. Enter or select the REG_DWORD value LDAPClientIntegrity and set it to 2.

4. Click OK.

5. Close the registry editor and reboot the computer.

To set domain controllers to enable LDAP signing,

1. Open the registry editor. (Type **regedit** at a command prompt.)

2. Select the HKEY_LOCAL_MACHINE hive and navigate to HKEY_LOCAL_MACHINE\SYSTEM\CurrentControlSet\Services\NTDS\ Parameters.

3. Enter or select the REG_DWORD value LDAPServerIntegrity and set it to 2.

4. Click OK.

5. Close the registry editor and reboot the computer.

Alternatively, the Group Policy Security Option "Domain controller: LDAP server signing requirements" can be set to Require Signing. In both cases, when LDAP signing is required, if the use of SSL is required, no additional packet signing will be done.

Determine Firewall Configuration

The examples shown in Table 3-4 illustrate the ports that would be used in the given case.

Side A of Firewall	Side B of Firewall	Ports
Exchange server	Global Catalog server	3268 and additional ports required by the Exchange server
Member server; User	Domain Controller necessary for authentication.	Authentication: 88 (TCP and UDP), 53 (TCP and UDP for DNS name lookup), 389 (TCP and UDP or 636 for locator pings), 445 (TCP and UDP for Microsoft-DS traffic)
User with account in domain A	Resources on member server in domain B	88 (TCP and UDP), 53 (TCP and UDP for DNS name lookup), 389 (TCP/UDP or 636 for locator pings), 445 (TCP and UDP for Microsoft-DS traffic)
Domain controller	Domain controller	Replication

Table 3-4.   Determining Ports

Protect Web Traffic

Some web communications, such as financial transactions or the sharing of confidential, private, or sensitive information, requires protection. The obvious choice is SSL.

Protect E-Mail

The first steps to protecting e-mail traffic are to provide gateway antivirus and spam filtering. Local antivirus products should also be installed and kept up to date. Sensitive e-mail data should be encrypted and/or signed.

Provide Protection for Critical Servers

Each server on the network plays some role. Typical roles are domain controllers, file and print servers, infrastructure servers, database servers, and so on. Specific instructions for securing these servers by role are provided in Chapters 5 and 8. However, there are physical and network infrastructure protective elements that need to be planned and implemented prior to server deployment.

Protect Domain Controllers

Protecting domain controllers consists of hardening the domain controller server as described in Chapter 5, protecting domain controller traffic as described in this chapter, hardening administration as described in Chapter 6, and ensuring physical protection. In the data center, domain controllers are protected from inadvertent physical attacks by sound data center security practices such as requiring authorization for entry, ensuring identification and authentication before entry, and restricting physical access to domain controllers via rack locks. When domain controllers must be deployed in remote locations where no data center exists, a different list of physical controls is necessary. This is especially true if domain controllers are Windows Server 2003 or Windows 2000 servers.

Secure Domain Controllers in the Data Center

In addition to normal data center access controls, the security of remote management of domain controllers and servers in the data center may be increased by providing a separate management network that is isolated from the rest of the organization's network. Terminal services, native to Windows 2000 and Windows Server 2003, can be used, and smart UPS or special remote management hardware such as a Compaq RILO board or a Dell DRAC III board can be used to provide remote restart. The remote management hardware can also provide other out-of-band management services. In the data center, this hardware should be connected via RS-232 or Ethernet to a dedicated network segment.

Secure Domain Controllers at Remote Locations

Windows NT 4.0 domain controllers do not all present an active, modifiable version of the domain directory. In Windows NT 4.0, the primary domain controller (PDC) maintains the only changeable directory. The remaining DCs are backup domain controllers. Physical access to these computers is less of a risk than physical access to an Active Directory domain controller. Physical access to either type of domain controller, however, poses a serious risk. Therefore, all domain controllers should be protected.

The security of domain controllers at these locations can be improved by taking these measures:

- Limit access to domain controller computers to authorized personnel. Provide physical protection in the form of a locked closet or enclosure.
- Only the domain controller's hardware and dedicated UPS systems should be in the enclosure. Sharing space with, for example, the telephone wiring closet is unacceptable.
- Require card-key or cipher-key access to the computers' enclosures.
- Build domain controllers off site.
- If domain controllers must be installed or rebuilt on site, do not leave systems unattended during the process.
- Deter booting into alternative operating systems by removing floppy drives and CD-ROMs and *not* allowing dual-boot systems.
- Secure backup media on site and secure archival copies off site.

- Provide procedures for restore operations, including who may conduct them and when, to prevent accidental restoration of old data over good current data.

- Use UPS systems to provide backup power.

- Specify procedures for repair and maintenance of DCs. Ensure all remote staff are knowledgeable in these procedures.

- Use remote administration where possible.

- Use SYSKEY on system restart. Options and best practices for using SYSKEY are discussed in the upcoming section "Use SYSKEY to Secure Reboot."

- Use a firewall.

- Configure the network infrastructure to allow communications with headquarters and other branches if permitted by policy, to take place over VPN tunnels.

- Block any other external requests for access to the domain controller or other local network servers and clients.

- Provide an option for out-of-band management.

- Wherever possible, provide dedicated domain controllers for remote offices.

Out-of-Band Management

Provide a modem for out-of-band management. This modem can be connected directly to a COM port on the domain controller or to a Compaq RILO board or Dell DRAC III board. This connection can be used to provide BIOS configuration, boot process monitoring, and on and off switching. To protect this connection from attack, keep the phone number of the modem private. Be aware that attack tools can discover phone numbers that dial modems, and mitigate this risk by requiring authentication and callback to a specific number.

Use SYSKEY to Secure Reboot

SYSKEY protects sensitive authentication data and can be configured to require the entry of a password or access to a floppy disk before booting. Using either of these methods adds a layer of physical security, since many attacks rely on shutting down the Windows operating system and rebooting it. Requiring a password before boot can thwart these attacks. At the very least, since the domain controller remains offline, staff will notice that there is a problem. If passwords are controlled, a compromised computer will not be accidentally rebooted.

Deciding which method to use is dependent on your evaluation of the risk exposure. Specifying the use of a known password requires that trusted personnel are available and know the password if the DC does require authorized reboots. Using a floppy disk has similar issues. The floppy disk must be protected and made available when needed for approved maintenance. It can be kept locked up, but still, someone at the remote location must be able to access it. A more secure option is to specify the use of a password stored on a floppy disk and then use special hardware such as a Compaq RILO board or a Dell DRAC III. With one of these boards in place, an image of the required floppy disk can be remotely distributed to the domain controller, hence placing reboot under administrative control from the remote location. After the DC has been rebooted, the image of the floppy disk can be removed. To configure these boards to work with SYSKEY, refer to the manufacturer's documentation. To configure SYSKEY,

1. At a command prompt, type **SYSKEY** and then press the ENTER key.

2. If this is a Windows Server 2003 or Windows 2000 computer, note that the Encrypt button is selected and cannot be deselected, as shown in the following illustration. SYSKEY is implemented by default. This behavior was not implemented by default for Windows NT 4.0 but can and should be added.

3. Click the Update button.

4. Select an option, as shown in the following illustration

5. Click Password Startup to require the entry of a password on server reboot. The password should be at least 12 characters long and can contain up to 128 characters. Make the password a strong password.

6. Click System Generated Password to require the system to generate a password to be used at startup. Select either Store Startup Key on Floppy Disk or select Store Startup Key Locally. (This is the default.)

7. Click OK.

Protect Infrastructure Servers

Servers that provide network services also require additional physical protection. These servers are DHCP servers, DNS servers, and WINS servers. Other servers, such as VPN servers, remote access servers, and RADIUS servers, also require protection. Follow physical security advice for securing domain controllers and use the information in Chapter 5 that specifically addresses the security of these servers by role.

Secure Network Infrastructure

Cabling and network devices must also be secured. Physical access to this equipment can enable an attack. While remote administration services on network devices must be protected from attack, physical protection is also required. Secure network infrastructure devices and wiring closets by requiring cardkey locks or cipher locks on doors and/or locks on racks. Provide UPSs for backup power. Require procedures that control who can perform administration and maintenance, and when they can be performed. For more information on securing these devices, see the book *Hardening Network Infrastructure*, referenced earlier in this chapter.

Protect Access to Client Systems

Client computers, by definition, appear to pose less risk. After all, ordinary users use them, and sound administrative and hardening procedures can reduce the risk. In many cases, sensitive data can be restricted to storage on servers protected in the data centers.

However, client computers can represent an enormous risk whether or not sensitive data is stored, viewed, or accessed from them and whether or not the individuals using them have access to sensitive data, or critical infrastructure operations. The first risk posed by client systems is, or course, that if they are compromised, some data of a critical or sensitive nature may be obtained. This can be data either that itself should not be obtained by unauthorized individuals or that may enable an attacker to further penetrate the network. A second risk, however, is that client systems, once compromised, will be used to attack other systems. A single computer infected with a virus or worm can infect many more on the network.

Client system hardening information is provided in Chapter 8; however, three things should be a part of the physical network infrastructure plan:

- Require the use of a personal firewall on systems that are not connected to the domain.

- Require the use of an up-to-date virus scanner. This should be part of your infrastructure plans regardless of client location and regardless of the use of gateway antivirus filters.

- Require physical security for all client computers.

Use Computer-Resident Firewalls

Firewalls are typically installed at the border of networks or network segments and are used to protect the computers and other devices inside the network. But firewalls can also be installed directly on computers. These computer-resident firewalls may be called *personal firewalls* if they are used on client computers or *basic firewall services* when they are implemented on servers. Such firewalls are especially useful when computers, such as those on home networks and at small businesses, are not behind a firewall device, or for computers that travel. Laptop computers are often removed from the organization's facilities and access the Internet from unprotected networks such as dial-up or high-speed networks at hotels and conference centers.

Examples of firewall products or processes that can block for Windows operating systems are

- The Internet Connection Firewall (ICF), a native firewall that is part of Windows XP and Windows Server 2003. The firewall is not enabled by default; however, the upcoming service pack 2 for Windows XP will enable the ICF when installed.

- Third-party firewalls such as those available from Computer Associates, McAfee, Symantec, Tiny Software, and ZoneAlarm (for all versions of Windows).

- Routing and Remote Access Service (RRAS) packet filtering, available on Windows 2000 and Windows Server 2003.

- Basic Firewall Services (preconfigured RRAS services), available on Small Business Server 2003.

- IPSec policies (Windows XP, Windows Server 2003, Windows 2000).

Physical Security Options for Clients

Client computers are located throughout the organization's facilities and travel with employees to their homes and beyond. There are many physical security options that can provide additional protection for client computers. The requirements that should be mandatory for client computers will depend on the physical location of the computers, the type of computer, and the data that may reside on the computer.

Physical Security Requirements for All Client Systems

All client systems should be protected from theft and from common physical attacks. Remember, it is not always the value of the computer or the data on the computer that makes it the object of an attack. Client computer systems can be divided into four types:

- **Low risk** Those desktops that are resistant to theft due to their size and weight, undesirable due to age or the nature of data that might be on them, and possibly protected by other sound security practices. These desktops are still vulnerable to physical attacks other than theft. They can still benefit from simple physical security efforts and should be protected.

- **High risk** Those desktops that are by their value, either in terms of cost or as data targets for theft, or those desktops in public locations or other areas where security in general is low.

- **Laptop computers** Computers that are built for mobility. The form factor is smaller, but laptops provide screens, keyboards, drives, and computing facilities similar to desktop systems.

- **Mobile computing devices** Handhelds such as PDAs and smart phones that are smaller and lighter in weight than laptops.

All of these client systems can benefit from the following physical protection. (Some systems may not have the devices present, or there may be no protective device designed for them.)

- Disabling CD-ROM/DVD autorun, or removing CD-ROM/DVD drives
- Removing floppy drives
- Disabling unused ports
- Locking or bolting nonmobile systems to the location where they are used
- Using cable and locks with laptop systems
- Providing locked containers such as drawers at the office, for mobile systems, when they are left unattended in the office

- Providing lockable cases for desktop systems so that hard drives and other components cannot be removed
- Securing access to ports to prevent the use of keystroke loggers, USB drives, and IRDA-enabled devices to transfer or record data

Physical Security Requirements for Laptop Computers and Other Mobile Devices

The most basic physical security requirement for laptop computers is the use of a cable and lock to physically secure the laptop. These devices can prevent the theft of laptop computers from offices as well as hotel and conference rooms. While the cables can be cut, tools for doing so are not usually toted by visitors, conference attendees, or hotel employees. Unfortunately, similar cables and locks do not exist for mobile computing devices such as smart phones and PDAs. These devices can be protected by using in-room or front-desk safes at hotels, and lockable cases.

The second physical security requirement for laptop computers should be a way to prevent the removal of the hard drive from the laptop. A cable and lock can prevent the theft of the laptop, but if it is the data the thief is after, then the cable lock will not usually prevent its theft. Many laptop computer hard drives are designed to be easily removed with the simple removal of a single screw. If the physical design of the computer does not provide a solution, the hard drive of the laptop can be removed and physically secured separately, or the entire laptop physically secured. The need to do this, of course, depends on the nature of the data on the drive, and evaluation of the possibility that such an attempt would be made. In a secure, or reasonably secure environment (could someone enter, flip over the laptop, unscrew the hard drive cover, and remove the hard drive and walk away without anyone noticing or responding?), perhaps the laptop can be left unattended. In others, a secure, locking drawer may be the best defense.

Finally, physical devices such as smart cards and biometrics can be good investments for mobile devices. Many products are available that delete data if several tries at authentication fail.

Physical Security Requirements for High-Risk Desktops

High-risk desktops are those that may have expensive components or may store or have access to critical and/or sensitive data. Some of these systems may be used for financial, research, or administrative purposes. Further security for these systems should be provided by physically securing their location. Access to areas of the organization where these computers are located should be restricted; they should be accessible only through key card– or cipher-locked doors. Physical devices such as smart cards or biometrics can provide additional security.

Chapter 4

Harden Logical Network Infrastructure

The logical network infrastructure describes the arrangement of computer and user accounts and defines the framework on which their management is based. It should be designed with security in mind. However, existing infrastructure can also be hardened. Hardening the logical network infrastructure consists of selecting the logical framework that provides the best opportunities for security and security management, and then hardening components that are specific to this infrastructure. In order to select and harden the logical infrastructure, you must know the opportunities that each possible choice presents. Many of the details of these opportunities (group policy, delegation, and so on) are detailed in other chapters, but in order to fully take advantage of them, you must provide the infrastructure on which they are built.

Windows systems have three possible logical organizational infrastructures:

- The Workgroup
- The NT 4.0–Style domain
- The Active Directory forest

Secure Foundations for Workgroup Computers

By default, Windows computers are installed as workgroup members. A *workgroup* is a logical grouping of computers that does not provide any centralized administrative structure or management advantages. A computer is made a member of a workgroup simply by recording the name of the workgroup in the computer's interface as shown in Figure 4-1. Computers that are members of workgroups are often referred to as stand-alone computers.

Workgroup Rationale

While it is tempting to insist that all computers be joined in a domain in order to provide centralized management of accounts and security settings, there are several reasons why this request cannot be granted:

- Windows 9*x* and Windows ME computers cannot be joined in a domain.
- In a small organization, perhaps ten computers or less, the requirements for establishing and maintaining a domain may be beyond the resources of the organization.
- In some circumstances, some computer roles may be best suited for stand-alone systems. Examples of stand-alone computer roles are firewall, VPN server, Routing and Remote Access server, certification authority. (These computer roles can also be held by domain member computers; the decision whether to make a computer stand-alone or a domain member depends on many things.)

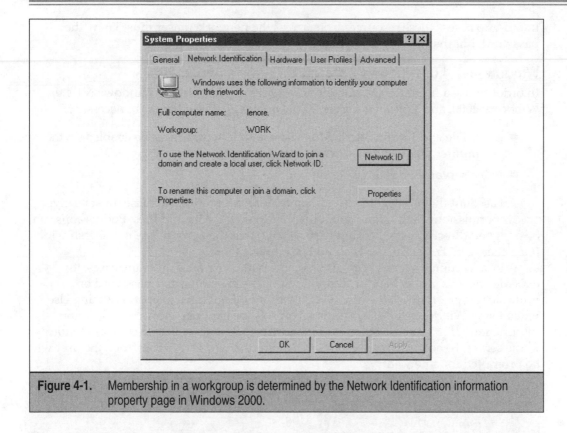

Figure 4-1.   Membership in a workgroup is determined by the Network Identification information property page in Windows 2000.

User Accounts in Workgroups

Windows 9x computers and Windows ME computers have a rudimentary user account database. An account can be set up and used to log on, but logon using an account is not necessary. Windows NT 4.0, Windows XP, Windows 2000, and Windows Server 2003 workgroup computers require a user account for logon, and each computer has its own user account database. Each workgroup member is a computer that has its own user account database. No centralized management exists.

Network Resources in Workgroups

File and printer resources on networked Windows computers can be made available to other computers via the File and Printer Sharing for Microsoft Networks services. If this network property is enabled, access to network resources can be gained.

Windows 9x and Windows ME

Resources on Windows 9x and Windows ME computers can be shared and made available by assigning a Read-Only password or a Full Control password to the share.

In order to access these resources from across the network, a user must know the password, but that user does not require an account on the system.

Windows NT 4.0, Windows 2000, and Windows Server 2003

In order to use a file share to remotely access files on stand-alone Windows NT 4.0, Windows 2000, and Windows Server 2003 computers, three things are necessary:

- The File and Printer Sharing for Microsoft Networks must be enabled on the computer where the files exist.

- The server service must be running.

An account that exists in the local, stand-alone computers database must be given access permissions to the share and to the underlying folder and files. Permissions can be assigned directly to the account or to a group that the account has membership in. (No other "DENY" permissions should be applicable.)

A local account that has been granted access must be used. In many cases, for expediency, a user may have an account with the same name and password on multiple servers. If this is the case, then the user will not have to enter anything else when using Windows NT 4.0. (Windows NT 4.0 does not use the account location information.) If the user is logged on, his cached credentials will be used to authenticate to the server. If, however, the account name or password is different, then the user will be prompted for a new entry.

HEADS UP!

Windows XP and Windows Server 2003 by default do not allow a blank password to be used for remote access. However, no such restriction is placed on Windows 2000 or Windows NT 4.0. If the account policy does not disallow blank passwords, they can be used remotely as well as locally. To gain access to a share on these computers, all the attacker needs to know is the user account name. Protecting shares is another good reason to configure all account policies to prevent blank passwords.

Windows XP Simple Sharing and ForceGuest

By default, Windows XP in a workgroup is configured to share network resources using the Simple Sharing mode and to use the ForceGuest security policy. Simple Sharing is unlike any other Windows systems used for accessing the file system across the network. When simple sharing is enabled, there is no Security tab in the interface and it is not possible to assign permissions by user group or user account. Instead, the Sharing tab has these options:

- **Share This Folder on the Network** The Everyone group is given Read permissions on the folder and its content (this is the default).

- **Share Name** The name of the share on the network.

- **Allow Other Users to Change My Files** The Everyone group is given Full Control permissions on folders and Change permissions on files.

If a share is configured, the only access that given is to the group Everyone. Since every account, including the Guest account, has membership in the Everyone group, this means that no matter which local account, even the Guest account, is used to access the share, permissions are the same (either Read or Change).

If the simple sharing option is removed, and access permissions are set using groups or user accounts, by default, access to resources across the network will only be that which the Guest account can obtain. This is because a security policy, called ForceGuest, is set. This policy ensures that the permissions set for the Guest account define the only network access allowed.

NOTE By default, Windows XP restricts access to the file system by the Everyone group. A comparison of permissions on Windows XP vs. Windows NT 4.0 or Windows 2000 shows far less access is available.

It is possible to change these defaults in two ways: either by joining the stand-alone computer to a domain or by changing the sharing mode and the ForceGuest policy. When XP Professional is joined to a domain (XP Home Edition cannot be joined to a domain), the simple sharing mode is no longer applied and the ForceGuest policy is removed.

Harden Workgroups

To harden the workgroup infrastructure, you must design and implement appropriate access to resources. Other server and client system hardening steps must also be followed. The following steps for hardening workgroup infrastructure should be part of your security practice and policy.

Prevent the Sharing of Resources from Client Computers

If the File and Printer Sharing for Microsoft Networks option is disabled in the network interface, this will prevent sharing. However, sharing is also necessary in order to do some remote administration and to run tools such as Microsoft Baseline Security Analyzer. Use the following guidelines to determine when to disable this feature:

- If computers such as laptops may be removed from the organization's network and be used on the Internet, then disable File and Printer Sharing.

- If alternative remote administration, such as terminal services can be used, disable File and Printer Sharing.

- If remote administration is not done, disable File and Printer Sharing.

- Since Windows 9x and Windows ME computers cannot be configured for granular network (or local) access control, it is critical that sharing not be allowed.

Disabling File and Printer Sharing is not the only way to prevent unauthorized sharing. Windows XP, Windows NT 4.0, Windows 2000, and Windows Server 2003 systems require Administrative privileges before a share can be created. If users do not have administrative privileges, they cannot set up shares. Any user of a Windows 9x and Windows ME computer, however, does have administrative privileges, since these systems do not distinguish between administrators and ordinary users.

HEADS UP!

Windows computers create default administrative shares for disk drives. Only members of the Administrators group can access these shares; nevertheless, the potential for broad access to disk contents is present and should be managed. More information on managing shares is in Chapter 10.

Use File Sharing Appropriately

Access to resources across the network is a central feature of, and the main reason for, early networks. Central file storage can make securing data easier, and it allows efficient backup. However, if not correctly done, sharing can provide easy access to sensitive and critical information. A server-class operating system should be used, and administration should be limited to trained and responsible individuals. The server should be hardened, and resources should be appropriately permissioned. Shares should be permissioned so that only authorized personnel have access and so that they have only the access required for their jobs. Windows NT 4.0 Server, Windows 2000 Server, and Windows Server 2003 all provide the ability to manage share access with this level of granularity.

Windows 9x and Windows ME are client operating systems and should never be used to share resources on the network. Windows XP Professional, Windows NT 4.0 Workstation, and Windows 2000 Professional are client systems but can be configured to securely share resources. In a very small network, they may be used as file servers if dedicated to this job, secured and administered as if they were servers.

Where stand-alone XP computers are not used as file servers, the ForceGuest security policy is a good one. With ForceGuest in place, access will be restricted to Read even if an organization's policy to disallow sharing of resources by client systems is not followed. This is true because the default permission for the group Everyone is Read. If a folder is shared, an attacker cannot change data or save and then run malicious code on the system. Guest-level access, however, is not appropriate where sensitive data might be accessed.

However, an organization may choose not to purchase a server-class operating system but instead dedicate a Windows XP computer for this purpose. In a very small network, this may be appropriate, if the computer is secured. To do so, the ForceGuest security policy should be disabled, as well as simple sharing, and the computer shares should be configured for granular access control.

If Necessary, Disable ForceGuest

Before granular access controls can control access to network shares, you must disable ForceGuest. To do so:

1. Open Start | Administrator Tools | Local Security Policy.

2. Expand Local Policies.

3. Select Security Options.

4. In the detail pane, double-click the Network Access: Force Network Logons Using Local Accounts to Authenticate as Guest.

5. Select the Disabled check box and click OK.

6. Close the Local Security Policy.

Disable Simple Sharing

The folder option, simple sharing, does not provide a security tab for shares. Granular permission setting is not possible. To disable simple sharing:

1. Open Windows Explorer.

2. Select Tools | Folder Options and then click the View tab.

3. Clear the Use Simple File Sharing (Recommended) check box.

4. Close Windows Explorer.

Create Local Accounts Only as Necessary

When Windows computers are in a workgroup, there is no central account database. Each Windows XP, Windows NT 4.0, Windows 2000, or Windows Server 2003 computer has its own local account database. In order to provide granular access to shared resources (in order to use something other than Simple Sharing on Windows XP), you must create local accounts on each server for each user who will be allowed to access resources on that computer. For example, if Chad and Nancy need to be able to access files on Server1 and Server2, they will each need to have access to an account on Server1, an account on Server2, and an account on the client computer that they use. Figure 4-2 shows such a design. In the figure, note that the account databases for Server1 and Server2 show accounts for Chad and for Nancy. Note also their accounts on client systems and note that Server3 does not have an account for them. They will be unable to access shares on Server3, unless they know the password and user ID of an account that exists there.

When many users need access to many resources across the network, observe these best practices:

- Require the use of an account on each system for each user who requires access.

- Make the correct setting of permissions on the resource. If only read access is required, set only this permission. Use proper techniques for providing access to resources.

- Do not establish accounts on all systems just "in case" access may be required.

- Do not use "shared accounts"; that is, do not create one account and allow all users to use that account to access resources.

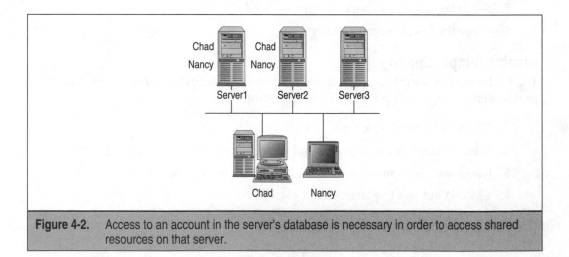

Figure 4-2.   Access to an account in the server's database is necessary in order to access shared resources on that server.

Secure Foundations for Windows NT 4.0–Style Domains

Windows NT 4.0 domains form a security boundary, provide a centralized account database, and afford the ability to centrally administer Windows computers that are domain members.

Central Administration

A Windows NT 4.0 domain controller hosts a central account database that can be used to access resources on all domain member computers. Windows XP Professional, Windows 2000, and Windows Server 2003 computers can be members in a Windows NT 4.0 domain. This means that it is not necessary to establish local accounts on servers for users in order to grant them access to resources. In addition to reducing the amount of administrative work, since control is centralized, it is easier to review for correctness, and to quickly make changes when users are hired, leave, or change jobs within the company. The more correct and up-to-date permissions are, the less opportunity there is for their misuse either accidentally or maliciously.

While multiple domain controllers can be part of a Windows NT 4.0 domain, only one domain controller is the Primary Domain Controller and contains the active account database. Backup Domain Controllers house a copy of the account database, but changes to the account database can be made only to the copy that exists on the PDC.

NOTE Domain member computers retain their local account database, and these accounts and groups can be used to grant or deny access to resources. In fact, best practices recommend that a local group be given the access, and that domain groups then be added to the local group. Members of the domain group thus are given access to resources on the local computer.

There are many other benefits of centralized administration:

- Account controls, while present on all computers that can become domain members, are easier to manage when they only have to be managed in one central location.

- Some user rights can be assigned or denied from the central location. An example of a user right that can be controlled centrally is the right to authenticate to the domain. An example of a user right that can be controlled locally is the right to log on locally. Both privileges, incidentally, are required in order for a user to log on from a workstation. If the user's right to log on to the workstation is absent, it will not matter that the user has a domain account and the right to use it.

- The System Policy tool can be used to create policies that can be automatically downloaded and secure member computers. A similar tool, available for Windows 9x, can be used to create a policy that can be distributed to Windows

9*x* computers when users log on to the domain. Care must be used when creating system policies, since users may log on to the domain from various client computers. System policies work by making changes to the client computer registry. Since the registries are different, and many security settings may differ within them, the use of system policies should be carefully architected and tested.

Security Boundary

Each Windows NT 4.0 domain stands separate from any other Windows NT 4.0 domain or Windows 2000 or Windows Server 2003 domain. An account in its central database must be used to access resources remotely, or an account on one of its member computers must be used. Accounts that exist in other domains cannot be used to access resources. This is what is meant by a security boundary. This does not mean that there are no built-in ways to access resources without the use of an account (see the "Use File Sharing Appropriately" section in this chapter and the "Restrict Anonymous Access" section in Chapter 2); instead, it means that having an account in another Windows NT 4.0 domain does not provide access to a separate domain. The security boundary can be extended by creating a trust relationship between two domains, but this requires administration action.

HEADS UP!

By contrast, a Windows 2000 or Windows Server 2003 domain has an automatically created trust relationship with every other domain in its forest. Because of the tight integration with Active Directory, domains are *not* security boundaries.

NT 4.0–Style Trusts

If an organization creates or acquires (via merger with or purchase of another organization) multiple Windows NT 4.0 domains, and if it requires that users with accounts in one domain access resources in another, then duplicate accounts must be created in the other domain(s) or a trust relationship must be established. Figure 4-3 shows the duplicate account scenario. In this scenario, our users Chad and Nancy have accounts in domains A and B but no account in domain C. They may be given access to resources in both domain A and domain B and not in domain C. This is similar to the workgroup situation.

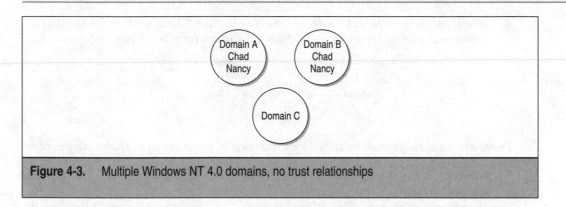

Figure 4-3. Multiple Windows NT 4.0 domains, no trust relationships

Several facts about Windows NT 4.0 trust relationships are important:

- Trusts are one-way. That is, one domain in the trust is trusted and its accounts can be granted access to resources in the other domain. The other domain is the trusting domain. Its accounts cannot be provided access to resources in the other domain. This relationship is shown here:

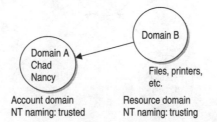

- A two-way trust is actually two one-way trusts. When users in both domains require access to resources in the opposite domain, a trust relationship can be set up in both directions, in which each domain is both trusted and trusting. This relationship is shown here:

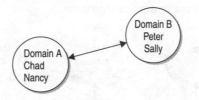

- Trusts are nontransitive. That is, if domain A trusts domain B and domain B trusts domain C, domain A and domain C have no trust relationship. This relationship is shown in the following illustration. Chad, with an account in domain C, can be given access to resources in domain B but not in domain A.

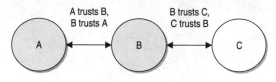

There are three basic trust models. Combinations of these configurations are possible.

■ **Master**   In the Master trust, a single domain's account database is used to provide the user accounts. Other domains are classified as resource domains and contain the resources (printers, files, folders, shares). The account databases on the domain controllers are not used for general user accounts. Access to resources in the resource domains is granted to user accounts in the master domains. This model is shown in the following illustration. Note that to create such a model, one-way trusts are created between the resource domains and the master domain.

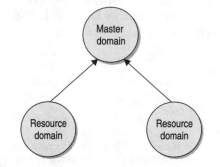

■ **Multimaster**   When a large number of accounts exist, two or more master domains may be used. The account database may be split for administrative purposes or because problems can occur with large account databases. This model is shown in the following illustration. Note that one-way trusts exist between each resource domain and all master domains and that two one-way trusts exists between the master domains.

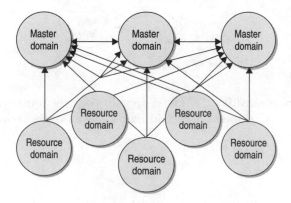

- **Complete trust**   In this model, there are no master domains. All domains have established two one-way trusts with every other domain. This model is shown in the following illustration:

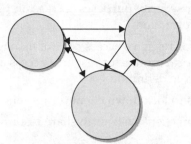

Harden Windows NT 4.0 Domains

Harden the logical infrastructure of Window NT 4.0 domains.

- If it is not necessary for users within one Windows NT 4.0 domain to access resources on another domain, do not create a trust relationship.

- If the trust is required in only one direction, create it in only that direction. A useful example of this is the use of a one-way trust to allow users in a domain on the internal network access to resources in a domain in the DMZ. However, since the trust can be created one-way, user accounts on the domain in the DMZ cannot be used to access internal resources. If the DMZ domain is compromised, its accounts cannot be used to access resources in the internal domain. This situation is shown in the following illustration. In the figure, Chad and Nancy can access the database in the DMZ, but even the Administrator account in the DMZ domain cannot be provided access to the internal domain.

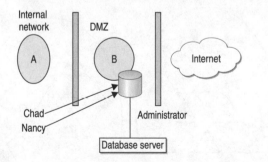

- Carefully design resource location and trust relationships to maximize your ability to isolate resources, yet provide appropriate access. For example, place sensitive data on servers in a domain that has few to no trust relationships with other domains.

- Carefully design resource location and trust relationships to maximize access using one account per user. For example, use a single domain where possible.

- Both consolidate resources into a single domain where possible and create unique domains for security purposes such as on perimeter networks and to isolate sensitive information.

- Use best practices for resource access control management. Best practices include the use of local groups for resource access and domain groups for user consolidation and role definition.

- Use system policies to lock down client computers.

- Do not use shares on client systems to share resources on the network. Period.

Secure Foundations for the Active Directory Forest

The third model for Windows logical network infrastructure is the Active Directory forest. In this model, any number of domains coexist with automatic, two-way trusts between them. User and computer accounts are created on one of the domain controllers (accounts can be created and modified on any domain controller in the domain) in the domain in the domain partition of the Active Directory database. Account information is replicated to all domain controllers in the domain. Because all domains in the forest trust each other, an account in any domain can be given access to resources in any other domain. Figure 4-4 provides an illustration of an Active Directory forest.

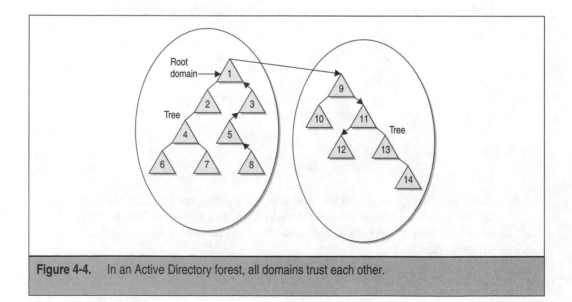

Figure 4-4. In an Active Directory forest, all domains trust each other.

The first domain created in the forest becomes the root forest domain and also the first domain in the first tree of the forest. (A *tree* is one or more domains that exist in the same namespace.) Domain naming in the Active Directory forest is based on the DNS-style name given to the first domain created in the forest. Hence, if the first domain is named adomain.local, that also is the name of the first forest tree. When a new domain is added to the forest, either it can start a new tree and therefore have its own unique namespace, or it can become a part of the adomain.local tree. As a member of the adomain.local tree, the new domain will append the tree name to its domain name. Figure 4-5 shows this situation.

Benefits of Centralized Administration

Because of the centralized account infrastructure and built-in trust relationships, Active Directory domains can benefit from many centralized administrative practices. These practices are implemented in three basic tiers:

- **Forest** At the forest level, several groups such as Enterprise Admins and Schema Admins provide forest-wide administrative rights. Many forest-wide applications such as certificate services, Microsoft Exchange, and Microsoft Internet Security and Acceleration Server require Enterprise Admin group membership in order to properly install them in a domain. Enterprise Admins also have administrative rights within all domains.

- **Domain** At the domain level, several administrative groups exist that can administer aspects of the domain. These groups do not have forest-wide administrative rights.

- **Organizational unit** Organizational units, or OUs, are created within domains. Administration of the users and computer accounts in these containers can be delegated. This is a useful way both to provide separate administration for natural political divisions of an organization and to delegate responsibility for many administrative tasks to appropriate departments. For example, the Help Desk may be delegated the ability to reset passwords on accounts in many OUs but not given the ability to reset administrator passwords.

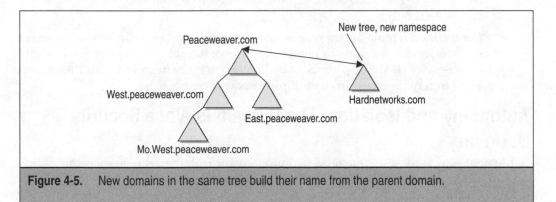

Figure 4-5.   New domains in the same tree build their name from the parent domain.

NOTE An additional level of potential centralized administration is the *site*. The site represents a physical division of the network, for example, a geographical location. A site can contain domain controllers from one domain, or from many. A domain may exist only in one site, or in many.

Many of the benefits of the Active Directory environment are available only when servers and clients are Windows 2000, Windows XP Professional, or Windows Server 2003, and still other benefits are possible when all domain controllers are Windows Server 2003. Each chapter in this book will clearly identify when and for which clients and servers benefits accrue. Some of the benefits of the Active Directory infrastructure are

- **Delegation of authority**   Delegation provides a way to give a group of users the ability to perform some administrative tasks, without making them full administrators. It also allows highly trained and paid administrators to concentrate on administrative tasks that require their abilities. A Delegation of Control Wizard provides the interface to delegate authority at the Site, Domain, and OU levels.

- **Group policies**   Group policies are administrative policies that can be used to install software, implement security policy, provide logon and logoff scripts, and carry out other duties. Group policies are linked to domains, sites, or OUs can provide a way to customize some elements of security for specific users and computers.

- **Single sign-on**   By default, any user with an account in a domain can log on from any client computer in any domain in the forest. Each user can be assigned access to resources throughout the forest and does not need to use a different password. Resources may be files, printers, and/or Active Directory–enabled applications.

- **Integrated Public Key Infrastructure**   If Windows certificate services are implemented with Active Directory, automatic certificate deployment is possible for computers in a Windows 2000 Active Directory and users and computers in a Windows Server 2003 Active Directory. Many other PKI-related features are also made possible such as smart card logon, key archival (Windows Server 2003 only), and the use of custom templates (Windows Server 2003 only.)

- **Centralized remote access management and policy**   Use of Microsoft Internet Authentication Services, an implementation of Remote Authentication Dial-In User Service (RADIUS), can be used to manage authentication, accounting, and audit of remote access from multiple remote access servers.

Autonomy and Isolation: The Domain Is *Not* a Security Boundary

Implement forests to reflect the need for autonomy or isolation. *Autonomy* is the ability to administer some subdivision of the logical infrastructure such as a domain. Administrative groups can administer this subsection with little need for external assistance. External administrative groups may be able to also provide direct administration. *Isolation* is the ability to administer some subdivision of the (or the entire) logical infrastructure. All administrative control rests with a single group. No external administrative groups are required, nor are they able to administer any part.

Domains in Windows forests are *not* security boundaries and do not provide isolation. While administrative groups and security policies are segmented by domain, it is not possible to isolate one domain from another. In Windows 2000 and Windows Server 2003, the forest is the security boundary.

Two factors make this so. First, enterprise-wide administrative groups have administrative control in all domains. Schema Admins, for example, can make changes to the Active Directory schema that then impact every domain. Enterprise Admins, by definition, can administer any domain, and membership in this group is necessary for specific services installation and operation. Second, because of the tightly integrated nature of Active Directory, it is possible, though not easy, for an administrator in one domain to gain administrative privileges in another.

This means that it is not possible to completely isolate domains within the same forest by technical means. You can, however, establish a policy that enforces autonomous domains, through means other than technical. That is, you can relegate the built-in forest-wide administration to only those duties that must be done, forbidding the use of enterprise-wide administrative action unless specifically approved. You can prohibit activity by domain administrators that might seek to compromise another domain. You can establish policy boundaries for domains and domain administrators. Much as you understand an administrator's ability to do harm by the very nature of that person's elevated privileges, much as you understand any human being's ability to do harm, you can mitigate that threat within the culture of your organization. You can make the rules and seek everyone's compliance. You can audit behavior, reward the good, and punish the bad. If autonomy is all you need, you can have it. However, you cannot enforce it by purely technical means.

HEADS UP!

For a domain administrator to gain access to another domain is not an easy task. It would require a level of knowledge and experience that most administrators will not have. It is not something that exists in the GUI. However, it is possible, so you must plan around it. If autonomy as described previously is all you need, then a single forest may be appropriate in your organization. However, if you need strict isolation between some aspects of your organization, then multiple forests may be the best solution. Examples of a need for isolation may be found in multinational companies, military operations, and financial organizations.

Establish Domains Based on Security Needs

In the early days of NT, domains were established without thought to overall organizational needs. Although there were many who planned this logical bit of the network infrastructure, there were many more who simply gave it no thought. You may find yourself in one of those latter environments. You may also find yourself the beneficiary of an Active Directory design that was given no thought either. Whether you have an existing Active Directory infrastructure or are migrating from earlier version of Windows, it is critical that domains represent need, not whim. It may be that only one domain is necessary in your entire organization, or that multiple domains are the best approach.

There are many reasons why a domain is created, including political, geographical, and security. The following list provides security reasons for establishing separate domains.

- **Security policies**   Security policy is part of a Group Policy Object (GPO), and while many security settings can be set per OU, some are pervasive for the entire domain. Domainwide settings are made in the Account Policy (Password Policy, Account Lockout Policy, Kerberos Policy), the User Rights Policy, and a few domain-specific security option sections of Group Policy.

- **Administrative autonomy**   Within an organization, there is often a need for autonomy. A department or division may require control of its users, computers, and resources. It may be possible to given them the autonomy they need within an OU, but it is more feasible to provide them within a domain. (See the preceding notes on autonomy and isolation.)

Establish OUs Based on Security and Administrative Needs

OUs can be used to administer security because

- Computer and/or user accounts can be contained within an OU.

- It is possible to delegate authority over objects within an OU.

- A GPO can be linked to OUs, making it possible to implement and maintain an administrative structure that provides for granular administration and security.

- Delegation of control can be provided at the OU level.

OUs should be established in order to provide administration over common users, computers, and user and computer groups. For example, it may be that control over users and computers in a specific department may be best and most securely exercised by a specific group of administrators, possibly those that also work for the department. The finance, human resources, and research departments are examples of such areas. Computer and/or user accounts within these groups may also require specific security settings that can be implemented via a common GPO. Likewise, computers that play a specific role (mail server, DNS server, database server, and so on) within the organization may require the enforcement of specific security settings. This activity can also be best served by placing computer accounts within an OU designed for the role. A unique GPO can be created and used to manage security for the computers. More information on computer roles and administrative authority can be found in Chapters 5, 7, and 8.

Locate Domain Controllers and Global Catalog Servers Only Where Required

Domain controllers are repositories for Active Directory and the locations where it can be expanded and modified. Access to a DC is required for logon, download of policies, and other activity. For the latter reason, in addition to placement at the main location of the organization, DCs are often conveniently placed where accounts exist in branch offices, divisional locations, and so on. For the former reason, placing DCs at remote locations is a security vulnerability. If high-speed connectivity exists, it may be possible to avoid the need to place a DC at every remote location. (But it may be necessary for other reasons.)

Global Catalog servers are DCs that also store a copy of the Global Catalog. The Global Catalog is a container in the Active Directory that contains partial information on every object in the Active Directory. Access to a Global Catalog server during logon is necessary when Universal groups (groups that can contain members from every domain in the forest) are used. Universal groups can be used in Windows 2000 domains in native mode (all domain controllers are Windows 2000) or in Windows Server 2003 domains at the Windows 2000 or above functional level. This is because the Security Identifier for each group the user is a member of must be obtained during logon. In Windows 2000, this information must be obtained from the GC. Therefore, in many cases, the domain controller at a remote site was also made a GC. Replication of information in the GC occurs between all GCs in the forest. Making many DCs GCs increases replication. Not having DCs and/or DCs and GCs locally present increases traffic and makes domain authentication failure more possible. When domain authentication cannot occur, users are still able to authenticate using cached logons. However, when cached logons are used, any new security policy is not downloaded, and there may be problems with network resource access. When problems with access occur and the reason is not understood, workarounds, which may not be well controlled, audited, or removed when no longer necessary, may be used. Therefore it is essential that domain logon be the norm, not the exception.

Configure Remote Windows Server 2003 DCs to Use Universal Group Caching

In Windows Server 2003, a Global Catalog server is not required to be present at remote locations. Instead, the system can be configured to cache Universal Group membership information on the local DC, where it is scheduled by default for update every eight hours.

To configure DCs for Universal Group Caching:

1. Log on as a member of the Domain Admins group in the root domain in the forest, or as a member of the Enterprise Admins group, or use the Run As command to switch your identity (run as a different user) to one of these.

2. Open Start | Administrative Tools | Active Directory Sites and Services.

3. Select the site where you wish to enable universal group membership caching.

4. In the details pane, right-click NTDS; then click Properties.

5. Select the Enable Universal Group Membership Caching check box as shown here:

6. In the Refresh Cache From box, select the site you want the previous site to obtain universal group membership from, or accept the default (the closest site will be used).

7. Close Active Directory Sites and Services.

Establish the Minimum Number of Additional Domain Trusts

Establish the minimum number of additional domain trusts. A reason for trust should be established, and trust relationships should be established that will provide only the access required. These are valid reasons for trusts:

- Each Windows 2000 or Windows Server 2003 forest is a security boundary. A user with an account in a domain of one forest cannot be provided access to resources in another unless either a separate account is established for the user in some domain in the other forest or a trust relationship is implemented. Likewise, if you have Windows NT 4.0 domains, the same is true.

- It is also possible that you may want to provide access to partners or need to merge resource access between your forest and that acquired during a merger or acquisition.

- Access may be required to resources in a forest established in the DMZ from user accounts in the forest established in the internal network.

- Access may be required between users in a partner's domain and a domain in a forest belonging to the other partner.

- Finally, because of the nature of Kerberos authentication across domains, you may want to establish a "shortcut" trust between two domains in the same forest. (A shortcut trust can improve performance, since it reduces the time it may take to authenticate using the normal process.)

Trust Relationships in Both Windows 2000 and Windows Server 2003

Three types of trust relationships are possible in both Windows 2000 and Windows Server 2003. When a trust is established, accounts in one domain can be given access to resources in another domain.

- **Built-in Active Directory trusts**   When a Windows 2000 or Windows Server 2003 domain is added to an Active Directory forest, a trust relationship is established between the new domain and its parent domain. (The parent domain is the domain just above the new domain in the Active Directory structure. This relationship is shown in the following illustration.) Because this trust relationship is two-way and transitive, trust exists between all domains in the forest.

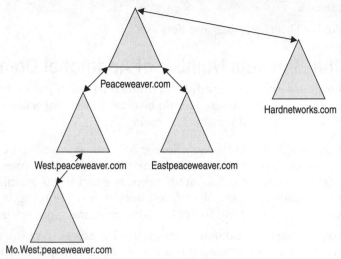

- **Shortcut trusts**   An explicit trust can be established between two domains in the forest. These trusts are one-way, NT 4.0–style trusts. This relationship is shown in the following illustration. If trust is required in both directions, then two one-way trusts must be established.

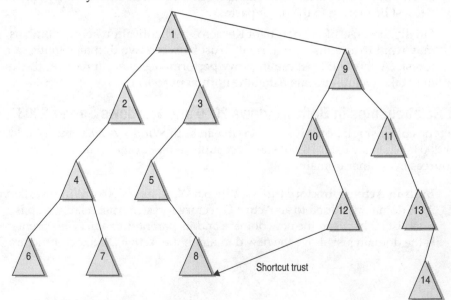

- **External trusts**   An explicit trust can be created between two domains in separate forests, or between a domain in a forest and a Windows NT 4.0 domain. These trusts are one-way, NT 4.0–style trusts. This relationship is shown in the following illustration. In the figure, note that the only access that can be established is of resources in the domain west.peaceweaver.com to user accounts in the domain east.trustworthycomputing.org. If trust is required in both directions, then two-way trusts must be established. (It is possible to establish a one-way trust or a two-way trust.) These trusts are not transitive. If trust between additional domains is required, then additional trust relationships must be established. An external trust is shown here:

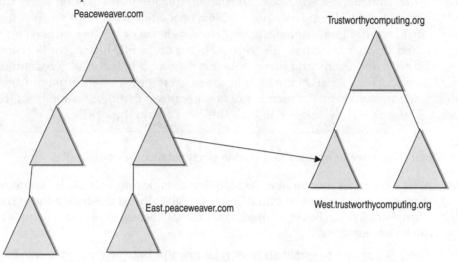

- **Realm trusts**   A realm trust is a trust established between a Windows Active Directory domain and a non-Windows, Kerberos realm, such as a Unix realm.

Trust Relationships in Windows Server 2003

In addition to domain, shortcut and external trusts, a new type of trust, the forest trust, can be established between two Windows Server 2003 forests. It is not possible to establish a forest trust between Windows 2000 forests. A forest trust is a trust relationship in which all domains in each forest trust all domains in the other forest. Forest trusts are transitive and two-way. Figure 4-6 shows a forest trust between peaceweaver.com and trustworthycomputing.org. Remember to use this type of trust sparingly.

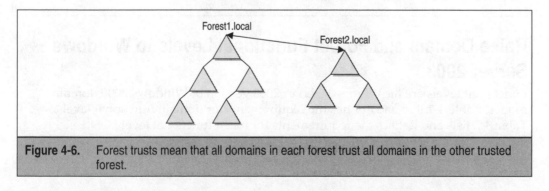

Figure 4-6.   Forest trusts mean that all domains in each forest trust all domains in the other trusted forest.

SID Filtering

An important consideration when establishing trusts between domains and forests is the property of SID Filtering. SID Filtering is automatically enabled between forests in a forest trust. This is important because SID Filtering prevents a user from a trusted domain from using SIDs that are identified as coming from the trusting domain. (SIDs include information that identifies the domain of their origination.) If SID Filtering was not enabled, user credentials from one forest might include SIDs from another forest. (This might occur because an account was moved and the former domain SIDs are included in the SID history, or because the SIDs are fraudulently and programmatically placed in the user's credentials.) SID Filtering evaluates all of the SIDs in a user's authorization information and drops SIDs presented by the member of another forest that don't come from that forest. The user's access token will therefore not contain these SIDs.

A forest trust may be applicable in some circumstances. For example,

- After a company merger, it is decided that a single forest would be appropriate. However, this may not be immediately possible. By establishing a forest trust, administration can be centralized, and ordinary access to resources across forests can be implemented.

- There is a reason to establish trust relationships between many, many domains within each forest.

HEADS UP!

Forest trusts require that the forest functional level be Windows Server 2003. Forest functional levels permit or exclude the implementation of many different functions. Domain functional levels are another possible restriction. Functional levels are changed by adjusting a setting; however, the forest and domain functional levels cannot be modified unless the statuses of all the domain controllers in the domain or forest, respectively, match requirements for the functional level.

Raise Domain and Forest Functional Levels to Windows Server 2003

Functional levels are the Windows Server 2003 version of Windows 2000 domain modes. Table 4-1 lists and defines the requirements for domain functional levels. Table 4-2 lists and defines the requirements for forest functional levels.

Functional Level	Domain Types Permitted
Windows 2000 Mixed	Windows NT 4.0, Windows 2000, and Windows Server 2003 domain controllers
Windows 2000 Native	Windows 2000 and Windows Server 2003 DCs only
Windows Server 2003 Interim	Windows NT 4.0 and Windows Server 2003 DCs only
Windows Server 2003	Windows Server 2003 DCs only

Table 4-1.   Domain Functional Levels

HEADS UP!

Once a functional level has been raised, it cannot be lowered. You cannot, for example, add a Windows 2000 domain to a forest that is at the Windows Server 2003 forest functional level.

To raise the domain functional level:

1. Log on as a member of the Domain Admins group to the Windows Server 2003 DC that is the PDC emulator. (To run the query in step 5, you may log on to any Windows Server 2003 domain controller in the domain; however, you should log on to the PDC emulator to raise the functional level).

2. Open Start | Administrative Tools | Active Directory Users and Computers.

3. Right-click the domain object and click Find.

4. In the Find drop-down box, select Custom Search and then click the Advanced tab.

Functional Level	Domain Types Permitted
Windows 2000	Windows NT 4.0, Windows 2000, Windows Server 2003 DCs
Windows Server 2003 Interim	Windows NT 4.0, Windows Server 2003 DCs only
Windows Server 2003	Windows Server 2003 DCs only

Table 4-2.   Forest Functional Levels

5. Check to be sure no Windows NT 4.0 domain controllers exist in the domain. Enter the following LDAP query, as shown in the following illustration:

(&(objectClass=computer)(operatingSystemVersion= 4*)(userAccountControl:1.2.840.113.556.1.4.803:=8192))

6. Click Find Now to produce a list of Windows NT 4.0 domain controllers in the domain. If you do not check for Windows NT 4.0 domain controllers and they do exist, raising the domain functional level will be possible, but Windows NT 4.0 domain controllers will now be orphaned and unable to participate in the domain.

7. Either open Start | Administrative Tools | Active Directory Domains and Trusts.

   a. Right-click the domain for which you want to raise functionality and select Raise Domain Functional Level from the context menu.

   b. In the Select an Available Domain Functional Level box, select either Windows 2000 native or Windows Server 2003, shown here, then click Raise.

    c. If a Windows Server 2003 level is chosen, and any Windows Server 2000 domains exist, the raising will be blocked; otherwise, the change takes place at the PDC emulator and then is replicated.

    d. Click OK in the warning box.

    e. Click OK in the confirmation box.

or use the Active Directory Users and Computers console:

    a. Right-click on the domain, and then select Raise Domain Functional Level from the context menu.

    b. Select the functional level required.

To raise the forest functional level:

1. Log on to the PDC emulator of the forest root domain as a member of the Enterprise Admins group. The change takes place on the Schema FSMO and then is replicated. If this operations master is not available, the functional level cannot be raised.

2. Open Start | Administrative Tools | Active Directory Domains and Trusts.

3. Right-click the Active Directory Domains and Trusts console and select Raise Forest Functional Level.

4. In the Select an Available Forest Functional Level drop-down list, click Windows Server 2003 and click Raise.

5. Click OK on the warning.

6. If an error message is received, and the functional level cannot be raised, click Save As in the Raise Forest Functional level dialog box, and a log will be saved that includes a list of all DCs that must be upgraded before you can raise the functional level. Otherwise, click OK in the confirmation box.

Use Selective Authentication

After a trust is established, you must grant access to resources in the normal manner. However, some access is available to users from the "trusted" domain immediately after the trust is established. This is because access, in many cases, is granted to the group Everyone, and this group will contain any account that can successfully authenticate with the exception of the Guest account. After a trust is established, all users in the trusted domain can authenticate. This default behavior may become a problem.

In Windows Server 2003 there is a solution. Selective Authentication can restrict trusts between Windows Server 2003 domains and forests. If selective authentication is established by the trust relationship, then you must explicitly grant the Allowed to Authenticate permission to those Windows user groups that you wish to have that ability. This right must be granted for each server in the domain involved in a domain trust, and each domain in a forest trust.

ONE STEP FURTHER

In addition to providing selective authentication, you can restrict access to servers and clients in Windows domains by denying the user the right to log on to the computer. This right is explicitly granted and can be explicitly denied. When this right is denied, it will not matter if the user has the right to authenticate to the domain or if selective authentication is applied. If the right to log on is denied and the user attempts to access resources on the server, the user will not be able to obtain access. Best practices suggest that the right be denied at the group and not the user level.

If a trust is already established, you can modify the Selective Authentication property by taking these steps:

1. Open Start | Administrative Tools | Active Directory Domains and Trusts.

2. Right-click the domain where the trust is present; then click Properties.

3. Select the Trusts tab.

4. Under either Domains Trusted by This Domain (Outgoing Trusts) or Domains That Trust This Domain (Incoming Trusts), click the trust to administer; then click Properties.

5. Select the Authentication tab.

6. Click Selective Authentication as shown in the following illustration.

7. Click OK to close and exit Active Directory Domains and Trusts.

The Impact of Selective Authentication

When Selective Authentication is used, the Allowed to Authentication permission must be granted to the groups of users that should have this permission. Although you can use the object picker to grant access to users on servers and in domains where they have not been granted the Allowed to Authenticate permission, these users will not be granted access to the objects until the Allowed to Authenticate permission is granted.

When a forest trust is in place, in order to grant access, use the Security tab of the resource, and then the object picker to select the group. The trusted forest must be selected in the location box of the object picker as shown in Figure 4-7, or you will not be able to search for groups to include.

On computers that are not Windows XP SP2 or Windows Server 2003, you cannot browse user and group names in order to select and then assign access. Instead, you must use a User Principal Name (UPN, or *user@domainname* format) or Windows NT 4.0–style name (*domainname\username*). Users wishing to use workstations in the trusting forest to log on to domains in the trusted forest (where their accounts are) must also use the UPN or Windows NT 4.0 format. Domain names will not be available from a drop-down list in the logon screen.

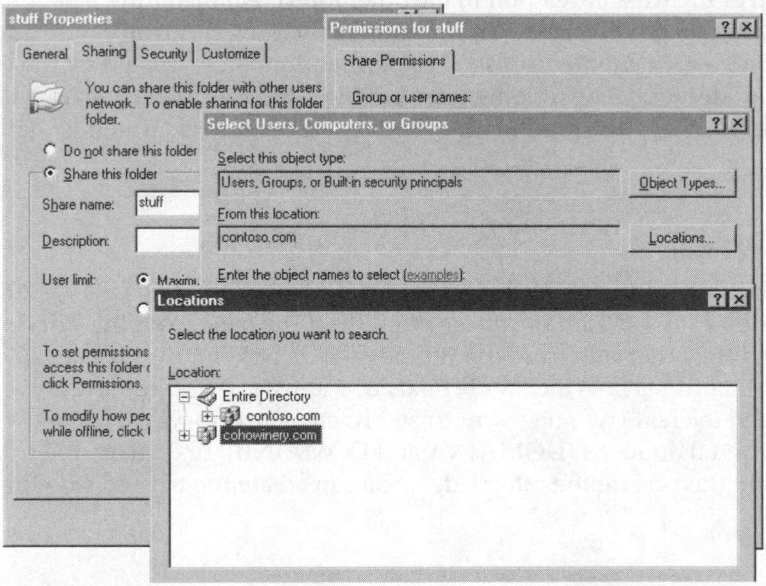

Figure 4-7. Use the object picker to search from groups in the trusted domain.

How to Establish an External Trust

The process for establishing an external trust varies depending on the operating system. However, there are several questions that you must answer before you begin:

- Should the trust be one-way or two-way? Do not provide a two-way trust if a one-way trust will do.

- If the trust should be one-way, which domain is trusted, and which trusting? This is important—choose wrong and it will not be possible to provide the access required, and in addition, you may grant access that may cause systems to be vulnerable to attack.

- Should selective authentication be used (Windows Server 2003 only)? If it will be used, then which servers will need to be configured?

- In Windows 2000 and Windows NT 4.0 trusts, where selective authentication is not a choice, how will you mitigate the risk?

HEADS UP!

A new trust nomenclature is present in Windows Server 2003. Instead of, or in addition to the old "trusted" and "trusting" conventions, trusts are referred to as outgoing or incoming. A new Trust Wizard is also available. When the wizard is started on a domain controller in one forest, trust is specified according to the direction of the trust in relation to the other forest. An incoming trust provides the current domain (the one you are running the program from) with additional access, or trust, in another forests. The current domain is trusted by the other (specified) domain. An outgoing trust provides the specified domain with access to resources in the current domain. The current domain is "trusting" of the other domain.

Windows NT 4.0

To create an external trust between a Windows 2000 or Windows Server 2003 domain and a Windows NT 4.0 domain, create one side of the trust from the Windows NT 4.0 domain, and the other side from the Windows 2000 or Windows Server 2003 domain. Remember that trusts in Windows NT 4.0 are one-way. If you require a two-way trust, you will need to create two one-way trusts. To create a one-way trust between two Windows NT 4.0 domains (DOMAINA and DOMAINB), first create the trusted side of the trust, and then create the other side. (You can create the trusted side first; however, you will have to wait for the trust relationship to be established, a matter of perhaps 15 minutes.) In this example, DOMAINA is the trusted domain and DOMAINB is the trusting domain.

1. Log on to the Windows NT 4.0 domain's PDC of DOMAINA as a domain administrator.

2. Click Start | Programs | Administrative Tools | User Manager for Domains to open the User Manager for Domains applet.

3. From the Policies menu, select Trust Relationships.

4. Click the Add button in the Trusting Domains text box.

5. In the Add Trusting Domains dialog box, enter the other Windows NT 4.0 domain name (DOMAINB) in the Trusting Domains text box.

6. In the Initial Password box, enter a password.

7. Confirm the password by entering it again, and then click OK.

8. Log on to the PDC of DOMAINB, the other Windows NT 4.0 domain, as a domain administrator and open the User Manager for Domains applet by clicking Start | Programs | Administrative Tools | User Manager for Domains.

9. From the Policies menu, select Trust Relationships.

10. Click the Add button next to the in the Trusted Domains text box.

11. In the Domain text box, enter **DOMAINA**.

12. Enter the password for the trust (the same password entered in step 6) and click OK.

13. Read the message noting the trust has been established, and then click OK.

14. Click Close.

Windows Server 2000

The Windows 2000 name for an external trust is an explicit trust. To create one:

1. Log on as a domain administrator.

2. Open the Active Directory Domains and Trusts console (Start | Administrative Tools | Active Directory Domains and Trusts).

3. Right-click the domain and select Properties.

4. Click the Trusts tab.

5. Click either Domains Trusted by This Domain or Domains That Trust This Domain, then click Add.

6. Enter the fully qualified domain name (FQDN) or NetBIOS name of the other Windows 2000 domain.

7. Enter a password for the trust and confirm it.

8. Log on as a domain administrator in the other Windows 2000 domain.

9. Open the Active Directory Domains and Trusts console (Start | Administrative Tools | Active Directory Domains and Trusts).

10. Right-click the domain and select Properties.

11. Click the Trusts tab.

12. Click either Domains Trusted by This Domain or Domains That Trust This Domain, then click Add.

13. Enter the full FQDN or NetBIOS name of the other Windows 2000 domain.

14. Enter the password for the trust (from step 7).

Windows Server 2003

To create an external trust between two domains, each in different Windows Server 2003 forests,

1. Log on as a domain administrator.

2. Open the Active Directory Domains and Trusts console (Start | Administrative Tools | Active Directory Domains and Trusts).

3. Right-click the domain and select Properties.

4. Click the Trusts tab and then click New Trust.

5. On the Welcome page, click Next.

6. Enter the FQDN or NetBIOS name of the specified domain (the other domain in the proposed trust relationship) and click Next.

7. On the Trust page shown in the following illustration, click External Trust and click Next. (If the domain is in another forest, and the forest functional level is not Windows Server 2003, then the trust will always be external and no Trust page will be present.)

New Trust Wizard   ⊠

Trust Type
This domain is a forest root domain. If the specified domain qualifies, you can
create a forest trust.

Select the type of trust you want to create.

○ External trust
An external trust is a nontransitive trust between a domain and another domain
outside the forest. A nontransitive trust is bounded by the domains in the
relationship.

○ Forest trust
A forest trust is a transitive trust between two forests that allows users in any of the
domains in one forest to be authenticated in any of the domains in the other forest.

< Back   Next >   Cancel

8. Select the Direction of Trust as shown in the following illustration. In this
example, a one-way outgoing trust is selected.

New Trust Wizard   ⊠

Direction of Trust
You can create one-way or two-way trusts.

Select the direction for this trust.

○ Two-way
Users in this domain can be authenticated in the specified domain, realm, or
forest, and users in the specified domain, realm, or forest can be authenticated in
this domain.

○ One-way: incoming
Users in this domain can be authenticated in the specified domain, realm, or forest.

○ One-way: outgoing
Users in the specified domain, realm, or forest can be authenticated in this domain.

< Back   Next >   Cancel

8. Select the Sides of Trust (see the following illustration). This action determines if both sides of the trust will be established from this domain. For this example, both the local domain and the specified domain were chosen. You must specify just the current domain (the local domain side of the trust), or to create both sides of the trusts, determine local and specified (the other domain) at the same time. In order to complete both sides of the trust, you must have the credentials of someone in the other domain that is authorized to create a trust (or they must be present). If you cannot provide these credentials, only attempt to create a trust for the local domain. You will need to have an authorized administrator complete the trust from the other domain.

9. If "Both This Domain and the Specified Domain" is selected, enter a user name and password for an account in the specified domain with authority to create a trust.

10. Select the scope of authentication. Scope can be either domain-wide or selective. Click Next.

11. Note the summary of your choices and click Next.

12. Note the Trust completion complete message and click Next.

13. Confirm the trust by clicking OK.

14. In the Trusts property page, note that the domain now shows up in the proper category.

Checklist for Hardening the Logical Network Infrastructure

The following checklist should be followed when hardening the logical network infrastructure:

- Plan domains and forests around administrative needs. For example, a domain can have only one password policy. If different password policies are necessary, more than one domain is necessary.

- Make new Windows domains, Windows Server 2003 domains.

- Work toward migration to 100 percent Windows Server 2003 domain controllers.

- Architect the proper number of forests for your organization in terms of the concepts of autonomy and isolation. If autonomy is all that is necessary, a single forest may be sufficient.

- Create a security policy that addresses issues of autonomy and isolation, that is, proper procedures for administrators, including what constitutes abuse of power, and what will happen should they choose to undertake such abuse.

- Use a separate forest in the Demilitarized Zone (DMZ).

- Establish the minimum number of trusts between domains of different forests.

- Use selective authentication.

- Raise domain and forest functional levels to Windows Server 2003 functional level, as they will enable important security functionality. Many optional security processes such as custom PKI templates and other options explained throughout the rest of the book can be obtained only with Windows Server 2003 functional level.

Chapter 5

Harden Network Infrastructure Roles

- Develop Security Baselines
- Limit User Rights
- Disable Optional Subsystems
- Disable or Remove Unnecessary Services
- Implement Miscellaneous Security Configuration
- Develop Incremental Security Steps
- Select Methods and Models for Security Deployment

omputer roles represent the computer functionality on the network. *Network infrastructure* roles are services such as DNS, WINS, and DHCP. These are important functions in a Windows network, and some or all of them will be present unless the network is very small. DNS, for example, must be present in a Windows Active Directory environment. WINS, the Windows Internet Name Service, provides name resolution for NetBIOS names, DNS provides IP address resolution, and DHCP can automatically provide IP addresses for clients. It is important to secure these services because unauthorized access and control of these services provides the opportunity for a number of malicious attacks.

The first step in hardening these roles, however, is to harden the basic operating system. The following information provides an introduction to a system that can be used to harden all Windows systems and specific steps for Windows DNS, DHCP, and WINS servers. The system defines the development of baseline security—common security steps that can be applied to Windows systems and still leave the computer able to boot and run. In order for most of these computers to then fulfill functional roles, the system requires the definition of incremental security settings and strategies for individual computer roles. This idea, the use of both baseline and incremental security definitions, is not new but was introduced as a system complete with templates and deployment strategies by Microsoft for Windows 2000 Active Directory domains. It is introduced here as a strategy that can be used within a workgroup, and the process for implementing it in a domain follows.

The entire process revolves around defining computer roles. Common sense tells us that all computers require some of the same security configuration and protection steps, while the different uses to which computers are put may dictate additional requirements. The first step in determining security requirements is to group computers loosely into large categories such as clients and servers. Each of these categories can be further broken down by the role that the computers play. Roles are such things as web server, domain controller, file server, and workstation. Infrastructure services are also computer roles. DNS, DHCP, and WINS are examples of infrastructure roles. Next, the easiest way to think about hardening computers is to develop baseline security goals for major categories and incremental security goals for specific roles. If you do so, you can apply quite strong security for the major categories and relax or increase security to accommodate the unique requirements of a computer role. To approach this task in a logical manner:

- Determine baseline security for each operating system.
- Determine the network roles that are present.
- Determine the operating systems that are used for each role.
- Develop incremental hardening criteria for each role.
- Determine which logical infrastructure model is used.

- Select appropriate models for deploying security.
- Develop structures such as templates, scripts, or Group Policy Objects (GPOs) that fit each model.
- Develop additional network infrastructure required to support the model.
- Deploy security.

To perform these steps in a network of any size is a large undertaking. In order to tackle such a project, it is helpful to address one small part of the picture by detailing the steps involved in securing network infrastructure servers in a workgroup. To do so requires developing both generic security steps and specific steps for each infrastructure role. The next step requires an understanding of various deployment models and how to secure them. After the appropriate model is chosen, the generic security template can be used to secure all computer systems, and new, incremental actions can be specified for each additional computer role. This process, of choosing the right infrastructure and developing incremental security steps for different roles, can be followed no matter which operating system is used and can be used when new operating systems and computer roles are added to the network.

Develop Security Baselines

Developing a security baseline is simply determining which security recommendations will be followed for all computers in a generic category. The first step is to use common security principles to develop a security policy. If a security policy exists, then you will need to check the recommended steps that follow against the security policy. Finally, the implementation details are developed by applying the policy to the operating systems that are used in the network. Table 5-1 lists areas that should be considered in developing the baseline. Many of these areas require their own chapter to define appropriate security. Following the table are hardening steps that may not be directly covered in other chapters. Since the goal of this chapter is to define security for network infrastructure servers, the baseline described here is for Windows servers. Additional information on defining security for specific infrastructure servers is defined in the section "Develop Incremental Security Steps." Where practical, the steps required to implement the baseline using local administrative tools are detailed or references are made to where implementation details can be found. Remember that the goal is to automate security, and techniques for doing so will be explained in the section "Select Methods and Models for Security Deployment."

You must also understand that not all of the baseline security recommendations may be available across all operating systems. It is also true that for different operating systems, different tools may need to be used. Wherever possible, these differences will be noted.

Hardening Step	Where to Find More Information
Implement a password policy	Chapter 2
Limit user rights	Section "Limit User Rights"
Restrict access to resources	Chapter 10
Harden communications	Chapter 11
Disable optional subsystems	Section "Disable Optional Subsystems"
Disable unnecessary services	Section "Disable or Remove Unnecessary Services"
Configure auditing	Chapter 13
Configure miscellaneous security	Section "Implement Miscellaneous Security Configuration"

Table 5-1. Security Baseline for Servers

Limit User Rights

User rights can be examined in Windows NT 4.0 from User Manager. Windows 2000, Windows XP, and Windows Server 2003 user rights can be examined and modified in the Local Security Policy (Figure 5-1) as well as via other tools. You cannot modify user rights on Windows 9x or Windows ME. You can use System Policies to restrict users' abilities to use some software.

NOTE The Windows XP and Windows Server 2003 Local Security Policy interface does not provide an Effective Settings column. The Effective Settings column in Windows 2000 displays the settings for user rights after the application of any applied Group Policies.

Baseline Modifications for User Rights

The list that follows considers rights exposed in the Windows Server 2003 operating system for easy adjustment. Some of these rights are not available or not modifiable in earlier operating systems. For example, the right to take ownership is inherently given to the Administrators group in Windows NT 4.0. You cannot adjust this right in the GUI. You can give users the right to take ownership of a specific resource, but you cannot assign this right across the entire operating system. However, Windows Server 2003 does provide a way to assign other groups this user right. Table 5-2 provides a listing of modifications to baseline user rights. The table does not include user rights that are by default restricted. Do not add groups to additional user rights.

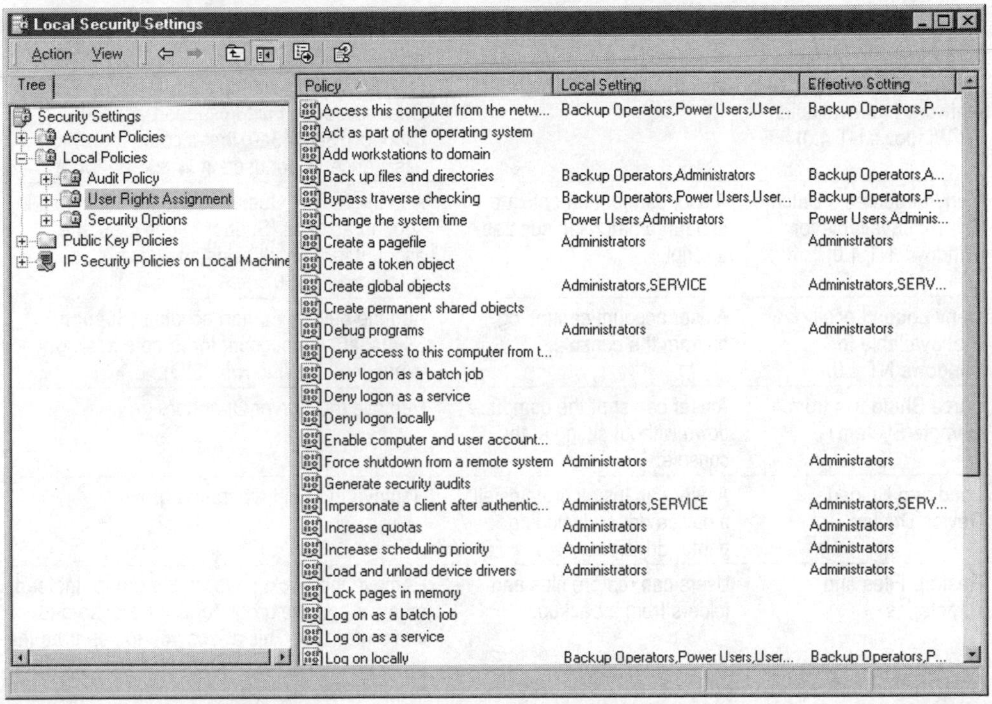

Figure 5-1. User rights

User Right	Description	Modification
Change the System Time	Users can change the time. The correct time is critical in order to ensure logs and audit logs record the correct time events.	Remove Power Users.
Debug Programs	Users can run a debugger. This ability provides the user with access to sensitive and critical operating system components. There is little need for this right on production systems.	Remove the Administrators group from this right—no user group should have this right in the baseline.

Table 5-2. Restrict User Rights

User Right	Description	Modification
Deny Access to This Computer from the Network (not available for Windows NT 4.0)	A user cannot connect from the network.	Add the following accounts: ANONYMOUS LOGON, built-in Administrators account, local Guest account, built-in support account (Support_388945a0, the account for remote assistance, is not used in Windows 2000).
Deny Logon as a Batch Job (not available for Windows NT 4.0)	A user cannot authenticate and run a batch job such as a script.	Add the built-in Guest account and the built-in support account (Support_388945a0, the account for remote assistance, is not used in Windows 2000).
Deny Logon Locally (not available for Windows NT 4.0)	A user account cannot log on from the console.	Add the built-in support account (Support_388945a0, the account for remote assistance, is not used in Windows 2000).
Force Shutdown from a Remote System	A user can shut the computer down without sitting at the console.	Remove the Server Operators group.
Load and Unload Device Drivers	A user can install or uninstall a device driver, including printer drivers.	Remove the Print Operators group.
Restore Files and Directories	Users can restore files and folders from a backup.	Remove the Backup Operators group. Instead, create a specific group for this purpose and add that group. This allows you to separate the privileges of backup and restore. You can then restrict physical access to backup media to only those with a right to back up, unless there is a verified need to restore. This will prevent inadvertent restoration of old data over good data and provides the opportunity to prevent an attack using this technique.
Shut Down the System	Users can shut down the system from the console.	Remove Power Users and Users. (Remember this is a baseline for servers; a baseline for workstations should not remove these groups.)

Table 5-2. Restrict User Rights *(continued)*

Modify User Rights Using the Local Security Policy

To modify user rights via the Local Security Policy on Windows 2000:

1. Open the Local Security Policy through Start | Administrative Tools.
2. Expand Local Policies, expand User Rights.
3. Double-click the user right to modify.

4. Select the user group or user to delete and click the Local Policy Setting check
   box to deselect, as shown here:

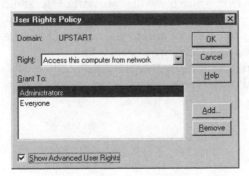

Or click the Add button, use the object picker to select the user or group to add, and
then click OK.

Modify User Rights Using User Manager for NT 4.0

To modify user rights:

1. Open the User Manager.

2. Select the Policy menu and then select User Rights.

3. Select the check box Advanced User Rights in order to display all user rights
   as shown here:

4. Select the right.

5. Add or remove users or groups.

Disable Optional Subsystems

Windows NT 4.0 was originally designed so that it could run programs developed for OS/2 or for POSIX 1.1 compliance. Two optional subsystems are still provided in the other Windows systems based on Windows NT technology. Updates to the POSIX files are also available as part of services for Unix. If you are using the Unix services in order to provide compatibility with Unix systems, the subsystem is not optional and should not be removed. The subsystems are not started unless a program is run that requires them. The idea behind disabling optional subsystems is that removing any part of the system that is not necessary strengthens security because it reduces the number of targets or opportunities. If these subsystems are present, there is always the risk that programs written to use these subsystems might be used to attack the operating system. Disabling these systems does not remove all risk; their code still remains on the system, and a vulnerability in them might still be used in an attack, although this becomes less likely.

The POSIX and OS/2 subsystems can be disabled by

- Deleting the Optional, POSIX, and OS/2 values at HKEY_LOCAL_ MACHINE\SYSTEM\CurrentControlSet\Control\SessionManager\ Subsystems

- Deleting the OS2LibPath entry at HKEY_LOCAL_MACHINE\SYSTEM\ CurrentControlSet\Control\SessionManager\environment

- Deleting the value OS/2 Subsystem for NT at HKEY_LOCAL_MACHINE\ SOFTWARE\Microsoft\

The POSIX and OS/2 code can be removed. Another method of ensuring the POSIX and OS/2 code is not available is to develop an installation configuration that does not include these files. However, since these files are part of the standard default installation, service packs and security patches may re-install the files. If you remove the files, remember to test new service packs and patches to see if the files are replaced and then develop a script or other methodology to deal with this.

POSIX- and OS/2-related flies are Psxss.exe, psxdll.dll, posix.exe, pax.exe, os2ss.exe, os2dll.exe, os2.exe, and os2ssrv.exe.

Disable or Remove Unnecessary Services

Services are developed to allow background software to run. Each service uses an account to authenticate to the operating system and then uses the security context of that account to do its work. Many, if not most, services run under the context of the local system account and have full control of the operating system. Two new accounts in Windows Server 2003, the network service account and the local service account, have reduced privileges and are used for many services. Do not arbitrarily change the account used to run a service, as you may cause the service to become inoperable.

The reason for disabling unnecessary services is that when running, the service can be exploited to cause harm to the system. Harm can be caused by simple misuse, or because there is vulnerability in the service's code. For example, the telnet service can be used to remotely access services. The vulnerability it introduces is that the logon credentials traverse the network in clear text. These are best practices for securing services:

- Do not install services that will not be used.

- Disable any questionable service (any service that is not required for the basic operation of the operating system) in baseline security.

- Enable services in computers that require that service.

- Determine what can be done to secure the use of the required services.

- Implement those processes.

NOTE   Some services are disabled or not installed by default in all Windows systems based on Windows NT technologies, and many more services are disabled by default in Windows Server 2003.

Table 5-3 lists the services that should be disabled for the server security baseline. A similar list can be used to prepare a baseline for clients; however, many services are server services and cannot be installed on clients, so it is unnecessary to include these services. The table provides a description of each service and notes operating systems versions where that service is not available. When examining the table, keep the following points in mind:

- Many of the services listed are not part of the Windows NT 4.0 or Windows 2000 operating system. Some of the features these services provide were bundled into other services prior to Windows Server 2003. By unbundling the services,

Microsoft provides more control. You can now disable some features without disabling others.

- You should, however, before arbitrarily disabling services, be careful to determine dependencies. Disabling some services will automatically prevent other services from running.

- Some services listed in the table are not installed by default; however, when they are part of a security baseline and disabling them is enforced, if the service is installed, it will not run.

HEADS UP!

The list of services provided in Table 5-3 that should be disabled in a security baseline seeks to disable the maximum number of services and still allow the Windows computer to boot and operate. It does not consider the services required for a domain controller to operate. You must create a different security baseline for domain controllers, and you should not attempt to dcpromo (promote a Windows 2000 or Windows Server 2003 server to DC) a server secured by this baseline. Remember, always test your security baseline in a test environment before using it in a production one.

Service	Description	Not Available
Alerter	Used to notify Administrator of events.	
Application Layer Gateway Service	A subcomponent of the Internet Connection Firewall that can be used to run vendor-produced protocol-specific APIs made to allow their protocols to be passed through the firewall.	Windows NT 4.0, Windows 2000
Application Management	Used during program install. Also used by Add/Remove programs to create a list of installed software.	Windows NT 4.0, Windows 2000
ASP .NET State Service	Used to run out-of-process session states for ASP.NET. If the server is not a web server, this service is not needed, and it may not be needed for some web servers.	Windows NT 4.0, Windows 2000
Automatic Updates	Used to automatically request information on and download and install security updates. Not recommended for environments over 25 workstations. Leaving the service enabled and configured requires each system to poll Microsoft periodically and can be a bandwidth issue. If updates are installed automatically, additional problems can occur. Updates should be tested before installing in production environments.	Windows NT 4.0, Windows 2000 prior to SP3 update

Table 5-3.   Windows Services That Can Be Disabled in the Security Baseline

Service	Description	Not Available
Background Intelligent Transfer Service	Background file transfer mechanism used with automatic updates.	Windows NT 4.0, Windows 2000
Certificate Services	Necessary for establishing a certification authority.	Windows NT 4.0 prior to the Option Pack
Client Service for NetWare	Access to file and print services on NetWare servers.	
ClipBook	Create and share pages of data for viewing by remote users. Might be used to expose sensitive data.	Windows NT 4.0
Cluster Service	Controls cluster server operations.	
Computer Browser	Also known as the Browser service. Maintains list of computers on the network and supplies that information to those programs that request it. May expose too much information to rogue computers on the network.	
DHCP Server	Allocates IP addresses and provides other network information.	
Distributed File System	Manages logical volumes distributed across a network. Is necessary for Active Directory SYSVOL shares.	Windows NT 4.0 base operating system
Distributed Link Tracking Client	Maintains links between NTFS file system files within computer or across computers in a domain. (Shortcuts and Object Linking and Embedding links can continue to work even if the target file is moved.)	Windows NT 4.0
Distributed Link Tracking Server	Stores information on files for each volume in the domain and enables the Distributed Link Tracking Client to track files moved within the same domain.	Windows NT 4.0
Distributed Transaction Coordinator	Coordinates transactions for distributed applications such as databases or message queues.	Windows NT 4.0 without SQL
DNS Server	Provides DNS name resolution.	
Error Reporting Service	Collects, stores, and reports Microsoft application errors to Microsoft. Many organizations do not want any information on their computer systems to leave their network. Using Group Policy, error reporting can be configured to report these types of error to an error reporting tool stored on a file server. Administrators can then filter what information is reported to Microsoft.	Windows NT 4.0, Windows 2000
Fax Service	Allows sending and receiving of fax messages.	Windows NT 4.0, Windows 2000
File Replication	Automatic copying of file changes to other servers.	Windows NT uses a different service (Directory Replicator)
File Server for Macintosh	Enables Macintosh users to access and use files on Windows.	

Table 5-3. Windows Services That Can Be Disabled in the Security Baseline *(continued)*

Service	Description	Not Available
FTP Publishing Service	FTP server.	
Help and Support	Runs Help and Support center applications such as remote assistance. Without the service, users can view .chm help files but cannot open or use the Help and Support Center.	Windows NT 4.0, Windows 2000
HTTP SSL	Enables IIS to use Secure Sockets Layer (SSL). A web server service only.	Windows NT 4.0, Windows 2000
Human Interface Device Access	Enables use of special input and output devices. If it is stopped, some buttons and controls on USB keyboards and speakers will not work.	Windows NT 4.0
IIS Admin Service	Necessary to administer IIS.	Windows NT 4.0
IMAP CD-Burning COM Service	Enables Windows Server 2003 CD-burning services. Does not affect third-party CD-burning products.	Windows NT 4.0, Windows 2000
Indexing Service	Indexes files.	Windows NT 4.0 prior to the Option Pack
Infrared Monitor	Enables file and image sharing via infrared.	Windows NT 4.0, Windows 2000, Window Server 2003 Web server or Enterprise versions
Internet Authentication Service	An implementation of RADIUS.	Windows NT 4.0 prior to the Option Pack.
Intersite Messaging	Enables messages between computers in Windows server sites. (Used for mail-based replication between Active Directory sites.)	Windows NT 4.0
Kerberos Key Distribution Center	Enables logon using Kerberos.	Windows NT 4.0
License Logging Service	Monitors and records client access licensing for IIS, Terminal Services, file and print sharing for some products that are not part of the operating system, such as SQL Server. Disabling this service does not disable license enforcing.	
Message Queuing	Tool for developing messaging applications for Windows.	Windows NT 4.0
Message Queuing Down Level Clients	Active Directory access for downlevel clients such as Windows NT 4.0 and Windows 2000.	Windows NT 4.0, Windows 2000
Message Queuing Triggers	Rule-based monitoring of message queues.	Windows NT 4.0
Messenger	Sends or receives messages from users and computers, or by the Alerter service. It is not related to the Windows Messenger (an IM product). This service, if accessible across the Internet, is used to pop-up Ads and notices that look as if they came from an Administrator.	

Table 5-3. Windows Services That Can Be Disabled in the Security Baseline *(continued)*

Service	Description	Not Available
Microsoft POP3 Service	E-mail transfers and retrieval services.	Windows NT 4.0, Windows 2000
.NET Framework Support Service	Provides the run-time environment for .NET, the Common Language Runtime (CLR).	Windows NT 4.0
NetMeeting Remote Desktop Sharing	Allows NetMeeting sessions to share the desktop across the network. This control of the user's desktop can be exploited.	Windows NT 4.0
Network DDE DSDM	Manages DDE network shares. Used by Network DDE to manage shared conversations. This service does not manage normal file shares.	
Network News Transport Protocol	Allows computer to act as a news server.	
Portable Media Serial Number	Retrieves the serial number of a portable music player connected to the computer.	Windows NT 4.0
Print Server for Macintosh	Allows use of Windows printers by Macintosh.	
Print Spooler	Manages local and network print queues.	
QoS RSVP	Provides network signaling and traffic control setup.	Windows NT 4.0
Remote Access Auto Connection Manager	Detects unsuccessful connection attempts to remote networks and computers. Offers alternative connections such as dial-up.	Windows NT 4.0
Remote Access Connection Manager	Manages dial-up and VPN connections from the computer to remote networks.	Windows NT 4.0 prior to the Option Pack
Remote Administration Service	Required by some remote administration tools.	Windows NT 4.0, Windows 2000
Remote Desktop Help Session Manager	Manages and Controls Remote Assistance.	Windows NT 4.0, Window 2000
Remote Installation (RIS)	Provides the ability to install Windows operating systems on Pre-Execution Environment (PXE)–enabled client computers.	Windows NT 4.0
Remote Procedure Call Locator Service	Enables RPC clients using the RpcNs family of APIs to locate RPC servers. It is used by few applications other than those available in 1995.	
Remote Server Manager	Is an interface for remote administration tasks and manages remote administration alerts.	Windows NT 4.0, Windows 2000
Remote Server Monitor	Provides monitoring of system resources.	Windows NT 4.0, Windows 2000
Remote Storage Notification	Notifies when secondary storage is accessed.	Windows NT 4.0
Remote Storage Server	Stores infrequently used files in secondary storage.	Windows NT 4.0
Removable Storage	Manages and catalogs removable media.	Windows NT 4.0.
Resultant Set of Policy Provider	Simulates Resultant Set of Policy (RsoP) for Group Policy settings.	Windows NT 4.0, Windows 2000

Table 5-3. Windows Services That Can Be Disabled in the Security Baseline *(continued)*

Service	Description	Not Available
Routing and Remote Access	Provides routing services, VPN, and NAT.	Windows NT 4.0 prior to the Option Pack
SAP Agent	Advertises network services on an IPX network.	
Secondary Logon (RunAs)	Allows a user to run software in the context of another security principal. This is often used by an Administrator while logged on as an ordinary user. However, it can also be used to bypass some third-party security software.	Windows NT 4.0
Shell Hardware Detection	Monitors and provides notification for autoplay hardware events. It detects pictures, music, or video files on removable media, and devices can autolaunch applications to play or display that content.	Windows NT 4.0., Windows 2000
Simple Mail Transport Protocol	Functions as an e-mail submission and relay agent.	
Simple TCP/IP Services	Provides support for Echo, discard, character generator, daytime, and quote of the day.	
Single Instance Storage Groveler	Integral component of RIS and reduces the amount of storage needed on the RIS volume.	Windows NT 4.0
Smart Card	Manages and controls access to smart card inserted in a smart card reader.	Windows NT 4.0
SNMP Service	Simple Network Management (SNMP) services requests for SNMP information, such as the status of network devices and the management of them. If not properly secured, it can be exploited to provide unauthorized individuals information about systems on the network or the ability to manage them.	
SNMP Trap Service	Receives Trap messages generated by SNMP service.	
Special Administration Console Helper	Used in Windows Server 2003 for remote management of servers that have received a stop error.	Windows NT 4.0, Windows 2000
SQLAgent	Job scheduler and monitoring service for SQL Server. Required for SQL replication and autorestart.	Unavailable on any OS unless SQL Server is installed
Task Scheduler	Used to configure and enable automated tasks.	Windows NT 4.0
TCP/IP Print Server	Enables TCP/IP-based printing using the Line Printer Daemon Service (LPDSVC) (required for printing to Windows printers from Unix computers).	
Telephony	Provides support for control of telephony devices and the ability to act as clients for services such as private branch exchanges (PBXs) and IP-based voice connections.	Windows NT 4.0
Telnet	Provides terminal sessions to telnet clients. Authorized users can run console-based applications remotely. Passes logon credentials in clear text.	Windows NT 4.0

Table 5-3.   Windows Services That Can Be Disabled in the Security Baseline *(continued)*

Service	Description	Not Available
Terminal Services Licensing	Provides license management for clients. Does not impact Terminal service in administration mode, the default installation of terminal services on Windows 2000 and Window Server 2003 computers.	Windows NT 4.0 except Terminal Services Edition
Terminal Services Session Directory	Can be used with clustered terminal servers to manage client access to virtual terminal services sessions.	Windows NT 4.0, Windows 2000
Trivial FTP Daemon (TFTP)	Provides FTP services that do not require user name and password. It is a part of RIS.	Windows NT 4.0
Uninterruptible Power Supply (UPS)	Manages UPS systems connected via a serial port.	
Upload Manager	Manages file transfers between servers and clients. Supports transfer of information between the computer and Microsoft to help users find drivers.	Windows NT 4.0, Windows 2000
Virtual Disk Service	Manages block storage virtualization. A vendor-neutral technology for managing logical volumes such as RAID.	Windows NT 4.0, Windows 2000
WebClient	Provides document access over HTTP using WebDAV (a file access protocol).	Windows NT 4.0, Windows 2000
Web Element Manager	Serves web administration interface access (to the Administration Web site) over port 8098.	Windows NT 4.0, Windows 2000
Windows Audio	Manages plug and play events for audio devices such as sound cards.	Windows NT 4.0, Windows 2000
Windows Image Acquisition (WIA)	Provides image acquisition services for scanners and cameras.	Windows NT 4.0, Windows 2000
Windows Internet Name Service (WINS)	Provides NetBIOS name resolution.	
Windows Media Services	Provides streaming media services over IP-based networks.	Windows NT 4.0
Windows System Resource Manager	Policy-based management of CPU and memory for applications or scenarios where multiple instances of the same service may be deployed (such as multiple instances of SQL server).	Windows NT 4.0, Windows 2000
WINHTTP Web Proxy Auto-Discovery Service	Implements Web Proxy Auto Discovery (WPAD), a protocol that allows an HTTP client to discover a proxy configuration.	Windows NT 4.0, Windows 2000
Wireless Configuration	Enables automatic configuration for IEEE 802.11 wireless adapters.	Windows NT 4.0, Windows 2000
World Wide Web Publishing Service	Is a web server.	Windows NT 4.0 prior to the Option Pack

Table 5-3.   Windows Services That Can Be Disabled in the Security Baseline *(continued)*

To disable services:

1. Open the Services console or tool.
2. Select the service to disable.
3. Use the Startup Type drop-down box to select Disabled.

Implement Miscellaneous Security Configuration

Some security baseline steps do not fit under the broad categories already mentioned. These opportunities for securing Windows can be accomplished via registry entries, or by using the Security Options portion of the Local Security Policy.

If you examine the Security Options section, you will also find many security steps that fall under the broad headings that are addressed elsewhere. For example, items that are related to authentication have already been addressed in Chapter 2, and items that refer to systems access will be discussed in Chapter 10. You should also be aware that Security Options Sections of the Windows XP, Windows 2000, and Windows Server 2003 Local Security Policy may differ both in number and in name. Most naming differences are self-explanatory, and therefore the nomenclatures of the latest version of Windows, Windows Server 2003, is used.

HEADS UP!

Avoid using a registry editor to make changes whenever possible. When the registry is edited directly, it is very easy to make an error. The error may mean that the change does not have the intended results, and it is not difficult to make the computer unbootable and unrecoverable. Changes are made as they are entered (there is no process of "saving" the registry before changes are put into effect). If editing the registry is the only way available, use caution, save the registry key before making the change, ensure you have current data backups, and wherever possible test the change on a test computer first and then use a tested script to apply the change to the production computer.

Do Not Display Last User Name

When the user name of the last user to log on is displayed, that is half the information required by an attacker to log on at the console. You may argue that this is not a huge risk, but still, it requires little effort to prevent. In addition, you will increase the user's ability to remember authentication credentials, as the information has to be entered for access. This knowledge is useful when troubleshooting problems but is often unknown by users because they do not have to enter it.

- Disable the Security option "Interactive Logon: Do not display last user name."
- Or use the registry entry: Add or configure the value DontDisplayLastUserName and set it to 1 at HKEY_LOCAL_MACHINE\ SOFTWARE\Microsoft\Windows Nt\Current Version\WinLogon.

Add a Logon Notice

Provide a legal notice that at least warns unauthorized users not to attempt to log on. In the past, attackers have gotten away with hacking systems by pointing out that a message "welcomed" them to enter the system.

- Add a logon notice to the Security option "Interactive Logon: Message text for users attempting to log on."
- Or use the registry entry: Modify the LegalNoticeCaption and LegalNoticeText values at HKEY_LOCAL_MACHINE\SOFTWARE\Microsoft\Windows Nt\ Current Version\WinLogon.

Develop Incremental Security Steps

Network infrastructure services such as DNS, DHCP, and WINS can be deployed on Windows NT 4.0 Server, Windows 2000 Server, and Windows Server 2003. Each infrastructure service enables the server to play a specific role. Addressing the unique role of each infrastructure server may require different steps.

Harden the Infrastructure Group

After developing the baseline, the first step is to secure infrastructure servers as a group. This means that you should review the base policy to determine if there are areas that can or need to be adjusted. The results of examining the sections of the baseline policy described in Table 5-1 are listed in Table 5-4.

Hardening Step	Modifications for Infrastructure Servers
Implement a password policy	The local password policy of critical servers should be adjusted to reflect a stronger password policy. Administrators accessing these servers have more power; it makes sense to make the accounts harder to access.
Limit user rights	User rights on these servers might also be restricted, but you may want to pay attention to how the services are used. For example, you might restrict logon rights and prevent users who do not need to log on to the server from accessing it. Perhaps a subset of administrators is the only group that needs to log on. If you can determine this, then provide access to only this group. Use of these services does not require authentication, so you may want to severely restrict logon rights.
Restrict access to resources	In addition to restricting logon access, access to files and registry keys may be more closely restricted.
Harden communications	Block ports (Windows Server 2003, Windows 2000, and Windows XP): Use IPSec policies to block access to all ports, but leave open ports that may be required for the service and for administration. For example, provide access to port 3389 TCP to allow remote administration via terminal services.
Disable optional subsystems	N/A
Disable unnecessary services	The services used to provide infrastructure services are disabled in the baseline. They should be enabled. In addition, it is possible in Windows 2000 and Windows Server 2003 to secure services so that only specific accounts can set the service to start as disabled, automatic, or manual and can stop and start the service.
Configure auditing	Some services provide the ability to log additional information.

Table 5-4.   Incremental Steps for All Infrastructure Servers

Harden DHCP

An interruption in DHCP service means that clients will not be able to obtain an IP address. Hardening DHCP means mitigating the risk of a Denial of Service (DoS) attack and protecting the DHCP server form unauthorized access. To do these things:

- Secure log access.
- Configure DHCP servers in pairs.
- Turn on extended DHCP logging.

Windows 2000 and Windows Server 2003 DHCP can be configured to perform dynamic updates and secure dynamic updates to Windows 2000 and Windows Server 2003 DNS. Windows 2000, Windows XP, or Windows Server 2003 clients can also be configured to perform dynamic updates. DHCP can perform dynamic updates for all Windows clients.

Ensure That Extended DHCP Logging Is Enabled

By default, startup and shutdown service events are recorded in the system events log file. Some versions of DHCP automatically log additional information to their own log files. This feature is configurable, although in some versions it cannot be disabled. Extended logging is important because it will contain detailed information about the activities of clients and does include both Media Access Control (MAC) and IP addresses. This information can help identify the source of an attack or a problem. MAC and IP addresses can, of course, be spoofed, but since not every address is spoofed, the extra information in these logs is invaluable. When DHCP extended logging is enabled, you must frequently archive the log, as it may grow quite large. (By default, in Windows Server 2003 logging will stop when less than 20MB of disk space is available. To archive the log, stop the DHCP service, copy the log, to removable media, delete the log from the DHCP folder and restart the DHCP service.

In Windows NT 4.0 DHCP audit logging is not enabled till post service pack 2. To enable logging:

1. Open the DHCP Manager.

2. Right-click the server and select Properties.

3. Select the Enable DHCP logging check box.

4. Click OK.

After applying service pack 4, DHCP logging is enabled by default and cannot be disabled, and new registry entries are added that allow setting of parameters such as the name of the log file and ways to manage the size of the log file. For more information, see Knowledge Base article 188027.

To turn on extended logging in Windows 2000 and Windows Server 2003,

1. Open the DHCP console through Start | Administrative Tools.

2. Right-click the DHCP server and select Properties.

3. Select the General tab and click Enable DHCP audit logging as shown here:

4. Click OK to close the property page.
5. A log file is created in %windir%\system32\DHCP.

Secure Log Access

Change the permission on the DHCP folder by removing access from the Server Operators and Authenticated Users groups. Only Administrators should have access to the logs.

Configure DHCP Servers in Pairs

Configure DHCP servers in pairs to mitigate the impact of a DoS attack. If only one DHCP server exists, an attacker who can successfully overwhelm that server can deny service to legitimate requests. If DHCP servers are configured in pairs, then even if one server is the victim of a DoS, the other will be able to provide addressing for legitimate clients. To configure DHCP servers in pairs, each DHCP server is provided some portion of the address pool set aside for DHCP assignment. An 80/20 split is usually recommended. For example, if the address range 192.168.5.100 to 192.168.5.200 is set aside for DHCP assignment, configure one DHCP server with a scope of 192.168.5.100 to 192.168.5.170 and the other with 192.168.5.171 to 192.168.5.200. Clients on the physical subnet with these servers will be granted an address by whichever DHCP server responds first. If one server is under attack, clients may obtain an address from the other server. (Of course, if both servers are under attack, then no client may be able to obtain an address.)

Use IPSec Policies

Windows Server 2003 and Windows 2000 DHCP servers can be further protected by developing IPSec policies block all access except that needed for administration and to provide the DHCP service to clients. Four filters are necessary, and a fifth is optional:

- A filter that blocks all inbound traffic
- A filter that allows access from the DHCP server to all domain controllers from any port to any port
- A filter to allow any traffic from *any* address, UDP ports 67 and 68 to the DHCP server
- A filter to allow port 135 traffic (used for the DHCP manager)
- If the Multicast Address Dynamic Client Application Protocol (MADCAP) is used, this service is part of the DHCP service in Windows Server 2003. Clients of either protocol may or may not be clients of the other. A filter must be created to allow access to UDP port 2535

Configure DHCP for Secure Dynamic Updates

Secure dynamic DNS updates are configured on the DNS server; however, the following items should be considered with respect to the DHCP server when this is done.

Install DHCP on a Member Server   If DHCP is installed on a Windows 2000 domain controller and secure dynamic updates are used, the DHCP server may have the ability to update client records that it does not have the authority to update. This is because the DHCP service uses the credentials of the local computer to make the changes. There are two ways to prevent this from happening: do not install DHCP services on a domain controller, or if you must install DHCP on a domain controller, configure a unique user account to use for applying updates and use **netsh** to configure the DHCP service to impersonate a user account in order to perform DNS registrations.

To configure DHCP:

```
netsh dhcp server set dnscredentials user_name domain_name password
```

To stop the DHCP server from using the user credentials for DNS registration:

```
netsh dhcp server delete dnscredentials dhcpfullforce
```

To determine which account is being used:

```
netsh dhcp server show credentials
```

Add DHCP Servers to DNSUPdateProxy Group   When multiple DHCP servers exist in an environment, any one of them may end up leasing an address to any client. If DHCP servers are not included in the DNSUPdateProxy group, then only the first DHCP server to lease the client an address can update the client's record in DNS. Since another DHCP server may eventually lease the client an address, this means the client's address may not be modified in DNS.

Enable DNS Dynamic Updates   Windows 2000, Windows XP, and Windows Server 2003 clients can dynamically update records in DNS. Windows NT 4.0 and Windows 9*x* clients cannot. However, DHCP is configured by default to update DNS addresses for these clients.

1. Open the DHCP console.
2. Right-click the server and click Properties.
3. Click the DNS tab.
4. Select Enable DNS dynamic updates according to the settings below as shown here:

5. Select either Always Dynamically Update DNS A and PTR records or Dynamically Update DNS A and PTR Records Only If Requested by the DHCP Clients (the default).

Harden DNS

The DNS server contains information about the structure of the network as well as the addresses for servers and workstations. Information can be found about services on the network such as mail and web servers. In addition, Windows 2000 and Windows Server 2003 DNS also includes information about services offered on the network such as domain controllers, Kerberos, and LDAP servers. To harden DNS:

- Implement DNS only when necessary
- Separate internal DNS and external DNS services
- Configure forwarders
- Use Active Directory–integrated zones
- Configure secure dynamic update
- Harden clients
- Configure multihomed DNS servers to listen on selected addresses
- Secure DNS zones

Implement DNS Only When Necessary

If you do not have Windows 2000 or Windows Server 2003 domains, a DNS server is not a requirement for the internal network. You may find that the DNS services of your ISP are adequate. However, DNS is a critical requirement of Windows 2000 and Windows Server 2003 domains and must be available.

Separate Internal DNS and External DNS Services

Comparatively few computers must be directly available from outside your network. For example, you may have a publicly facing web server and mail server. You protect intranet web services by hosting them on internal computers that are inaccessible from the Internet. Do the same for your DNS services. Host information that must be externally available in an external DNS server, and host information about your internal network in an internal DNS server. The external DNS server can be available on your perimeter network, or you may choose to have your ISP host those addresses on their DNS servers. Protect your internal DNS server by blocking port 53 at the internal firewall. Figure 5-2 shows this design. In the figure, the internal DNS server is accessible to all clients on the internal network. But it is not available from the external network. Port 53 is open on the internal interface of the firewall to allow request for information on external DNS servers, but port 53 access to DNS1 is blocked on the external interface of the firewall to prevent requests for information from the external network to pass through to the internal DNS server.

Use Active Directory–Integrated Zones

Active Directory–integrated zones provide redundancy and can provide extra security for host records.

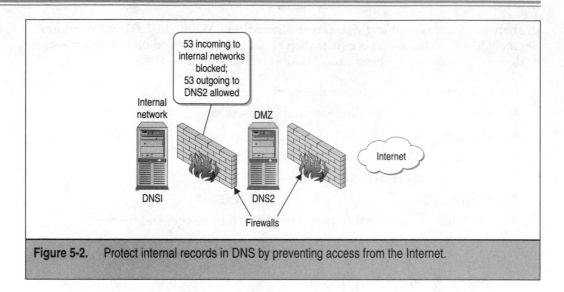

Figure 5-2. Protect internal records in DNS by preventing access from the Internet.

- If Active Directory is used, DNS can be configured to either be a standard DNS server or be integrated with Active Directory. Unless application partitions are configured (this is possible only in Windows Server 2003 domains), DNS information is replicated to every domain controller in the domain and therefore the need for secondary zones may be unnecessary. When DNS is integrated with Active Directory, additional security benefits are possible.

- Replication of DNS data between domain controllers is encrypted by default using a 128-bit or 56-bit key. Any domain controller can serve as a DNS server if DNS services are installed.

- Domain controllers mutually authenticate using Kerberos for RPC replication before replication can occur. (SMTP replication is authenticated with the use of certificates.) Zone transfers are not mutually authenticated.

- Integrated zones can be configured for secure dynamic update. Secure dynamic update protects DNS from attacks seeking to change the IP address listed in DNS. If dynamic updates alone are used, a rogue computer could be given the same name as an existing computer and use dynamic updating to modify the IP address in the DNS server.

Integrated zones are configured during installation of DNS, but the zone type can be changed:

1. Open the DNS console through Start | Administrative Tools.
2. Right-click the zone and select Properties.

3. On the general page, click the Type: Change button.

4. Select Active Directory Integrated as shown here:

Configure Secure Dynamic Update

Secure dynamic update can be configured when Active Directory–integrated zones are used. Using secure dynamic updates provides control over who can modify the IP address recorded in DNS for the computer. Once this setting is enabled, rogue computers can be prevented from changing addresses in DNS. In order to modify an address in DNS, a computer must

- Be a member computer in the domain where the DNS server resides.

- Be authenticated.

- Have permission to access and modify the information. By default, the group Authenticate Users is given the Create permission on the zone. This means that any authenticated user or computer can create a new object in the zone. The user that creates the object becomes the owner and has permission to change the settings. You can change the default behavior for the zone by changing these permissions. You can also explicitly set permissions for specific objects in the zone.

To change to secure dynamic update, change the Dynamic Updates drop-down box on the General page of DNS properties to Only Secure Updates (see the preceding illustration).

Reserve FQDN in DNS

Secure dynamic update prevents rogue computers from changing the IP address of DNS clients on the network. What about servers that have not been introduced to the network yet? To reserve these names, you can configure the fully qualified domain name of the server as a record in DNS and set permissions on this record to allow IP address assignment by specific computers or users.

Configure Forwarders

Internal clients should not access DNS services on the external network. Instead, set the internal DNS server to forward requests to the external DNS server for resolution and configure internal clients to make requests for DNS services to the internal DNS server. To configure forwarders for Windows 2000 and Windows Server 2003 DNS:

1. Open the DNS console from Start | Administrative Tools.
2. Right-click the server and select Properties.
3. Select the Forwarders tab.
4. Select the Enable forwarders (Windows 2000) box.
5. Add IP addresses for DNS servers that are available to act as forwarders.
6. Click Add.
7. Click OK.

Windows Server 2003 provides an additional option, conditional forwarders. You can configure DNS to forward requests for specific domains to specific DNS servers.

Windows NT 4.0 DNS forwarders can be configured in the Forwarders dialog box in the DNS administration tool. The information can be configured using the **forwarders** command in the boot file. (The boot file must be located in the %windir%\system32\ DNS folder and named boot.) An example of the **forwarders** command in the boot file to use a list of servers as forwarders is

```
forwarders 192.168.7.89 192.168.7.90
```

Harden DNS Clients

In addition to general client hardening:

- Configure DNS address of DNS server in the client interface.
- Ensure clients use only secure dynamic update.
- Set clients to react to name conflicts.

Configure the DNS Address of the DNS Server in the Client Interface   Configure the DNS address of the internal DNS server directly in the client interface. The address can be configured in the standard installation image for clients to automate the task. Even if DHCP is used, directly configuring the DNS server address on the client will override any address supplied by DHCP. While it is easier to change the DNS server address of clients by assigning it via DHCP, that is the problem. If the DHCP server is compromised, the DNS address supplied to clients can be changed. Clients will then seek DNS resolution from the attacker's DNS server, thus possibly obtaining spoofed addresses for critical services, or obtaining no address at all, resulting in a DoS.

Ensure That Clients Use Only Secure Dynamic Update   By default, Windows XP, Windows 2000, and Windows Server 2003 clients will attempt a nonsecured dynamic IP address update; if that fails, they will attempt a secure dynamic update. However, that behavior can be changed. To do so, change the value UpdateSecurityLevel to 256. This prevents a nonsecure dynamic update. (The value of 0 is the default, and a value of 16 specifies the use of insecure dynamic update only.)

The registry key location of the value is HKEY_LOCAL_MACHINE\SYSTEM\CurrentControlSet\Services\Tcpip\Parameters.

Set Clients to React to Name Conflicts   During IP address registration, if a host with its IP address listed in an insecure dynamic update zone discovers that another computer has registered the first host's name with another IP address, the first client will overwrite the IP address with its own. When secure dynamic update is configured, it will not be successful. You can configure the client to back out of an attempt at modifying the IP address and enter an error message in the Event log when it finds a name conflict. To do so, set the value DisableReplaceAddressesInConflict to 1. The value is located at HKEY_LOCAL_MACHINE\SYSTEM\CurrentControlSet\Services\Tcpip\Parameters.

Configure Multihomed DNS Servers to Listen on Selected Addresses

If DNS servers have multiple network interfaces, manage their accessibility by restricting the DNS service to listening on a single address. Other addresses might be used by management networks. To set this address in Windows 2000 and Windows Server 2003:

1. Open the DNS console through Start | Administration Tools.
2. Right-click the server and select Properties.
3. Select the Interfaces tab.
4. Select Only the following IP addresses.
5. In the IP address box, enter the IP address to use and click Add.
6. Click OK.

In Windows NT 4.0, configure this setting by using the Interfaces dialog box of the DNS administration tool.

Secure DNS Zones

In order to secure DNS zones, secure Registry DNS entries, secure dynamic updates, and restrict zone transfers.

Secure Registry DNS Entries   DNS entries are located in the registry at HKEY_LOCAL_MACHINE\System\CurrentControlSet\Services\DNS\. To secure DNS registry entries, maintain permissions on the key.

By default, permissions on this key are enabled in

- Windows NT 4.0
- Windows 2000
- Windows Server 2003

Restrict Zone Transfers   Zone information is transferred from primary DNS zones to secondary DNS servers in order to duplicate the same information on multiple DNS servers. Zone transfers are not necessary for communicating zone information between DNS servers when zone information is integrated with Active Directory. However, even Active Directory–integrated DNS zones can be configured to do a zone transfer.

Zone transfers should be restricted. If zone transfers are freely available, it is possible for an intruder to obtain all DNS information by simply requesting a zone transfer. Recording the IP address of authorized DNS secondary zone servers on the primary DNS servers will restricts zone transfers. Remember to change the IP address of these servers in DNS if it changes. Take the following steps to restrict zone transfers.

In Windows NT 4.0:

1. Click Start | Administrative Tools | DNS Manager.
2. Right-click the Primary zone icon and select Properties.
3. Click the Notify tab.
4. In the notify list, add the names of Secondary DNS servers that are allowed to do zone transfers.
5. Click the check box Only Allow Access from Secondaries Included on the Notify List.
6. Close the console.

In Windows 2000 and Windows Server 2003:

1. Open the DNS console.
2. Right-click the DNS zone and click Properties.
3. Select the Zone Transfers tab and select the Allow Zone Transfers check box.
4. Click Only to the Following Servers.

5. Add the IP address of one or more DNS secondary servers or click Only to Servers Listed on the Name Servers tab.

6. Click OK to close the property pages.

You can also use the **dnscmd** command to add servers to the list by identifying the DNS name of the zone and the IP address of the secondary DNS server in the command:

```
dnscmd dnserver_name_zone /SecureList Secondary_server_IP_address
```

Carefully Review Requests for Zone Delegation   Management of part of your DNS infrastructure can be delegated. The zone can then be located on a separate DNS server, which may be under the management of a different department or different individuals. In fact, this is one method that may be used when adding Active Directory to a network in which DNS is already established. A zone is delegated and then implemented in Windows DNS for use as the DNS server for the Active Directory–based domains. Turning over administration of delegated zones should be carefully considered to make sure that the DNS server will be properly secured and that only trained and authorized administrators will be able to manage it.

Back Up Zone Information   A backup of zone information should be made so that a server can be restored if necessary.

Harden Security Settings in DNS Configuration

Secure the DNS cache against pollution, consider disabling recursion, and adjust root hints if necessary.

Secure DNS Cache Against Pollution   When a request for a DNS address is made of a DNS server and the server does not have the address, it will attempt to obtain that address from other DNS servers and then add that address to its cache in case it is requested again. If an attacker can pollute the cache by providing an incorrect address, clients might be directed to a rogue server or a DoS condition can occur if the IP address is unreachable.

When the DNS cache is secured against pollution, the risk of an incorrect address being added to the cache is reduced. This is because the DNS server will not cache an IP address unless the address is received from the DNS server authoritative for that domain. Take these steps to secure the DNS cache against pollution:

- In Windows NT 4.0, add the value SecureResponses and set it to 1. The value should be added to HKEY_LOCAL_MACHINE\System\CurrentControlSet\Services\DNS\Parameters.

- In Windows 2000 and Windows Server 2003, the setting Secure cache against pollution is enabled by default. This setting is found on the Advanced tab of DNS server properties as shown in Figure 5-3.

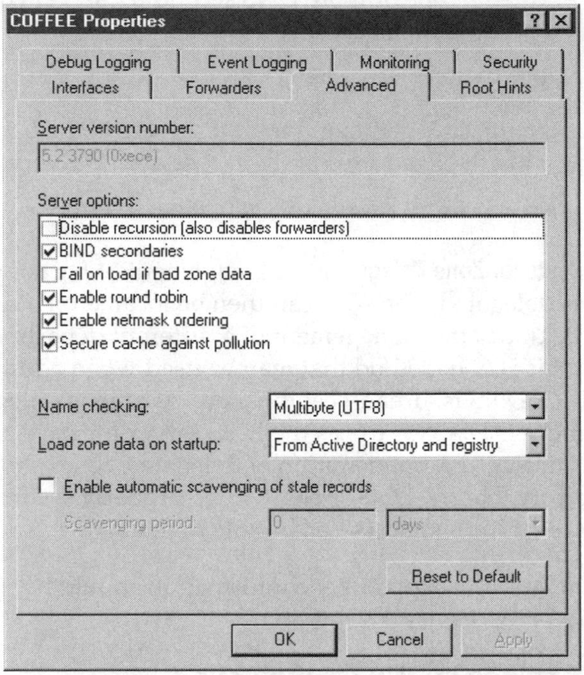

Figure 5-3. Secure DNS cache against pollution.

Disable Recursion When Possible   Recursion is enabled by default so that the DNS server can provide recursive queries for its clients. DNS servers use iterative requests to communicate with each other. If the DNS server is not required to provide recursive queries, disable this capability. When recursion is enabled, an attacker might flood a DNS server with recursive queries and deny access to legitimate clients. Recursion is necessary if DNS servers use forwarders. When using the DNS server on the internal network to service internal network clients, while forwarding requests for external clients to Internet-based DNS servers, recursion is required. However, any flooding attack using recursive inquires will have to come from within your network if you do not make the internal DNS server accessible from the Internet.

To disable recursion, check the Do not use recursion on the Windows 2000 Server Options area of the Advanced property page.

Configure Root Hints If Necessary   If an internal root is present in your internal DNS infrastructure, configure root hints on other DNS servers to point to this root, rather than to Internet root servers. This prevents internal information from going to the Internet.

To configure root hints on Windows 2000 and Windows Server 2003, use the Root Hints tab of the DNS server properties pages. Use the Add button to add a root or select the root listed and use the Remove button to remove it.

Harden WINS

WINS servers may need to be accessible from the Internet, or they may need to replicate information with WINS servers at remote locations. WINS partners transfer NetBIOS names and addresses for servers and clients. That information should not be shared across the public network. Take the following steps to secure WINS server traffic.

Restrict Replication of WINS Data to WINS Replication Partners

Restrict the replication of data between WINS servers to WINS servers that are defined in the WINS interface. This will prevent a rogue WINS server from being used to gain access to NetBIOS names of computers on your network. To restrict replication:

1. Open the WINS console.
2. Right-click.
3. Select the Replication Partners.
4. Select Replicate Only with Partners.
5. Click OK.

Place Internet-Accessible WINS Servers on the Perimeter Networks

Placing WINS servers on the perimeter protects intranet resources while providing WINS resolution for the clients connecting to resources in the perimeter network.

Secure Traffic Between Intranet and Perimeter WINS Servers

If replication between the WINS server in the intranet and perimeter network is required, use the WINS snap-in and select Replicate only with Partners in the Replication Partners Property dialog box. Make sure to do so on both WINS servers. Use pull replication from the intranet servers, and secure traffic by using IPSec.

Secure Traffic Between WINS Replication Partners

Use VPNs to secure traffic between WINS replication partners that share information over the Internet.

Use IPSec Policies to Restrict Access to the WINS Server

The following filters are required:

- A filter to block all inbound traffic
- A filter to allow access from the WINS server to all domain controllers from any port

- A filter to allow access from any computer on any port to port 1512 TCP (WINS resolution server)

- A filter to allow access from other WINS servers to port 42 TCP (WINS replication partner) on the WINS server

Select Methods and Models for Security Deployment

As you can see, how security hardening is applied and exactly what needs to be done will depend on the operating system used, the specific service, and whether or not the server is joined in a domain or part of a workstation. If these servers are member servers in a Windows 2000 or Windows Server 2003 domain, Group Policy can be used to automatically deploy much of the security hardening. If Windows NT 4.0 domains are used, some hardening may be automatically deployed via the use of System Policies. If servers are workgroup members, you may be able to use the Security Configuration and Analysis tools or you may need or choose to develop your own scripts. You can also manually configure each server. Regardless of the logical model, additional steps may be needed to complete the job.

Many, if not most, security hardening steps, whether they involve configuration changes made via administrative Group Policy or System Policy, are carried out by making changes to the Windows registry. In some cases, you may have to directly edit the registry or make direct changes to some other file. Never directly edit the registry unless no other option is available. If multiple computers must have registry changes and no automated tool is available, prepare and test a script. A script can be used on multiple machines and will always make the same change. It is both cumbersome and error-prone to manually configure the registry. The information that follows details when to use which tool. The next section provides information on how to use Security Configuration and Analysis, **secedit**, and security templates to provide security for Windows 2000, Windows XP, and Windows Server 2003 workgroup computers. Other automated tools, such as System Policy and Group Policy, require domain membership and are described further in Chapter 8, where an implementation model for hardening all computers by role is detailed. Use Administrative tools for making changes to security for services. To select tools and models, use the following guidelines:

- Use basic administrative tools when configuring a simple change on a single computer. It's quick and easy to identify that you are making the correct change. Basic administrative tools are those identified in the Administrative Tools menu. They exist for an explicit reason and typically are used by making changes to property pages, or by running wizards that step you through the configuration process. Windows services, DNS, WINS, and DHCP have their own administrative tools.

- Use scripts to apply changes to the registry. Changing registry settings can be automated in a script.

- Use System Policy in Windows NT 4.0 domains. System Policy provides a way to apply a set of registry changes at logon and can be used to effectively manage multiple computers and users.

- Use Security Configuration and Analysis and security templates where appropriate. Security templates can be used to apply security in Windows NT 4.0 (post service pack 4), Windows Server 2003, and Windows 2000. Security templates are applied via the Security Configuration and Analysis tool, by using the command-line tool **secedit**, or in Windows 2000 and Windows Server 2003 domains, by importing the security template into a GPO. The Security Configuration and Analysis tool can be used to configure only one computer at a time, but a script can use **secedit** to automate the application of security templates. Use Group Policy in Windows Server 2003 and Windows 2000 domains.

- Use Group Policy in Windows 2000 and Windows Server 2003 domains. Group Policy can automatically distribute security policy to Windows 2000, Windows Server 2003, and Windows XP Professional systems that are joined in the domain. It is possible to design a hierarchical arrangement of GPOs to explicitly secure different types of systems that are used for different roles.

- Use combinations of tools to address the security of the multiple systems that may exist on the network.

Use Tools to Set General Security Settings in Windows NT 4.0

One of the complaints often made about Windows NT 4.0 security is that no single tool exists that could be used to apply security. Instead many GUI-based tools must be learned, and direct registry entries configured, in order to apply the required and recommended security settings. However, Windows NT 4.0 System Policies can be used to manage some Windows NT 4.0 security settings and Security Templates, and Security Configuration Manager, a Windows NT 4.0 version of Security Configuration and Analysis, can be used post service pack 4.

NOTE To be used, Security Configuration and Analysis must be installed post Sp4. Once it is installed, the file permission settings interface changes to look similar to Windows 2000. In order to properly manage file permissions remotely, make sure that the Security Configuration and Analysis tool is configured on the remote administration computer.

Use System Policy to Restrict Application Usage

The System Policy Editor can be used to create a file that sets Windows NT 4.0 security and user desktop configuration settings. The file must be named ntconfig.pol. To manage Windows 9x computers, a Windows 9x version of the tool can be used to create a config.pol file. Additional template files are provided for managing Microsoft Office. A version of the tool can be used to manage settings for Microsoft Office in Windows Server 2003 and Windows 2000. Be sure to use the correct tool to create files that manage each operating system.

HEADS UP!

If the ntconfig.pol file is present in the netlogon share of a Windows NT 4.0 domain controller in a Windows NT 4.0 domain, Windows NT 4.0 and Windows 2000 and Windows XP clients will read the file and apply its policies by making registry changes. There is no easy way to back out of such changes. Deleting the policy file does not remove changes that have already been made. To recover from a bad policy file, create a new policy file that corrects the changes, or directly edit the registry on the affected computers. Always thoroughly test the file in a test environment before deploying. While System Policies are not as powerful as Group Policies, System Policies can disable a computer so that it is unusable.

The tool can be used in registry mode to edit the registry of the local machine. To use the tool to create an ntconfig.pol file:

1. Open the System Policy Editor through the Administrative Tools menu or use the command-line tool poledit.exe.

2. Select the File menu and choose New Policy.

3. Use the Edit menu to add specific computers or user groups to the policy file. In this way, you can create policies that will affect only these specific users and computers.

4. Double-click the Computer icon or User icon as shown here to open the default policy.

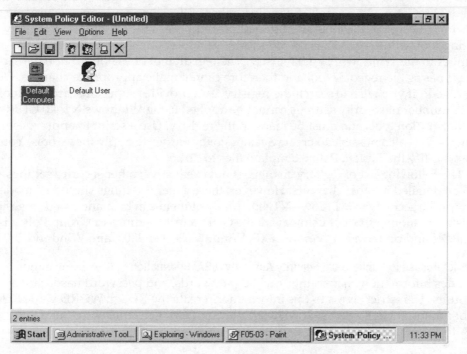

5. Expand sections in the policy to view possible settings.

6. Check boxes for settings are clear, checked, or gray. A box in gray means that the policy will not change the current registry setting. If a box is checked, the setting will be set; if it is clear, the setting will be undone in the registry. Clicking the check box repeated times will cycle among these three options.

7. Click OK to return to the policy editor.

8. Select the File menu Save As selection and enter the name **ntconfig.pol** for the file.

9. Ensure that the location where the file will be saved is the %windir%\System32\ Repl\Import\Scripts folder of the domain controller.

10. Click Save.

11. Click File | Exit to close the file.

NOTE The Import\Scripts path is shared as \\PDC_server_name\Netlogon$. This is the netlogon share. If the file is not present, the policy will not be read and applied by clients.

Use regedt32 to Apply Security Settings

Windows XP and Windows Server 2003 combine the best features of the regedit and regedt32 registry editing tools. Executing either of the commands opens the same tool. In NT 4.0, however, the tools are different. Regedit.exe is the Windows 9*x* registry editing tool, while regedt32 is the Windows NT 4.0 version. Never use regedit to make changes to the Windows NT 4.0 registry. The regedit tool does not provide the same data types as the regedt32 tool and therefore cannot make appropriate changes. Do use regedit if you wish to search the registry, as it provides superior searching tools.

A number of security settings cannot be applied using Windows NT 4.0 GUI-based administration tools and must be made in the registry. Use a script to apply these changes. It is also possible to create System Policy entries to apply these tools. You must modify the System Policy template files to do so.

The following list of registry changes is not exhaustive; other security settings will be detailed in other chapters. However, these general settings should be made to improve security in Windows NT 4.0. (Many of them can be made by editing the registry in another OS, but using available GUI security settings or Group Policy is available and preferred in Windows XP, Windows Server 2003, and Windows 2000.)

Restrict Access to Public Local Security Authority (LSA) Information   LSA information includes information on accounts, cached passwords, and password hashes for service accounts. To restrict access to this information, create the REG_DWORD value Restrict_Anonymous at HKEY_LOCAL_MACHINE\SYSTEM\CurrentControlSet\Control\LSA to 1.

Enable Strong Password Checking: Install passfilt.dll   The add-on passfilt.dll, when installed, prevents the addition of a password that does not meet the following criteria:

- Uses at least three of the following—uppercase letters, lowercase letters, numbers, or special characters
- Is at least six characters long
- Does not use the user's name or any portion of the user's full name

To install passfilt.dll, add the string passfilt.dll to the list at the value NotificationPackages at HKEY_LOCAL_MACHINE\SYSTEM\CurrentControlSet\Control\LSA.

Restrict Null Session Access over Named Pipes   Named pipes are used for network connections to services. Restricting anonymous access to these connections can prevent unauthorized network access. To restrict access, remove all values in the NullSession Pipes and Null SessionShares values at HKEY_LOCAL_MACHINE\CurrentControlSet\Services\LanmanServer\Parameters\.

Set Permissions on Run and Run Once Keys   If a program path is copied to the Run or Run Once keys in the registry, the program will run the next time the computer is booted. To mitigate the chance of this happening, change the permissions on Run, Run Once, Uninstall, and AEDebug to Everyone Read at HKEY_LOCAL_MACHINE\Software\Microsoft\Windows\CurrentVersion\. (These values do not exist on all Windows operating systems.)

Set Paging File to Be Cleared on Shutdown The paging file caches data used during the computer's operation. It is not accessible while the computer is running; however, when the computer is shut down, it is an ordinary file. If the computer is booted to another operating system, then data in the file might be accessible. To ensure that it is not, set the system to clear the file at shutdown by setting the value ClearPageFileAtShutdown to 1. The location of this value is HKEY_LOCAL_MACHINE\CurrentControlSet\Control\SessionManager\MemoryManagement.

NOTE The page file can get quite large. When it is cleared at shutdown, the system may take longer to boot.

Use Security Templates to Define Security Settings

A *security template* is a text file that details security settings using a syntax that can be loaded by various tools and used to apply security settings. Figure 5-4 is a partial view of a security template file. Several default security templates ship with Windows XP,

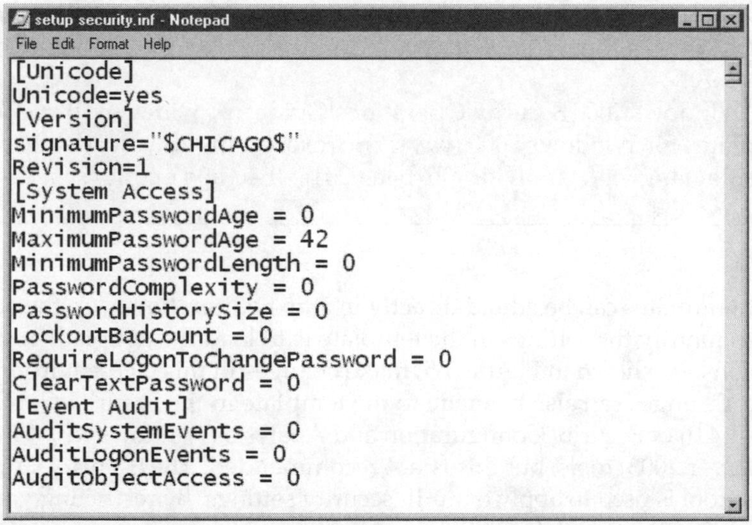
setup security.inf - Notepad
File Edit Format Help
[Unicode]
Unicode=yes
[Version]
signature="$CHICAGO$"
Revision=1
[System Access]
MinimumPasswordAge = 0
MaximumPasswordAge = 42
MinimumPasswordLength = 0
PasswordComplexity = 0
PasswordHistorySize = 0
LockoutBadCount = 0
RequireLogonToChangePassword = 0
ClearTextPassword = 0
[Event Audit]
AuditSystemEvents = 0
AuditLogonEvents = 0
AuditObjectAccess = 0

Figure 5-4. A security template file

Windows Server 2003, and Windows 2000 systems. Security templates for Windows NT 4.0 are available with the Security Configuration Manager tool. Rather than rely on default templates, however, download templates provided by Microsoft as part of practical documents describing security measures for the company's operating systems. Other institutions, including the National Security Agency (www.nsa.gov) and the Center for Internet Security (www.cisecurity.org), have written security templates, and existing templates can be extended, or new ones written, by anyone who cares to learn the syntax. Basically, if a change can be made by editing the registry, that change can be incorporated into a security template.

Important Microsoft Security Documents

The Microsoft documents include more than the templates and should become part of your security library. Each document is a book in itself and provides hundreds of pages of security-related information. Some of the documents you can download follow.

The "Windows Server 2003 Security Guide" provides templates and instructions for securing Windows Server 2003 (www.microsoft.com/downloads/ details.aspx?displaylang=en&familyid=8a2643c1-0685-4d89-b655-521ea6c7b4db).

The "Windows XP Security Guide" provides instructions and templates that can be used to secure Windows XP (www.microsoft.com/downloads/details .aspx?displaylang=en&familyid=2d3e25bc-f434-4cc6-a5a7-09a8a229f118).

The document "Threats and Countermeasures: Security Settings in Windows Server 2003 and Windows XP" details every security setting (www.microsoft .com/ downloads/details.aspx?displaylang=en&familyid=1b6acf93-147a-4481-9346- f93a4081eea8).

The "Windows 2000 Security Operations Guide" provides similar information and templates for Windows 2000 (www.microsoft.com/downloads/details .aspx?displaylang=en&familyid=f0b7b4ee-201a-4b40-a0d2-cdd9775aeff8).

Security templates can be edited directly in a text editor; however, the easiest and safest way to modify the settings in the template is to load the template in the Security Templates console, shown in Figure 5-5, make changes in this GUI environment, and save the file. Changes can also be made to the template in the Security Configuration Manager (NT 4.0) or Security Configuration and Analysis (Windows XP, Windows 2000, Windows Server 2003) tools, but this is not recommended. The Security Configuration and Analysis tool is used to apply or audit security settings. By restricting your changes to directly editing the templates in the Security Templates console, you will always know exactly which settings have been applied or are being audited, since you can

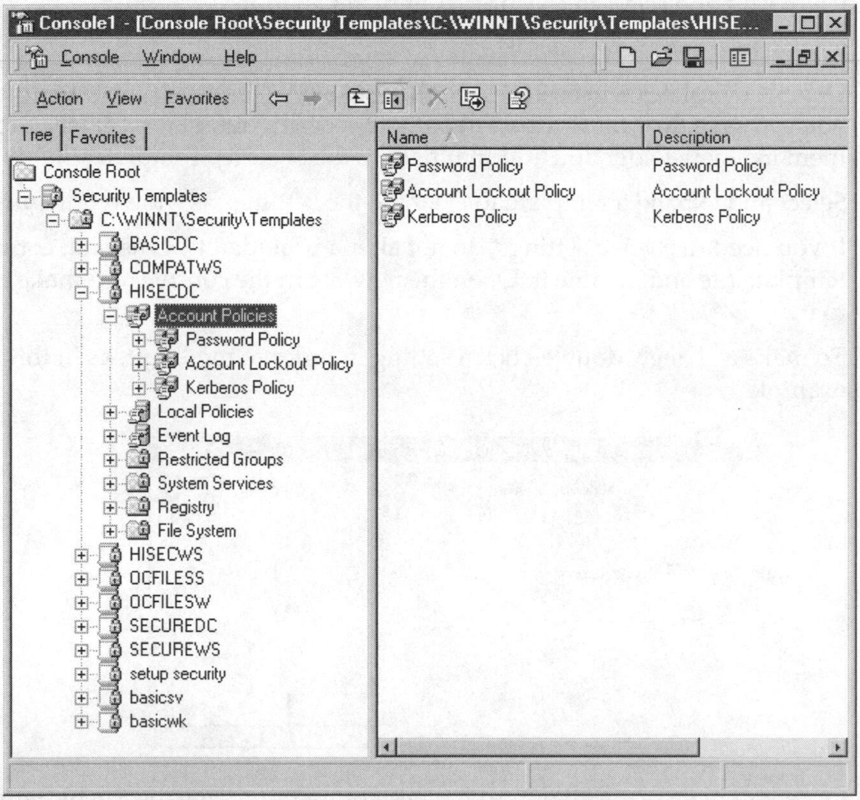

Figure 5-5.   The Security Templates console

point to a template. If, for example, you create a security template called "FileServer" to be used to secure computers that fulfill this role, you can store the original template and always use it on any server to consistently apply security. You can also make it available to the IT auditor to be used in an audit for compliance to security policy. If you modify the template in the Security Configuration and Analysis tool, forget to export the new template, and then replace all copies of the original with it, you have no record of what you have done. More information on how to use these tools to apply security consistently is provided in Chapter 8.

To edit a template in the Security Templates console,

1. Enter **mmc** after clicking Start | Run.

2. Use the File (Windows Server 2003, Windows XP) or Console (Windows 2000) menu and select Add, Remove Snap-in.

3. Click Add and select the Security Templates snap-in.

4. Click Close and then click OK.

5. Default templates will be added to the console. To use additional templates, you can save their files to the %windir%\security\templates folder or locate them in a new folder and add that path to the Security Templates snap-in.

6. Select and expand a template to examine the settings, as shown in Figure 5-5.

7. If you need to change settings, do not alter a provided file. Instead, copy the template file and rename it. Open the new file in the console and make changes to it.

8. To make a change, double-click a setting in order to modify it, as in this example:

9. Once you have made all of the changes you require, save the file by right-clicking the template and selecting Save As, entering a name, and clicking Save.

Once you have determined that a security template is appropriate for the operating system and the computer's role on your network, it can be used to apply security in a consistent fashion. It can also be used to analyze the security settings of a specific computer. Security templates are, however, basically a list of security options that have been preset. You can and should edit them to make them specific to your environment. You must, at the very least, understand what the changes they will make will do, and test them prior to using them to apply security in your production environment. This is especially true if you plan to use Group Policy to deploy them, because you can easily and quickly deploy security settings that might cause problems on your network.

The security areas that may be defined in security templates are similar to those defined in the Local Security Policy; they do not, however, provide opportunities for specifying IPSec policies. Security templates also provide additional areas for definition. Security Template areas are listed and defined in Table 5-5.

If you or anyone else adds security specifications to the security template, these settings will not be viewable in the Security Templates console unless additional work

Area	Description
Account Policies	Password policy, Account Lockout policies, Kerberos policies. Kerberos policies are applicable only on domain controllers and are ignored everywhere else.
Local Policies	Audit policy, User rights, Security options (numerous registry settings that can provide additional security such as clearing page file upon shutdown, logon messages, and so forth).
Event Log	Configure event log size and retention method, restrict access.
Restricted Groups	Restrict membership in groups.
System Services	Set the service boot options: automatic, manual, disabled. Set security (establish who can start, stop, or adjust boot options for a service).
Registry	Set permissions and audit settings on registry keys.
File System	Set permissions and audit settings on file folders and files.

Table 5-5.   Security Template Sections

is done. In addition to defining what will be displayed in the GUI, the new settings must be registered on any machine that might be used to view them. This means that there may be additional settings in any template that are not viewable when you load them into the console. The settings, however, if entered with the proper syntax, will be applied when the template is applied.

HEADS UP!

Since all security settings defined in a template will be applied, whether or not they are viewable in the console, you may inadvertently apply settings. This may or may not cause a problem but certainly has the potential for causing havoc. Do not apply any template without thoroughly examining the text file and making sure you understand exactly what changes will be made. Even templates downloaded with Microsoft documents may have additional items. (These items are thoroughly described in the documents and will be reviewed in Chapter 8.)

The use of Group Policy to deploy security is described in Chapter 8. Basic instructions for using security templates with the Security Configuration Manager, Security Configuration and Analysis, and **secedit** follow.

HEADS UP!

When security templates are used to deploy security in an automated fashion, for example, by using Group Policy, you can easily *cripple* an entire organization's network, making thousands of machines so secure that no one can use them. This warning should mean two things to you: First, thoroughly test security changes before deploying. This means using them in a test network that is representative of the production network. It also means using a staged production implementation and having a backout plan. Second, protect access to tools that might enable the clueless or the malicious to use security templates.

Use Security Configuration and Analysis or Security Manager

Both of these automated tools are quite similar to use, and so only instructions for Security Configuration and Analysis will be provided. Do remember, however, that registry settings in each operating system may vary. Use the correct tool, and use templates developed for the operating system you wish to secure.

The Security Configuration and Analysis tool must be loaded into an MMC console before it can be used. Before using the template, consider how you might back out the new security settings if they prove to be harmful. One way to do so is to create a template that changes settings back to the way they were before the changes. Keep this in mind when developing security templates. If you develop a "rollback" template at the same time as you create the one that will be used to apply settings, you will be able, in most cases, to return the computer to its state before you applied your settings. As a final recovery step, ensure you have current system backups. You can create a rollback template for Windows Server 2003 as described in the section "Use Secedit." To use the Security Configuration and Analysis console to apply a security template:

1. Add the Security Configuration and Analysis console to an MMC console.

2. Create a new database by right-clicking the Security Configuration and Analysis container and clicking Open database.

3. In the File Name box, enter a name for the new database and click Open.

4. Browse to the location of your template file, select it, and click Open. The database is created and instructions displayed as shown next.

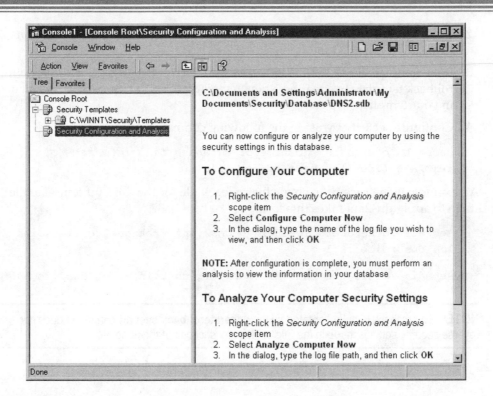

5. Right-click Security Configuration and Analysis and select Configure Computer.

6. Click OK when asked to confirm the location of the error log.

7. Wait for the configuration to complete and then close the console.

Use Secedit

Secedit is a command-line tool that can be used to apply security templates, refresh security policy, and analyze security. It can be used in a script to automate this process. To use it on a single machine to apply a security template,

1. If the template is for a Windows Server 2003 computer, create a rollback template using the following command:

```
secedit /generaterollback /cfg name_of_template_file /rbk file_
name_to_use_for_generated_template_file /log name_to_use_for_
logfile
```

2. Examine the rollback template by opening it in the Security Templates console to ensure it is a valid file.

3. If the template is not for a Windows Server 2003 computer, create your own rollback template by creating a new template that reverses the settings made in your template.

4. Configure security by using the following command line:

```
secedit /configure /db name_of_database_file /cfg name_of_
template_file /log name_of_log_file
```

An example using **secedit** to create the rollback file for the dns2.inf template file and then to apply dns2.inf takes this form:

```
secedit /generaterollback /cfg dns2.inf /rbk dns2rollback.inf /
log dns2rollback.log

secedit /configure /db dns2.sdb /cfg dns2.inf /log dns2.log
```

NOTE   The rollback template created by the **generaterollback secedit** command does not reverse security settings made in the File or Registry sections of the template.

Chapter 6

Secure Windows Directory Information and Operations

- Secure DNS
- Place AD Database and SYSVOL on a Drive Separate from the System Partition
- Physically Secure Domain Controllers
- Monitor and Protect Active Directory Health
- Secure Active Directory Data—Understand Active Directory Object Permissions

Active Directory (AD) provides directory services for Windows Server 2003– and Windows 2000–based domains. It also serves as the basis for security by providing authentication, distribution of security policy, and delegation of administrative authority. While Windows NT 4.0–based domains use a different directory infrastructure, many of the basic security structures supervised by Active Directory exist in Windows NT 4.0 domains. Knowledge of these structures, including basic information on user rights, groups, and object permissions, and of the similarities and differences in their implementation by the different Windows operating systems is important to anyone charged with securing a Windows network. Without this knowledge, those seeking to secure Windows can be blindsided by poor implementations that weaken, rather than improve, security.

This chapter will primarily discuss securing Active Directory operations information, because the Active Directory is a much more complex directory infrastructure than the Windows NT 4.0 directory, which is also described where relevant.

Because Active Directory provides the framework upon which a large part of the Windows security infrastructure can be based, it must be properly administered and secured. If it is not, it can easily be accidentally or maliciously destroyed. Improper or lax administration may introduce weak security controls in order to provide efficiency. Lack of attention to securing AD operations leaves it unnecessarily exposed to attack, or can prevent security controls from operating.

If your responsibility is securing Windows networks, an understanding of how Active Directory works, and how it differs from the Windows NT 4.0 directory infrastructure, should be part of your Windows security knowledge. Understanding AD security will allow you to fully utilize this tool to secure your Windows networks and to protect the security policy and data that resides within AD.

Active Directory operations consist of the manual and automatic updating of AD data; replication; the downloading of software, scripts, and security policy from Active Directory to domain member computers; authentication; and control over user rights and permissions via access control lists (ACLs) on AD objects.

Importance of Replication to Security

The Active Directory database resides on Windows 2000 and Windows Server 2003 domain controllers. Changes to AD data are replicated between domain controllers. Some data is replicated only between domain controllers in a domain, some to all domain controllers in the forest. Some data, such as Universal group membership and portions of different objects in the AD, is replicated between Global Catalog (GC) servers (a special function assigned to some domain controllers). While some data can be changed from only one location, for the most part, data can be changed at many different locations and is then replicated across the directory infrastructure. User account information, for example, can be changed at any domain controller in the domain and will eventually replicate to each domain controller in the domain. This process, multi-master replication, is the "active" in Active Directory. It is possible, at any one point in time, that data is actively being modified and updated across multiple servers.

This process is the exact opposite from Windows NT 4.0 directory services. A Windows NT 4.0 domain consists of one Primary Domain Controller (PDC) but can have many Backup Domain Controllers (BDCs). Only data on the PDC can be modified. Data on the BDCs is static. It is updated only via replication from the PDC.

In addition to the replication of data in the directory, both Windows domains' structures also utilize a file replication service. Windows NT 4.0 provides the Directory Replicator service. This service can be configured to replicate small files between Windows NT 4.0 servers and to Windows NT 4.0 workstations. It is often used to replicate logon scripts and the ntconfig.pol Systems Policy file. Active Directory domains use the File Replication service (FRS) to replicate Group Policy information. Both FRS and the Directory Replicator service can also be configured to replicate files that have nothing to do with directory or security policy.

Replication, therefore, is a process essential both to the AD and to directory operations in a Windows NT 4.0 domain. Without it, security policy cannot be distributed, nor can user changes such as password changes and/or modifications to account settings be distributed. A breakdown in replication of any type means a breakdown in security. Monitoring replication is a large part of monitoring AD health.

To secure directory operations and information:

- Secure DNS.
- Place AD Database and SYSVOL on separate drives.
- Physically secure domain controllers.
- Monitor and protect (Active) Directory health.
- Provide a strong domain controller security policy.
- Protect directory communications.
- Manage administrative authority.

Secure DNS

DNS is critical for proper Active Directory operations. Securing DNS will ensure that records important to Active Directory functioning and health are not modified by unauthorized persons or processes. Monitoring the proper functions of DNS will provide early warning of DNS problems. Information on Securing DNS can be found in Chapter 5. Information on monitoring DNS function is included in the later section "Monitor and Protect Active Directory Health."

Place AD Database and SYSVOL on a Drive Separate from the System Partition

Separating the AD database and SYSVOL from the system can help prevent problems due to space. The AD database will grow in size and needs additional free space to operate efficiently. In addition, a Denial of Service attack is easy to generate by filling up the print spool with large print files. If the database and SYSVOL are on the same drive, they may run out of space to operate. If they are on different drives, this attack will not directly cause them a problem.

NOTE   While the obvious solution may be to disable the spooler service on a DC, in some companies, the DC also does serve as a print server. It never hurts to take a step that is easy, such as placing the database on a separate drive. You can more closely control the available space for the growing AD, and where the spooler service must be run, avoid the possible DoS.

During the dcpromo process, when there is an opportunity to select a location for the database and SYSVOL, choose a separate drive. The preferred method for relocating the database and SYSVOL is to decommission the domain controller and the dcpromo again and select the new locations. If this cannot be done, you can move both manually, but the process, especially that required to move SYSVOL, is involved. To move SYSVOL, refer to the instructions in the Active Directory Operations Guide, a document that can be downloaded from www.microsoft.com/downloads/ details.aspx?FamilyID=4a82eccc-76d6-4431-aac4-1ef1ba11dbea&DisplayLang=en. To move the database, use ntdsutil.exe. Always use ntdsutil.exe to move the database, as this will modify the registry information on the location of the database.

1. Determine the size of the ntds.dit (the database) file by locating it in the %systemroot%\NTDS folder in Windows explorer.

2. Make sure the size of the new drive volume is large enough for the file and for projected growth and operations. Use the formula "add 20% or 500MB," whichever is greater, to the size of the database.

3. Back up the system state. This will back up the database, the SYSVOL and Netlogon folders, and other critical system files.

4. Restart the domain controller in Directory Services Restore Mode:

   a. Restart the DC.

   b. When the screen for restarting the OS appears, press F8.

   c. From the menu, select Directory Services Restore Mode.

5. Change to the directory location of the current ntds.dit file.

6. Run the **dir** command and make a note of the current file size.

7. At the command prompt, type **ntdsutil.exe** and press ENTER.

8. At the ntdsutil prompt, enter **files** and then press ENTER.

9. At the File Maintenance prompt, enter **move db to** *drive:\path*, where d*rive:\path* is the drive letter and path for the new location of the database.

10. If desired, move the logs to the new location too by entering the command **move logs to** *drive:\path*.

11. After all moves are complete, at the File Maintenance prompt type **quit** and press ENTER.

12. Type **quit** and press ENTER again to exit ntdisutil.

13. Check the permission on the new location. The permissions on the file should be Administrators and SYSTEM Full Control; inherited permissions are not allowed.

14. Check the integrity of the database by using the **ntdsutil** command again. Enter the command and then at the ntdsutil prompt, type **files** and press ENTER.

15. At the File Maintenance prompt, type **integrity** and then press ENTER.

16. If the check succeeds, type **quit** and press ENTER; then type **quit** and press ENTER to exit ntdsutil.

17. Restart the DC in normal mode.

18. If errors occur, or if you check the event log and discover errors, you may need to restore from your backup.

19. If there are no errors, back up the system state so that you have a backup of the registry with the new file location.

Physically Secure Domain Controllers

Physical security is more than physical access controls such as locked doors and cases. Physical security also encompasses protection from environmental extremes and natural disasters such as flooding. Secure all domain controllers by providing these things:

- **Physical barriers to DC access** When DCs are located at a site with a data center, DCs should be located within the data center. If DCs are located at a site where there is no data center, DCs should be placed in a locked room or at least a locked cabinet. Additional protection can be provided by using locking cases, securing access to power sources, and providing alarms. Where possible, use card key locks or cipher locks. Cipher locks improve security, as they also require authentication measures beyond simple possession of a key or card. In the data center, use locking racks to provide two layers of protection. In the remote site, use locking cases and locked enclosures.

- **Physical protection for network infrastructure** Access to network infrastructure provides an attacker many possible venues of attack. Secure cables, routers, switches, and other devices should be located in the same locked location with the DC. If they cannot be locked in the data center or remote site server location, then separate, locked enclosures should be provided. Do not store network infrastructure equipment in telephony cabinets. The telephony provider will require access to these locations and should not have access to your network infrastructure.

- **Security for DC backup media** Backup media contain sensitive data, including the account database. Backup media might be used to install the system on another computer and attack the contents of AD without interference. Backup media might also be used in an attempt to restore old data over current data, thus disrupting normal operations. An important part of managing backup media is to store backups offsite. An important part of protecting against inadvertent or malicious tampering with media and with DCs is to carefully control the media. Require authorized administrative signature before any backup media are returned from offsite, and secure the returned media.

- **UPS or other power control and backup** Clean power is important to the operation of any computer. Providing power free from spikes and brownouts ensures an environment where normal processing can occur. Power problems can corrupt Active Directory. Proving power backup is critical. Although years can pass between incidents of power blackouts, it only takes one to damage or corrupt data. In addition, without power, normal operations cannot occur. Critical systems may need to be in operation 24 × 7.

- **An operational policy for DC access and maintenance** The policy should specify who may enter locked areas and who may work on DCs; it should describe procedures that detail how systems are managed. Limit the number of administrators with physical access to DCs. Not all administrators require this access. The policy and procedures should also indicate how compliance is assured and audited.

In addition to the preceding, take these further measures:

- **Secure remote access to DCs.** Remote access is often defined as any access that is not local. Ensure that remote access, such as that from the Internet or across other forms of connectivity, is prevented or secured. See the section "Protect Active Directory Communications."

- **Secure remote administrative processes and hardware.** Windows Server 2003 provides special tools for remote administration, including terminal services, remote assistance, and even out-of-band remote control. Other third-party tools may be used, as may special administrative networks. It makes no sense to provide physical security and not secure these types of access.

- **Require the use of smart cards for local logon.** While implementing smart cards across your infrastructure may be a daunting task and require much widespread approval, cooperation, training, and funding, implementing and requiring smart card logon to domain controllers can be an effective way to protect them.

- **Inspect blueprints and remodeling history of potential server locations.** While a great deal of attention is spent on the location, design, and maintenance of a data center, servers are often placed in remote sites without even a cursory examination of the physical location. These rooms should not be located near or below rooms where things such as chemicals, water heaters, maintenance closets, and other potential hazards exist. Beware of remodeling that does not remove, but merely covers up, water pipes.

- **Remove floppy drives and CD-ROMs on DCs that are not kept in data centers.** Doing so can prevent physical attacks that attempt to boot or load another operating system. If an alternative OS can be loaded, most of the protections offered by the Windows OS controls are useless. (Encrypted files are still protected from access.)

- **Make sure DCs cannot be dual-boot systems.** If they are, it's possible to attack the domain controller by booting to the alternative system, obtain data such as the password database, and then attack it.

- **Disable remote boot if servers will not be remotely managed.** Remote boot can be used in an attempt to install an alternative OS. Remote boot, however, can provide a means by which to securely administer remote DCs. It's not the possibility for remote boot that is a security issue, it's the fact that it might not be securely managed or that, because it is not used at all, it is ignored and might be used in an attack. Remember to follow the adage, "If it is not used, disable or remove it so that it at least cannot be used against you."

- **Use a BIOS password.** This can prevent the unauthorized boot of a DC. Use caution. If a BIOS password is implemented, someone must be available in order to boot the computer. In addition, many manufacturers provide workarounds that bypass BIOS passwords.

■ **Use a SYSKEY password entry or floppy disk choice.** Once again, someone will need to be present to boot systems.

Monitor and Protect Active Directory Health

Active Directory health is a view of Active Directory that indicates how well it functions. To monitor and protect the health of the Active Directory, you will need to

■ Monitor DNS

■ Monitor replication

■ Monitor client authentication

■ Monitor Group Policy operation

Monitor DNS

Windows NT 4.0 can operate without DNS; however, without DNS, Active Directory and thus Windows Server 2003 and Windows 2000 domains cannot operate at all. In fact, many authentication issues and problems with replication can be traced to problems with DNS. Therefore, the proper functioning of DNS should always be monitored, and any improper operations corrected immediately.

Take these steps to monitor DNS:

■ Examine Event Viewer events.

■ Examine DNS records and make manual tests.

■ Use support tools to examine DNS.

Windows Server 2003 and Windows 2000 domains include a DNS event log. Windows NT 4.0 DNS messages will be recorded in the systems log. DNS errors can mean problems for authentication and security policy distribution. Monitoring the logs for errors should be an essential part of the monitoring process. Example error conditions to filter for are listed in Table 6-1. This list does not list *all* possible DNS errors.

DNS records can also be manually inspected to determine their accuracy. In a large environment, this is not a practical way to monitor DNS, but it is an effective one. A knowledgeable administrator can quickly spot incorrect information.

Support tools are those tools available in the support directory of the server installation CD-ROM. These tools are not installed by default, and you should use caution in installing them. Do not blindly install them on every server. These powerful tools can be used for good or for evil. Do not give an attacker tools. In many environments,

Error Number	Description	Value
1056	DHCP service present on a domain controller	May provide improper access to DNS host records.
4011	Failure to update _ldap record in DNS	LDAP requests will not reach the proper server, or an attempt at spoofing an LDAP server has occurred.
5781	Failure of DNS registration	If DNS registration fails, clients may not be able to access domain controllers or servers. Failure can also indicate a failed attack on DNS.
6524	Zone transfer failure	Changes to DNS information isn't getting to approved DNS secondary servers, or an attack on DNS failed.

Table 6-1. Some DNS Errors to Watch For

the best strategy is to have the tools available on a CD-ROM, or on administrative workstations only, and never to leave the tools on production domain controllers. Many of these tools were developed to troubleshoot problems, that is, someone has already determined that there is a problem but wants to find out exactly what it is so that it can be fixed. You can and should use tools periodically to find out if there are problems. It is not necessary to use all of these tools to monitor AD health, but you should be familiar with them all, since once a problem is discovered, it should be fixed as soon as possible. If you have time to use only one tool, use DCDiag. DCDiag can indicate if DC operations are running properly. If its tests find problems with DC operation, you can then use other tools to discover problems with DNS and replication.

Use DNSLint to Detect Problems with DNS

The DNSLint utility is a Windows Server 2003 support tool but can be obtained for use with Windows 2000 DNS. It is a diagnostic tool that can point out DNS problems. It does not fix them. The tool is described in Knowledge Base (KB) article 321045. A description of the DNSLint utility and a link to the download location are provided in the article. When run, DNSLint provides an HTML report or a text file that lists problems with DNS, such as

■ **Are CNAME or host (glue or A) records for domain controllers missing?** When a Windows client needs to find a domain controller in the local site, it locates the GUID for the domain, then resolves the associated CNAME, and then obtains the IP address for the domain controller from the associated glue record. The CNAME record identifies a device on the network but does not provide an IP address. The glue record ties or glues the computer name with the IP address. If either is missing, the client will not be able to locate the domain controller. This can cause problems with authentication, security policy download, and so forth.

- **Are Server Locator (SRV) records missing?** These records, such as _ldap, kerberos, gc, and _msdts, must be available in order for clients to locate domain controllers and global catalog servers. Without the records, authentication to the domain cannot occur.

- **Is TCP/IP properly configured?** If the primary or alternative DNS server identified in the client TCP/IP configuration is not authoritative for the client's domain, when the client boots it will not find the correct DNS server and hence not find the location of a DC in its domain. Without this, the computer and its users cannot authenticate to the domain.

- **Does lame delegation exist?** Lame delegation is a situation where a DNS server delegates authority of a subdomain to another DNS server but this new server cannot be located or is not configured to be authoritative for the subdomain. Once again, the result is that a DC cannot be located to provide authentication, and of course, no security policy will be downloaded to the client.

- **Are DNS servers responding?** After locating the IP addresses of the DNS servers for the domain, DNSLint checks to see that they are locatable and responding to requests for DNS information.

- **Is information consistent on all DNS servers authoritative for the domain?** If IP addresses, for example, are different for the same computer, then inconsistent results are going to occur.

DNSLint also identifies the information listed about the DNS server in its SOA record and lists all servers listed as authoritative for the domain, the host or A records for the DNS server, and any Mail Exchange (MX) and glue records for mail servers in the domain. You should examine this information against your documentation to determine if any rogue DNS servers or mail servers may be in existence.

To use DNSLint, issue the following command at the command line:

```
dnslint /d domain_name
```

where *domain_name* is the name of the domain. This general command will check for lame delegation and related DNS problems. You can use the **/s** switch to indicate the IP address of the DNS server; otherwise, DNSLint will use the Internet to do an Internic **whois**. (the Internic is the organization responsible for delegating authority for IP address assignments. The **whois** command attempts to find the IP address of a DNS server authoritative for the domain included in the command. Figure 6-1 displays the partial results of using the **dnslint** command:

```
dnslint /d microsoft.com
```

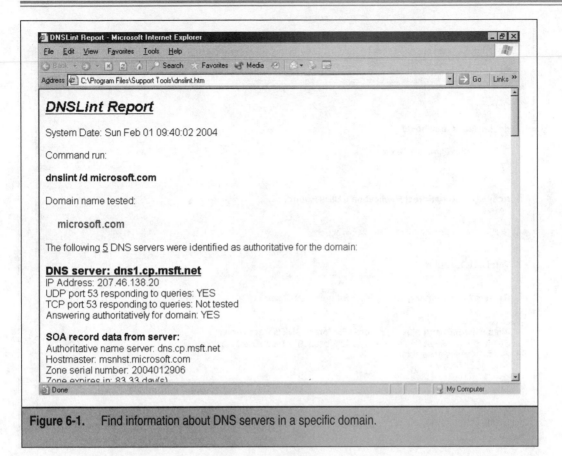

Figure 6-1. Find information about DNS servers in a specific domain.

In Figure 6-2, the command **dnslint /ad /s localhost /v** was used to obtain information about Active Directory and cancel the Internic lookup.

Note that in Figure 6-3, the report indicates a missing CNAME for the domain controller cream.contoso.com. This error means that there is missing information in DNS and that this DC cannot be used for authentication. In this particular case, the report was run after running **dcpromo** on cream, but before rebooting. After a reboot, the information was registered in DNS and **dnslint** was able to locate the CNAME record in DNS.

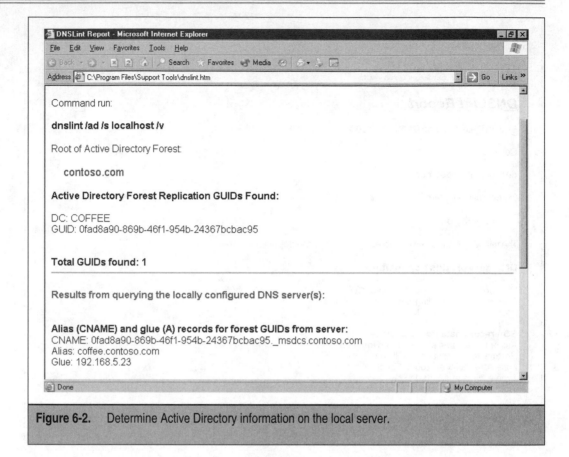

Figure 6-2. Determine Active Directory information on the local server.

Here are additional uses for DNSLint:

- Use DNSLint to verify a list of defined DNS records by putting the records in a text file and using the switch **/ql**. In the following example, the *server_file_path* specifies the path and filename of the text file:

```
dnslint /ql server_file_path
```

- Use the **/v** switch to report information on screen while the report is being generated.
- Use the **/r** switch to identify the path of the report file.
- Use the **/t** switch to generate a text file and an HTML file report.
- Use the **/c** switch to look for SMTP records and test connections for Pop3, SMTP, and NNTP.

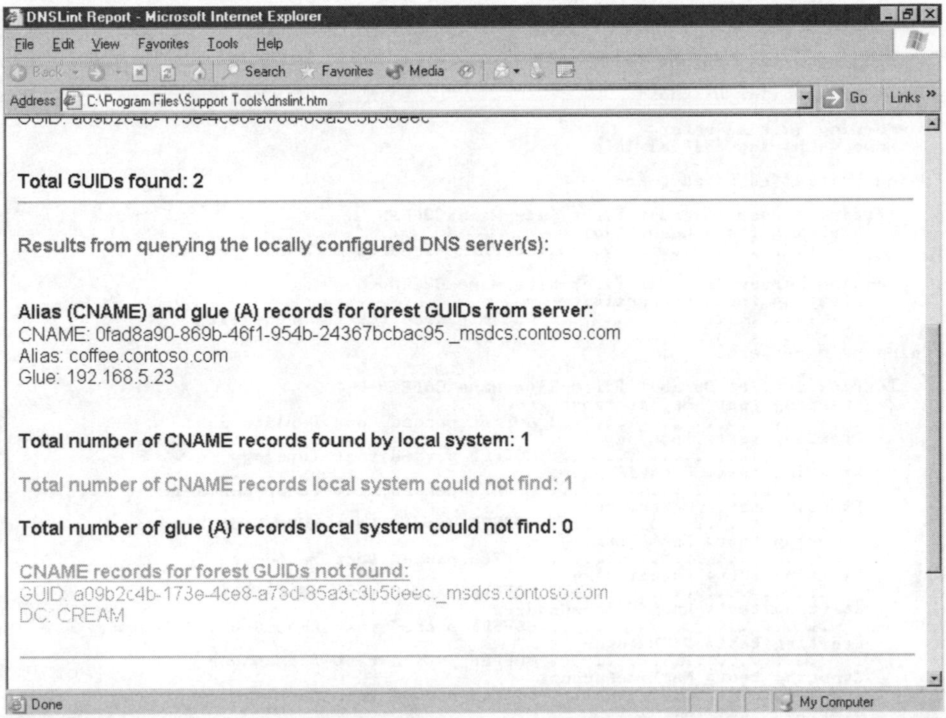

Figure 6-3.   The **dnslint** command will point to errors in DNS.

TIP   Use the following KB articles to learn more about DNSLint: 321045, "Description of the DNSLint Utility." and 321046, "How to Use dnslint to Troubleshoot Active Directory Replication."

Use DCDiag to Discover DC Problems

DCDiag is a multipurpose domain controller diagnostic tool. Use DCDiag to periodically test DC-specific functions. Since many DC functions rely on DNS, if the DC operations are functioning smoothly, you can eliminate many potential DNS problems. That DC operations are broken, however, is not proof positive that the problem is DNS-related.

To run all tests on all DCs, as shown in Figure 6-4, use the command line:

```
dcdiag /a /c
```

```
Command Prompt                                                    _ | 6 | X |

C:\Program Files\Support Tools>dcdiag /a /c

Domain Controller Diagnosis

Performing initial setup:
   Done gathering initial info.

Doing initial required tests

   Testing server: Default-First-Site-Name\COFFEE
      Starting test: Connectivity
         ......................... COFFEE passed test Connectivity

   Testing server: Default-First-Site-Name\CREAM
      Starting test: Connectivity
         ......................... CREAM passed test Connectivity

Doing primary tests

   Testing server: Default-First-Site-Name\COFFEE
      Starting test: Replications
         ......................... COFFEE passed test Replications
      Starting test: Topology
         ......................... COFFEE passed test Topology
      Starting test: CutoffServers
         ......................... COFFEE passed test CutoffServers
      Starting test: NCSecDesc
         ......................... COFFEE passed test NCSecDesc
      Starting test: NetLogons
         ......................... COFFEE passed test NetLogons
      Starting test: Advertising
         ......................... COFFEE passed test Advertising
      Starting test: KnowsOfRoleHolders
         ......................... COFFEE passed test KnowsOfRoleHolders
      Starting test: RidManager
         ......................... COFFEE passed test RidManager
      Starting test: MachineAccount
         ......................... COFFEE passed test MachineAccount
      Starting test: Services
         ......................... COFFEE passed test Services
      Starting test: OutboundSecureChannels
         ** Did not run Outbound Secure Channels test
         because /testdomain: was not entered
         ......................... COFFEE passed test OutboundSecureChannels
      Starting test: ObjectsReplicated
         ......................... COFFEE passed test ObjectsReplicated
      Starting test: frssysvol
```

Figure 6-4. DCDiag can test all DCs for proper functioning.

To run a specific test, use the following command at the command line:

```
dcdiag /test:test_name
```

Here are some useful tests:

- **Frsevent**   Looks for errors in the File Replication System (FRS)
- **Services**   Checks to see that appropriate domain services are running
- **Advertising**   Checks to see that each DC is advertising itself as a DC
- **Replications**   Tests for timely replication between domain controllers
- **RegisterinDNS**   Checks to make sure the server can register in DNS

Figure 6-5 shows the results listing the coffee.txt file. The command that follows was entered at the command prompt to test the operation of DC-related services on the DC coffee and place the results in a text file:

```
dcdiag /s:coffee /test:services > coffee.txt
```

TIP   KB article 265706, "DCDiag and NetDiag in Windows 2000 Facilitates Domain Join and DC Creation," provides in-depth information on DCDiag and NetDiag.

Use Netdiag to Test Client-to-DC/DNS Connectivity

Netdiag is similar to DCDiag but tests client-to-DC/DNS connectivity. Run **netdiag** from a client. Useful **netdiag** tests are listed in Table 6-2.

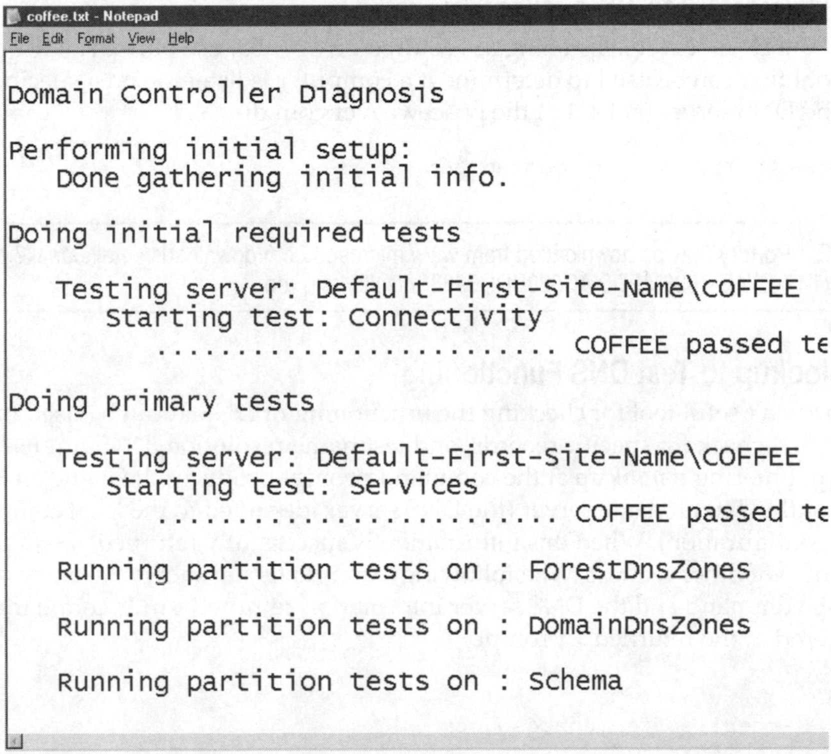

Figure 6-5.   Checking the operation of DC-related services

Command or Test Name	Results
netdiag /d:*domainname*	Tests if a client can access a domain controller
netdiag /test:*testname*	Runs the test *testname*
/l	A switch that will output data to the **netdiag** log file
dsgetdc	A test that will test the network card, computer domain membership, and access to the DC
dclist	Lists domain controllers
DNS	Tests DNS function
Kerberos	Tests Kerberos

Table 6-2.   Netdiag Examples

Use Portqry to Test DNS Availability

To test if the DNS server is listening as required on port 53, use **portqry**. Portqry is a simple tool that can be used to determine if a computer is listening on a specific port. To test the DNS server on DC1 in the peaceweaver.com domain,

```
portqry -n coffe.contoso.com -p udp -e 53
```

> **NOTE**   Portqry may be downloaded from www.microsoft.com/downloads/details.aspx?familyid= 89811747-C74B-4638-A2D5-AC828BDC6983&displaylang=en.

Use Nslookup to Test DNS Functioning

Nslookup is a useful tool for checking the functioning of DNS. It can be used to locate DNS servers, check for specific records, and test name resolution. DNSLint uses **nslookup**. Entering **nslookup** at the command prompt produces the name and IP address of the default name server (the DNS server identified in the local computer's TCP/IP configuration). When this information is successfully returned, a ">" prompt allows entry of other requests. The following example listing shows the entry of the **nslookup** command and the DNS server information returned. An **ls** command has been entered at the returned > prompt.

```
nslookup
Default Server: coffee.contoso.com
Address: 192.168.5.23
>ls -t a peaceweaver.com
```

CAUTION   The **ls** command works by doing a zone transfer. If you have restricted zone transfers, as you should, then this test will not work unless it is done from one of the DNS name servers authorized to request and receive a zone transfer. You should never allow unrestricted zone transfers. You can use **nslookup** from a computer that is not authorized, as a check on this setting. If the **ls** test works, the DNS server is not securely configured.

Monitor Replication

If Active Directory replication and FRS replication are not operational, new security information is not available. Ensure replication is functioning correctly.

In order for Active Directory replication to occur, the DC must be able to find its replication partners. Replication partners are those domain controllers assigned to conduct replication with each other. The assignment can be automatic, or manual. The DC knows its partners and uses DNS to find them. Always ensure that DNS is functioning properly and that all DC records are available in DNS.

TIP   KB article 178169 lists the records registered in DNS by Windows 2000 DCs when the netlogon service starts. You can use this list to verify that appropriate and correct records are being registered for a DC, but a simpler solution is to use DNSLint to automatically verify all records for all DCs.

Use DNSLint to Determine if SRV Records for Replication Partners Exist

The DNSLint utility can be used to test replication. It tests to see that all DC SRV records are registered on the correct DNS server and that all replication partners are listed and accessible. In essence, DNSLint simulates the process used by DCs to locate their replication partners and reports any problems. The DNSLint **/ad** switch uses LDAP to connect to the root forest of AD and gets the GUIDs for all DCs in the forest, then queries DNS to resolve the CNAME and obtain the alias and then the IP address of DCs. In order to obtain this information, DNSLint must authenticate to the domain, if it finds **netlogon** problems, these will also be reported. Use the following command to run the test:

```
dnslint /ad IP_address_of_the_forest_root_DC /s IP_address_of_the_DNS_server
```

Figure 6-6 shows the results of issuing this command in the test domain.

Use Replmon.exe to Examine Replication and Set Up Notifications

The Replication Monitor (**replmon**) can be used to find information about replication partners and replication. To use the tool:

1. Type **replmon** at the command prompt in the support tools directory or double-click the **replmon** command in the file system.

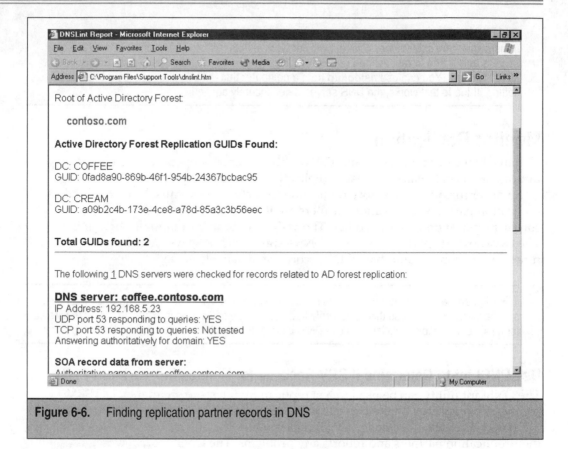

Figure 6-6. Finding replication partner records in DNS

2. Right-click the monitored servers node and select Add Monitored Server; then click Next.

3. Select the Add the Server Explicitly by Name choice or the Search the Directory for the Server to Add choice, and select the domain name. Click Next.

4. Enter the name of the server that you want to monitor, or select it by expanding the site.

5. Click Finish.

6. Repeat for each DC. Information about each DC is displayed in the GUI, as shown here:

7. From the View menu, select Options.

8. Select Show Transitive Replication Partners and Extended Data.

9. Check Notify When Replication Fails After This Number of Attempts and enter a number in the text box.

10. Use the dialog box to set up e-mail notification, as shown here:

11. Click OK to close the Options page.

12. Expand a server container. Select any partition to view the replication status in the detail windows, as shown here:

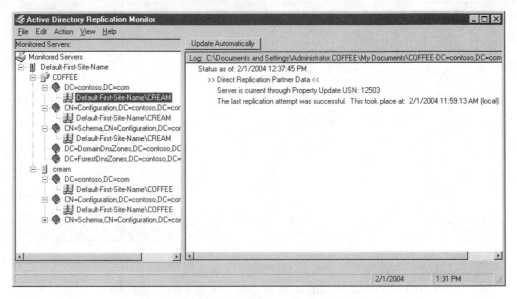

13. To obtain a comprehensive report, select a server and then select the Action menu. Select Server, and then select Generate a Report. Enter the name for the report and click Save. The following dialog box appears that allows you to select details for the report:

14. Click OK to generate the report.

Use Repadmin to Check Replication Links

The command-line tool **repadmin** can check replication links and replication latency, as well as summarize information on replication and replication exchanges. To test for replication success as shown in the illustration:

```
repadmin /showreps domain_controller_name
```

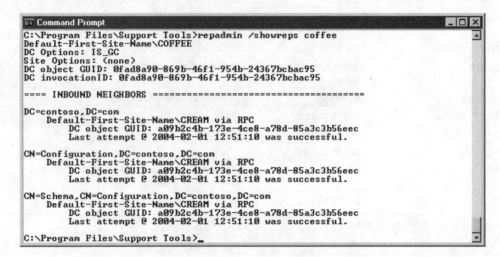

To display replication statistics as shown in the illustration:

```
repadmin /replsummary domain_controller_name
```

```
Command Prompt                                                       _ □ ×
Replication Summary Start Time: 2004-02-01 13:44:15

Beginning data collection for replication summary, this may take awhile:
 . . . .

Source DC          largest delta  fails/total  %%  error
 CREAM                  53m:05s      0 /   3     0

Destination DC     largest delta  fails/total  %%  error
 COFFEE                 53m:05s      0 /   3     0

C:\Program Files\Support Tools>
```

Test FRS Replication and GPO Health

Group Policy Objects are replicated as part of AD replication; however, the template files associated with the GPO, and critical for its correct operation, are replicated via FRS. Files that are important to GPO processing are stored in the SYSVOL share and its subfolders. Table 6-3 lists the subfolders.

Folder	Files	Use
User	Registry.pol	Registry settings for users
User	(.aas extension files may be present)	May contain these application advertisement files used to implement application installation via Group Policy
Documents and settings	Fdeploy.ini	Status information about folder redirection options
Microsoft/remoteinstall	Oscfilter.ini	User options for operating system installation through the Remote Installation service (RIS)
Microsoft/IEAK	(may be present)	Settings for Internet Explorer maintenance snap-in
Scripts	(various files may be present)	All Group Policy–based scripts
Machine	Registry.pol	Registry settings for computers
Scripts startup	(may be present)	Startup scripts
Scripts shutdown	(may be present)	Shutdown scripts
Applications	(may be present)	
Microsoft\windows NT\secedit	Gpttmpl.ini	The default security configuration settings for a Windows 2000 domain controller
Adm	(.adm files)	All of the .adm files for this GPO

Table 6-3.   SYSVOL Subfolders

The synchronization of this information can be tested by using the GPO tool. If the information is not synchronized, it may just mean replication latency, or it may mean problems with FRS replication.

The Windows Server 2003 Resource Kit tool sonar.exe can be used to look for FRS replication problems. The tool reports information on traffic, backlogs ,and even free space available for the SYSVOL share. To run the tool, double-click the sonar.exe file, click View Results, then click Refresh All. If left running, sonar will periodically run its tests. Sonar will monitor FRS in the domain by querying AD and then displaying the information it has received (see Figure 6-7). You can log statistics.

A more sophisticated tool, Ultrasound, is available to provide more comprehensive health status information on FRS.

Use the File Replication and Directory Service Events Logs

Problems that can prevent replication are reported in the Directory Services event log. Problems with FRS replication are reported in the File Replication event log. Error 1925, for example, indicates a replication failure and often points out the reason, such as a DNS lookup failure.

Replication errors are also reported in the logs. For example, error 1311 indicates that replication configuration information in Active Directory Sites and Services doesn't

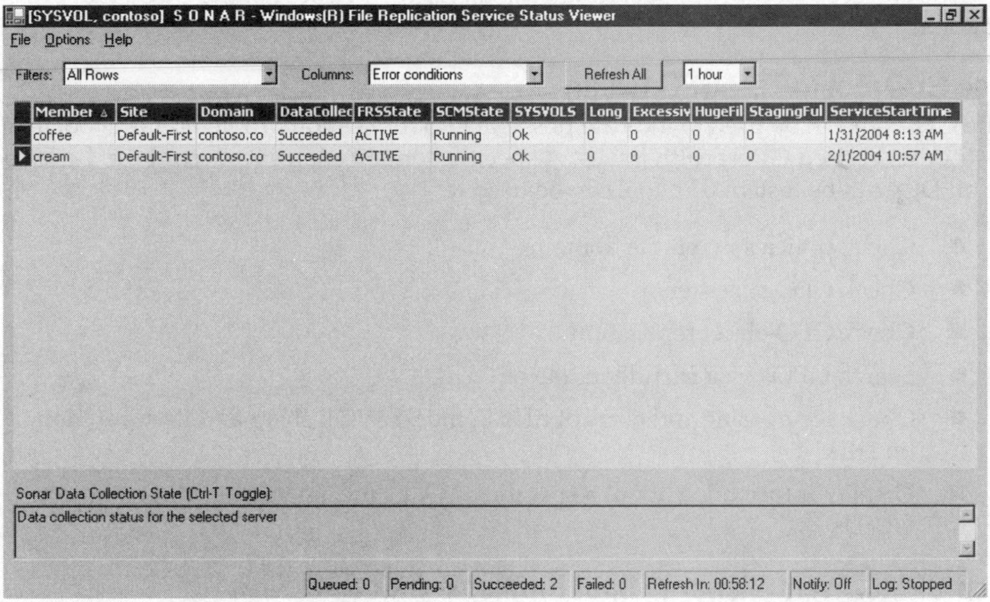

Figure 6-7. Test FRS with sonar.exe.

reflect the actual physical topology of the network. It might indicate a DC is offline, or point to a configuration problem. Error 1265 indicates DNS lookup failure or an unavailable RPC server. It can also indicate authentication failure between the DC and one of its replication partners.

Monitor Group Policy Operation

Group Policy failure means that security settings are not applied to computer and user accounts in the domain. Group Policy operations should be periodically tested to ensure application of security policy.

Use GPResult to Determine if Policies Are Being Applied

How do you know if Group Policy security settings are being applied? The GPResult tool is available for Windows 2000 and for Windows Server 2003. The Windows 2000 GPResult tool produces a list of the Group Policy settings applied at a single computer. You must be locally logged on to that computer using the user ID and password for the user you want to test results for. The Windows Server 2003 version reports more information and actually provides information similar to that provided by RSOP.

Use the correct tool for each operating system. Each tool does list the GPOs that are applied.

Use GPOTool to Test GPO Health

The GPOtool can be used to indicate possible FRS replication problems. GPOtool also tests other related GPO health issues. A specific domain controller record can be tested, or all DCs can be tested. GPOtool can be used to

- Check policies in remote domains
- Check GPO consistency
- Check GPO object replication
- Search GPOs by a friendly name or GUID
- Check for missing and corrupt files in the SYSVOL share and its subfolders on DCs
- Display information about a specific GPO, including version and extension GUIDs

Use GPMC/Event Viewer to Spot Problems with GPO Files

The Group Policy Management Console (GPMC) is a new tool that can be used to work with Group Policies. File access problem events are indicated in the Group Policy Results report. They are also listed in the Application Event log of the DC's Event viewer.

GPMC can be used to manage Group Policy Objects in Windows 2000 and Windows Server 2003 domains; however, more extensive capabilities are possible for Windows Server 2003 domains.

TIP Download GPMC from www.microsoft.com/downloads/details.aspx?FamilyId=C355B04F-50CE-42C7-A401-30BE1EF647EA&displaylang=en.

Use System File Checker to Verify Client File Versions

The System File Checker (SFC) utility can be used to check for missing client files and to verify the proper version of the file is in place. Files related to client-side processing are located in the %windir%\system32 folder and are

- Userenv.dll
- Scecli.dll
- Dskquota.dll
- Fdeploy.dll
- Appmgmts.dll
- Gptext.dll

Use RSOP to Test Group Policy Application

Resultant Set of Policy (RSOP) is an additional Group Policy tool that can be used to poll existing GPOs and report their potential impact on computers and users. It can also be used to identify which GPOs will be applied to all user and computer accounts in a specific domain, site, or OU. RSOP used on Windows 2000 does not confirm that a GPO is applied; however, logging mode on Windows Server 2003 and Windows XP does. To use the tool:

1. Click Start, then Run.

2. Add the Resultant Set of Policy snap-in to an existing MMC.

3. Right-click Resultant Set of Policy and then click Generate RSOP data, and click Next.

4. Click Logging Mode, Review Policy Settings Applied to a Specific Computer and User, and then Next.

5. Select This Computer, or else select Another Computer and enter or browse to another computer on which to RSOP.

6. If desired, select Do Not Display Policy Settings for the Selected Computer in the Results (Display User Policy Settings Only) and then click Next.

7. Select a user from among those displayed, or select Do Not Display User Policy Settings in the Results (Display Computer Settings Only) and then click Next.

8. Review a summary and then click Next.

9. Click Finish when processing is complete.

10. Expand containers to view results in the details pane, as shown here:

You can also run RSOP for a specific domain or OU. To do so:

1. Open Active Directory Users and Computers.

2. Expand the Domains container and right-click the domain you wish to run RSOP on, or else right-click the OU to run RSOP on.

3. Select All Tasks and then click Resultant Set of Policy (Planning).

4. Select user and computer groups. In Planning mode, the results will show an estimate of what will be applied to the user and computer groups selected.

Use GPMC to Monitor GPOs

When the GPMC tool is added to a Windows Server 2003 DC, it extends the information that can be collected about GPO processing. In addition to gathering RSOP information on the "potential" impact of Group Policy, you can determine which policies have been successfully applied. You can view success and failure by examining the GPO records in the GPMC console, and you can generate reports that actually visit the specified computer to determine Group Policy application. This makes troubleshooting Group Policy application on client computers easy, as it can be done remotely. It also can be used to monitor Group Policy application, as it can be used to determine if policies are being applied as expected.

A number of reports can also be produced using GPMC. The scripts that produce these reports are defined in the %programfiles%\gpmc\scripts\gpmc.chm file on a computer on which GPMC has been installed. Table 6-4 identifies several reports and how they might be used to monitor Group Policy.

Report	Usage
List all GPOs in a Domain	Are GPOs that are supposed to exist present? Are any rogue GPOs present?
List Disabled GPOs	Why are they disabled? Are they supposed to be? Are some enabled that should be disabled?
List GPOs at a backup location	Are GPOs all backed up?
List GPOs by Security Group	Which security group will have the GPO applied. Is this correct? Is some group that shouldn't be filtered, filtered?
List GPOs orphaned in SYSVOL	Files may exist, but AD has no records. Should these be active GPOs?
List GPOs without security filtering	Lists GPOs not applied to any security group.
List Unlinked GPOs in a Domain	It is possible to create a GPO that is not linked to a container, and it is possible to remove all links. If a GPO is not linked, Group Policy is not applied. Should these GPOs be linked?

Table 6-4. GMPC Reports Useful in Monitoring Group Policy Application

Use GPMonitor to Report Group Policy Refresh Information

GPMonitor is a Microsoft Windows Server 2003 Resource Kit tool. It installs a gpmonitor service on the client. This service collects data, and the tool provides a viewer that can be used to look at the data. By installing the tool on a representative client, you can monitor policy refreshes. From this information, you can determine if client application of Group Policy is occurring and is being properly refreshed. When security policy changes are made, check the log from this tool to determine if changes are reaching clients. Remember, installing the service on a single client tells you only what is happening on that client. It would not be efficient to monitor application at all clients, but by monitoring application at representative clients, you do gain valid information. A problem on one client may indicate widespread problems that need to be investigated. If no problem is recorded on this client, however, that fact does not prove that all clients are receiving new policy.

Set Up Verbose Logging

Information on Group Policy processing is logged for Group Policy client extensions (CSEs), GPMC, and GPOEdit. CSEs are the portions of Group Policy that are present on the clients. The location of the logs is listed in Table 6-5. Verbose logging on the client side can often reveal problems with Group Policy processing.

CAUTION   Do not turn on verbose logging arbitrarily. You will only fill up the drive of clients with information that probably will never be reviewed.

To set up verbose logging requires extensive registry modification on the client as listed in Table 6-6. This should not typically be done, because it will produce extensive log information that will not be used. However, it is useful when troubleshooting issues such as why Group Policy security settings are not being applied on a specific client. Verbose logging can also be used as a monitoring tool by selecting a random client and examining the logs.

Log	Log Name	Location
Group Policy Core and Registry CSE	userenv.log	%windir%\debug\usermode
Security CSE	Winlogon.log	%windir%\security\logs\winlogon.log
Folder Redirection CSE	fdeploy.log	%windir%\debug\usermode
Software Installation CSE	appmgmt.log	%windir%\debug\usermode
Windows issues	MSI*.log	%windir%\temp\

Table 6-5.   GPO CSE Log Locations

Log	Key	Location
Group Policy Core CSE	UserENvDebugLevel = REG_DWORD ox10002	HKEY_LOCAL_MACHINE\Software\ Microsoft\Windows NT\Current Version\ Winlogon
Security CSE	ExtensionDebugLevel = REG_DWORD ox2	HKEY_LOCAL_MACHINE\Software\ Microsoft\Windows NT\Current Version\ Winlogon\GpExtensions\{827d318e-6eac-11d2-a4ea-00c04f79f83a}\
Folder Redirection CSE	FdeployDebugLevel = REG_DWORD 0x0f	HKEY_LOCAL_MACHINE\Software\ Microsoft\Windows NT\Current Version\ Diagnostics
Software Installation CSE	Appmgmtdebuglevel = d	HKEY_LOCAL_MACHINE\Software\ Microsoft\Windows NT\Current Version\ Diagnostics
Windows Installer CSE	Logging = voicewarmup Debug = 00000003	HKEY_LOCAL_MACHINE\Software\ Policies\Microsoft\Windows\Installer
GPMC errors	gpmgmttracelevel = 1	HKEY_LOCAL_MACHINE\Software\ Microsoft\Windows NT\Current Version
GPMC error and verbose logging	Gpmgmttracelvel = 2	HKEY_LOCAL_MACHINE\Software\ Microsoft\Windows NT\Current Version\ Diagnostics
GPMC output to log file only	Gpmcmtlogfileonly = 1	HKEY_LOCAL_MACHINE\Software\ Microsoft\Windows NT\Current Version\ Diagnostics
GPO Editor core entries	GPEditDEbugLevel = REG_DWORD 0x10002	HKEY_LOCAL_MACHINE\Software\ Microsoft\Windows NT\Current Version\ Winlogon
GPO Editor CSE specific	GPTextDebugLevel = REG_DWORD 0x1002	HKEY_LOCAL_MACHINE\Software\ Microsoft\Windows NT\Current Version\ Winlogon

Table 6-6. Turn On Verbose Logging

Provide a Strong Domain and Domain Controller Security Policy

Security policy for domain computers, including DCs, is configured automatically by Group Policy. Two different Group Policy Objects (GPOs), which are present by default, affect the security of DCs and their operations. When Windows computers based on NT technologies are in a workgroup, their security policy is determined by local security settings defined in the registry, or within the Local Security Policy or local GPO. When they join a domain, their security settings are modified by policy defined at different levels of the Active Directory hierarchy. By default, the source of these security settings is that defined in two default GPOs: the Domain Security Policy and the Domain Controller Security Policy.

Local Group Policy vs. Domain Group Policy

The local GPO is the set of security settings defined for the local machine. Most discussions of Group Policy define it as a domain-based process that can be used to secure and manage computers joined in a domain. The objects used to define the security settings that will be applied are called Group Policy Objects. Strictly speaking, however, the local GPO is part of Group Policy, but the local GPO is neither reliant on nor modified by joining the computer to a domain. However, the local GPO's impact on the security of the computer most probably is modified by joining the computer to the domain. The Windows 2000 Local Security Policy console, in fact, indicates this effect by providing information on the settings both in the Local Security Policy and in the effective security policy, the policy as applied due to Group Policy downloaded from the domain. It's as if the local GPO is infrastructure designed to fit into the domain model, but used nevertheless without it.

Group Policy is applied at boot and at logon; it is refreshed when changes are made. One part of Group Policy, the Security Settings part, is refreshed every 18 hours whether or not changes are made. Thus Group Policy is a very powerful tool that can be leveraged to set and maintain security.

All GPOs can be examined and configured by using the Group Policy Editor. However, the Domain Security Policy and the Domain Controller Security Policy can also be accessed from the Administrative Tools menu. The Domain Security Policy Account Policy (password, account lockout, and Kerberos) specifies the account policy used for the domain. When users log on using their domain accounts, the domain policy specifies the account policy that is used. The rest of the Domain Controller Security Policy can be used to secure domain controllers. To do so, use the other areas of the GPO, such as User Rights and Security Policy.

Minimize User Rights

User rights should always be restricted to those and only those user groups that need the rights. The default assignments can be tightened and reviewed against the organization's security policy. The policy may, and should, require different settings depending on the computers that will be impacted by the User Rights settings. For example, in many organizations users are required to turn off their desktop computers at day's end, and laptop users will always require this ability. However, only IT administrative staff should have the right to shut down servers.

The User Rights section of the Default Domain Controller Security Policy defines the user rights for the domain. The User Rights section defined in the Domain Security Policy and in other GPOs defines user rights for the local accounts in the local account database of computers joined to the domain. If a user uses a domain logon account at a computer console, his user rights are defined by the Default Domain Controller Security Policy. However, if he uses an account from the local computer account database, his rights are defined by the Default Domain Security Policy and any GPOs present in the OU hierarchy that the computer account is contained within.

The first step in minimizing user rights is not to give rights arbitrarily. Default settings may be adequate, or even too broad. Do not give users additional rights without thorough investigation. User rights associated with logon were reviewed in Chapter 2. Additional user rights to reduce are listed in Table 6-7.

User Right	Restriction	Operating Systems
Shut Down the System	Remove this right from the Account Operators group and the Print Operators group. Allow user groups to have this privilege on desktops and laptops if this is the organization's policy.	All built on NT technologies
Backup Files and Directories	The Backup Operators group has this right by default, as do Administrators. On some critical servers, the Backup Operators group may be removed, requiring a member of the Administrators group to back up the system.	All built on NT technologies
Restore Files and Directories	Backup Operators and Administrators have this right by default. Set up a separate user group and provide them this right. Remove Backup Operators. This separation of privileges can help prevent inadvertent or malicious application of old data to functioning servers.	All built on NT technologies
Deny Access to This Computer from the Network	Add the local Administrator account. This will prevent the success of attacks on the computer based on knowledge of the known SID for this account, or simply on knowledge of the Administrator password. The account can still be used at the console. Add the Support_388945a0 account to prevent access using this account. This account can be programmed for use by help services, and an attack could be launched using such a program. Add the Guest account and all *non*–operating system service accounts used to run local services. These accounts are actually normal user accounts, and their passwords might be obtained in a number of attacks. By denying remote access using these accounts, you can prevent attacks that might do so. Use caution to determine if this account might be "legitimately" used for remote access. In that case, do not deny remote access.	Windows Server 2003, Windows XP, Windows 2000

Table 6-7. Minimize User Rights

User Right	Restriction	Operating Systems
Access This Computer from Network	In Windows NT 4.0, Administrators and the group Everyone have this right. Remove the group Everyone and replace with authorized groups. This may vary by server. Be careful—if appropriate groups are not included, you may interfere with necessary operations. Other Windows systems based on NT technologies add the Authenticated Users group. On these systems, you can modify this right by using the Deny right.	All based on NT technologies
Debug Programs	Remove the Administrators account in production systems. This right is not necessary for production operation. The right may be necessary for debugging programs, and for some extreme troubleshooting efforts on production machines. If it is necessary, it can be added for troubleshooting; it should not exist otherwise. Some known attacks leverage this right. Without it, the attack will fail.	All based on NT technologies

Table 6-7.   Minimize User Rights *(continued)*

Lock Down Security Options

Security Options define additional security settings. These settings can be configured in the registry but are much easier to set in the provided GUI. In addition, when set in a GPO, the settings can be downloaded to multiple computers via Group Policy, thereby eliminating the need for computer visits, third-party products, or homegrown scripts. Security Options that affect authentication are covered in Chapter 2, those that impact data access, in Chapter 10, and those dealing with communications are discussed in Chapter 11. Additional restrictions for domain controllers are listed in Table 6-8. Similar restrictions can be applied to servers.

Security Option	Recommendation	Discussion
Accounts: Guest Account Status	Disabled	Disable the guest account to prevent access from those that do not have proper credentials.
Accounts: Rename Administrator Account	Rename	Renaming the Administrator account will not stop a determined attacker; however, it does prevent canned scripts that use the name Administrator. Use in conjunction with restrict anonymous settings to prevent discovery of the new name for this account.

Table 6-8.   Restrict Security Options

Security Option	Recommendation	Discussion
Devices: Prevent Users from Installing Printer Drivers	Enable	If enabled, this right is restricted to Server Operators and Administrators. Users won't be able to install printers. A malicious person might disguise attack code in a printer driver, and simple disk space attacks can be mounted that cause a DoS by filling up the printer spool, and hence the disk, by submitting large print jobs. If no printer is, or should be, installed on the server, then prevent this attack by enabling this setting.
Devices: Unsigned Driver Installation Behavior	Do not allow installation	Unsafe drivers can cause problems with the operation of the system. This is especially important for DCs. You may have to adjust this policy if a driver you absolutely need is not signed. The policy can be set to allow installation, then returned to the do not allow installation setting.
Domain Controller: Allow Server Operators to Schedule Tasks	Disabled	Restrict task scheduling to Administrators. Scheduling tasks on a domain controller should be restricted. This option applies only to domain controllers.
Interactive Logon: Require Domain Controller Authentication to Unlock Workstation	Enabled	When the console is locked, logon may occur using cached logon credentials. If, for example, the cached logon credentials are present for account Jane, and Jane's account is disabled, Jane will still be able to log on, since her account is not checked but the cached credentials are used. Enabling this requirement forces access of Jane's account, and Jane will not be able to log on.

Table 6-8. Restrict Security Options *(continued)*

ONE STEP FURTHER

Windows NT 4.0 does not have anything like Security Options defined in a GUI. Instead, security settings can be made directly in the registry. A list of appropriate registry settings comparable to the Security Options section is defined in the Windows NT 4.0 Baseline Security Checklist at www.microsoft.com/technet/treeview/default.asp?url=/technet/security/chklist/nt4svrcl.asp.

In addition to those Security Options visible in the Group Policy Editor, additional registry settings can be distributed via Group Policy by adding the registry information to a security template and importing this template into a GPO. Examples of such settings can be found in the security templates provided with Microsoft white papers on securing XP, Windows 2000, and Windows Server 2003. These specific settings harden TCP/IP against some known denial of service attacks and are defined in the KB article 315669 for Windows 2000 and KB article 324270 for Windows Server 2003.

Figure 6-8 shows a snapshot of the area of a security template where registry settings are defined. You can see the example settings, as well as some that are displayed in the GUI. You can also, with some additional work, make the new settings show up in the Security Options section, but the work will have to be done on each computer. It is not necessary if all you want to do is apply the settings. If they are in the template and the template is either manually applied or imported into a Group Policy, the settings will be applied. More information on using security templates is provided in Chapter 8.

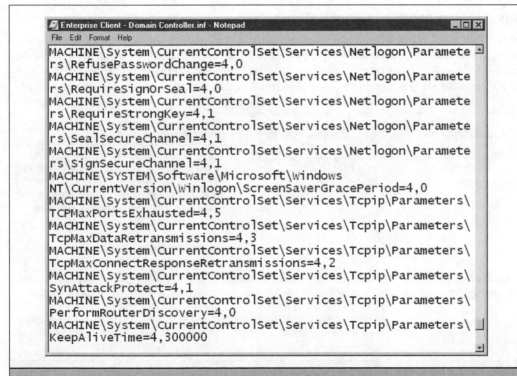

Figure 6-8.   All registry settings in the security template will be applied.

Protect Active Directory Communications

Protecting Active Directory communications means ensuring that replication data and other communications with the AD are secured. Chapter 5 discusses options for protecting this data, including the use of VPNs, SSL, and IPSec and the use of perimeter network forests with trust relationships with internal forests instead of allowing replication between domains from the same forest over the internal firewall. It also discusses the ports used for Active Directory communications. Chapter 11 discusses how to harden and securely implement these communication processes.

LDAP traffic with Windows Server 2003 domain controllers can also be secured by using the Security Options described in Table 6-9. If legacy clients such as Windows 98 are used in LDAP communications, you cannot require these settings.

Manage Administrative Authority

Managing administrative authority is an important process in securing the entire Windows network and is covered in detail in Chapter 8. However, there are specific AD related administrative concepts that are critical for the security of Active Directory.

Restrict Membership in Forest Groups

Several security groups have access forest-wide. These groups, Enterprise Admins and Schema Admins, assign immense power. Restrict membership in the Enterprise Admins group. Follow information provided on Administrative Authority in Chapter 8. Remove any accounts that are members of the Schema Admins group. An account can be added

Security Option	Recommended Setting	Discussion
Domain Controller: LDAP Server Signing Requirement	Require signing unless legacy clients exist.	LDAP traffic between Active Directory and administrator workstations can be protected by requiring digital signing of LDAP packets. If an attacker alters the packet and puts it back on the network, the digital signature will be incorrect and the packet will be dropped. However, when the domain controller requires LDAP signing, there can be problems if legacy clients exist.
Network Security: LDAP Client Signing	Negotiate signing if some domains will require it and some will not. Require signing if all domains require signing. If legacy clients are used, then set to None.	When LDAP signing is required by domain controllers, workstations must be able to conduct it. If they cannot, there will be failure in authentication, Group Policy, and logon scripts. If legacy clients are used, LDAP signing cannot be required.

Table 6-9. Protect LDAP Communications

when it is necessary to modify the schema. Windows 2000 schema additions cannot be removed. By removing membership in the Schema Admins group, you will prevent inadvertent additions, and if you require a policy review before changes to schema are made, you can, if policy is enforced, prevent unauthorized additions. Windows Server 2003 schema additions can be disabled; however, many applications that make schema additions add a large number. Avoid the necessity to disable them by managing membership in Schema Admins and by enforcing a strict review of any proposed additions.

Restrict Delegation of Authority

The Delegation of Control Wizard can be used to assign administrative duties to any user or group. This should not be done lightly. However, it is a powerful tool that can be used to grant the minimum amount of authority necessary to groups of users that require the ability to perform some administrative task. Help Desk employees, for example, may require the ability to reset users' passwords but do not require full administrative privileges.

Restrict Group Policy Administration

The ability to administer Group Policy confers the ability to set and modify security policy. The right to do so can be used to cripple operations in a Windows domain or OU, either maliciously or by simple ignorance. This ability should be restricted to trained, authorized Group Policy administrators.

Secure Active Directory Data— Understand Active Directory Object Permissions

The data stored in the AD can be protected by protecting AD communications and infrastructure as previously outlined in this chapter as well as in Chapter 5. In addition to securing the database and its operation, you should pay attention to the ACLs on individual Active Directory objects. These ACLs both provide security for the object and provide permissions that permit manipulation of the object. The use of permissions to manage objects is discussed in Chapter 8.

Chapter 7

Harden Administrative Authority and Practice

 Delegate and Control Administrative Authority

 Define Secure Administrative Practices

Administrative authority defines the scope of administrative responsibility assigned to specific administrative roles. A simple division of administrative roles into *service administration* (administration of the Active Directory infrastructure) and *data administration* (administration of the data within the Active Directory) is one way to define these roles. This concept, which applies the security principal of role separation, should be extended. In addition to closely defining administrative roles, define policies and procedures for secure administrative practices. The first consideration should be to specify the types of administrative roles required and then develop a plan for delegating and controlling administrative authority. Before implementing the plan, define secure administrative practices. Secure administrative practices include hardening administrative workstations and protecting administrative communications.

Delegate and Control Administrative Authority

Many users need elevated privileges in order to perform their responsibilities, but most users do not need full administrative responsibility in the forest, domain, or organizational unit (OU), or even on the computer that they use. Use this principle, the principle of least privilege, to provide users with only the rights and privileges they need to do their job. This ensures that the risk of accidental or malicious abuse of privilege is manageable.

What Is an Administrator?

What is an administrator? To many IT pros and end users, an IT administrator is a user with supreme powers. She can do what she wants to on the computers on which she is an administrator. Those that have been around IT implementations of any size understand that the modern enterprise segregates administration into network infrastructure management and systems management. Knowledgeable Windows pros know that Windows systems management has a variety of classifications, such as Enterprise Admin, Domain Admin, local Administrator, Server operators, database administrator, and so forth. However, all of these "administrator" positions reek with authority.

Is this the only definition of administrator? Windows 9*x* and Windows Millennium computers don't define the concept at all. By default, any individual in possession of the computer can perform any role, from user to administrator. He can adjust network settings, view all data on the hard drive, install software, and configure device settings, all without meeting any requirement such as authentication or authorization. Windows NT 4.0 requires authentication, provides options for authorization based on user accounts, and defines several administrative roles. Windows 2000 introduces the ability to granularize administrative responsibilities ad infinitum. It is possible to provide permission to perform a single administrative task such as password reset, or even the ability to modify only telephone numbers in user accounts. If you use the delegation of authority concept to distribute administrative authority across a large number of individuals, at what point do you label a user an administrator, as opposed to an individual with an "elevated privilege"?

This is not as esoteric a discussion as it might seem. If you are to define secure administrative practices, you must be able to define the groups and individuals that these concepts apply to. In this chapter, you will find explicit directions for defining administrative roles and securing administrative practices based on those roles. Before you use these procedures to secure administrative practices in your environment, you will need to determine how well your administrative roles match those defined here.

Windows NT 4.0 and products built on its technologies have always had the ability to support this activity. It was, however, more difficult and not quite as flexible a process on Windows NT 4.0. Two questions form the cornerstones on which the process is built:

- What exactly does the user need to be able to do (what is the list of the minimum privileges that a specific user must have)?
- How can you technically enforce that role?

Define User Roles

In many networks, there are only two classes of users; administrators and end users. Role definition is simple: Administrators manage, configure, maintain, and operate the network and its systems. Users do business-related work. However, this model is not sustainable. It is impossible to provide enough qualified and fully trained administrators to perform for users all of the network administrative duties, and it's a bad idea to give a large number of people full administrative privileges.

The Help Desk role illustrates this dilemma. Help desk personnel require the ability to do things such as reset passwords, unlock accounts, and perhaps modify network configurations. (You may define their duties differently.) In order to provide them with these privileges, the typical response is to make them a member of the Domain Admins group. This gives them far too many privileges. They can, for example, create users, add users to groups, add and configure printers, and create shares and modify permissions on them.

In addition to administrative role definition, the principle of least privilege should be applied to ordinary users. Access to specific applications and resources (files, printers, databases, and so on) on the network should be restricted to those who need access. By default, much access is provided to implicit groups, such as Everyone and Network. Membership in these groups is automatic, according to some characteristic of the user. For example, remote connections to a file server become members of the Network group. While you cannot remove or add user accounts to these implicit groups, you can define user roles and use user rights, access controls, and optional Windows operating system configurations to closely define a role for each type of user on the network.

Clearly, an alternative to the simple two-tier user or administrator role definition is necessary. Windows systems provide several ways to implement a granular approach to user roles, both administrative and process oriented.

Define Administrative Roles

The first step in defining administrative roles is to list the user roles that exist and the duties they perform on the network. By default, these roles will assume some dissection of administrative responsibility. Use the following process:

1. Use the operating system predefined administrative roles.

2. For workgroup computers and for Windows NT 4.0 domains, define additional roles by creating custom groups and assigning user rights and resource permissions to fit.

3. For Windows forests (Windows 2000 and Windows Server 2003), use the document "Best Practices for Delegating Active Directory Administration" (http://www.microsoft.com/downloads/details.aspx?FamilyID=29dbae88-a216-45f9-9739-cb1fb22a0642&displaylang=en) to define administrative roles.

4. For Windows forests, use the Delegation of Control Wizard to implement the roles you defined in step 3.

Use Operating System Predefined Administrative Roles   Eventually, you will have to define roles that precisely fit the way that you need to administer your network. However, step 1 in hardening Administrative Authority is to use those roles that are predefined. Use the roles defined in Tables 7-1 and 7-2. Table 7-1 lists groups that are present by default on a workgroup computer. Table 7-2 defines the groups present in domains and forests. Default administrative groups are listed and identified with respect to which operating system they exist in. The designation "All" in the operating system column indicates that the group is present in all Windows computers based on Windows NT technology. If groups exist only in workgroups, domains, or forests, that information is added. Windows 9x and Windows Millennium computers do not use the concept of Windows group. All users by default act as administrators on the local computer, and these computers cannot be joined in the domain.

TIP Rights are different than permissions. Rights authorize users to perform an action on a system. Permissions are associated with a specific object. Thus, a member of the Administrators group has the right to add users to groups. She also has the Full Control permission on many system files and registry keys that members of other groups do not. Rights can override permissions. For example, the right to back up files and directories empowers the holder to make backup copies of files that they do not have any permission to access. When selecting predefined group membership, it is important to understand what rights and permissions that group holds. It is equally important when defining custom groups, and in troubleshooting authorization and access problems.

Role	User Rights*	Default Membership	Operating System
Administrators	All powerful on the local system.	Administrator, Domain Admins if computer is member of a domain.	All
Backup Operator	Back up and restore files. Log on locally. Shut down systems.	None	All
Debugger Users	(Can debug processes on this machine, both locally and remotely. Added with Visual Studio.)	Local Administrator account	Windows XP, Windows Server 2003
Guests	Log on locally to a workstation (client system).	Guest	All Workstations
HelpServicesGroup	Can run applications that are part of the Windows Help and Support Center.	SUPPORT_388945a0	Windows XP, Windows Server 2003
Network Configuration Operator	Manage networking features.	None	Windows XP, Windows Server 2003
Performance Log Users	Remote access to schedule logging of performance counters.	Network Service account	Windows Server 2003
Performance Monitor Users	Remote access to monitor the computer.	None	Windows Server 2003
Power User	Change system time, force shutdown of remote system, create and manage user accounts. Lock the machine, create common groups, share and stop sharing of directories (Windows NT).	None	All

Table 7-1. Predefined Administrative Roles for Servers and Clients Whether or Not They Are Joined in a Domain

Role	User Rights*	Default Membership	Operating System
PreWindowsCompatible Access	Membership provides access equivalent to Windows NT 4.0 with respect to access to information on user accounts and groups and certain access to files and registry keys.	Everyone (Windows 2000) Authenticated Users (Windows Server 2003) If the Permission Compatibility option is selected during dcpromo	Windows 2000, Windows Server 2003
Remote Desktop Users	Can log on remotely and access and use the local computer console.	None	Windows XP, Windows Server 2003
Replicator	Replicate files and directories with other authorized systems.	None	All
Users	Run applications, manage files, access computer from network.	Domain Users if computer is joined in a domain	All
Windows Authorization Access Group	Provides access to the Token-Groups-Global_and_Universal (TGGU) attribute. TGGU enumerates membership in groups. Access to this attribute is necessary for some applications to run and is granted by default to members of the PreWindowsCompatibleAccess group.	Enterprise Domain Controllers	Windows Server 2003

Table 7-1. Predefined Administrative Roles for Servers and Clients Whether or Not They Are Joined in a Domain *(continued)*

*Basic user rights given to all users, such as log on locally, access the computer from the network, and so forth, are not listed for each user group, since all users are by default members of the Users group.

Role	User Rights	Default Membership	Operating System
Account Operators	Create and manage user and groups accounts for the domain.	None	All
Administrators	All powerful on the local system.	Administrator	All
DHCP Administrators	Administer DHCP.	None	Windows Server 2003, Windows 2000

Table 7-2. Predefined Administrative Roles in Windows Domains and Computers

Role	User Rights	Default Membership	Operating System
DHCP Users	View-only access to DHCP server information.	None	Windows Server 2003, Windows 2000
DNS Administrators	Administer DNS.	None	Windows Server 2003, Windows 2000
Domain Admin	Manage the domain.	Local Administrator group for all computers joined in the domain	All
Domain Guests	Log on locally to workstations.	Guest	All
Domain Users	Log on to workstations.	All user accounts	All
Enterprise Admins	Administer the forest, including the ability to perform some administrative tasks that Domain Admins cannot, and to administer all domains in the forest.	Local Administrator Account of forest root domain	Windows 2000, Windows Server 2003
Group Policy Creator Owners	Create and administer group policy.	Local Administrator account	Windows 2000, Windows Server 2003
Incoming Forest Trust Builders	Can create the incoming portion of a trust. The trust provides potential access for the local domain's users to be given access to the other domain.	None	Windows Server 2003
Print Operators	Create, delete, and manage printer shares. Log on locally, shut down system.	None	All
Schema Admins	Modify, add schema classes and attributes.	Local Administrator account in forest root	Windows Server 2003, Windows 2000
Server Operator	Log on locally to servers, back up and restore files (NT 4.0), change system time.	None	All

Table 7-2. Predefined Administrative Roles in Windows Domains and Computers *(continued)*

Harden Default Administrative Roles   The default rights assignments provided for standard groups can be further restricted, and this should be the first step in hardening administrative roles. Since each operating system has some differences in user groups and rights, each of the items in the following list indicates a specific operating system, if the modification is unique to that OS. Keep in mind that the reason for restricting access is to fulfill the requirement of least privilege. This may also be fulfilled by creating special administrative groups and giving them access instead of providing access to the entire Administrators group.

- Restrict Windows NT 4.0 Replicator group membership to an account created to run the Replicator service.

- Modify User Rights assignments according to computer role. Many steps for doing so will be included in Chapter 8; however, a good example is to remove the right of user groups to "Access This Computer from the Network" from any Windows NT 4.0 RAS server and from all client computers operated by ordinary users, and to restrict the administrative groups that can exercise it. Log on locally should also be restricted according to computer role. In general, when administrative roles are created for specific server types, then access to servers should be restricted to those roles.

- Restrict the right to Shut Down from a Remote System. If computers are not managed remotely, then this right should not be available. Sensitive servers may, by policy, be managed directly from the console. In this case, the right is not necessary and should be removed from any group's list of user rights.

- Remove any membership in the Schema Admins group. Doing so will prevent accidental or many malicious additions to the schema, since an account must first be added to the group. The ability to add membership should be controlled, and that policy requires examination; testing and approval of all schema changes should be established.

- On Windows Server 2003, grant the user right Allow Logon Through Terminal Services to only the Administrators group. (If users require this access, they should be added to the Remote Desktop Users Group.)

- Remove the Administrators group from the Debug Programs user right. Do not assign this right to users on a production system, unless and until it is necessary to do so.

- Remove the Print Operators group from the Load and Unload Device Drivers right on critical print servers. Requiring a full administrator to perform this action can help prevent the loading of damaging print drivers.

HEADS UP!

You should carefully consider the server's situation before removing the right to shut down from a remote system. Some critical servers in remote location are administered remotely. The ability to shut down these systems remotely is critical and should not be removed. The reason for preventing anyone from exercising this right is to prevent malicious or accidental shutdowns. As usual, the risk of having this right available must be weighed against the right of not having it available. It may be necessary to grant this right to a limited number of administrators so that they can complete a repair or take a system offline that may come under attack or that may be trojaned and used to attack other systems. Where these types of processes are required, use custom groups and assign the right.

To modify user rights in Windows NT 4.0:

1. Open the User Manager or User Manager for Domains program via Start | Programs | Administrative Tools.

2. Click the Policies menu and select User Rights.

3. Click the Show Advanced User Rights check box, shown here:

3. Select the User Right to modify.

4. Select the group in the Grant To box and click Remove.

Alternatively, if the Security Configuration Manager is used, create and apply a Security Template designed for server, workstation, or DC hardening.

To modify User Rights in Windows XP, Windows 2000, and Windows Server 2003 stand-alone systems, use one of three methods:

- Modify a Security Template created for managing servers or clients and apply the template using Security Configuration and Analysis.

- Modify the local group policy, Gpolicy.msc.

- Modify the Local Security Policy, reached through Start | Programs | Administrative Tools.

To modify user rights in Windows XP, Windows 2000, and Windows Server 2003 systems joined in a domain, use Group Policy. User rights for the domain are managed in the default Domain Controller Group Policy, under Local Policies and then User Rights Assignment. User rights applied to the local accounts (when used to log on) of member servers and clients can be modified in a GPO linked to the OU where the computer accounts reside.

Establish Custom Workgroup and Windows NT 4.0 Domain Administrative Roles   Creating custom groups can create additional administrative roles in Windows NT 4.0 computers and domains. An ordinary local group (can be used only on the local computer) or global group (can be used throughout the domain) can be granted user rights using User Manager. The group can also be provided a higher level of access to files and registry keys, as desired.

Unfortunately, it is hard to create useful custom administrative roles in Windows NT 4.0 because the range of user rights is small, and there is limited access to directory, computer, and user management through the use of permissions. (In Windows NT 4.0, permissions are used only to provide access to objects such as printers, files, folders, and registry keys. Directory objects in Windows Server 2003 and Windows 2000 Active Directory can be administered by applying permissions.) User rights, for example, are often implicit, not explicit. You cannot, for example, create a Help Desk group and give them just the right to reset passwords without granting them more administrative privileges. The Account Operators group can manipulate user groups, but there is no explicit Windows NT 4.0 User Right that can be used to confer that right on a custom group. Administrators can share folders, but there is no User Right that can be assigned a custom administrative group.

Potential custom administrator groups are possible. For example, a custom global group with the ability to administer a specific server or type of server can be created and given membership in the local Administrators group of that server. Another custom global group that needs to administer specific file and print servers can be used to provide access to appropriate files and folders on that server, and can be given the User Right to Access This Computer from the network. The right of the Users group to access the server can be removed. Ordinary users then would not be able to access the servers, but members of this new custom group would. To harden administrative roles in Windows NT 4.0, use custom groups to define administrative roles for specific types of servers or operations.

Define Additional Roles for Windows Forests   Windows 2000 introduced the Delegation of Control Wizard. Use of the wizard allows the creation of special administrative roles. For example, the Help Desk group just mentioned can be created in Windows 2000 and Windows Server 2003 domains and given explicit rights to do things like reset passwords. There is no need to make help desk operators members of the Administrator group. Creating and using additional administrative roles in Windows forests usually requires the design and implementation of an OU hierarchy and the use of the Delegation of Control Wizard to delegate administrative authority at the OU level.

TIP   Security-sensitive information on accounts should not be modified by account operators or help desk operators. Security-sensitive information is information such as whether or not the account is trusted for delegation, whether or not it requires a password, or modifications to the UPN.

The problem with the Delegation of Control Wizard is that the choices are many, and the documentation somewhat limited. The wizard works by allowing administrative assignment of Active Directory object permissions. Each object has common permissions and some specific to its object type. It's easy to create an administrator for an OU by assigning all permissions on all OU objects. It's harder to determine what permissions to assign in order to make more granular decisions. The Microsoft document "Best Practices for Delegating Active Directory Administration" (URL provided previously, under "Define Administrative Roles") provides sound instruction for making these determinations, including a reference on precisely which permissions to delegate to create the roles. The document recommends the forest administration roles in Table 7-3 (data management) and Table 7-4 (service administration) for Windows Server 2003 and Windows 2000 forests. Its appendix defines the Active Directory permissions to delegate to provide each role the ability to perform its job.

When reviewing these recommended roles, note how they help administrative roles fulfill the security principles of least privilege and role separation. Role separation seeks to divide, where possible, operations into functions and assign different parts of each function to different groups of individuals.

Role	Definition	Tip
Account Admins	Manage user accounts. Create, delete, move users accounts. Modify non-security information such as phone numbers on accounts. (Account support such as password reset may be assigned to the HelpDesk Operator role.)	Use the built-in Account Operators group and define members per OU for servers that are the responsibility of specific business units.
Application-Specific Admins	Manage application-specific data and possibly servers on which the data and application reside.	N/A
Business Unit Admins	When multiple business units share a common forest, separate data administration by granting this group responsibility for its own domain data and resources. Resources may be defined by collecting resources in specific domains or OUs and delegating authority to the specific Business Unit Admins group.	N/A
Help Desk Operator	Perform functions such as modify network settings on user computers, reset passwords, and unlock accounts.	In many organizations, create many instances in order to limit user access according to business unit. In all cases, however, provide functionality at the OU level to prevent operators from having access to administrative accounts.
Resource Admins	Manage a collection of servers that host a similar role, or set of services. For example, web server administrators should be provided administrative control to all web servers, and database administrators to database servers, but membership in these groups may be exclusive. Administrative control may include membership in the local administrators group on the server, or only administrative control of some service running on the server.	Examine processes, not server roles. For example, an application that requires several levels and servers may require database servers, application servers, and web servers. It may be best to create a group to administer the application (see the Application-Specific Admins group) and provide them with control over the specific servers that are part of the application process, rather than provide separate groups access to the different types of servers.

Table 7-3.   Roles for Data Administration

Role	Definition	Tip
Security Group Admins	Manage security groups required by a business unit. This would include user as well as administrative groups. Security groups are used to grant users rights as well as access to resources.	Create these groups per OU hierarchy that belongs to a business unit, then delegate the ability to create and manage users and groups.
Server Operators	Manage servers.	Use the built-in Server Operators group and define membership on local servers by using the Security Policy of the GPO linked to OUs.
Workstation Admins	Manage workstations. Members of local Administrator accounts on these workstations.	Create multiple groups if necessary to granularize control per business unit or even within business units.

Table 7-3.   Roles for Data Administration *(continued)*

Role	Definition	Tip
Backup Operator role	Back up system state.	Backing up system state includes the backup of Active Directory.
DNS Management	Install DNS server service. Configure forwarding and root hints, and configure zones and use of the forest-wide DNS application partition.	N/A
Domain Configuration Operators	Add additional DCs to a domain. Transfer and seize domain operations master roles. Raise domain functional level. Manage default domain controllers OU. Manage information in systems container. Restore AD from backup if necessary.	Each domain should have its own Domain Configuration operators group. Domain-specific AD configurations such as managing the caching of the universal security group membership information and refreshing this cache immediately is an example of a domain-specific duty that should be assigned to domain controller administrators.
Domain Controller Administrator	Manage DCs. Install and modify software, install service packs and hotfixes, configure directory service setting in registry, maintain and back up event logs, manage directory service file and sysvol, start and shut down domain controllers.	Use the default Domain Admins group.
Forest Configuration Operators	Create and delete child domains. Trust management. Create and manage cross-reference objects. Transfer and seize forest-wide operations master roles. Modify LDAP policy settings. Raise forest functional level.	Cross-references (references to directory partitions that are stored in the cross-reference object in the partition container) are important, as they allow proper location of directory partitions. (On which domain controllers can a specific partition be found? Where is a global catalog server?) If references can be changed, then it is possible to misdirect or DoS necessary access. LDAP policies prevent LDAP operations from adversely affecting DC performance (making it more resistant to DoS attacks). A default policy exists, but additional policies can be created using the **ntdsutil** command.

Table 7-4.   Roles for Service Administration

Role	Definition	Tip
Replication Management	Creation and maintenance of replication topology and monitoring of replication. Includes creation and deletion of sites, associating subnets to sites, adding and removing site links and site link bridges, modifying replication schedules, forcing replication.	It might be tempting to combine replication management with replication monitoring. Don't. In most cases, when monitoring is performed by a separate group, management is better.
Replication Monitoring	Monitor replication.	N/A
Schema Management	Extension and modification of the schema.	Use the built-in Schema Admins group.
Security Policy Administrator	Manage Domain security policy settings, including password, account lockout, and Kerberos policy, and manage Domain Controllers GPOs for every domain in the forest.	Domain and domain controller GPOs establish security policy that can impact the entire Active Directory infrastructure; therefore, they should be managed by one instance of forest-level administration.
Service Admin managers	Create and manage service administrator accounts and groups.	Creating and managing accounts and groups is a data admin role; however, allowing a data admin group to manage service admin accounts is not a good idea. The two roles, data admin and service admin, should remain separate.

Table 7-4.   Roles for Service Administration *(continued)*

HEADS UP!

Managing some aspects of domains should be delegated to forest-level administration. The Take Ownership user right, for example, while applied at the domain level, provides the holder with the ability to take ownership of any object on the DC, including any directory partition in the Active Directory. Likewise, the domain user right Load and Unload Device Drivers empowers an individual to add code that runs at kernel level. Security policy that impacts domain-wide and potentially forest-wide operations should be delegated to a single instance of forest-level administration, not parceled out in multiple domain-by-domain assignments.

Define Nonadministrative Roles

Nonadministrative role definition is important as well. Like administrative role definition, it includes elements of user rights, and object permissions. However, the most important user right for nonadministrative roles is the ability to run applications.

Controlling the ability of users to run applications often also involves controlling access to files, folders, registry keys, and Active Directory objects. Role definition, therefore, for nonadministrative users is defined in Chapters 9 and 10.

Define Technical Controls

Technical controls are those that can be enforced using technology. By creating custom groups and giving them rights and privileges, you can create technical controls.

Create Service Administration Roles in the Forest Root Domain

Service administration is a forest-level operation, and therefore the groups that implement it should be created in the forest root domain. To do so:

1. Create an OU in the forest root domain. The name "Service Management" is a good name for this OU.

2. Create each service administration group in the OU.

3. Protect the role instances by making the groups that are not default administrative groups, members of some group that is one, in order to protect them with the AdminSDHolder object. (The Print Operators group is a good choice, since is the least used.)

4. Add the approved user accounts to membership in the role groups.

NOTE   A process that runs on the Primary Domain Controller (PDC) emulator periodically checks and applies a standard security descriptor to the accounts that are members of default administrative groups. This occurs so that if the security descriptor is inadvertently or maliciously changed, it will be overwritten. (If the security descriptor is modified, the account might become unusable.) The process runs 15 minutes after system startup and every 30 minutes after that. The master security descriptor is stored as the security descriptor of the AdminSDHolder object (CN= AdminSDHolder,CN=System,DC=*domainname*). Administrative groups protected in Windows 2000 are Enterprise Admins, Schema Admins, Administrators, Domain Admins, Server Operators, Backup Operators, Print Operators. Windows Server 2003 also protects the Account Operators group members.

Create Data Administration Roles in Appropriate Domain OUs

Data administration groups typically manage domain-level data for users, groups, resources, and applications. Therefore, these groups should be implemented at the domain level. In many cases, multiple business units share a single domain; therefore, each business unit may manage an OU hierarchy. OUs should be structured to support administrative requirements and group policy requirements. Figure 7-1 illustrates such a hierarchy.

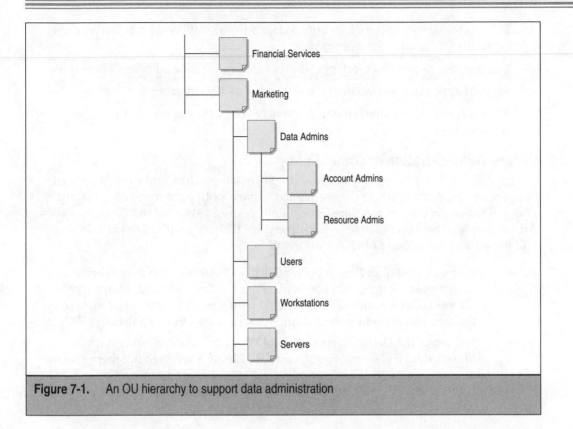

Figure 7-1.   An OU hierarchy to support data administration

To implement data administration roles:

1. Create an OU structure. A possible structure might include

   - An OU for every business unit
   - A child OU of each business unit OU in order to store data administrator group roles
   - A child OU of each business unit OU to store business unit user accounts
   - A separate child OU for each business unit to store business unit resources such as workstations and servers
   - Child OUs of these child OUs as appropriate. For example, the OU for the storage of administrative roles may include child OUs for common account groups, one for Account and Resource groups for specific resources, and so on.

2. Create security groups for various data administration roles in the business unit's OU created for this purpose.

3. Delegate Active Directory permissions that fulfill data administration roles.

4. Add approved user accounts to data administration groups.

5. As necessary, add authorization for access and management of specific resources.

Secure Administration of Group Policy

Group Policy is used to apply security settings, install patches, and control behavior of users on the network. It makes sense to define a policy for managing Group Policy. Two of the custom roles are Group Policy Administration and Security Policy Administration. Several practices will help ensure that only authorized administrators will have access to Group Policy Administration.

■ Limit membership in Group Policy Creator Owners group to the service administrators designated as Security Policy Administrators. Membership in Group Policy Creator Owners enables full administration of group policy in the domain, including the default domain and domain controller GPOs.

■ When using the Delegation of Control Wizard, do not provide data administrators Full Control over their OU. Limit them by giving them specific administrative duties. Full Control would include the administration of GPOs linked to their OU and OUs in its hierarchy. Administration of these GPOs should be delegated to specific data administrators by delegating Group Policy administration permissions.

Use Delegation of Control Wizard to Implement Custom Roles

The Delegation of Control Wizard can be used at the site, domain, or OU level to delegate an aspect of administrative authority. In its default implementation, the wizard can be used to delegate data administration. It uses a text file that can be customized so that the wizard can be used to delegate additional tasks. To use the wizard is simple. To use it properly is difficult if you do not know which permissions to delegate. The ability to use it should be restricted to knowledgeable, trustworthy administrators, and the precise permissions that are to be granted should be defined by security policy. In the Best Practices document mentioned previously, the precise permissions are defined that will enable the creation of its recommended administrative roles. The following example implements a portion of the Replication Management role for the contoso domain.

1. Right-click the contoso domain in Active Directory Users and Computers and select Delegate Control, and then click Next.

2. Click the Add button and use the Object Picker to select the Replication Management group, and then click Next.

3. Click Create a Custom Task to Delegate, as shown here, and then click Next.

4. Click This Folder, Existing Objects in This Folder, and Creation of New Objects in This Folder, as shown here, and then click Next.

5. Select the Monitor Active Directory Replication and Manage Replication Topology Permissions, as shown here, and then click Next.

6. Review choices and click Finish.

7. Open Active Directory Sites and Services, right-click a site that includes contoso domain controllers, and click Delegate Control. Then click Next.

8. Use the object picker to select the Replication Management group and click Next.

9. Click Create a Custom Task to Delegate, and then click Next.

10. Click Next.

11. Click the Full Control permission, as shown here, and then click Next.

12. Review your selections and then click Finish.

This implementation is not complete, nor is it perfect. Two specific problems are present. First, granting Full Control of the Site may be granting more access than is necessary for replication management. Second, it is also necessary to grant permissions on the Schema object and on the Configuration object. To complete the implementation, you must either modify the operation of the Delegation of Control Wizard to include the ability to do these things or use the ACL editor to complete the implementation. (You can also use the ACL editor it to provide all of the permissions necessary to this group.)

Edit dssec.dat to Unfilter Specified Permissions

Some common tasks are preprogrammed into the Delegation of Control Wizard. Others are not. It is possible to add tasks to delegate, or to add options. To do so, it is helpful to realize that not all permissions are viewable in the wizard because some are filtered. Those filtered are listed in the dssec.dat file, which appears in the %systemroot%\ system32 container. This file lists the filtered permissions in Active Directory. If permission is listed here with a value of 7, the property is filtered. To remove the filter and provide the property so that it can be delegated, change the 7 to a 0.

In Windows 2000, for example, you cannot delegate the ability to unlock a locked account. Help desk operators may require this ability. To provide the option to delegate the task:

1. Open the dssec.dat file in Notepad on a Windows 2000 domain controller.

2. Navigate to the heading [User] (hint: search on "[U"").

3. Select the setting lockoutTime=7.

4. Change the 7 to a 0, as shown here:

```
groupsToIgnore=7
instanceType=7
isCriticalSystemObject=7
isDeleted=7
isPrivilegeHolder=7
l=7
lastKnownParent=7
lastLogoff=7
lastLogon=7
legacyExchangeDN=7
lmPwdHistory=7
localeID=7
lockoutTime=0
logonCount=7
mail=7
```

5. Save the file.

6. In the Delegation of Control Wizard, add the Help Desk group.

7. In the Object Type box, select Users and then select the property-specific check box.

8. In the Permission list, select the ReadlockoutTime and WritelockoutTIme permissions.

9. Close the wizard.

Use ACL Editor and Adsiedit.msc to Create Custom Roles

The Delegation of Control Wizard operates by assigning permissions on objects in the Active Directory. These permissions can be added and removed by using ACL editors on objects displayed in Active Directory Sites and Services, and Active Directory Users and Computers, and by using adsiedit.msc, a support tool provided in the support folder on the installation CD-ROM. The appendix of the Best Practices document lists all of the permissions required in order to use the ACL editors to implement the role. Applying permissions using ACL editors is similar to manipulating file permissions. To determine what permissions to add, use the Best Practices guide. While the preceding example granted Full Control on the Site object, the example that follows details how to provide more granular control using adsiedit. It does not implement every permission listed in the document. To apply permissions using adsiedit.msc,

1. Click Start | Run, enter **adsiedit.msc**, and then click OK.

2. Right-click the ADSI Edit root and select Connect To.

3. Click OK to select the connection point as the DC component.

4. Right-click the ADSI Edit root and select Connect To.

5. Use the drop-down box in the Connection Point area to select Configuration, and then click OK to add this to the interface. Repeat, if desired, to add other components.

6. Expand the configuration container.

7. Adsiedit will be displayed in an MMC console, as shown here:

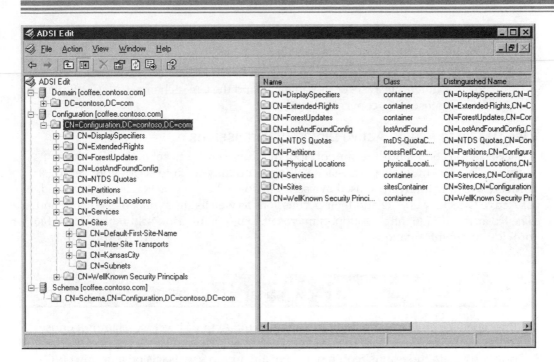

8. Right-click the DC=contoso, DC=com object and select Properties. Then select the Security tab.

9. Click the Advanced button.

10. Use the object picker to add the Replication Management group.

11. On the Object tab, add the Manage Replication and Monitor Replication permissions, and then click OK three times.

12. Repeat for other child domains.

13. Expand the Configuration container, right-click the CN=Configuration, DC= contoso, DC=Com container, and select Properties. Then select the Security tab.

14. Click Advanced and use the object picker to add the Replication Management group.

15. On the Object tab, add the Manage Replication and Monitor Replication permissions, and then click OK three times.

16. Expand the CN=Configuration, DC=contoso,DC=com container.

17. Right-click the site container and click Properties; then select the Security tab.

18. Click Advanced and use the object picker to add the Replication Management group.

19. Select the Object tab and select the Create Site objects and other settings as identified in the guide. Click OK three times.

20. Repeat the process to add permissions on the CN=Sites, CN=Subnets container, the CN=Inter-Site Transports container, and the CN=Schema, CN=Configuration, DC=Contoso, DC=com container.

Use Dsacls to Assign Active Directory Permissions

Dsacls.exe is a command-line support tool that can be used to set active directory permissions. To automate permission settings, you may want to script your settings. Dsacls.exe commands can be used in a script to do so. To use **dsacls** requires knowledge of Active Directory objects and their permissions as well as the syntax of the command. The KB article 281146 (http://support.microsoft.com/default.aspx?scid=kb;en-us;281146) provides more information.

HEADS UP!

Improper use of **dsacls** can be as damaging to the Active Directory as improper use of the registry editors. Both require intimate knowledge and correct application in order to obtain the results required. Do not attempt to use **dsacls** on a production domain unless and until you have tested commands in a test forest.

Use Dsrevoke to Revoke Permissions Granted by the Delegation of Control Wizard

Dsrevoke is a command-line tool that can be used to remove access control entries (ACEs or permissions) applied on a domain object or OU object. **Dsrevoke** removes only permissions. If user rights have been granted to an administrative role, use Security Policy to remove these user rights. Specify the OU hierarchy to search and remove permissions from, or the command will search the entire domain and all OU hierarchies within that domain. The command can also be used to simply list the permissions granted on domains and OUs for a specific user group. To use the command to remove permissions for the Accountants user group in the Financial OU in the contoso domain, issue the command

```
dsrevoke /remove /root:OU=Financial,DC=contoso,DC=com contoso\Accountants
```

You can also look for or revoke permissions granted to a specific user account. Figure 7-2 displays the partial results of issuing the command

```
dsrevoke /report /root:OU=Financial,DC=contoso,DC=com contoso\Luke
```

```
Command Prompt                                                    _ □ ×

C:\stuff>=dsrevoke /report root:OU=Financial,OU=contoso,OU=com contoso\Luke


ACE #1
Object: OU=Financial,DC=contoso,DC=com
Security Principal: CONTOSO\luke

Permissions:
  CREATE CHILD
  DELETE CHILD
ACE Type: ALLOW

ACE inherited by all child objects


ACE #2
Object: OU=Financial,DC=contoso,DC=com
Security Principal: CONTOSO\luke

Permissions:
  DELETE
  READ CONTROL
  WRITE DAC
  WRITE OWNER
  CREATE CHILD
  DELETE CHILD
  LIST CONTENTS
  VALIDATED WRITE ACCESS
  READ PROPERTY
  WRITE PROPERTY
  DELETE TREE
  LIST OBJECT
```

Figure 7-2. Use **dsrevoke** to report permissions granted on objects in Active Directory.

TIP Download dsrevoke.exe and instructions (dsrevoke.doc) from http://www.microsoft.com/ downloads/details.aspx?FamilyID=77744807-c403-4bda-b0e4-c2093b8d6383&displaylang=en.

Define Secure Administrative Practices

Administrative practices include any action that may be carried out by any administrator. However, since many different types of administrative roles exist, be sure to align administrative practices with these roles. While there are general practices that are relevant for all administrative roles, some administrative tasks are not as sensitive as others. One approach to security administrative practices is to divide administrative practices into five risk models. The risk models can then be used to determine which steps to take in order to secure administrator workstations, protect administrative logons, and secure administrative communications. These risk models are defined:

- **Very high-risk administration roles** Administrators are responsible for high-risk operations such as management of the root certification authority.

- **High-risk data center administration roles**   These administrators manage domain controllers, database servers, perimeter servers, e-mail servers, remote access servers, and so on that exist in the data center.

- **High-risk non–data center administration roles**   Business units may be located at remote sites or require isolation of critical or sensitive servers outside of the data center. Examples are domain controllers at remote sites, departmental database servers, and smart card or biometric registration servers. Business units may also be dealing with sensitive data, data too sensitive to risk placing it in the data center. By policy, this data is secured outside the data center and only authorized business unit employees are given authority to administer the systems.

- **Medium-risk administration roles**   Non-IT administrators such as help desk operators may carry out specific administrative operations. While these operations may be sensitive, such as password reset, they are limited. Help desk operators, for example, are not given authority to reset service administrator account passwords.

- **Low-risk administration role**   Business units may be delegated authority to manage user accounts for their own units. Account creation and management may be carried out from workstations located within the business unit.

Very High-Risk Administration

High-risk systems often require unique physical security as well as a high level of administrative practice security.

Secure Administrator Workstation

Very high-risk administrative roles demand either administration directly at the computer console or administration via a dedicated administrative network. When administrative workstations are used, they should be isolated from the administrative functions designed for the rest of the data center. It is often required that the administrative workstation be secured in the same manner as the very high-risk system. This should include secure installation practices and secure maintenance practices, as well as location in the same area as the high-risk computer. If administrative workstations are not located in isolated environments with the high-risk system, they should be isolated from mundane administrative workstations and dedicated to the administrative activity.

An example of a very high-risk system is a certification authority (CA). While some CAs must reside online to service certificate requests, some, including the root CA, require isolation.

Best practices for securing the root certification authority (CA) state that

- The CA should be dedicated.

- The CA should be offline (no network connection ever).

- The CA should be kept in a vault, or at least, a secure, isolated room should be dedicated to the CA.

- Access to the vault or room should be severely restricted.

- Vault or room access should be via cipher locks.

- The CA certificate and keys should be kept in a hardware device, not on the CA computer.

An administrative workstation is not used. In fact, the CA computer should not have a network card. Secure administrative procedures are used, and all administration is done from the CA console.

Other CA computers that are maintained online may also require console-only administration. If they are administered via a workstation, a dedicated management network may be implemented. More information on why CAs should be secure and how to secure them is provided in Chapter 12.

Physical security for the workstation consists of

- A BIOS password

- A required syskey Windows boot password

- A smart-card, token, and/or biometric for administrator logon

- Removal of floppy, CD-ROM, or other removable drives

- Disabling of USB, serial, and other communications ports in the BIOS

- Physical removal of USB, serial, or other ports as possible

- Hardware locks on cables and drives

- Physical locks that prevent theft of the workstation

- Alarms that warn of computer movement

Protect Administrative Logons

Administrative logons should be secured with the use of smart cards or strong password policies and by protection the transfer of logon credentials over the network.

Use Smart Cards   The additional physical security provided by requiring a smart card, token, and/or biometric for logon is a sound investment. While card readers are not expensive, some biometrics are. Neither will be available from every workstation in the organization. The ability to use smart cards is built into Windows 2000 and Windows Server 2003 domains (an enterprise CA must be implemented). Also provided is support for client smart card logon for Windows XP and Windows 2000 Professional systems joined in these domains. Additional third-party devices and software is available for all Windows systems, including fingerprint, facial recognition, iris and retinal scan, tokens such as secure-ID, and proximity cards. While it may be expensive and require large time outlays to implement such systems enterprise wide, their use for administrative logons to high-risk and very high-risk systems is neither cost prohibitive, difficult, nor time consuming to deploy.

If Windows-based smart cards are implemented, an additional secure practice may be implemented via Group Policy. The following items can be configured to ensure the use of smart cards for logon to designated administrative workstations.

Set these Security Options in the GPO linked to the OU where administrative workstations accounts reside:

In a Windows Server 2003 domain, enable the Interactive Logon: Require Smart Card option and set the Interactive Logon: Smart Card Removal Behavior option to "Force Logoff." Setting these options will both require a smart card be used (preventing the use of a password) on these workstations and force logoff if the smart card is removed.

In a Windows 2000 domain, the Security Option "Interactive logon: Smart card removal behavior" should be enabled.

HEADS UP!

Thoroughly investigate the impact of **runas** (the secondary logon service) on smart card operations or the use of biometrics. Frequently, administrators are advised to use a normal user account logon to do normal user activities on the network and to then use **runas** and their administrator account logon to perform administrative tasks. However, many security devices cannot be used to protect the **runas** logon. That is, even if accounts and workstations are capable of requiring the use of the device, using the runas option will void the device requirement. This means that the security gained by insisting on the use of the device may be negated. Windows 2000 **runas** cannot require the use of smart cards; however, Windows XP and Windows Server 2003 have that ability built in. In high- and very high-security requirements, especially where dedicated administrative workstations are used, disable the **runas** service and require administrators to log on using their administrator accounts.

In both domains, administrative accounts can be individually required to use a smart card for interactive logon. That is, if special administrative accounts are designated to administer high-risk workstation, these accounts can be required to use a smart card. To do so, open the account property pages by double-clicking the account in Active Directory Users and Computers, selecting the Account tab, and then selecting the account option Smart Card Is Required for Interactive Logon as shown in Figure 7-3.

Restrict Logon Access to Administrator Workstations   Restrict administrative workstations to specific user accounts. That is, you can prevent unauthorized individuals from using their assigned accounts to log on to the administrative workstation. To do so, configure the user right Allow Logon Locally by removing the listed groups and adding in the group that represents the administrators allowed to use the workstation. Also adjust the user right Access This Computer from the Network by removing all groups and adding back only a designated administrative group or account authorized to do remote administration or security scanning of the administrative workstation.

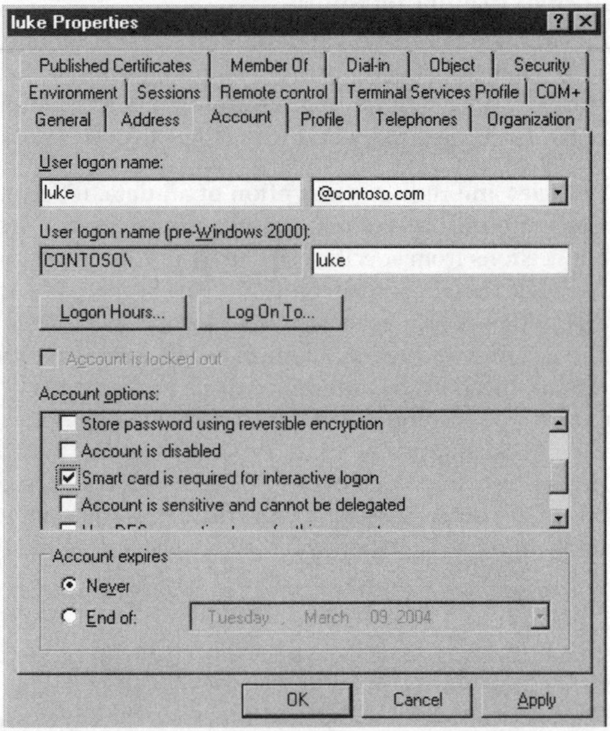

Figure 7-3.   Require smart card logon for specific administrator accounts.

Set Strong Password Policy   Alternatively, or until hardware-based or biometrically based logon can be identified, implement a strong password policy for administrator logon. As you know, password policies are domain specific. That is, technical controls for passwords and account lockout must be consistent across the domain.

Setting technical controls for service administrators, therefore, may be easy, since service administrator accounts should reside in the root forest domain. Since all accounts in the root forest domain represent higher risk than those in other domains, setting a restrictive password policy for this domain should be required.

Setting technical controls for data administrators may not be so easy, since these accounts may reside in child domains where most users are not performing high-risk activity and a more relaxed password policy may be required. In these domains, strengthen password policy by requiring that administrators use longer, more complex passwords. You cannot restrict them via normal technical controls, but you can audit passwords for length and complexity to ensure compliance.

Secure Administrative Communications

Where administrative functions use workstations and network connections, the data the passes between the client and server computers may be at risk. Sensitive data, including authentication data, configuration information, and so forth, regularly travels across the network. There are several ways to protect this data:

- **Use IPSec policies and require encryption of all data.** IPSec policies can be used to protect administrative connections with servers. IPSec policies can authorize connections from specific computers (for example, the administrative workstation) while denying other connections. Alternatively, they can restrict the use of specific ports, for example, those used to administer servers, to access by the administrative workstation, while allowing other types of necessary communications by authorized users of the server. Mutual computer authentication is required and therefore supports the requirement that authorized administrative workstations be used. Protect access to the administrative workstation, as IPSec does not require user authentication. Access to workstation and server does, of course; it's just not an additional component of IPSec. If a user can log on to the workstation and server, she can use the IPSec connection.

- **Use SSL.** If web servers are administered remotely, administrative connections can be required to use SSL. Both server and client certificates can be required for access to administrative tasks, while ordinary web server communications can take place in the normal manner. Using SSL can provide mutual computer authentication (server to client and client to server) and/or encryption of all data that passes between them.

- **Use VPN.** When administrative workstations are used to access systems that exist in different networks, a VPN connection may be the solution. Though VPN connections generally extend from a client to a VPN server on the edge of a network, you can extend the secure connection by requiring IPSec from the VPN server to the server to be administered. VPNs are also strong choices for securing all communications between the organization's sites, especially if these connections take place over the Internet.

- **Use out-of-band connections.** Emergency Management Services (EMS) is a new feature of Windows Server 2003 that provides assistance for remote administration. It enables Server 2003 boot without video card and legacy keyboard controller support. Using EMS, an administrator can administer a server as if she had a local console connection. Startup and shutdown, as well as system recovery tasks, can be accomplished. There is even a Special Administration Console (SAC). EMS requires, and other remote administration tasks can use, out-of-band hardware-based connections. Out-of-band connections are modems, service processors (dedicated and separate circuits that can be used to provide connectivity independently of the computer's normal processors) or terminal concentrators (hardware devices used to provide serial access to several servers from a single networked device). The use of these connections can protect administrative activity, since they do not flow over the normal TCP/IP network (however, you will need to carefully secure these connections as well).

- **Use a dedicated administrative network.** A dedicated administrative network places administrative workstations on a network separate from the organization's primary network. Servers are connected to both networks. This process secures administrative access, since remote access to administrative workstations is possible only from other administrative workstations, or from compromised servers. Server compromise may be the goal of attacking the administrative workstation; so removing it from the normal network prevents that avenue of attack. If a server is compromised, then there is access to the administrative network, but the goal of getting there has already been at least partially accomplished. (It is possible that other servers will then be at risk, so the server-to-workstation attack venue is not as silly as it seems.)

- **Require the use of VPNs or IPSec policies in conjunction with Terminal Services or disable Terminal Services in administration mode.** Use these additional security methods because Terminal Services cannot provide server authentication. A spoofed terminal server could be used to obtain logon credentials from a client. Prevent the use of remote desktop connections, including remote assistance, by deselecting the Turn On Remote Assistance and Allow Invitations to Be Sent from This Computer and Allow Users to Connect Remotely to This Computer check boxes on the Remote tab of the System properties, as shown here:

Securing management communications is vital to protecting high-risk systems. Information on SSL, IPSec, and VPNs can be found in Chapter 11. The details of EMS are located in Chapter 13.

Additional Security for Administrative Practices

There are many other issues that require consideration in order to secure administrative practices. Use the following list:

- Require background checks on administrators before hiring and periodically thereafter.

- Monitor and audit administrative work. Administrators make errors, and administrators may also be attackers. You must be able to trust administrators; however, use the adage "trust but audit."

- Reduce membership in administrative groups. The delegation of administrative roles increases opportunities for the proliferation of administrative accounts. However, the goal is to have as few administrators of any one type as is possible. It is preferable to have a large number of administrators, each with limited administrative responsibility, than a smaller number of administrators who all have extraordinary access and control. Instead of, for example, 15 Enterprise Admins in the forest, it is better to have two administrators in each of the designated service admin and data admin roles (for a total of 36) defined previously in this chapter. In this case, not only do fewer individuals have total control, but checks and balances between administrative roles can be defined that may prevent, or make it easier to discover, malicious action.

- Ban the use of PDAs and smart phones as administrative access points. It may be more difficult to secure communications with these instruments, and it is definitely harder to secure the devices themselves.

- Require and provide security training that supports the very high-risk administration role.

- Provide policy that identifies who has authority to require the management changes that each administrator has the ability to make. In other words, separate the role of the change maker from that of the change decision maker. While this is not always possible when troubleshooting network issues, it is possible when ordinary change processes are required. For example, the decision to add a user account to a service or data administration role should not be the responsibility of the service administrator who has authority to do so on the system. Policy should identify who has the authority to request such changes.

- Take systems offline to troubleshoot them. If there is any possibility that the computer has been compromised, do not troubleshoot while it is connected to the network. You cannot rule out the possibility that the impact of your operations may allow an attack to proceed; after all, you do have powerful administrative authority. Attack programs may require this authority to proceed.

- Secure administrative tools and their use. Do not install special administrative tools on high-risk systems. Where possible, use them from remote workstations. Use security features provided with administrative tools. Limit their access to approved administrators by restricting access via file permissions and software restriction policies. Disable or remove, if possible, parts of tools that are not required and that may provide vulnerabilities. Protect insecure tools via other means. For example, secure telnet access by using IPSec.

- Secure the use of tools that can be used in the Microsoft Management Console (MMC). You can do so by limiting access to administrators that require it, and by developing customs MMCs that include only the tools that specific administrators need. Set the mode of the MMC console to reduce users' ability to add administrative functionality to it. Restrict access to snap-ins and tools in Group Policy. Use the principle of least privilege: provide access to specific tools to only those who have authority to use them. For example, the use of the DNS administration console can be restricted to use by DNS administrators.

To change console mode and restrict changes to the console:

1. Open a new MMC console by entering **MMC** in the Start | Run text box and clicking OK.

2. Select the File menu (the Console menu in Windows 2000) and select Options.

3. Select the Do Not Save Changes to this Console box.

4. Select the console mode from the drop-down box in the Console tab, as shown here:

Choices are as follows:

- **Author Mode**   Full access including the ability to add and remove snap-ins.

- **User Mode - Full Access**   Provides full access to management configuration but users cannot add or remove snap-ins.

- **User Mode - Limited Access, Multiple Window**   Users have access to only the areas of the console tree that were visible when the console was saved. Users can open new windows but cannot close windows.

- **User Mode - Limited Access, Single Window**   Users have access to only the areas of the console tree that were visible when the console was saved. Users cannot open new windows.

5. Click OK to close the property box.

To restrict access to the MMC console and to specific snap-ins using group policy:

1. Open the GPO linked to the OU where the user account exists for editing.

2. Navigate to the Microsoft Management Console through User Configuration | Administrative Templates | Windows Components, as shown here:

3. To prevent all users in this OU from creating console files or adding or removing snap-ins, double-click the "Restrict the user from entering author mode" policy and select Enabled on the Settings tab. Then click OK. Users

can open consoles that are not opened in author mode such as those on the Administrative Tools menu or those designed for them that are configured to be opened in user mode.

4. To restrict users to using only some specific snap-ins, double-click the policy "Restrict users to the explicitly permitted list of snap-ins." Click Enabled on the Settings tab and then click OK to prevent access to all snap-ins. You must then define which snap-ins are permitted in the Restricted/Permitted snap-ins folder. Alternatively, you can allow access to all snap-ins (the default) and then prohibit access to specific snap-ins using the Restricted/Permitted snap-ins folder.

5. Open the Restricted/Permitted snap-ins folder.

6. Select a snap-in to control.

7. Double-click the snap-in and click Enabled to permit the use of the snap-in or Disabled to prohibit its use. Click OK. The enabled or disabled function will be shown in the interface, as shown here:

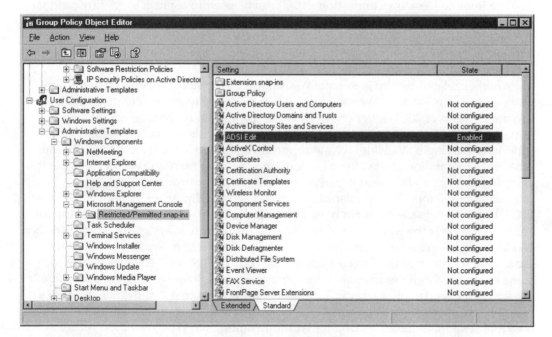

High-Risk Data Center Administration

Administration of servers in the data center is high risk if the activity can impact either sweeping areas of the organization's network or sensitive or critical or sensitive servers or data. Many of the items outlined for protecting very high-risk administration practices are applicable. Use the following recommendations to reduce security operations or practices as required; however, never reduce security for convenience.

Secure Administrative Workstations

Workstations used to administer high-risk data center services should already be located within the data center, but it is unlikely that a single workstation will be dedicated to administer a single server. Normal data center physical security, not the extremes of very high-risk operations, should apply. Changes may be simple things such as not requiring a BIOS password, even the manual input of an operating system boot password for syskey. Nevertheless, the workstation should be dedicated to administrative practices and follow practices for very high-risk situations where practical.

Secure Use of Terminal Services

Windows 2000 provides two Terminal Services modes: Administrative and Application. Administrative mode allows only two connections by Administrators. Terminal Services communications can be secured by configuring the encryption level. Windows XP and Windows Server 2003 include the Remote Desktop and Windows Server 2003 provides Terminal Services Configuration.

The Remote Desktop Connection (RDC) can be used to connect to XP Professional systems running the Remote Desktop service and to Windows Server 2003 servers running Terminal Services. The Remote Desktop Web Connection is another way to connect to Terminal Services. RDC provides full access to file system, ports, printers, audio, and smart card signon.

Another related service is Remote Assistance, the Remote Desktop Help Session Manager service. Remote Assistance provides the ability to invite remote control over a Windows Server 2003 server or Windows XP computer. Invitations can be sent via e-mail or Messenger (and even by saving the invitation file to a network share or otherwise making it available). While access is validated via password, the individual making the invitation creates the password and there are no requirements to make it complex, or to prevent insecure transmission of the password.

Remote Desktop for Administration can be used to administer Windows Server 2003. Terminal Services does not have to be installed or running; Remote Desktop for Administration is the equivalent of Windows 2000 Terminal Services in Administration mode. In addition to the typical Terminal Services connection, Remote Desktop for Administration can be used to connect to the "real" console of the server to provide the same experience as if the administrator were connected directly to the console using the server's keyboard and mouse. This allows items that are not allowable through normal Terminal Services or Terminal Services for Administration, since those ran in a virtual session. Remote Desktop for Administration, like Windows 2000 Terminal Services in Administration mode, provides limited connections (two in the latter, three in the former). To use Terminal Services for user connections, you must install Terminal Services.

TIP To use Remote Desktop for Administration and access this console, use the /**console** switch: enter **mstsc.exe /console** at the command prompt.

To secure Terminal Services manually:

1. Open the Terminal Services Configuration console, and right-click Connectoids in the details pane of the Connection folder.

2. Select the General tab and use the Encryption level drop-down tab to select High (128-bit, RC-4 encryption), as shown in the following illustration. The default client compatible setting allows the client to establish the encryption level. Legacy clients are not capable of using high encryption levels and should not be used to administer servers.

3. Click the Logon Settings tab and check the Always Prompt for Password box, as shown here:

4. Click the Client Settings and disable Drive Mapping, as shown in the following illustration. Enabling drive mapping allows the client to access drives on the client computer that will engage in a Terminal Services session with the server. This also empowers a connection from the server to the client, and therefore a possible client compromise if the server has been trojaned or otherwise compromised.

5. Click the Permissions tab. Note that Administrators have full control. Remove Remote Desktop users' access if those administering servers will be members of the local administrators group. Otherwise, leave or adjust the Remote Desktop group permissions and ensure that authorized nonadministrators are member of the Remote Desktop group. The Remote Desktop group is a group for designating which nonadministrative users can access the server using RDP. Membership in this group is not necessary for members of the local Administrators group.

To ensure consistency across servers, use Group Policy to secure Terminal Services. Terminal Services settings are located in the both the Computer Configuration and User Configuration folders under Administrative Templates | Windows Components | Terminal Services.

High-Risk Non–Data Center Administration

When domain controllers must be located in branch offices or other sites outside of the data center, administration practices must be reviewed with this fact in mind.

Secure Administrative Workstations

If local workstations are used to administer high-risk servers at remote locations, then the local workstation must also be secured. Do not use workstations in publicly accessible locations. Provide a workstation within the locked server room provided for the server, or if this is not possible, require administration at the server console. Alternatively, remote servers such as domain controllers can require headless operation and remote administration by employees located within the data center at headquarters. In this case, no local administrative workstation is required.

Protect Administrator Logons

Require the use of smart card logon where possible for local administrative operations. Where this is not possible, require the use Kerberos with a backup of NTLMv2.

Secure Administration Communications

Secure communications with at least the use of IPSec policies.

Additional Security for Administrative Practices

Protect access to secured servers by providing a locked room or enclosure and not colocating servers with telco equipment. Provide security for cabling, routers, switches. Include firewall access to the LAN and provide all other normal security defenses. Do not allow direct access to the local LAN from the Internet. If administration is to be remote, provide out-of-band access, as through a dial-up modem or other dedicated line.

Medium-Risk Administration

Medium-risk server administration does not require the high level of security discussed previously. It is often necessary to reduce security requirements in order to enable the delegation of authority and the smooth functioning of operations. Medium-risk situations may not require the same level of security as high-risk situations; however, many of those security steps are still valid. Consider carefully the impact of reducing securing requirements. The following may be potential modifications to security policy for medium-risk administration situations.

Secure Administrative Workstations

Dedicated administrative workstations are not the rule here. Instead, ordinary desktop computers that also serve as normal workstations are used by individuals whose administrative duties may not require full-time dedication. Nevertheless, their computers should be hardened wherever possible to protect them from attack. Require Windows 2000 or Windows XP Professional for these workstations, as these systems can be more easily and more completely secured.

If PDAs and smart phones are allowed for administrative purposes, they can be used via Terminal Services connections. However, security should not take a back step to convenience. Specifically, to secure PDAs:

- Use a power-on password. This feature is not enabled by default. Enable it.

- Require extended authentication, such as RSA tokens or biometrics. Many of these can be set to destroy all data if a number of incorrect authentication attempts are made.

- Require encryption of PDA data. Purchase third-party products that require validated logon within a short time frame. If the time requirement is not met, the encrypted database is destroyed.

- Label PDAs with subscription services tags. These services provide a number to call if the PDA is found. While only an honest person will call, many PDAs are turned in to lost and found departments but never returned to owners because there is no identifying information.

- Require physical protection of the PDA. Policy should require that PDAs be kept in locked drawers or safes when not in use. Carry PDAs in locking briefcases or at least cases that close rather than hang open.

- Provide a VPN client for the PDA and require its use for all connections used for administration.

- Store as little confidential information as possible on the PDA. Instead, require that data be manipulated at the server.

- Protect against rogue synchronization. Require synchronization with a specific desktop and harden the desktop.

- Use antivirus protection.

Protect Administrator Logons

Use Administrator accounts only for administrative functions. Administrators of medium-risk systems typically will not use dedicated administrative workstations. Instead, they must also use their computer for e-mail and other applications. Require administrators to use a normal user account for normal activity and use the secondary logon commands when performing administrative chores. These are common secondary logon tools:

- Windows NT 4.0 Resource Kit provides the **su** command. Resource Kit tools are available to TechNet subscribers and purchasers of the Resource Kit.
- Windows 2000 includes the **runas** service.
- Windows XP and Windows Server 2003 include the Secondary Logon Service.

The services differ. To use **runas** on Windows Server 2003 or Windows XP:

1. Navigate to where you can see the application from the Start button, and then hold down the left SHIFT key and right-click to produce a shortcut menu.
2. Click the runas option.
3. Select The Following User and enter the user name and password of the account you wish to use, as shown here:

4. Click OK.

To use **runas** at the command line, enter the **runas** command followed by authorization information and the name of the program to run under that account's authority. You will be prompted for a password. To open a command prompt with the local administrator authority on the computer computer1, use

```
runas /user:computer1\administrator cmd
```

To open a copy and use the Computer Management console as the administrator FredB in the peaceweaver domain, use

```
runas /user:peaceweaver\FredB "mmc %windir%\system32\compmgmt.msc"
```

Wherever possible, require Windows 2000 Professional or Windows XP Professional for these workstations, since the authentication process can be more securely configured.

Require longer, more complex passwords for these administrators. Since their accounts probably reside in domains right along with ordinary users, the same technical password policy will apply. However, there can be a separate, tougher security policy for administrators. You will have to enforce this policy, however, by alternative means.

Secure Administration Communications

In medium-risk administrative situations, where workstations are used for more than one purpose and are not located on dedicated administration networks, it makes sense to secure the communication channel between the workstation and the server. Use VPN connections when communication across public networks. Use SSL in administering web sites, and use IPSec to secure communications directly between server and client.

Additional Security for Administrative Practices

Administrators of medium-risk servers may require more constant and careful supervision and education. Regardless of the server managed, the user should be aware of the risk to security that thoughtless actions may pose. Training in security awareness, best practices, and how to spot intrusions and attacks, especially social engineering attacks, should be provided.

If administrators are responsible for creating and managing accounts and resource permissions, they should be required to follow policies that identify who may require them to add or change accounts or permission settings on resources.

Low-Risk Administration

Low-risk administration is often data administration that impacts user accounts or data of reduced sensitivity. Because the risk to operations, critical servers, and sensitive data is less, the security for administrative practices may be reduced. However, always remember that often access to critical servers is provided; for example, access is given to domain controllers in order to create and manage user accounts. While these data administrators do not have extensive privileges on DCs, they still have access to them.

Secure Administrative Workstations

Provide high-security hardening for these workstations. Physical security can include locks that prevent their movement and settings that include locking screen savers and smart cards or other more secure authentication practices where possible. Workstations should not be in public areas, and access to the workstations can be restricted by locking offices where they are located.

Protect Administrator Logons

Use ordinary accounts to access e-mail and other mundane applications. If hardware devices are not used for authentication, use **runas** to perform administrative duties.

Secure Administration Communications

Require IPSec policies to secure communications between workstations and servers.

Chapter 8

Harden Servers and Client Computers by Role

- The Role-Based Hardening Process
- Determine Computer Roles
- Design Role-Based Hardening Infrastructure
- Adapt Security Templates
- Implement the Hardening Plan Using Group Policy

erver and client computer roles define the purpose and use of computers on the network. If your goal is to secure every computer, you will find that this task becomes much easier when approached with the computer role in mind. While all computers share common security requirements, there are also security needs that must be considered in terms of the role each computer plays. The simple strategy presented in this chapter can form the security framework on which your computer-level hardening efforts can be based and on which you can build a sustainable security program. While it emphasizes server roles, a similar process can be followed to develop role-based security for client computers.

To begin:

- Understand the simple role-based hardening process.
- Divide computers into role categories.
- Address hardening infrastructure issues.
- Adapt security templates.
- Implement the hardening plan.

The Role-Based Hardening Process

The role-based hardening process works this way: First, it defines a baseline security standard for one or more top-level computer roles. Top-level roles for servers are usually defined separately for member servers and for domain controllers. The baseline hardens the generic Windows computer on which the top-level role runs. The computer boots and runs, but may not be able to do much else. Think of such a computer as you might a firewall that allows no traffic to pass through it. Until the firewall is configured to allow some traffic through, it is functionally useless. The proper way to configure the firewall is to allow only approved, necessary traffic through. This "loosening" of security is necessary to allow the organization behind the firewall to communicate with its partners, customers, and remote employees, as well as the general public. Without this step, the organization cannot function. The organization realizes it's taking a risk, but it's a manageable and acceptable risk because it has been mitigated by the initial hardening process.

The next step of the role-based hardening process is similar to opening required communication ports on the firewall. It defines the steps necessary to remove some aspect of hardening so that the business of the organization can continue. It does not apply to all computers all of the changes necessary. This would unnecessarily weaken security across the board. Instead, the role-based hardening process defines the steps necessary to enable each computer to perform its role. This step may also define further hardening that is specific to the computer's role. For example, many steps for hardening the DNS server are outline in Chapter 5. These steps cannot be applied at the baseline level, because the service that they are applicable to is disabled on the baseline level.

When security templates are used to implement such two-phase hardening, the baseline templates are called *baselines,* and the role-based templates are called *incremental templates.* Throughout this chapter, the term incremental templates will be used when the security template method of applying role-based security is defined. The more generic term, role-based security template, is used to mean any methodology for defining role-based security, including a simple recording of requirements in a document.

HEADS UP!

The words "security baseline" can be interpreted in at least two different ways. The Microsoft definition, and the one used in this book, is a list of hardening steps that strongly secure the computer. It implies that you may need to add functionality back to the computer in order to use it on the network. Another definition for security baseline is the set of hardening steps that provide a "minimal" level of security. Security baselines of both types are defined by numerous documents, which are accompanied by security templates that fulfill the baseline. These documents and templates can be downloaded for free from the Internet. Do not get confused by these different definitions. The "minimal" level templates will not work if used in the hardening solution defined in this chapter.

In essence, the database server and the web server and the file server all are first hardened to the same specification, but then each is configured independently so that they can do their own jobs. This means that a vulnerability that is specific to the file server only cannot be exploited on the database server. By first locking everything down and then opening only the things that are necessary for a specific computer role, the risk picture for the entire network is reduced.

Security baselines represent the ultimate locked-down computer configuration for standard base Windows computer roles. Second-tier, or "incremental," levels must be developed for more specific roles. It is even possible that third-tier security levels may be developed. For example, a client, or desktop, baseline might be developed to harden all desktop computers. An incremental level might be developed for most users—those that have requirements for standard applications. This incremental security level might be too restrictive for laptops, and therefore a third level might be defined.

Determine Computer Roles

It's easy to make a list of the computer roles on your network. It's harder to determine those that share similar security requirements. The idea, after all, is not to develop unique hardening steps for each computer role, but to develop a common security baseline or two that can be applied to large groups of computers, and then to develop additional security strategies for smaller subsets of computers. While this may seem like a time-consuming task, several Microsoft white papers propose a hierarchy of computer roles and provide security templates that can be used to implement the roles. In a Windows Server 2003 or Windows 2000 domain, these templates can be easily adapted to a specific enterprise, thus reducing the initial investment in role definition.

Table 8-1 summarizes both the Microsoft-defined roles and some additional roles. Modify this table by adding any unique roles used on your network and crossing out roles that you do not need. This will be helpful both when obtaining and developing security definitions for each role and when defining the architecture needed to support their implementation.

Top-Level Computer Roles

Microsoft defines two top-level, basic computer roles on the Windows network: Server and Domain Controller. While domain controllers are servers, the role that they play is so specialized, and their basic security needs so different from those of other servers, that their role is best set apart at the top level.

TIP Do not apply the member server baseline security template to any server that will be promoted to be a domain controller. Promotion will fail. Instead, apply the domain controller baseline security template.

Top-Level Roles	Second Level	Third Level
Server	Infrastructure Servers File Servers Print Servers IIS Servers Remote Access Servers Certificate Services Servers Bastion Servers* Database Servers Mail Servers IAS Servers	DNS, WINS IAS, RRAS, VPN SMTP, FTP
Domain Controller	N/A	N/A
Client	Desktop Machinery Control Systems	Laptop

*Bastion Servers are servers especially hardened to exist on the pubic side of the firewall and as such must be considered separately from the Active Directory–based implementation defined in the rest of this chapter.

Table 8-1. Computer Roles

In order to complete the role-based security paradigm, I have added the Client, or Workstation, top-level role.

Second- and Third-Tier Computer Roles

The second and third tiers for servers and clients represent what most people think of as computer roles. These roles are for database servers, file and print servers, and so forth. The second tier may be further divided.

You can define as many computer roles as you require. You may determine, after analyzing their security needs, that two or more computer roles require the same security. If you do, create a category that can serve both roles. For example, the table separates the File Server and Print Server roles. However, in your environment, you may decide that both types of servers will receive the same security hardening, or that the differences are so minor that to separate them results in more work without providing any additional security benefit.

Design Role-Based Hardening Infrastructure

No matter what specific hardening standard you adopt, you must adopt a way to apply the standard. In order to implement security for each role, you must provide the infrastructure necessary to do so. Windows computers may be hardened in the following ways:

- Manual configuration using GUI tools, one thing at a time, one computer at a time

- Direct registry editing, one computer at a time

- Some combination of GUI tools and registry editing

- System Policies deployed in a Windows NT 4.0 domain

- Security templates applied using Security Configuration Manager directly on a single Windows NT 4.0 computer or applied via scripting to multiple Windows NT 4.0 computers

- Security templates applied using Security Configuration and Analysis directly to a single Windows XP, 2000, or Server 2003 computer or applied via scripting to multiple computers

- Security templates imported into a Group Policy Object (GPO) and applied to multiple computers in a Windows 2000 or Windows Server 2003 domain via Group Policy

- Some combination of automated and manual tools

In order to ensure appropriate hardening for all Windows computers, the last bullet in the list will most likely represent the strategy used. It is to your benefit, however, to automate as much of the process as possible. There are three major automated strategies and hence three different infrastructure requirements that can be used. Common to two of these strategies is the use of security templates:

- The automation of the application of multiple security templates via scripting
- Automation of the application of multiple security templates via Active Directory

The third strategy consists of using Windows NT 4.0 System Policies—a strategy that does not incorporate security templates.

TIP   You do not need to use security templates to automate the deployment of security settings throughout the domain using Group Policy. However, using security templates allows you to create a flexible means of defining security according to computer role, and provides a method for documenting, auditing, reproducing, and maintaining security across many domains.

Automate the Use of Multiple Templates via Scripting

In a Windows 2000 or Windows Server 2003 domain, it is easy to use Group Policy to apply template security settings. However, in a Windows NT 4.0 domain, or in a workgroup setting, a Group Policy distribution is not possible. In these cases, the command-line version of the GUI tools (Security Configuration Manager, Security Configuration and Analysis), secedit.exe, can be used to apply security templates to the local computer via the command line. Once you have tested the security templates designed for each computer role, you can apply the templates to multiple computers via scripts that utilize the **secedit** command. Scripts can be distributed in any manner that you choose and configured to run via manual choice, automated script, use of the run once registry key, and so forth. Secedit is available for Windows NT 4.0, Windows XP, Windows 2000, and Windows Server 2003.

The syntax of the command is fairly simple. There are several forms of the **secedit** command, each of which can use several switches. Subcommands are listed and described in Table 8-2, while the parameters are listed and described Table 8-3. Sample commands follow the tables.

Subcommands	Explanation
/analyze	Compare the security settings on a computer to settings in a template that has been loaded in a database.
/configure	Configure a computer by applying the settings in the template.

Table 8-2.   Secedit Commands

Subcommands	Explanation
/import	Import a template into the database.
/export	Export the settings in the database to a template.
/validate	Validate the syntax of a template.
/GenerateRollback	Produce a template that will, when applied, reset settings to the way they were before the template was applied. The command is available only with Windows XP and Windows Server 2003.

Table 8-2.   Secedit Commands *(continued)*

TIP   When a new template is added to the database, either by using the **import** subcommand or by using the **/cfg** switch together with the **analyze** or **configure** command, the settings are combined with the existing settings, if any. Where there is a conflict, the latest template added wins. Otherwise, settings from both templates will be applied.

Here are examples of the command:

```
secedit /configure /cfg mytemplate.inf /areas REGKEYS FILESTORE
```

Applies the registry key and file permission settings from the mytemplate.inf template.

Switch	Description
/db	Name the database used in the analysis.
/cfg	Indicate the template to import into the database and do the analysis against.
/log	Specify the name of a log file that can be used to log status of the process. (If no file is indicated, data is entered in the scesrv.log file in the %windir%\security\logs directory.)
/quiet	Prevent comments to the screen.
/areas	Indicate area of the template to be used. Areas are SECURITY POLICY—Account policies, audit policies, event log settings, and security options GROUP_MGMT—Restricted group settings USER_RIGHTS—User rights REGKEYS—Registry permissions FILESTORE—File system permissions SERVICES—System services
/overwrite	Empty a database prior to importing a new template.

Table 8-3.   Secedit Switches

```
secedit /analyze /db mydatabase.sdb /cfg mytemplate.inf /overwrite /log
mylogfile.txt /quiet
```

Analyzes the settings in mytemplate.inf against those in the database mydatabase.sdb and logs to mylogfile.txt.

TIP   SCM for Windows NT 4.0 was released as a separate download at the time of service pack 4 for Windows NT 4.0. The use of secedit.exe at the command line and the use of the GUI tools are built into Windows XP, Windows Server 2003, and Windows 2000. SCM for Windows NT 4.0 can be downloaded from ftp://ftp.microsoft.com/bussys/winnt/winnt-public/tools/SCM/.

Use an Active Directory Hierarchy and Group Policy Approach

Group Policy can be used to apply security settings. Settings configured in a GPO can be applied to all users or to some subset of users with domain accounts and computers joined in the domain. Security settings are also periodically refreshed, and thus a security policy can be easily maintained. The application process is simple and elegant in its design and can be easily granularized to support different security policies for the different roles that computers play.

Use Group Policy to Apply Security Settings

You do not have to do anything to apply security settings via Group Policy. However, to apply the security settings that meet your organization's security policy, and to protect each computer with security appropriate for its role and its users, does require you to understand and adjust Group Policy. At a bare minimum, the security settings in the two default GPOs—the domain and domain controller GPOs—should be inspected and tailored to the needs of your organization.

Better still, use Group Policies functional rules set to develop a sound implementation of security tailored to computer roles. Two important concepts are

- Where in Group Policy settings can be made
- How Group Policy works when multiple GPOs are used

Group Policy Security Settings Location   Four areas of a Group Policy Object (GPO) can be used:

- Computer Configuration, Windows Settings, Security Settings
- User Configuration, Windows Settings, Security Settings
- Computer Configuration, Administrative Templates
- User Configuration, Administrative Templates

The methodology described in this chapter for downloading and applying new security settings that are role-specific relies primarily on the development of security templates for import into Group Policy. It is important to realize that the settings in a template have no effect on the user security settings opportunities in a GPO, or to the Computer Configuration, Administrative Templates section of the GPO. The concept of applying security by computer role can be extended to cover these settings, but you must configure them separately.

Once you have determined the settings required for each computer role, to implement the settings via Group Policy you will need to import security templates into a GPO. You may need to manually configure security applications in other sections of the GPO.

What Happens When Multiple GPOs Are Used?   By default, security settings for a computer are applied at boot. The following locations for Group Policy–related security settings are checked, and settings applied in the following order:

1. The local Group Policy

2. A GPO lined to the site in which the computer is authenticating

3. A GPO linked to the domain

4. A GPO linked to the OU hierarchy within the computer account

An OU hierarchy consists of the top-level OU together with its child OUs. For example, the OU Division1 in the following illustration is a top-level OU, as it is not a child OU of any other OU. Division1 has two OUs in its hierarchy, Production and Clerical. The OU Division2 is not part of the hierarchy; it is another top-level OU. Computers with accounts in either the production or clerical OU will receive security settings from GPOs linked to the Division1 OU as well as their own OU. This means that these computers will potentially receive security settings from a number of OUs.

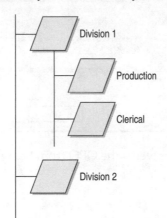

Settings are applied in the following order:

1. The local Group Policy

2. A GPO linked to the site in which the computer is authenticating

3. A GPO linked to the domain

4. A GPO linked to the OU hierarchy in which the computer account exists

5. The Division1 OU

6. The Clerical or the Production OU

If an OU, domain, or site has multiple OUs linked to it, then all GPOs are applied in the order in which they exist in the GUI. There are strict rules for how settings are applied. The primary rule is that all settings from all GPOs are applied but if there is a conflict, the last setting applied wins. That is, if a setting in the Clerical OU GPO and a setting in the domain GPO are in conflict, the setting in the Clerical OU will be applied and win, unless an exception is encountered. These are the exceptions:

- Account Policy for domain accounts is always configured in the domain GPO. Change made to GPOs linked to OUs affect local computer account logons, not domain logons.

- User rights for domain-wide activity are always configured in the domain controller GPO. (User rights that apply to local computers can be impacted by User Rights settings in GPOs linked to OUs.)

- The No Override Option (Group Policy property page Options button), as shown here, will prevent another GPO from overwriting the policy so protected.

- The Disabled option prevents the GPO from being applied at all.

- The Block Policy Inheritance check box on the Group Policy Property page, as shown here, will prevent the inheritance of a GPO from the previous hierarchical object:

- No Override overrules Block Policy. That is, if a GPO linked to Clerical OU has the Block Policy setting, but a GPO linked to the Division1 OU has the No Override option set, the GPO linked to the Division1 OU will be applied.

Use Security Templates with Group Policy

The portion of Group Policy reached through Computer Configuration | Windows Settings | Security Settings includes sections that are also represented in security templates. (The Security Settings section also contains additional settings.) These settings can be directly manipulated in the GPO, however, best practices are to use a Security Template to develop the settings. Test the settings on non-production computers, and then import the settings into the GPO.

To import security templates into a GPO:

1. Open a GPO in the Group Policy Editor, right-click the Computer Configuration, Windows Settings, Security Settings node, and select Import Policy.

2. Select, or browse to and then select, the security template file and click Open to import the template into the GPO as shown here:

There are many advantages to using a security template, including

- A record of changes that were applied.
- A way to audit that security is getting applied (use Security Configuration and Analysis on the computer).
- An opportunity to test on a single machine even before testing in a test domain (You know changes are applied and their effects. You eliminate the possibility that the security changes aren't being made because Group Policy isn't working.)

Use the Active Directory Hierarchical Approach to Security Application

You can use Group Policy to distribute security settings by computer role to as many of the computers in your enterprise as you desire. To do so, follow these steps:

1. Create a baseline security template, both in the principle policy and in the actual security template file.
2. Define computer roles and develop incremental template definitions that modify baseline settings to allow the role to function, or that specifically add hardening for the role.
3. Create a security template file that implements what it can from step 2.
4. Create an OU hierarchy, or use an OU hierarchy, that supports implementation of these templates.
5. Import appropriate templates into GPOs in the hierarchy.

Sample baseline and incremental security templates for common computer roles are supplied by Microsoft and can be downloaded along with documents that describe them and outline the process of implementing such a hierarchical application of security based on computer roles. Adjust the templates for security policy differences between the template implementation and your organization's security policy. The later section "Implement the Hardening Plan Using Group Policy" takes the information from the three documents and details what an OU infrastructure might look like.

Use Windows NT 4.0 System Policy

In a Windows NT 4.0 domain, System Policy can be used to provide configuration settings to Windows 98 and Windows NT 4.0 computers. If Windows XP, Windows 2000, or Windows Server 2003 computers are members in a Windows NT 4.0 domain where System Policy is deployed, they will read and apply the policy. You should use the System Policy Editor tool, poledit, from each specific OS, on that OS to create the file used.

System Policy, however, is not Group Policy. You will not find a one-to-one match of items that can be controlled. System Policy allows you to use a GUI to select lockdown settings, create a policy file, place it in the netlogon folder, and automatically modify the registry settings for Windows computers and users when they log on. It can be used to lock down the desktop and apply some security settings. You can distribute different policies to different Windows user groups, and you can create a unique policy for specific computers (not groups of computers).

Create a System Policy to Manage Desktop Settings

While it's impossible to implement a full-blown security configuration using default System Policy capabilities, it is possible to create a standard desktop, and also to modify restrictions based on Windows groups. Here's how to implement a couple of basic computer security settings for Windows NT 4.0 computers.

TIP Note that all check boxes are grayed. Boxes have three different settings: Clear means a setting will not be set, checked means it will be set, and gray means that nothing will change. Remember, a registry values has a setting already, even if it is null. When a System Policy is applied, you may not want to change the underlying setting.

---

1. Open the System Policy Editor program via Start | Programs | Administrative tools.

2. Select New Policy from the File menu.

3. Double-click the Default Computer icon, as shown here:

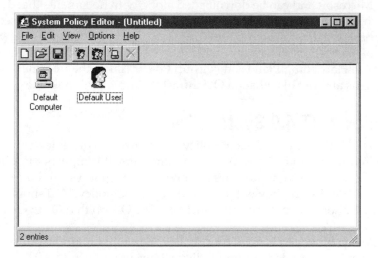

4. Expand the Windows NT System node, as shown here:

5. Click the Logon Banner check box.

6. Use the default caption and text or enter the approved logon banner for your organization as shown here:

7. Select "Do not display last logged on user name."

8. Click OK to close the Default Computer Policy.

A policy for a specific computer can be created by first using the Edit menu to add a computer and then creating a policy for that computer. Windows NT 4.0 does not understand the concept of a group of computers; therefore, there is no provision in System Policy for applying settings to some computers and not others. It is possible to implement some computer role differentiation in a large environment by establishing separate domains for computers that play different roles, such as servers and desktops. It is also possible, in a small environment, to create a separate policy for each computer that requires one. However, neither of these options is particularly attractive.

User groups, however, are a part of Window NT 4.0, and you can create a separate System Policy on a group-by-group basis. In the following example, a policy is created for the Accountants group. The policy prevents members of this group from seeing Network Neighborhood, modifying display settings, running registry tools, or running applications that are not on the approved list. To create this policy:

1. Select the Edit menu and then select Add Group.

2. Click the Browse button and select the group from the Add Groups window.

3. Click Add and then click OK to select the group.

4. Double-click the new group icon, as shown here:

5. Expand and select Control Panel items, as shown here:

6. Expand the System\Restrictions items, as shown here:

7. Use the Show button to open the list of Allowed Applications window and add approved applications, as shown here:

8. Click OK to close the policy.

Configure Settings to Take Advantage of Application Order

While only one System Policy file for each operating system type is possible within a domain, it is possible for the different parts of the policy file—the different policies within it—to conflict with each other. Conflicts can arise between the two default parts, Default User and Default Computer, and any other part, such as a part for a specific computer, a specific user, or a user group. To use the order of policy part application to advantage, you must understand how it works. Following are the rules.

- If a specific computer policy part exists for a computer, it will be applied when the computer authenticates (Windows NT 4.0) to the domain, or when it connects to the domain for user logon (Windows 98).

- If no specific computer policy part is present, the Default Computer policy will be used.

- If a specific user policy is present, that will be applied, and no policy created for a group (even if the user is a member of a group) will be applied.

- If no specific user policy is present, the Default User policy will be applied, followed by any policies for groups the user is a member of.

- If separate policy parts are configured for multiple groups, and users have membership in more than one group, they will be affected by settings in both groups. Policy parts will be applied, one at a time, and the last part applied will win if there is any conflict. If, for example, the setting to prevent the use of registry editing tools is checked in the first policy part applied and grayed out in the second, the use of registry editing tools will be restricted. However, if the restriction is checked in the first policy part and unchecked in the second, then registry tools use will not be restricted. If the order of application is reversed, then registry tool use will be restricted.

Because the order of policy parts created for specific groups can result in unintended configurations, it's important to consider the order of their application. To adjust the order:

1. Open the Options menu and select Group Priority.

2. Select a group, as shown here:

3. Click the Move Up button or the Move Down button until the group is positioned as desired.

4. Select another group if necessary and repeat until all groups are in the order desired.

5. Click OK to close the window.

When policies are complete, save the file. In this example, the System Policy Editor for Windows NT 4.0 was used. The file should be saved to the net logon (%windir%\ system32\Repl\Import\Scripts) directory as ntconfig.pol. Alternatively, in order to copy the file to other domain controllers via replication, the file should be saved into the replication scripts folder (%windir%\system32\Repl\Export\Scripts) and replication configured. If replication is correctly configured, the ntconfig.pol file will be copied to the net logon folder of each domain controller. This not only speeds implementation of the original file but also allows you to update all copies easily and automatically when changes need to be made.

Expand the Usefulness of System Policies

System Policy files can also be created to manage settings for Windows 98 computers. The policy file should be created on a Windows 98 computer using the Windows 98 version of the poledit.exe program and saved to the netlogon or replication scripts folder of the Windows NT 4.0 DC as config.pol.

Many of the settings in System Policies are directed toward desktop management, and not specifically toward security. Settings are included in .adm files. Additional .adm files are available, and you can build custom .adm files to configure any security elements that can be applied by modifying the registry (.adm files are available for use in configuring Microsoft Office). Additional .adm files can be added to the System Policy Editor:

1. Select the Options menu, and then select Policy Template.

2. Select a template and click Remove to remove it, as shown here:

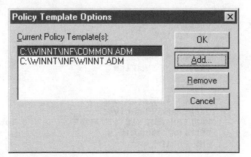

3. Click Add, and then browse to the location for the new .adm file.

4. Select the .adm file and click Open to add it to the policy.

5. Click OK to close the window.

System Policy files are special text files included in the %windir%\inf folder. You can use a text editor to add additional registry key settings to the .adm file and therefore increase the ability of this tool to secure computers in the NT 4.0 domain. You must first understand the syntax required. Figure 8-1 displays a portion of the common.adm file. Note that the first part indicates the location of the policy, in the Shell folder. Next the "restrictions" category, which is also viewable in the GUI of the System Policy, is listed, followed by the registry key. Finally the value name is present.

To add new restrictions, you will have to understand the necessary registry edit and the syntax of the System Policy file. Some instructions are available in the document "Guide to Windows NT 4.0 Profiles and Policies." The document is a collection of KB articles, and KB 185589 includes a section called "Creating a Custom .adm file." You can find explicit directions in the Windows 95 Resource Kit and the Windows 32-bit Software Developers Kit.

TIP System Policy has limited use as an implementation tool for security based on network role. However, it can be used to provide some security, especially if customized policies are developed. It also provides an opportunity to lock down the desktop.

```
Common.adm - Notepad
File  Edit  Search  Help
CATEGORY !!Shell
        CATEGORY !!Restrictions
                KEYNAME Software\Microsoft\Windows\CurrentVersion\Policies\Expl(
                        POLICY !!RemoveRun
                        VALUENAME "NoRun"
                        END POLICY

                        POLICY !!RemoveFolders
                        VALUENAME "NoSetFolders"
                        END POLICY

                        POLICY !!RemoveTaskbar
                        VALUENAME "NoSetTaskbar"
                        END POLICY

                        POLICY !!RemoveFind
                        VALUENAME "NoFind"
                        END POLICY

                        POLICY !!HideDrives
                        VALUENAME "NoDrives"
                        VALUEON NUMERIC 67108863          ; low 26 bits on (1 bit
                        VALUEOFF NUMERIC 0
                        END POLICY

                        POLICY !!HideNetHood
                        VALUENAME "NoNetHood"
```

Figure 8-1. The System Policy file is a text file that uses a specific syntax.

Adapt Security Templates

Group Policy provides the perfect opportunity to develop a full-blown role-based security implementation. The key is the development of incremental templates that can be applied to all servers, and of incremental templates that can be applied to all computers that meet specific role definitions. It's clear, however, that the security templates provided with the operating system are not granular enough. Use the Microsoft-provided templates to your advantage. You can examine the configured templates and adjust them to meet your security needs.

Make sure to select the right templates for the operating system. Operating systems differ, and a setting available in one might be unavailable in another. Additionally, similar settings may be configured differently. Using the wrong template for the operating system can even be detrimental to the overall health of the system. If you are going to import templates into policies and therefore unleash their settings into the production network, take the precaution of establishing different OUs for computers that ordinary users use.

Three documents and three sets of templates exist:

- The "Windows Server 2003 Security Guide" provides templates and instructions for securing Windows Server 2003 (www.microsoft.com/downloads/details.aspx?displaylang=en&familyid=8a2643c1-0685-4d89-b655-521ea6c7b4db).

- The "Windows XP Security Guide" provides instructions and templates that can be used to secure Windows XP (www.microsoft.com/downloads/details.aspx?displaylang=en&familyid=2d3e25bc-f434-4cc6-a5a7-09a8a229f118).

- The "Windows 2000 Security Operations Guide" provides similar information and templates for Windows 2000 (www.microsoft.com/downloads/details.aspx?displaylang=en&familyid=f0b7b4ee-201a-4b40-a0d2-cdd9775aeff8).

Additional documentation on the settings for Windows Server 2003 and Windows XP are described in "Threats and Countermeasures: Security Settings in Windows Server 2003 and Windows XP," which details every security setting (www.microsoft.com/downloads/details.aspx?displaylang=en&familyid=1b6acf93-147a-4481-9346-f93a4081eea8).

Before using the templates in a production network, customize them for your environment and test them. Here are some steps to be used in the development process:

1. Select baseline templates for different computer groups. Baseline templates for generic servers and domain controllers are available. Don't forget to select a baseline template for each different operating system for which they are available and for which you have member computers in your domains.

2. Select an appropriate template for each computer role used on your network. If a template does not exist, create a new template.

3. Review baseline templates to ensure they meet your needs. Baseline templates, while they have the most items configured, are probably the easiest to configure. They attempt to turn off or lock down every setting and have been thoroughly tested to ensure that the Windows computers they are designed for will run after the templates have been applied.

4. Configure your password and account lockout policy in the baseline domain controller templates. These parts of the template are not configured in the provided baseline templates, perhaps because each organization usually has its own password policy and setting a default might arbitrarily change what is approved for use.

5. Add a local, default password policy to the baseline policies. Remember that these password policies will affect only user accounts that are local to the server or workstation used.

6. Review all security template settings for conflicts with the organization's security policy.

7. Examine each role-based template, looking for ways in which it can be used to further lock down computers on the network.

Examine and Modify Baseline Templates

Examine each baseline template that you will use. The baseline template for Windows Server 2003 is used in this example. The Windows Server 2003 template selection is the most comprehensive, as it recognizes difference in security needs and provides a set of templates for three different scenarios:

- **Enterprise Client** Template settings assume all member servers are Windows 2000 or Windows Server 2003.

- **Legacy Client** Template settings assume some member servers may be Windows NT 4.0.

- **High Security** Template settings assume no legacy clients exist and that a need for the highest security is present.

To work with templates, add them to their own folder on a computer in the test network and open them in the Security Templates console. In the example used in this chapter, templates are added to the TestTemplates folder. When the Security Templates console is opened, it loads templates in the default location. To work with templates in other locations, add the path to the console.

1. Right-click the Security Templates container in the console and select New Template Search Path.

2. Browse and select the new location, then click OK to add the path.

3. Expand the path and select the template to work with, as shown here:

Examine each section of the baseline template to ensure it does not conflict with your security policy. Remember, baseline settings are modified by settings in incremental templates. If policy requirements exist for specific server roles, settings should be modified in templates designed for those roles. In the following example, the High Security – Member Server Baseline template is used. If you cannot use this template in your environment, adjust the appropriate template using these guidelines.

Examine Account Policy

The Account Policy consists of the Kerberos Policy, the Password Policy, and the Account Lockout Policy. No settings are made in the provided templates. Make the following modifications:

- The Kerberos Policy is irrelevant. It is used only in the domain policy.

- The Password Policy should be strengthened to at least match the domain policy. The Password Policy defined in the baseline template will impact only logons using accounts local to member servers. However, it is important that these logons meet strict requirements.

- The Account Lockout Policy should be set to lock out accounts after five attempts. The duration should be until reset, and the account lockout count should be reset after five minutes. Remember, these settings impact only logons using local accounts. An attacker wishing to produce a widespread denial of service attack on the network would have to target many servers. By setting the policy, attempts at guessing administrator passwords for member servers will most likely be thwarted.

Examine Local Policies

Local Policies are Audit Policy, User Rights Assignment, and Security Options. Audit Policy settings, as shown in Figure 8-2, turn on most auditing requirements. Leave these settings as defined.

User Rights assignments reduce access to servers. Examples of settings changes include

- Removing Server Operator rights to Administrative access

- Denying Guest and ANONYMOUS LOGON access to the servers from the network

- Denying Guest logon as a batch job and through Terminal Services

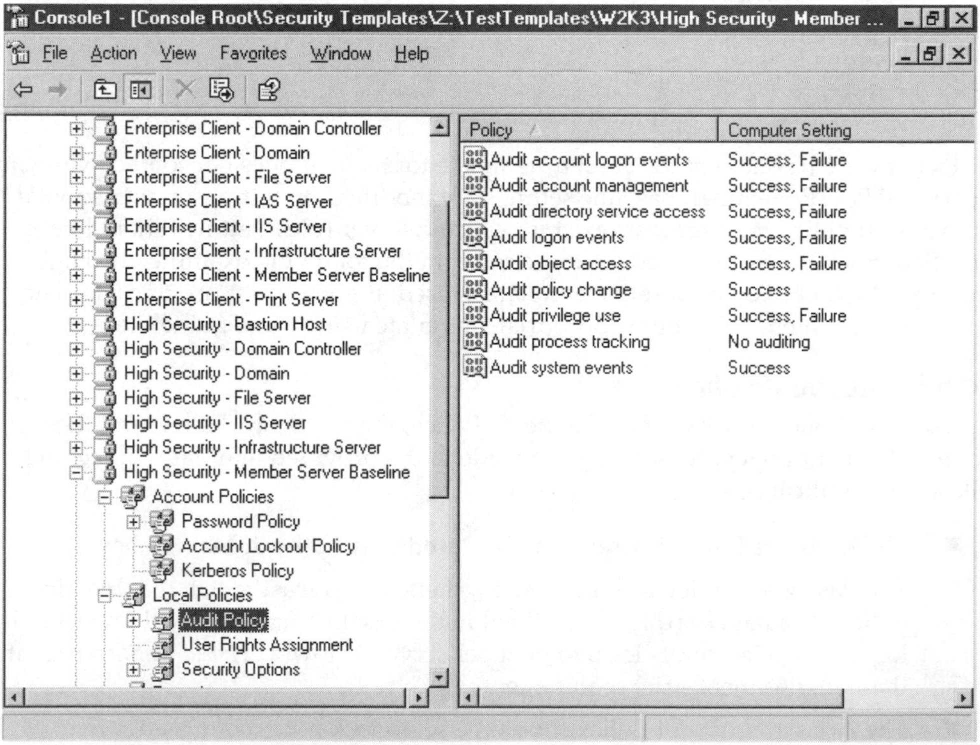

Figure 8-2. Audit Policy settings are configured in the baseline template.

- Restricting the right to log on locally to only Administrators and Backup Operators
- Security Options settings include
  - "Shut down system immediately if unable to log security audits." This setting does exactly what it appears to do: if the Security event log fills up, the system stops. An attacker may seek to cover her tracks by first filling up the audit log with mundane events. If the log settings prevent the log entries from being overwritten with new events, then the attacker can accomplish this goal, and no audit events will be available. Without audit events, in-place alarms may not be triggered, and determining how the attack occurred or what was done is more difficult.

HEADS UP!

If the setting "Shut down system immediately if unable to log security audits" is enabled, and if the Security Event Log is not monitored, archived, and cleared on a regular basis, the operation of the server will be interrupted. Worse, if this setting is applied and administrators are not aware, or are not fully aware, of its implications, then servers may eventually experience mysterious outages, and needless hours of troubleshooting and lost productivity will occur. Do make sure that logs are increased in size and that a procedure for archiving and clearing log files is followed. Do provide training for administrators in what security settings are applied and what their impact may be.

- Many additional settings as recommended throughout this book.

Examine Event Log Policies

Log sizes are increased, and the guest group is prevented from accessing the log. The retention method is specified as needed.

Examine Restricted Groups

No restricted groups are set. This setting can be used to restrict membership in local computer groups, allowing domain administrators to prevent local Administrators from adding local accounts to local administrative groups. This is important because an attacker might successful gain access to a local administrator account and then seek to hide activity on the server by creating a new account and placing it in the local

Administrators group. The attacker might then return at a later time and use this account. Even if the password on the local Administrators account is changed, the attacker still has administrative-level access. If the Administrators group's membership is restricted, the next time the security policy is applied, the rogue account will be removed.

Examine System Services

Significant changes are made to the operation of services. In this section, most services are disabled and only critical services are started. No changes should be made here unless it is determined that some service is used by all member servers in the domain.

Examine Registry and File System Settings

No permission settings are made for registry or file system settings.

Examine and Modify Role-Based Templates

Role-based templates are incremental templates and are applied to only member servers that fulfill that specific role. You may need to create additional role-based templates for use in your organization. The following role-based templates are provided for Windows Server 2003:

- File Server
- IIS Server
- Infrastructure Server
- Print Server

Role-based templates should be used to relax security so that a server may fulfill its role, or to tighten security specifically for that role. An example of relaxed security can be found in the Infrastructure Server template. This template changes the DHCP server, WINS server, and DNS server services to Automatic from their Disabled status in the baseline policy. An example of increased security would be adding groups to the Restricted Groups section of the policy. In areas where role-based templates do not change the security settings of baseline templates, the settings are left as Not Defined. Figure 8-3, for example, shows the settings for the Infrastructure template's Audit Policy. All settings are "Not Defined." This does not mean that there is no audit policy for the infrastructure servers, merely that the policy set by the baseline template, if applied, will remain in place.

Be sure to thoroughly examine role-based security templates. You may find that the incremental changes addressed are simply making services automatic.

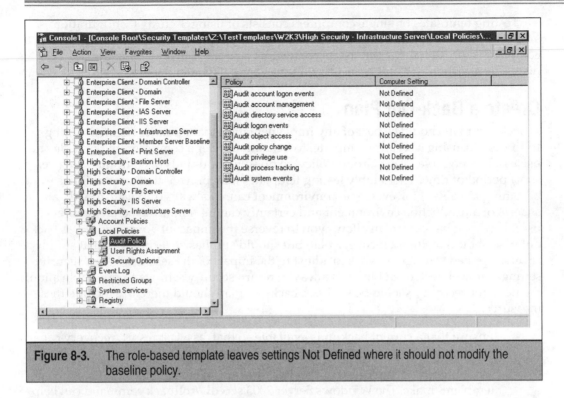

Figure 8-3.   The role-based template leaves settings Not Defined where it should not modify the baseline policy.

Implement the Hardening Plan Using Group Policy

Once computer roles have been defined and security templates created or adapted for the baseline policy as well as each role, implementation is easy. Follow these steps:

- Ensure that a backout plan is available.

- Test baseline templates to ensure computer functionality after its application. Test by applying templates to a single computer.

- Apply role-based templates and test the function of the role. Test by applying incremental templates to a computer that has had the baseline template applied.

- Test templates in a test domain by importing into GPOs linked to appropriate Active Directory objects.

- Roll out into production by importing tested templates into GPOs linked to OUs in your hierarchical design.

Testing templates on single computers consists of using Security Configuration and Analysis, as previously described, to apply the templates and then testing the computer's functionality. Sections on creating a back-out plan and using the OU hierarchical structure to apply security settings are detailed in the next section.

Create a Back-Out Plan

A back-out plan should be part of any implementation that modifies security settings. It is possible, using a security template, to instantly render a computer inaccessible and useless. It is possible, using Group Policy, to do so to thousands of computers in a very short period of time. Thoroughly testing templates may prevent these possibilities from becoming a reality. However, a test environment cannot always duplicate exactly all aspects of a production environment and certainly cannot mimic the behavior of every user. Having a back-out plan allows you to reverse the impact of your changes. A back-out plan should include a recovery plan but should emphasize techniques that simply reverse applied settings, or ways to adjust to the impact of the settings. When security settings are well tested, and there is a way to return security settings to pre-application, the need for recovery should be slight. A back-out plan should therefore include these measures:

- Ensure that a current backup is available so that, as a last resort, recovery can be made.

- Create security templates that "undo" the settings that baseline and incremental templates make. The Windows Server 2003 **secedit /rollback** command can help, but for earlier versions of security templates, an undo template can also be created manually. Remember to make these undo templates before applying the others. Remember to test their effectiveness in the test domain before applying them in a production environment.

- Detail workarounds that might work around unexpected and expected issues. Consider, for example, the earlier discussion of the "Shut down system immediately" security option, which brought up the possibility of uninformed Administrators being caught unawares. The solution to their dilemma lies not in reversing the setting, but in education and training and in immediate action to archive the log, clear it, and get the server functioning again.

Import Templates into Appropriate GPOs

This is the final implementation step. It cannot be performed unless an OU infrastructure has been developed with computer security management in place. Many possible designs can be used to implement this step, either a domain-wide structure that places all server accounts in OUs beneath a single top-level OU created for servers, or, for instance, a design in which multiple top-level or server hierarchy OUs are created, one for each business unit.

Figure 8-4 illustrates the former approach. In this drawing, the OU W2K3 is the top-level OU for Windows Server 2003 servers. Note that the member server baseline security template is designated for import into a GPO linked to this OU. No server accounts are added to this OU. Beneath this OU are several role-based server OUs. The server accounts for servers that play each role are included within each OU. For each OU, the appropriate security template is designated for import into a GPO linked to the OU.

Figure 8-5 illustrates the latter approach. In this drawing, two divisions, Division1 and Division2, each have their own W2K3 OUs. Beneath the W2K3 OUs are role-based server OUs. Security templates are designated for import into respective OUs.

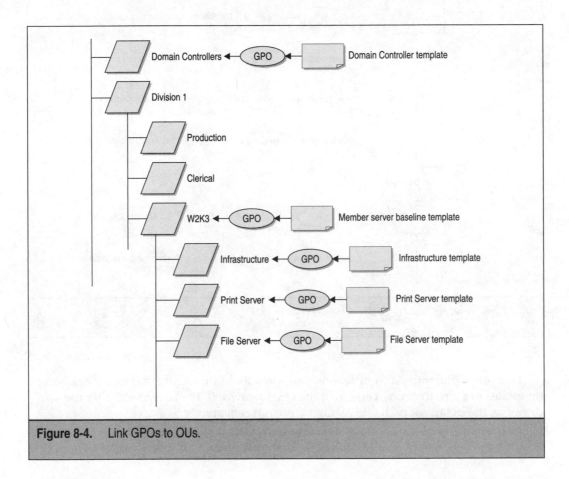

Figure 8-4.   Link GPOs to OUs.

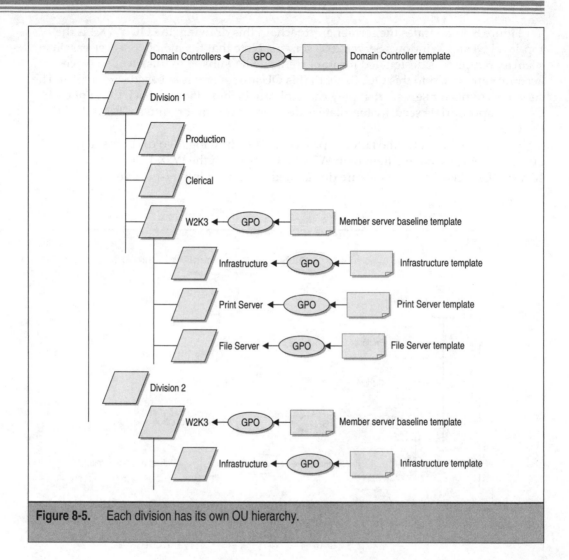

Figure 8-5. Each division has its own OU hierarchy.

Figure 8-6 illustrates a comprehensive approach. In this figure, a plan for applying templates to more than one version of the OS is provided. In order to simplify the drawing, the details of each OU hierarchy are not repeated.

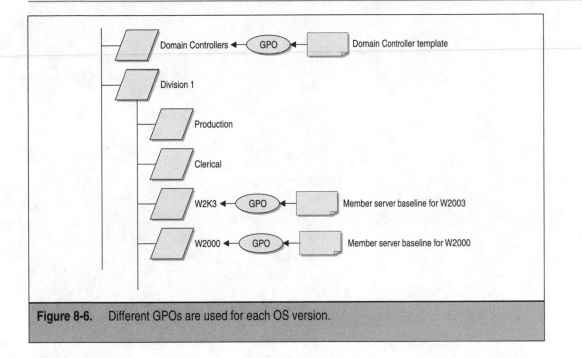

Figure 8-6.   Different GPOs are used for each OS version.

Chapter 9

Harden Application Access and Use

- Restrict Access with Administrative Templates
- Restrict Access with Software Restriction Policies
- Develop and Implement Desktop Computer and User Roles
- Use Group Policy Management Console to Copy GPOs

Do not forget that the reason for hardening computer systems is to provide secure platforms on which work can be done. Users of desktop systems must be able to run applications and to access and store data. Some users, such as those that work remotely, must also have the ability to modify some configuration settings. To harden desktop systems, you must strike a balance between usability and security. To do so, provide users with the ability to do their job but restrict access to data, applications, and configuration settings. Strategies for hardening data access are detailed in Chapter 10.

Restrict Access with Administrative Templates

Administrative templates (.adm files) are at the heart of Windows NT 4.0 System Policies. They are still used to manage configuration settings and access to configuration settings for Windows 2000, Windows XP, and Windows Server 2003. The .adm files are part of Group Policy and should be used to further harden servers and desktops. Additional .adm files are available for most currently available versions of Microsoft Office.

To use .adm files on Windows NT 4.0 and Windows 98, use the System Policy Editor as described in Chapter 8. To use .adm files on Windows XP, Windows 2000, and Windows Server 2003, use Group Policy. To use .adm files for Microsoft Office, a version of the System Policy Editor is available, and some .adm files available for Office can be added to Group Policy.

Group Policy exposes the .adm file settings so that they may be easily configured in a familiar GUI setting. The settings can be manipulated in the Administrative Templates nodes of both User and Computer Configuration areas of Group Policy. To make modifications:

1. Open a GPO in the Group Policy Editor.

2. Navigate to the Computer Configuration or User Configuration Administrative Templates section.

3. Expand a section, as shown in the following illustration, and double-click a setting in the details pane.

4. Change the setting to Enabled, Disabled, or Not Configured, as shown here:

Unlike security settings, each administrative template is accompanied by an Explain tab, as shown in Figure 9-1. The Explain tab details the default settings, explains what Enable and Disable will mean, and indicates if settings exists both in computer and user configuration sections.

TIP   The Enabled, Disabled, and Not Configured choices roughly correspond to the checked, unchecked, and grayed statuses of the settings in a System Policy. As in the System Policy, the Disabled and Not Configured choices are actually different, and the impact of each is clear when you consider the application of multiple templates. When multiple GPOs are applied, a Not Configured setting has no impact on the computer to which the GPO is applied. A Disabled setting, however, may have an impact if it is part of the last GPO applied. The rule is that, when there is no conflict, settings in all GPOs are applied, but if there is a conflict (one GPO says disabled, another says enabled), it is the last GPO applied that wins.

Harden Operating System Configuration

The Computer Configuration, Administrative Templates area of Group Policy can be used to harden operating system utilities and to restrict access to operating system configuration. Both are important. If you harden computer systems but allow access to

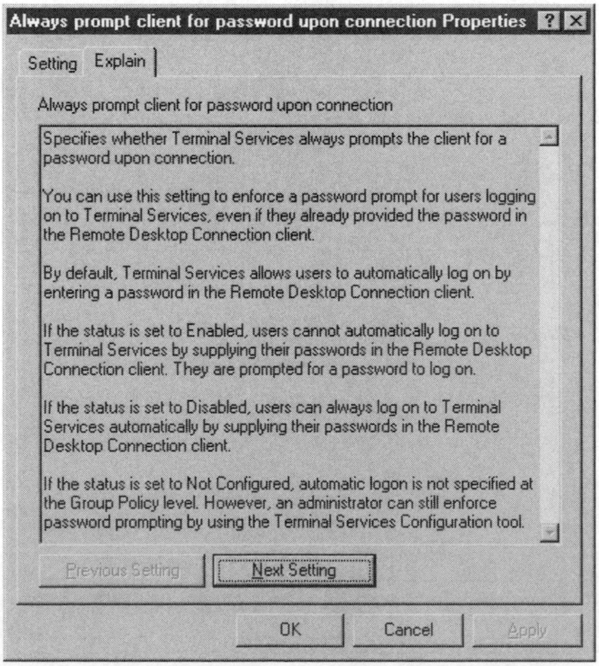

Figure 9-1.   Use the Explain tab to determine the effect of Enable and Disable.

these controls, users will remove or modify system settings. Deciding how much to harden, as well as designating who should be able to modify settings, is not an easy process. Ultimately, you will need to develop multiple hardening scenarios based on user needs and desktop uses. However, there are many restrictions that can and should be made unless a compelling reason for not making them can be defined.

NOTE   Administrative templates cover more than security choices. Many configuration settings can be manipulated here. Use templates to implement standards across the network for desktop computers.

Your approach to hardening desktop configuration settings should be the same as your approach to servers and networks: lock them down, then allow choices or relaxation where justified. Even though there has been progress toward this goal, you will find there is much work that can be done by using administrative templates. Windows Server 2003, for example, implements many default settings that are in line with the security recommendations made in this book. However, these same settings are not the defaults for other Windows versions. Using Group Policy to implement sound security choices can improve security for these clients and can ensure secure defaults on Windows Server 2003 remain in place. Table 9-1 lists and describes a number of essential computer hardening steps that should be made.

Section	Setting	Action	Result
Windows Components, NetMeeting	Disable Remote Desktop Sharing	Enable	Users cannot share their desktop for remote access.
Internet Explorer	Security Zones: Do not allow users to change policies	Enable	Prevents users from changing Security Zones settings. Administrators should establish settings. If users can change these settings, they can reduce security and therefore increase risk.
Internet Explorer	Security Zones: Do not allow users to add/delete sites	Enable	Prevents users from adding or removing sites from zones. If user can add sites, for example, they might place a site in a zone where less restrictive settings exist, thus making them more vulnerable to an attack.
Internet Explorer	Disable Automatic Install of Internet Explorer Components	Enable	Prevents IE from automatically installing a component. When a user visits a web site that requires an IE component, IE can automatically download it. If this setting is enabled, the user will be prompted. This does not prevent the user from installing the component; it does, however, make them choose to do so.

Table 9-1.   Important Administrative Template Settings

Section	Setting	Action	Result
Internet Explorer	Disable Periodic Check for Internet Explorer software updates	Enable	IE automatically will check for new software updates every 30 days. Enable this policy to prevent the automatic check.
Application Compatibility	Prevent access to 16-bit applications (User Configuration and Computer Configuration)	Enable	Prevents the ntdvm.exe subsystem (DOS subsystem) from running. 16-bit programs require this to run. Many, exploits use 16-bit code, which cannot be run if ntdvm is disabled. In addition, early versions of software restriction policies had no impact on 16-bit software, so this option might be a workaround.
Internet Information Services	Prevent IIS installation	Enable	Prevents installation of IIS or components that require IIS.
Task Scheduler	All settings (User Configuration and Computer Configuration)	Enable	Prevents users from modifying current tasks, creating new tasks, running existing tasks manually, and deleting tasks.
Terminal Services, Client Server data redirection	All settings	Enable or Disable to restrict redirection	Clients can redirect ports, clipboard data, audio, drives, and printers to terminal servers. Redirection, especially of clipboard data, or drives could mean potential compromise of client systems and should therefore be carefully considered in terms of risk and user requirements.
Terminal Services, Encryption and Security, RPC Security Policy	Secure Server (Require Security) (W2K3 Server Required)	Enable	Requires encrypted and authenticated RPC sessions. RPC sessions are used to administer and configure Terminal Services.
Terminal Services, Encryption and Security	Always prompt client for password upon connection (XP Terminal Services)	Enable	Requires the user to enter a password on connection even if a password is supplied in the Remote Desktop Connection client.
Terminal Services, Encryption and Security	Set client connection encryption level (User Configuration and Computer Configuration)	Enable	Enforces an encryption level for all data. Set to High (if FIPS compliant if required) and therefore support a policy requiring that only clients capable of using this level can connect.
Windows Installer	Disable Windows Installer	Enable "for non-managed apps only"	Prevents installation of Windows Installer–based applications except those offered by systems administrator.

Table 9-1.   Important Administrative Template Settings *(continued)*

Section	Setting	Action	Result
Windows Installer	Always installed with elevated privileges (User Configuration and Computer Configuration)	Enable	User does not have to be an administrator to install. Make sure to couple with the preceding setting, "Disable Windows Installer."
Windows Installer	Remove browse dialog box for new source	Enable	Prevent users from browsing to a location for installation files. Instead, users must select from components offered.
Windows Installer	Cache transforms in secure location on workstation	Enable	Protects transforms (instructions for modifying a program's settings during installation). Malicious changes to transforms could affect application reinstalls or removals, leaving the application or computer vulnerable to attack.
Windows Messenger	Do not allow Windows Messenger to be run (User Configuration and Computer Configuration)	Enable	Prevents Windows Messenger from running. Internet messengers (IMs) can be a boon to productivity or a time waster. They can also be a source of Trojans, worms, and viruses. IMs, like any other tool, should be managed. Disable Windows Messenger until a management strategy is developed.
Windows Update	Configure Automatic Updates	Disable	Prevents automatic updates. A policy for updating desktop computers should be designed and implemented. However, the default setting is to check for the existence of updates, which means polling of Microsoft sites over the Internet, not a good use of bandwidth. (Note: for small offices and home use, automatic updating directly from Microsoft is a sound strategy.)
System, Logon	Do not process the run once list (User Configuration and Computer Configuration)	Enable	The Run Once value in the registry can store a list of programs to run when the system starts. Enable this setting to ignore this list. The Run Once list is often the site used by attackers to get malicious code run on the computer. By ignoring this list, you avoid such attacks. However, if you use programs that must use this list to load, you will also prevent them from running.
Remote Assistance	Solicited Remote Assistance	Disable	Prevents users from soliciting remote assistance. Remote assistance solicitation can provide a non-Administrator access to the user's desktop.

Table 9-1.   Important Administrative Template Settings *(continued)*

Section	Setting	Action	Result
Remote Assistance	Offer Remote Assistance	Enable, Allow helpers to remotely control the computer and identify helpers	Set a list of approved helpers who can remotely control the computer.
System Restore	Turn off configuration	Enable	System restore allows restore of system configuration without loosing user data. Users should not be able to configure system restore.
Error Reporting	Report Errors	Disabled	When enabled, system errors and application errors can be reported to Microsoft via the Internet. This provides Microsoft with useful information but also means unapproved communications.
Network, Network Connections	Prohibit use of Internet Connection Sharing on your DNS domain network	Enable	Prevents sharing of an Internet connection from this computer. Internet connection sharing can make any Windows 2000 or Windows XP Professional or XP Home computer a gateway. Is relevant to only the DNS domain the computer is connected to when the setting is made.
Network, Network Connections	Prohibit installation and configuration of Network Bridge on your DNS domain network	Enable	Prevent converting desktop computer into gateway between two network segments via installation of Network Bridge.

Table 9-1. Important Administrative Template Settings *(continued)*

HEADS UP!

Windows Messenger is an application and is an Internet messenger (IM). Do not confuse this with the messenger service. The messenger service is not an IM; instead, it is used to transmit alerts and administrative messages. Both should be disabled. Windows Messenger, here in Administrative Templates, and the messenger service in the Services portion of Security Settings.

Harden User Settings

Administrative templates should also be used to implement configuration settings for users. Basically, settings in the User Configuration | Administrative Templates section of a GPO apply on a user-by-user basis, instead of being applied to every user of the computer. If a computer plays a specific desktop role, you may want to ensure that settings are applied across the board for all of its users. On the other hand, there may be a need to decide settings on a user-by-user basis. When configuring administrative template settings, remember that GPOs apply, not to user groups, but to those users with accounts within the site, domain, or OU to which the GPO is linked. Keep in mind that some settings appear in both computer and user configuration sections. If they are configured in both places and there is a conflict, in most cases, the computer configuration will apply. (The Explain tab of the specific setting provides definitive information.) As with Computer Configurations, there are User Configuration settings that should be set unless there is a very good reason not to. Table 9-2 lists and describes those settings.

Section	Setting	Action	Result
Windows Components, NetMeeting, Application Sharing	Disable application sharing	Enable	Prevents users from sharing applications.
Windows Components, NetMeeting, Application Sharing	Prevent Desktop Sharing	Enable	Prevents users from sharing the desktop.
Windows Components, NetMeeting, Application Sharing	Prevent Sharing Command Prompts	Enable	Prevents users from providing a command prompt to other users. (Command prompts can be used to start applications.)
Windows Components, NetMeeting, Application Sharing	Prevent Sharing Explorer windows	Enable	Prevents users from sharing Explorer windows. Explorer windows can be used to launch applications.
Windows Components, NetMeeting, Options Page	Hide the General page	Enable	Prevents users from changing bandwidth and personal identification. If users can change personal identification, it will be harder for other users to know who they are communicating with.

Table 9-2. Important User Administrative Template Settings

Section	Setting	Action	Result
Windows Components, NetMeeting, Options Page	Hide the Security page	Enable	Prevents users from changing security and authentication settings.
Windows Components, Internet Explorer, Internet Control Panel	Several pages	Enable	Prevents users from configuring security, privacy, content connections, programs, and advanced.
Windows Components, Internet Explorer, Offline Pages	Disable adding channels	Enable	Prevents users from adding channels. Channels are connections that update local content periodically to the desktop. Information such as weather, stock quotes, and so forth may appear as the result of channel additions.
Windows Components, Internet Explorer, Browser menu	Tools menu: Disable Internet Options menu option	Enable	Prevents users from changing default home page, connections, and proxy settings from the Tools menu.
Windows Components, Internet Explorer, Browser menu	Help menu: Remove "Send Feedback" menu option	Enable	Prevents user from sending feedback to Microsoft from the Help menu.
Windows Components, Internet Explorer, Browser menu	Disable Context menu	Enable	Prevents users from running commands by right-clicking while pointing to a web page.
Windows Components, Internet Explorer	Disable changing certificate settings	Enable	Prevent users from downloading certificates, remove approved publishers and change settings for certificates. Certificate presence or absence can mean the difference between secure communications and not with trusted web sites. If users can download certificates, they can create a trusted relationship with web sites whose certificates do not chain to an accepted certification authority.

Table 9-2.   Important User Administrative Template Settings *(continued)*

Section	Setting	Action	Result
Windows Components, Internet Explorer	Do not allow AutoComplete to save passwords	Enable	Prevent users from allowing auto-entry of their passwords in forms on Internet sites, and from saving passwords to disk. A user should always have to enter a password; this can prevent a malicious program from harvesting passwords. User passwords should not be saved to disks.
Windows Components, Internet Explorer	Configure Outlook Express	Enable and check "Block attachments that could contain a virus"	Prevents user from opening or saving attachments that might contain a virus.
Windows Explorer	Remove "Map Network Drive" and "Disconnect Network Drive"	Enable	Prevents users from using these settings to change network shares that they are connected to. Also disables commands from the toolbar and from My Network Places. Does not prevent users from connecting to other computers.
Windows Explorer	Hide these specified drives in My Computer	Enable	Removes drive icons from my computer and Windows Explorer. Does not prevent access to drives from other resources.
Windows Explorer	Remove Security tab	Enable	Removes the Security tab and prevents changing security or viewing security on items in Windows Explorer.
Windows Explorer	Remove CD burning features	Enable	Removes CD burning features from Explorer. (Does not prevent use of third-party CD-ROM-burning software.) A malicious user could use these features to remove a large quantity of confidential information. While third-party software can be used, the user would still have to install the software.
Windows Explorer	Remove Publish to the Web from File and Folder Tasks	Enable	Prevents users from using these quick ways to post data to a web site.

Table 9-2.   Important User Administrative Template Settings *(continued)*

Section	Setting	Action	Result
Microsoft Management Console	Restrict the user from entering author mode.	Enable	In author mode, a user can add additional snap-ins, etc.
Microsoft Management Console	Restrict users to the explicitly permitted list of snap-ins.	Enable and use the Restricted/ Permitted snap-ins folder to designate permitted snap-ins	Permits users to use snap-ins such as the Certificates snap-in, but prevents use of other snap-ins.
Windows Media, User Interface	All settings	Enabled	Prevents users from changing security settings such as by allowing scripts to run, or from accessing settings based on skin (Set and Lock Skin).
Windows Media Player, Networking	Hide Network tab	Enable	Prevents users from configuring network settings such as ports for receiving streaming media.
Start Menu and Task Bar	Remove links and access to Windows Update	Enable	Prevents user connections to Windows update site. Update should be under administrative control.
Start Menu and Task Bar	Remove programs on Settings menu	Enable	Removes Control Panel, Printers, and Network Connections from settings on the Start menu and from My Computer an Windows explorer. Also prevents associated programs, such as control.exe, from running. Control Panel programs may be usable by other means.
Start Menu and Task Bar	Remove Run menu from Start menu	Enable	Removes the run command from the Start menu, Internet Explorer, and the Task Manager. Users will also not be able to access a UNC share or local drives, or folders from the Explorer address bar.
Control Panel, Add/ Remove Programs	Remove Add/Remove Programs	Enable	Prevents use of Add/Remove Programs for adding and removing programs. Does not prevent use of other means to install software.

Table 9-2.   Important User Administrative Template Settings *(continued)*

Section	Setting	Action	Result
Control Panel, Add or Remove Programs	Hide the Set Program Access and Defaults page	Enable	Removes Set Program Access and Defaults button from Add or Remove Programs bar. Prevents users from changing default programs for things like web browsing and e-mail.
Network, Network Connections	Prohibit advanced TCP/IP advanced configuration, or Prohibit access to properties of a LAN connection.	Enable	Prevents configuration of DNS, WINS, and/or other network settings by administrators. Couple with Enable Windows 2000 Network Connections Settings to prevent local Administrators from accessing this as well.
Network, Network Connections	Enable Windows 2000 Network Connections settings for Administrators	Enable	Prevents administrators from changing network configuration if specified in Prohibit sections. (In Windows XP, these settings will not have an effect on Administrators unless this setting is Enabled.)
System, Power Management	Prompt for password on resume from hibernate/ suspend	Enable	Requires users to enter a password when the system resumes from hibernate. Otherwise, when the system resumes, the desktop is not locked. If a user was logged on, then he is still logged on, and anyone present can impersonate him on the system.

Table 9-2.   Important User Administrative Template Settings *(continued)*

Use Additional .adm Files

By default, several .adm files are already available in Group Policy. To add additional .adm files, such as those provided for Microsoft Office 2003, follow these steps:

1. Open the Group Policy in the Group Policy Object Editor.

2. Right-click the Computer Configuration | Administrative Templates (or User Configuration | Administrative Templates) node and select Add/Remove Templates.

3. Click the Add button, as shown here:

4. Select the template and click Open to add it to the GPO.

5. Click Close to close the Add/Remove Templates dialog.

To create your own .adm files requires knowledge beyond the scope of this book; however, you can find information on doing so in the white paper "Implementing Registry-Based Group Policy" at www.microsoft.com/windows2000/techinfo/howitworks/management/rbppaper.asp.

Harden Applications

Administrative template settings can be used to restrict access to and harden the use of system utilities and built-in desktop applets. But other applications need hardening and restricted access provisions as well. Some applications provide .adm files that can be used for this purpose. Other applications have their own ways of exposing configuration settings. You will have to seek documentation and assistance from the software manufacturers.

The provided administrative template files also do not provide a way to modify all of the settings. For example, you can use existing templates to make some IE security settings, but you cannot add web site URLs to security zones, or define security settings on a zone-by-zone basis. You may develop your own .adm files and add them to Group Policy, or use the Internet Explorer Administration Kit (IEAK) to deploy a customized, locked-down browser.

Use IEAK to Deploy Internet Explorer

Proper configuration of Internet Explorer should be a major focus in your plans to secure the desktop. This is because many attacks use the technologies deployed in IE and because settings for IE are shared with Microsoft Office. If service packs and security fixes for IE are not in place, and if care is not taken in locking down IE, desktop systems are vulnerable to numerous types of attacks.

Your objective, just as elsewhere, must be to deploy a hardened version of IE, and to maintain it by keeping users from making configuration changes and by updating IE as service packs and security patches become available. Group Policy can assist you in preventing user access to the security features of IE and in deploying IE service packs. Group Policy, however, does not provide a way to do some of the security configuration such as the identification of security zone configuration and the identification of specific web sites for each zone.

However, many features of IE can be locked down only by deploying a hardened version. The best way to do so is to use IEAK. A copy of IEAK can be obtained by ordering the CD-ROM or by downloading (www.microsoft.com/windows/ieak/downloads/default.asp). IEAK is a set of tools that can be used to deploy and administer IE. The product and license are free, but you must be licensed to use it to distribute IE.

After you obtain IEAK, you use it to build a custom distribution package. You can also use the included Profile Manager tool to make changes to IE after its distribution. Many of the settings that can be preconfigured for your custom distribution can be imported from the local computer's IE configuration. The first step, therefore, is to customize the local IE browser so that it meets your security policy. Next, run the Customization Wizard to create the custom IE package. Finally, distribute the package and prepare to maintain IE settings using Group Policy, System Policy, and/or Profile Manager.

Configure the Local Internet Explorer Browser   The goal of configuring IE is to lock down features that pose a security risk. However, many of the features that do so, such as cookies and active scripting, are widely used on the Internet. When IE features are locked down, it may not be possible to use these sites. What gets locked down is a matter for policy and may vary depending on the users. For an example of a good server IE management policy, examine the Windows Server 2003 Enhanced Security Configuration paper at www.microsoft.com/downloads/details.aspx?FamilyID=d41b036c-e2e1-4960-99bb-9757f7e9e31b&DisplayLang=en. The paper is accompanied by VB scripts and sample IE .adm files.

The following tables list and describe security enhancements for client computers. Use these lists to configure IE on the computer that will be used to develop the IE package. The following recommendations are similar to those implemented for IE on Windows Server 2003. Test these options to determine if they are fully useful in your environment. They will prevent some usability (many sites use scripts to display .pdf files, load documents in a view within IE, and so forth), but they will make desktops less vulnerable. You may also need to adapt your list for the version of IE used. Table 9-3 lists configurations for the Security tab of the Internet Options dialog box (accessible through Tools | Internet Options), and Table 9-4 lists configuration for the Advanced tab. You must also configure IE by adding appropriate sites to the local Intranet and Restricted Sites zones. And configure connection settings and other nonsecurity settings required by your organization.

Setting Group	Option	Recommendation
.NET Framework–reliant components	Run components not signed with Authenticode	Disable
	Run components signed with Authenticode	Disable
ActiveX control and plug-ins	Download signed ActiveX controls	Disable
	Download unsigned ActiveX controls	Disable
	Initialize and script ActiveX controls not marked as safe	Disable
	Run ActiveX controls and plug-ins	Disable
	Script ActiveX controls marked safe for scripting	Disable
Downloads	File download	Disable
	Font download	Prompt
	Java permissions	High safety
Miscellaneous	Access data sources across domains	Disable
	Allow META REFRESH	Disable
	Allow scripting of Internet Net Explorer Web browser control	Disable
	Display mixed content	Prompt
	Don't prompt for client certificate selection when no certificate or only one certificate exists	Disable
	Drag and drop or copy and paste files	Prompt
	Installation of desktop items	Disable
	Launching applications and unsafe files	Prompt
	Launching programs and files in an IFRAME	Disable
	Navigate subframes across different domains	Disable
	Software channel permissions	High safety
	Submit nonencrypted form data	Prompt
	User data persistence	Disable
Scripting	Active scripting	Disable
	Allow paste operations via script	Disable
	Scripting of Java applets	Disable
User Authentication	Logon	Prompt for user name and password

Table 9-3. Internet Explorer Security Settings Recommendations

Setting	Option	Recommendation
Browsing	Disable script debugging	Check
	Enable install on demand (Internet Explorer)	Unchecked
	Enable install on demand (other)	Unchecked
	Enable third-party browser extensions	Unchecked
Security	All Items	Check

Table 9-4. Internet Explorer Advanced Options Recommendations

To set privacy settings, for example:

1. Open the Privacy page through Tools | Internet Options and click the Advanced button.

2. Select Override Automatic Cookie Handling.

3. Under First-Party Cookies, select Accept, and under Third-Party Cookies, select Prompt, as shown in the following illustration. (First-party cookies are those from the web site visited; third-party cookies are not. They may be cookies from sites advertising on the visited web site.

Use the Customization Wizard to Create a Custom Internet Explorer Package The Customization Wizard can make many changes to the look and feel of IE. You may want to investigate its use to modify the favorites and toolbar, as well as for branding. Only security issues are covered here. These are the security-related configuration choices:

- **Certificate Customization** Specify which Certification Authorities are Trusted.

- **Authenticode Customization**   Specify software publishers and their credentials, for example, credentials for internal developers.

- **Security Zones**   Harden security settings on a per-zone basis and specify web sites for each zone.

- **Privacy Settings**   Including the level of cookie use permitted.

- **Content Ratings**   Prevent viewing of sites that are deemed offensive.

To use the Customization Wizard:

1. Start the Microsoft Internet Explorer Customization Wizard through Start | Programs | Microsoft IEAK 6 and then click Next twice.

2. Accept the default destination folder for the files that will be created, or browse to a location you have prepared.

3. Click the Advanced Options button to set a location where you can download the most current versions. By default, the new files will be downloaded from the Internet. (You must use this default at least once to obtain the latest files.)

4. Click OK, and then click Next.

5. Check that the target language is correct, and then click Next.

6. Select the location where files will be published for use. If you select for download, you must have a URL ready. You can also elect CD-ROM or indicate that a location for network download will be used, as shown in following illustration. Having made this choice, click Next.

7. Select the areas to customize, as shown in the following illustration. Areas of customization are described in Table 9-5, and several are detailed in the steps that follow.

IE Customization	Definition
Setup Customizations	Additional products to be installed during setup.
Corporate Install Features	Location, silent install.
Automatic Digital Signing	Sign the files produced with your certificate. You must already have a certificate and provide information on its location.
Connection Manager	Specify the addition of connection manager profiles (produced with the Connection Manager Administration Kit [CMAK]).
Browser Customizations	Modify the look and feel of the browser.
URL Customizations	Home page, support page, welcome pages can be added.
Favorites and Links	Specify favorites and links to include, for example, local intranet sites.
User Agent String	Customize what the browser sends to servers to identify itself.
Connections Customizations	Custom connection settings, proxy settings.
Certificate Customization	Change accepted CAs, intermediate CAs.
Security Zones and Content Ratings	Set zones and content rating information.
Programs Customization	The default programs that should be used for e-mail, calendar, contact list.
Outlook Express Customizations	User interface, custom messages.
Policies and Restrictions	Preset and lock down user systems.

Table 9-5.   Internet Explorer Customization Wizard Topics

8. Click Next twice to begin the download of files. If this is your first use of the wizard and IEAK was downloaded from the Internet, you may need to click the Synchronize All button to begin the download of files. When all files are updated, each will sport a green circle with a checkmark, as shown in the following illustration. Click Next twice.

9. Select Completely Silent Installation (user is not aware) or Hands Free (the user sees dialog boxes but cannot change anything) installation mode.

10. Select "Enable logon after restart with user-level access" for Windows 2000 and Windows NT users. (Without this selection, logon after installation is required to be by a user with Administrative privileges.) Click Next.

11. Select Remove the Windows Update Option from the Tools menu. You should configure updates via Software Update Services or a third-party product, and not allow users to visit the Windows Update site. Conversely, you can point the browser to an alternative site, such as an internal site designated for updates.

12. If you do not have an internal location set up for distribution of additional IE-related downloads, check the box Download Components from Microsoft after

Install, as shown in the following illustration. After IE installs, additional software may be required. You can use an internal site or point the browser to Microsoft. Click Next.

13. Select the installation directory and then click Next.

14. Set Corporate install options and then click Next twice.

15. Set custom URLs for home page, search page, and support pages by entering the URLs, and then click Next.

16. Enter a URL for your own custom welcome page. This is a good place to provide information on acceptable use, list support numbers, describe policies, and so forth. Then click Next. The welcome page is shown only the first time IE is used.

17. Do not enter a custom user agent string unless you wish to track use of your customized browser. You cannot remove the default string, and any company tracking site statistics can read the string. Click Next to continue.

18. Click Import the Current Connection Settings from This Machine, as shown in the following illustration. (The current settings on the Tools, Internet Options, Connection page including the Advanced button settings such as proxy server information, will be imported.) Use the Modify Settings button to verify the correctness of these settings or to change them. Click Next.

19. Click Import Current Certification Authorities to import the information in the local browser.

20. Click Import Current Authenticode Security Information to import the information in the local browser.

21. Use the Modify Settings button, as shown in the following illustration, to validate or modify the settings. Click Next.

22. Click Import the Current Security Zones and Privacy Settings to import this information. Use the Modify Settings button to verify and modify settings.

23. Click Import the Current Content Ratings Settings. Use the Modify Settings button to verify and modify settings. Click Next twice.

24. Click Import the Program Settings to import this information. Use the Modify Settings button to verify and modify settings.

25. Set accounts (e-mail and news) and make any custom settings for Outlook Express if it will be used. Set also the need to use Secure Password Authentication if required. Regardless of your choice of settings, click Disable Access to Accounts, as shown in the following illustration. This will prevent users from changing account settings, removing them, or adding them. If users can add accounts, they can configure access to alternative e-mail accounts. These accounts may be a source for possible viral or worm infections, since the e-mail may come directly from a server not under your control. Continue

entering OE custom settings as required through four more pages, clicking
Next to move forward through them.

26. Enter Outlook Express and address book customizations if required and then
    click Next.

27. Click Display All IEAK Policies if client machines are Windows 98 or Windows
    ME. Otherwise, select Display the Subset of IE Policies for Non-Admin Users.
    Then click Next.

28. View and configure the range of configuration settings if necessary, as shown
    in the following illustration; however, where Windows NT System Policies or
    Windows 2000 and Windows Server 2003 Group Policies will be used, skip
    these settings. Click Next.

29. Click Next to generate the package, and then click Finish when the process is complete.

Use the Profile Manager to Modify Internet Explorer Settings after Deployment   Profile Manager can be used to create an .ins file that will be used to update IE. The file can be located on your network, and you can specify a schedule to be used for browser update. Essentially, the process requires that an .ins file be created prior to running the Customization Wizard. You point to the file from within the wizard. Then when browsers seek updates, they look to that location. Hence, you only need modify the file as necessary, and browsers will be automatically updated the next time they look for an updated file. You can also use Profile Manager to set up IE for modification, even if you did not originally do so before deploying IE. To set up and use Profile Manager changes:

1. Run the IE Customization Wizard at least once to set up the folder path and structure.

2. Run the IEAK Profile Manager from Start | All Programs | Microsoft | IEAK 6.

3. On the Profile Manager File menu, select Open and point to the .ins file to modify or click New to create a new .ins file.

4. Change settings by selecting items in the left-hand pane and modifying them in the right, as shown here:

5. Make sure to open the Wizard Settings | Automatic Browser Settings option and check Enable Automatic Configuration. Add the URL where new INS files can be found.

6. Use the File menu Save As command to save the file.

7. Copy the new .ins file and cab files to a location and test them. If everything works well, then copy to the distribution point.

Digitally Sign Files   To distribute a custom IE via a URL and to automatically update configurations, you must digitally sign the files you create. If you do not, the default IE security settings will not allow the download and installation of these files. You can sign files during the production of the customized files or afterward; however, you must obtain a digital signing certificate. You can obtain a certificate from a public certification authority or from a private CA.

Distribute Internet Explorer   IE can be installed using a number of methods. The files created by the wizard can be placed on CD-ROMs and distributed, or posted for download to a web site. Setup for either option can be made easy by writing a batch file that contains the setup command. Information on using this command is included with IEAK.

Seek Information and Help from Third-Party Application Providers

The following list is a list of areas to explore and questions to ask that will improve the security of applications used on your network:

- What is the software development company doing to promote secure coding or to ensure that they produce robust, secure products?

- What is their response to notification of a vulnerability problem with their code?

- Is the product certified for operation on the version(s) of Windows you use? Certification means that the product was developed to the Microsoft specifications, including requirements for operation by nonadministrators if the product is meant for their use (if administrator privileges are not required to run the application). If the product is not certified, what help is available (workarounds, registry settings) to empower ordinary users to use the application?

- Are security settings locked down by default?

- What security settings are available for customization?

- How is authentication handled? Is there a default password? What protocol is used for authentication? Can the application be adapted for use with other mechanisms than user name and password?

- How is data stored?

Restrict Access with Software Restriction Policies

Software Restriction Policies can be used to prevent access to applications on Windows XP Professional and Windows Server 2003. They can be used on a per–desktop system configuration, or they can be implemented as part of Group Policy and applied per OU. When they are used via settings on an individual computer, only computer-wide settings can be made (an exception allows you to exempt the Administrators group). However, when Group Policy is used, both user and computer policies are possible, thus allowing you to develop different policies based on computer or user accounts.

To create a Software Restriction Policy, open a GPO in the object editor and right-click the Computer Configuration (or User Configuration) Windows Settings | Security Settings | Software Restriction Policies node and then select New Software Restriction Policies. Follow the steps outlined under the headings that follow to implement a general-purpose policy to let only approved software run. For more help with the nuances of software restriction policies, see the Microsoft white paper "Using Software Restriction Policies to Protect Against Unauthorized Software" at www.microsoft.com/technet/treeview/default.asp?url=/technet/prodtechnol/winxppro/maintain/RstrPlcy.asp.

Set Security Level to Disallowed

The first step in creating a software restriction policy is to understand the words Microsoft chooses to describe them. This will clarify the descriptions that follow and make it easier to document and configure policies. The word choices make creating policies more difficult than it should be. Instead of identifying software as allowed or restricted, Microsoft refers to software as either disallowed or unrestricted. Get it? Software that you want to run must be set as unrestricted. Software that should not run is disallowed. If you can remember that, you'll find the actual implementation of a policy easy.

Next, I recommend that you use the policy to prevent all software from running and then allow only selected software to run. (The alternative is to allow all software to run and then prevent selected software from running.) Setting the security level of the policy enforces the setting. Setting the security level to Disallowed (no software can run unless it is unrestricted by policy) means that you must identify and unrestrict all software that should be allowed to run. A number of exceptions and default settings make this easier than it seems but also require you to understand the process thoroughly in order to make it work well. However, this is preferable to the default, or "unrestricted," security level that requires you to identify only the software that cannot be run. There are too many ways around these rules, and of course, it is impossible to identify all of the software you want to ban.

Setting the security level to Disallowed will not prevent the operating system from running, as default rules and exceptions allow it to do so. However, you must write rules in order to allow software to run.

To set the security level:

1. Double-click the Security Levels folder as shown here:

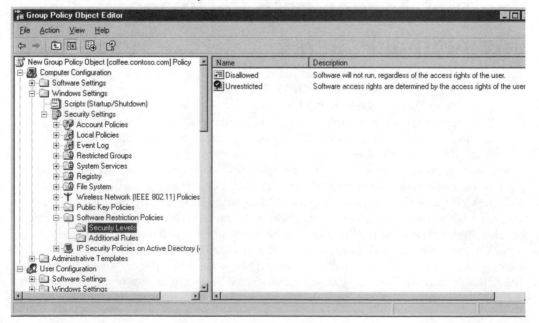

2. Double-click Disallowed.

3. Click the Set as Default button, and then click Yes at the prompt.

Set Policy Options

Before you write rules to specify applications allowed to run, there are several policy options you should configure.

Exempt Administrators When Using Workgroups

No doubt you may easily make the policy too restrictive. To test the policy in a workgroup, exempt the local Administrators group. This way, you can log on as an administrator to correct a policy that is too restrictive. To do so, open the Enforcement Properties window from the details pane and select All Users Except Local Administrators, as shown in Figure 9-2.

Exempt DLLs

You must define what is meant by software. Many Windows applications have an executable file or two but also include many DLLs, files that are not executable on their own but that do contain code. If you do not exempt DLLs, you will need to identify not

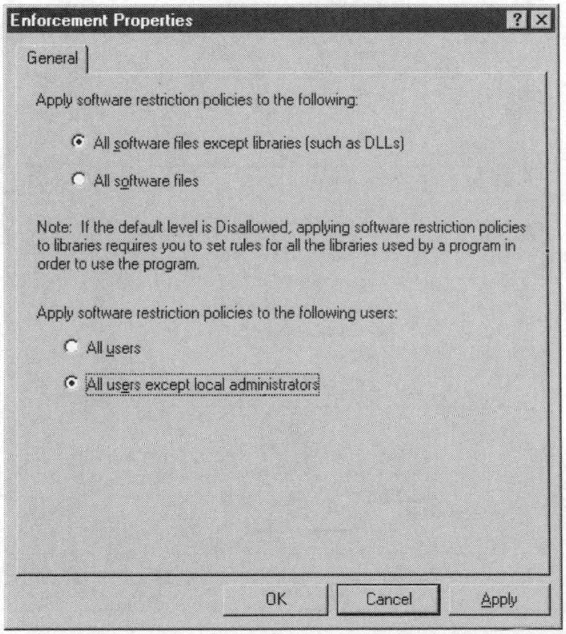

Figure 9-2.   Exempt Administrators in workgroup policies.

only executable files but possible hundreds of DLLs. The DLLs exemption is configured on the Enforcement properties dialog box. as shown in Figure 9-2.

Identify What File Types Are Software

The Designated File Types Properties page, as shown in Figure 9-3, lists the file types that are defined as software. You can add a file type by entering the extension in the File Extension box and clicking Add.

Restrict Identification of Trusted Publishers to Enterprise Administrators

Trusted publishers are certificate holders trusted to produce secure software. The publisher certificates identified can be used to identify software that you will allow to run on the computer. Only enterprise administrators for domains and local Administrators for workgroups should have the choice to accept certificates for trusted publishers. Configure this setting from the Trusted Publisher Properties page as shown in Figure 9-4. While you are on this page, protect desktops from compromised certificates by selecting Publisher and Timestamp as settings to use to determine if a certificate has been revoked.

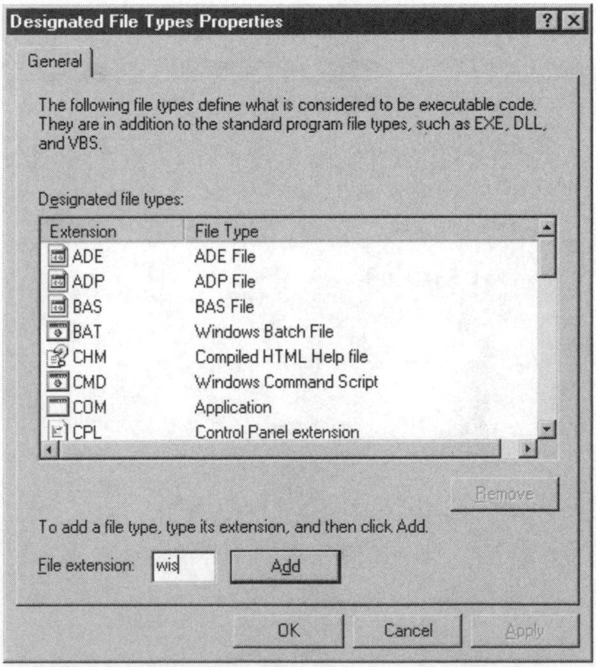

Figure 9-3. Manage file types defined as software.

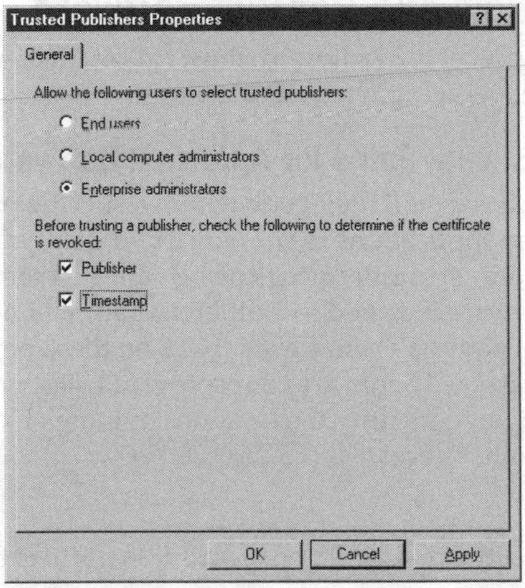

Figure 9-4. Configure revocation settings and other trusted publisher settings.

Provide Workarounds for Exempted Software

Some types of software are exempt by default. This makes it easier to set up a disallowed security level—you don't have to identify or understand all of the code required just for Windows to run on a specific computer. Before you scoff at the exemptions, imagine trying to write rules that allow all critical drivers to run. Since many computers use different drivers, this would be a nearly impossible task.

Nevertheless, you may want to explicitly prevent some of the exempted software from running. You can do so by creating rules that identify the software and then set the rule security level to Disallowed. Ordinarily, you would write rules with a security level of Unrestricted, in a policy whose policy security level is Disallowed, but this case is the exception, since some software will be exempt from the Disallowed policy security level and run anyway.

The following types of software and settings are exempt:

- **Four path rules** Leave these in, or Windows may not run.
- **Drivers or other kernel-mode software** If you need to disallow a specific driver, write a rule.
- **Programs run by the SYSTEM account** Nothing can be done here.
- **Macros in Microsoft Office 2000 or Office XP** Use macro security in Office to control this.
- **Programs written for the Common Language Runtime (CLR)** Use Code Access Security Policy to manage this.

Write Rules to Allow and Restrict Software

When the policy security level is disallowed, most rules will be written to allow software to run. Use the following types of rules.

Write Path Rules to Exempt Paths for Approved Software

Many software applications install their code within a specific path. A path rule is perfect for allowing these applications to run, since you don't have to identify every single executable file and write a rule specifically enabling it to run. Do, however, realize that the same software installed to a different path will not run and that any software installed to this path will run. Check ACLs on these paths. If users have write permission, they can easily subvert your software rules by installing software to allowed paths. Don't forget to identify the locations of things like logon scripts, virus scanning software, and other items.

To write a path rule:

1. Right-click the Software Restriction | Additional Rules folder and select New Path Rule.

2. Use the Browse button to browse to the top level of the software installation path. (Alternatively, you can enter the path.)

3. Set the (rule) security level to Unrestricted, as shown here:

4. Click OK to complete the path rule.

If you need to create registry path rules, you will need to enter the registry path manually. To do so, use the format

```
%[Registry Hive]\[Registry Key Name]\[Value Name]%
```

A few rules must also be followed:

- Value must be REG_SZ or REG_EXPAND_SZ.
- Spell out the hive, hence HKEY_LOCAL_MACHINE, not HKLM.

Write Certificate Rules for Approved Software Signed with an Acceptable Certificate

Certificate rules can be used to approve software signed by an accepted certificate. A copy of the certificate must be available when writing the rule.

1. Right-click the Software Restriction | Additional Rules folder and select New Certificate Rule.
2. Use the Browse button to browse to a copy of the certificate file.
3. Set the (rule) security level to Unrestricted.
4. Click OK to complete the rule.

Use Hash Rules to Prevent Drivers and Other Software from Running

Hash rules create a hash of the software and then use that hash to identify the software when it attempts to run. If the hash matches, the software will be ruled by the security level of the hash rule. If the hash rule security level is Unrestricted, the software will run. If it is Disallowed, it will not. So in our example, if there is a driver that you do not wish to run, you can create a hash rule and set the security level to Disallowed. Even if an administrator installs the driver, the driver cannot run. However, if a new version of the driver is created, it will be able to run, since its hash will not match that of the previous version. To create a hash rule,

1. Right-click the Software Restriction | Additional Rules folder and select New Hash Rule.
2. Use the Browse button to browse to a copy of the file.

3. Note that a hash is created and entered in the File hash text box, as shown in the following illustration. If you do not have a copy of the file but can obtain a copy of the hash, you can insert that here instead.

4. Set the (rule) security level to Disallowed.

5. Click OK to complete the rule.

Create Internet Zone Rules to Allow Installer-Based Programs to Install

Internet zone rules can be used to restrict or allow the installation of software from web sites. The software, however, must use the Windows installer to install. This rule can be used effectively, though, when the policy security level is disallowed but you need to allow an application of your creation to install from a URL on your intranet. To write the rule:

1. Right-click the Software Restriction | Additional Rules folder and select New Internet Zone Rule.

2. Select the zone from where software may be installed, as shown here:

3. Set the (rule) security level to Unrestricted.

4. Click OK to complete the rule.

Develop and Implement Desktop Computer and User Roles

Inaction is a common reaction to knowledge of the plethora of choices that administrative templates and software restriction policies present. Administrators can become overwhelmed by the sheer number of choices and by the need to customize such control for the sheer number of uses for desktop computers. Truly, there is no one desktop strategy that fits all needs.

The solution to this dilemma is to understand that the definition of computer roles and the development of security settings to match them do not end with servers. Desktop computers also play roles on the network. Your job is to define those roles and develop hardening strategies based on those roles. In a Windows NT 4.0 domain, roles can be implemented using System Policies. In a Windows 2000 or Windows Server 2003 domain, implement roles using Group Policy for Windows 2000 and Windows XP Professional clients. To do so:

- Define custom GPOs by configuring user and computer Administrative Template settings. At least one GPO is necessary for each specific desktop role.

- Add software restriction policies to GPOs where required.

- Create OUs, at least one for each role.

- Link custom GPOs to OUs.

- Add appropriate computer accounts into the respective desktop role OUs.

Study Common Desktop Scenarios

Understanding and developing a list of desktop roles is only the beginning. Thousands of configuration choices must be made in order to develop a GPO that makes sense for each role. In addition, the infrastructure necessary to support the deployment of GPOs to the right computer is not a trivial task. However, there are sample GPOs and scripts that can help. Studying these samples and implementing them in a test environment can help in two ways. First, you may discover predefined roles that match your needs, and second, you can use the existing definitions to test the infrastructure necessary to support implementation.

One example of predefined desktop roles is outlined in a Microsoft white paper. Accompanying sample GPOs and a script can be used to implement a test environment. Microsoft calls its desktop roles "common desktop scenarios." Download the documentation and GPOs from www.microsoft.com/downloads/details.aspx?FamilyID=354b9f45-8aa6-4775-9208-c681a7043292&DisplayLang=en. The six desktop roles defined in the document are described in Table 9-6.

TIP   An Excel spreadsheet that lists and compares differences among Windows XP, Windows Server 2003, and Windows 2000 options in Group Policy is located at www.microsoft.com/downloads/details.aspx?familyid=ef3a35c0-19b9-4acc-b5be-9b7dab13108e&displaylang=en.

Use the materials to set up an environment where you can not only view proposed desktop security settings, but see how they work. To do so, join desktop systems to the domain and place computer accounts where they will be affected by each scenario, and then use each desktop both in the way it should be used and in an attempt to do things that you should not.

Role	Description
Lightly Managed	For power users and developers. Users still have much control over their desktop. Supports free seating, or the ability to sit at any computer and access resources, applications, and data.
Mobile	For users with laptops who may connect via the LAN or remotely via dial-up or other technologies. Supports locally cached data. Also for remotely connected users such as those who work from home or from remote offices.
Multi-user	Desktop customization per user is possible, but not of network configuration, hardware, or system settings. Good for lab or library settings. Supports free seating. Data is not locally cached when users log off. Write access to local computer is restricted. Highly secure.
App-Station	Computer highly restricted. Only one or a few applications can be used. Highly secure.
Task Station	Computer highly restricted. A single task or application is available. Good for floor station, order entry station, etc.
Kiosk	Public area unattended computer such as airport check-in computer. Highly secure. One user account, auto-logon. Simple operation. Users cannot make changes to user or system settings. No data is saved to the disk. Cannot be shut down or logged off.

Table 9-6.   Microsoft Example Desktop Roles

Use Group Policy Management Console to Copy GPOs

Any settings you make in the Administration files in a GPO will be applied only to user or computer accounts that reside in the OU to which the GPO is linked. If, for example, you have desktop computer accounts in multiple business unit OU hierarchies and want to apply the same desktop hardening configuration, you must apply it to GPOs linked to the respective OUs.

To repeat security settings configuration in multiple GPOs (using the Security Settings portion of the Computer Configuration | Windows Settings node of a GPO), you can import a tested security template. To repeat administrative template settings, there is no comparable process. You can, of course, link a GPO to multiple OUs, but this is not always a good solution, especially if OUs exist in different domains. However, a new tool, the Group Policy Management Console (GPMC), can be used to copy GPOs for use elsewhere. GPMC was released as a free download shortly after Windows Server 2003 became available. GPMC runs only on Windows Server 2003 and Windows XP. However, it can be used to administer Group Policy for Windows 2000 domains, though not all features are available. In addition to making it easy to copy and move GPOs, GPMC can be used to inspect GPOs.

TIP Download GPMC from www.microsoft.com/downloads/details.aspx?FamilyID=c355b04f-50ce-42c7-a401-30be1ef647ea&DisplayLang=en.

When GPMC is installed, the process for access to GPOs is changed slightly on the computer on which GPMC is installed. For example, instead of accessing a GPO by selecting the GPO tab of the properties pages of an OU, domain, or site, you use the GPMC. On computers on which GPMC is not installed, access remains as per the older means.

To install GPMC, download the .msi file and run it. To copy a GPO from one OU to another, you can drag and drop the file. To copy a GPO to another domain, you must use the Import command.

Chapter 10

Harden Data Access

- Use the NTFS File System
- Use DACLs to Secure Data
- Use EFS to Secure Data

It is easy to forget that a major reason for hardening computers and networks is to protect the data that is stored on them. We spend so much time talking about and learning how to perfect network perimeter defenses and control access to the computer, that we often forget the reason for this protection: our data. Sound perimeter, computer, and applications controls do assist in providing confidentiality and integrity for our data. If an attacker cannot get into your network, he cannot steal or damage the data on it. If an attacker cannot connect to a specific computer, she cannot steal or directly damage the data on it. However, once the attacker breaks through network defenses, once she penetrates controls on the network interface of a computer, what prevents her from damaging and stealing its data? Application-level defenses may prevent the success of an attack based on using that application, but file system permissions and encryption can add another layer of defense. In addition to other defenses, you must develop protection for the data that resides on your systems.

TIP Don't confine your idea of data to documents, spreadsheets, and reports. Think also of configuration data, objects in the Active Directory, and even your ability to protect access to output devices such as printers. Once you understand how to use discretionary access control lists (DACLs), you can provide protection for those items as well.

On Windows systems that are built on Windows NT technologies, the NTFS file system can be used to provide discretionary access control lists (DACLs) and encryption can be used to provide greater protection.

Use the NTFS File System

In NTFS, some default DACLs are set to protect Active Directory objects and registry keys. If the NTFS file system is used, additional protection is also available, including these forms:

- If NTFS is selected during installation, default DACLs for drive roots and operating system files are applied.
- Permissions can and should also be managed to assist you in providing protection for application and data files.
- The Encrypting File System (EFS) can be used to encrypt files.

No hardening effort is complete without putting these capabilities to good use.

TIP If FAT or FAT32 is selected during installation, the file system can be converted to NTFS. The operation will convert the drive to NTFS and leave your data intact. While it is very unlikely that you would experience any problems, you should, nevertheless, back up your system and data as a precaution. You should also ensure that any applications that you run can run on NTFS (some very old applications do not). You must then set appropriate DACLs for drive roots and operating system files.

To convert a file system to use NTFS:

1. Do a complete backup.

2. Open a command prompt.

3. Enter **convert** *drive_letter*: **/fs:ntfs**, where *drive_letter* is the drive letter to convert followed by a colon; for example, **convert C: /fs:ntfs**.

Use DACLs to Secure Data

A DACL, or discretionary access control list, is a list of access control entries (ACEs) that specifies who can do what with a specific object. In the Windows OS, objects are files, folders, shares, printers, registry keys, and Active Directory objects. Each type of object has its own set of possible permissions.

HEADS UP!

The Windows 9*x* and Windows ME operating systems do not use the DACL concept and therefore are not discussed in this chapter. Access to every object and part of the standard Windows 9*x* and Windows ME computer is available to anyone who has physical access to the computer, since no logon is required and no file permissions can be set.

ACEs define the security principal (user, group, or computer), whether or not the permission is allow or deny and no matter what the permission is. (SACLs, or system access control lists, are similar and are used to generate audit information. As such, they will be described in Chapter 13.) ACEs may be set by object owners, and by anyone with the permission permission. The local administrators group, by default, has this permission.

To properly use DACLs to secure Windows data, you must first understand the basic permission principal. In all cases where DACLs are properly used, there are three options:

- **Explicit allow**   Permission is granted, an ACE exists
- **Explicit deny**   Permission is refused, an ACE exists.
- **Implicit deny**   Neither an allow nor deny ACE exists; therefore, no permission exists.

HEADS UP!

It is possible to code an application in which a NULL DACL is applied. A NULL DACL is different from an empty one. An empty DACL does not list a group or user account that has access to the object. In this case, no group or user has access. The object owner can give a group or user access (by creating an appropriate ACE), but until he does so, no one has access. (In addition, an administrator, or someone with the take ownership right, can take ownership and set an ACE that provides access.) A NULL DACL is the opposite; it defaults to provide default full control to anyone. Applications should not be written which assign NULL DACLs to objects, and this is an item that should be included in any software security review.

It is not necessary to deny access, since access is implicitly denied to those who do not have specific access allowed. The explicit deny can be used to prevent access by users whose membership in one group might allow them access, but who should not be allowed access to a specific object. An example of such usage is provided in the later section "Use DACLs for Separation of Duties."

DAC vs. MAC

According the National Institute of Science and Technology (NIST), in special publication 800-7 "Security in Open Systems" (http://csrc.nist.gov/publications/nistpubs/800-7/), a Discretionary Access Control (DAC) ". . .is used to control access by restricting a subject's access to an object. It is generally used to limit a user's access to a file. In this type of access control it is the owner of the file who controls other users' accesses to the file."

Using a DAC mechanism, as Windows does, allows users control over access rights to their files. When these rights are managed correctly, only those users specified by the owner may have some combination of read, write, execute, etc. permissions to the file.

Another mechanism is the mandatory access control (MAC), in which the system, not the owner of the data, controls access to the data. Current Windows implementations do not use this mechanism.

Use Inheritance to Manage Permissions

In addition to permissions granted directly on objects, permission inheritance plays a role. Permission inheritance means that permissions are, by default, inherited from objects that exist above the current object in the object hierarchy. This means, for example, that permissions set on a file folder may be applied to subfolders and files beneath that folder. It means that permissions set on the root of a drive may be applied to every folder, subfolder, and file on the drive. Inheritance makes it easier to set permissions, and permission inheritance makes it possible to make a mess of the intended permission settings for folders and file.

NOTE   Imagine having to explicitly set permissions on every file or registry key; you just would never get the job done. It's much easier to set permissions for a large group of objects by setting them at some hierarchical level, and then, if necessary, set individual additional privileges for objects beneath that level.

The permissions that are available on any specific object are a combination of inherited and explicit permissions. You determine these "effective" permissions differently depending on the objects and the operating system used. Inheritance of permissions can be also be blocked in some versions of Windows. Table 10-1 lists information about inheritance as it is handled by the different Windows versions.

Feature	OS
Permission inheritance is available.	NT, Windows 2000, Windows Server 2003, XP Professional
Inheritance can be blocked.	Windows 2000, Windows Server 2003, XP Professional
Inherited permissions are stored with the object.	NT 4.0
Preferred order of ACEs: access deny ACEs first in the DACL.	NT 4.0
Preferred order of ACEs: noninherited access denied ACEs are first, followed by noninherited access allowed, followed by access denied inherited.	Windows 2000, Windows Server 2003, Windows XP

Table 10-1.   Permission Inheritance

HEADS UP!

Because noninherited permissions (the permissions assigned directly to the object) are evaluated first in Windows 2000, Windows XP, and Windows Server 2003, it is possible that an inherited Deny permission will never be evaluated. This is because these OSs evaluate noninherited ACEs first and this process may result in granting access. If it does, the inherited permissions will never be evaluated.

An example of such a problem can be shown by comparing two sets of permissions. First, assume this example is being applied on a Windows XP Professional computer. In the first set, a folder named Accounts Payable is assigned the permissions Administrators Allow Full Control, Accounts Payable Clerks Allow Change, and Accounts Receivable Clerks Deny Full Control. A file in this folder inherits these permissions and is also given the additional permission Account Receivable Clerks Allow Change. Henry, who is a member of the Accounts Receivable Clerks group, uses an application and attempts to read a file in the Accounts Payable folder. The ACEs on the file are evaluated first. So, in our example, the permission on the file, which allows Accounts Receivable Clerks group change permission, is evaluated first. Since the change permission includes the read permission, Henry is granted access. The inherited permissions are not evaluated.

In the second set of permissions, permissions are replaced entirely by a new set. The same folder, the Accounts Payable folder, is assigned the permissions Administrators Allow Full Control, Accounts Payable Clerks Allow Change, and Accounts Receivable Clerks Deny Full Control. A file within the folder inherits these permissions and is also given the permissions Auditors Allow Read. Henry, who is a member of the Accounts Receivable Clerks group and the Users group and no others, uses an application and attempts to read a file in the Accounts Payable folder. The ACEs on the file are evaluated first. The permission Auditors Allow Read is evaluated but does not apply to Henry because he is not a member of the group Auditors. Next the inherited permissions are evaluated. The Deny permissions are evaluated first. The Accounts Receivable Deny Full Control permission is evaluated, and Henry is denied access.

Now imagine this scenario if implemented on Windows NT 4.0. Because the processing of inherited permissions is different, a Deny permission either inherited or directly applied on the file will be evaluated first. Henry will not be able to access the file.

Avoid Inadvertent Incorrect Permission Application

The different permission features can cause some confusion and misunderstanding of how permissions work. More important, any misunderstanding could mean a misconfiguration that might prevent authorized users from accessing objects, or provide unauthorized users with access. Misunderstanding or simple ignorance could also allow applications to order ACEs in a way that perverts their interpretation. To avoid this issues, use these simple rules:

- Apply recommended hardening for Windows NT 4.0. Default file system root and system permissions for Windows NT 4.0 are weak and require modification. See the later section "Harden File System DACLs."

- Restrict user permissions on file system roots and system folders. Only administrators should have the ability to change permissions here, and administrators must be thoroughly trained before obtaining the ability to modify these permissions.

- Where possible and necessary, protect folder-based permissions from changes due to inheritance by blocking inheritance. See the later section "Block Inheritance of Permissions."

- Use Deny permissions sparingly and review their application. Remember, it is possible that a Deny permission may not be the first permission evaluated. If an Allow permission is evaluated first, access will be granted. All applicable permissions are not read and then selected; only as many permissions as are necessary to provide or deny the requested access are evaluated.

- When writing code that may order ACEs in DACLs, follow the Windows preferred ACE order for the operating system.

Assign Permissions Based on User Role

Use the role-based approach to permissions. That is, provide each user with only the access required to do his job. When designing permissions infrastructure:

- Determine what access to which objects is required for a specific role.

- Create additional custom Windows groups as necessary to fulfill each role.

- Assign permissions to groups, not users.

- Add user accounts to the groups whose role they must perform.

Determine Required Access

Determining who requires access to what is the difficult part of permissioning. You will have to use Windows documentation, application documentation, and organizational information to determine the required access. Data owners should be required to provide information on who within the organization requires specific access to specific data.

Create Additional Windows Groups as Necessary

Administrative groups and how to delegate administrative duties are defined in Chapter 7. Many other custom windows groups will probably be required, but the exact groups will be dictated by the organization's composition, business model, and other unique requirements. Group scope will also impact group creation.

Stand-alone Windows computers based on NT technologies have only one type of group scope—the local group. Groups are created in the local account database, and local accounts can be added to these groups. Accounts with membership in groups have object access and user rights assigned to the group.

Windows NT computers joined to a domain have three group scopes: local, global, and domain local.

- Local groups are those groups created in the local account database. They can be granted access only to objects on the same local computer. Their membership can be local accounts, domain accounts from the domain the local computer is a member of, and domain accounts from trusted domains.

- Global groups are created in the domain database that is shared by all domain controllers. These groups can be given access to any domain member computers' resources and to any trusted domain member computers. Members are domain user accounts.

- Domain local groups in Windows NT are simply an extension of the local group concept. They are local groups created on domain controllers. However, since the domain account database is replicated to backup domain controllers, local groups created on DCs can be granted access to resources on any domain controller in the domain.

Windows 2000 and Windows Server 2003 domains also have global groups, but two additional group scopes are available:

- Domain local groups for Windows 2000 and Windows Server 2003 represent different group scope. They are created in the account database of the domain controllers but can be given access to objects on any domain member computer. Members can be domain accounts and domain global groups.

- Universal groups can be granted access to any resource in the domain and can have as members any domain member from any domain in the forest, and any global group. Universal groups are possible only when a domain is in Windows 2000 Native mode or at the Windows Server 2003 functional level.

The ability of groups to nest memberships from other groups varies depending on the OS and domain mode or functional level. In a Windows NT 4.0 domain, the only nesting is of Windows global groups into local groups. In a Windows 2000 or Windows Server 2003 mixed-mode (or mixed functional level) domain, the same is true. However, a Windows 2000 Native mode domain, or a Windows Server 2003 domain at Windows 2000 and above functional level, also allows additional nesting. Universal groups can be nested in local and global groups, global groups in global groups, and domain local groups within other domain local groups.

Assign Permissions to Groups, Not Users

In all versions of Windows domains, the preferred group and permission management structure can be remembered by using the acronym AGLP. It stands for this process:

- Assign *Permissions* to *Local* groups.
- Nest *Global* groups within *Local* groups.
- Place *Accounts* in *Global* groups.

If this simple structure is followed, many benefits accrue:

- The list of ACEs in a DACL is shorter, and performance is improved.

- It is easy to assign a new employee the access he requires. Simply provide him membership in the group or groups that have been assigned permissions and user rights that he requires.

- It is easy to remove a departing employee's access by disabling his account and then simply removing his membership from all groups. (When permissions are assigned to accounts, deleting an account immediately may not be best practice, since this may leaves orphan SIDs on objects throughout the entire Windows infrastructure.)

- It is easier to adjust permissions for employees that change jobs within the organization; simply remove membership from groups necessary for the old assignment, and add membership to groups required by the new one.

Add Users to Groups According to the Roles They Must Perform

Once the catalog of necessary permissions and user rights for specific roles has been determined and the proper group assignment and group infrastructure implemented, it is a simple task to add users to the required groups.

Use DACLs for Separation of Duties

Using DACLs to implement the security principle "separation of duties" is a step few organizations take but many should. This is how to set it up:

1. Determine where separation of duties is present—for example, between accounts payable clerks and accounts receivable clerks.

2. Determine objects that each should have access to but the others should not.

3. Create a group to represent each role, for example, a Payables Clerks group and a Receivables Clerks group.

4. Give each group the Allow permissions on the objects it should have access to.

5. Give each group Deny Full Control on the objects the other group should have access to.

This is an example of how it works:

1. Alice is hired to work in the Accounts Payable department. She is added as a member of the Payables Clerks group. She is able to access appropriate files and other resources.

2. Alice changes jobs. She now works in the Accounts Receivable department. IT was not notified, and her membership is not removed from the Payables Clerks group. IT is told to add Alice as a member of the Receivables group.

3. While membership in the Receivables Clerk group is appropriate and necessary for her new job, if she retains membership in the Payables Clerk group, then she has access permissions assigned to both groups. This would be a violation of the principle of separation of duties. Alice might be able to issue a fraudulent purchase order and a fraudulent payment on that purchase order. However, since the Deny Full Control permission is assigned to the Payables Clerks group for objects the Receivables Clerks require access to, Alice will be denied access to those objects. She will not be able to do her job. Since she cannot do her assigned job, action will have to be taken. The action required is to remove her from the Payables Clerks group.

Block Inheritance of Permissions

Permission inheritance can be blocked in Windows Server 2003, Windows XP, and Windows 2000. When inheritance is blocked, the objects do not inherit permissions assigned higher in the object hierarchy. A good example of this feature is its application to protect system files. The WINNT or WINDOWS folder is the folder where operating system subfolders and files are stored. Different permissions are applied here than at the root, and they are protected from change via inheritance from drive root permissions settings, as shown in Figure 10-1. The Allow Inheritable Permissions from the Parent. . . check box is unchecked.

If you must set critical folder permissions that should not be modified by changes to folders higher in the object hierarchy, uncheck this box on the Advanced Security Settings Permission page for folders in Windows Server 2003 and XP, and on the general Security page in Windows 2000. You can also block permission inheritance for registry keys and Active Directory objects. Windows NT 4.0 permission inheritance cannot be blocked. Inheritance in printer permissions is not possible.

Use Apply To Appropriately

When adding permissions, Windows 2000, Windows Server 2003, and Windows XP systems allow setting of the Apply To property. The Apply To property allows setting permission applicability to a variety of possible scenarios. Use the setting that gives exactly the assignment required for each case. For example, folder permissions can be assigned

- This folder, subfolder, and files
- This folder only
- This folder and subfolders
- This folder and files
- Subfolders and files only
- Subfolders only
- Files only

Maintain Proper Permissions

Once permissions are set, they should remain. Unfortunately, permissions may be modified for many reasons. Changes to permissions may be made in an attempt to troubleshoot access or application failures, to provide temporary access, or during program installation. There are three ways to ensure appropriate permissions are maintained:

- Use proper change management procedures and processes. Change management should be formally organized and carried out. When proper procedures are followed, the reasons for changes are evaluated, and if approved, implemented with proper testing and accompanied by documentation. No change should be made without using approved procedures.

- IT should conduct periodic sampling for adherence to approved settings. This can easily be automated using security templates.

- IT should make proper audits. Whether internal or external auditors get involved, appropriate permissions can be checked as part of every IT audit.

The topics of change management and audits are covered in Chapters 13 and 14 respectively.

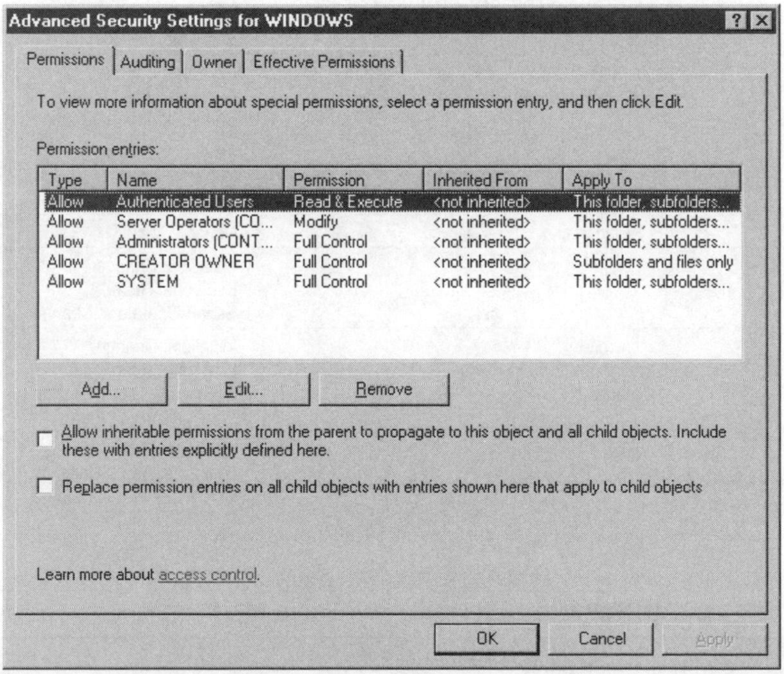

Figure 10-1. Permission inheritance is blocked for the WINDOWS folder.

Secure File Systems and Data

Object permission basics apply to file system objects, to folders and files. Each file and folder permission setting should be considered, designated, implemented, and maintained appropriately.

Harden File System DACLs

Default file and registry DACLs are set appropriately for Windows Server 2003, Windows 2000, and Windows XP. However, Windows NT 4.0 file system DACLs are weak. Table 10-2 lists the Microsoft-recommended modifications. Note that the changes are for a Windows NT 4.0 domain controller, and that the Installers group is a not a standard Windows group but a placeholder for a recommendation made in the white paper "NSA Windows NT System Security Guidelines." The Installers group is used to represent all users who have privileges to install applications or systems software. Recommendations are similar for NT Workstation and Server and are located in the Baseline Security Checklists available from www.Microsoft.com/technet/security.

Folder	Subfolder/Files	Recommended ACEs
C:\	Root and IO.SYS and MSDOS.SYS, AUTOEXEC.BAT, CONFIG.SYS	Installers: Change Everyone: Read Server Operators: Change
	BOOT.INI, NTDETECT.COM, NTLDR	None
C:\	TEMP	Everyone: (RWXD) (not specified)
C:\	WINNT and control.ini WINNT is also shared as ADMIN$	Installers: Change Everyone: Read Server Operators: Change
\WINNT	Win.ini	Installers: Change Public: Read Server Operators: Change
\WINNT	Netlogon.chg	None
\WINNT	\config	Installers: Change Everyone: Read Server Operators: Change
\WINNT	\cursors\ \fonts\ \media\	Installers: Change Everyone: Read Server Operators: Change Power Users: Change
\WINNT	\help	Installers: Change Everyone: Add & Read Server Operators: Change Power Users: Change
WINNT	\inf	Installers: Change Everyone: Read
WINNT\inf	*.ADM files	Everyone: Read

Table 10-2. Permission Hardening for Windows NT 4.0

Folder	Subfolder/Files	Recommended ACEs
WINNT\inf	*.PNF	Installers: Change Everyone: Read Server Operators: Change
\WINNT	\media*.RMI	Everyone: Change
\WINNT\profiles	\profiles	Installers: Add & Read Everyone: (RWX) (not specified)
\WINNT\profiles	...\all usrs	Installers: Change Everyone: Read
\WINNT\profiles	...\Default	Everyone: Read
\WINNT	\repair	None
\WINNT	\system	Installers: Change Everyone: Read Server Operators: Change
\WINNT	\system32	Installers: Change Everyone: Read Server Operators: Change Backup Operators: Change
\WINNT\system32	Files	Everyone: Read Server Operators: Change
WINNT\system32\	$winnt$.inf	Installers: Change Everyone: Read Server Operators: Change
WINNT\system32\	AUTOEXEC.NT, CONFIG.NT	Installers: Change Everyone: read Server Operators: Change
WINNT\system32\	Cmos.ram, midimap.cfg	Everyone: Change
WINNT\system32\	Localmon.dll, decpsmon.*, hpmon.*	Installers: Change Everyone: Read Server Operators: Change Print Operators: Change
\WINNT\System32	\Config	Everyone: list
\WINNT\SYSTEM32	\Dhcp	Everyone: Read Server Operators: Change
\WINNT\System32	\drivers	Everyone: Read
WINNT\System32	\LLS	Installers: Change Everyone: Read Server Operators: Change
\WINNT\System32	\OS2	Everyone: Read Server Operators: Change
\WINNT\System32	\RAS	Everyone: Read
\WINNT\System32	\Repl	Everyone: Read Server Operators: Change
\WINNT\System32\Repl	Import, export, scripts (import\scripts is the netlogon directory)	Everyone: Read Server Operators: Change Replicator: Change

Table 10-2.   Permission Hardening for Windows NT 4.0 *(continued)*

Folder	Subfolder/Files	Recommended ACEs
\WINNT\System32	\Spool, \drivers, \prtprocs	Installers: Change Everyone: Read Server Operators: Full Print Operators: Change
\WINNT\System32	\printers\, \tmp\	Installers: Change Everyone: (RWX) (not specified) Server Operators: Full
\WINNT\System32	\viewers\	Everyone: Read Server Operators: Change
\WINNT\System32	\wins	Everyone: Read Server Operators: Change
C:\...	*.EXE, *.BAT, *.COM, *.DLL	Everyone: Execute

Table 10-2. Permission Hardening for Windows NT 4.0 *(continued)*

Add File System DACLs to Converted or Formatted NTFS Drives

When Windows 2000, Windows Server 2003, and Windows XP systems are installed, default file system DACLs are applied. However, when systems are upgraded to these operating systems, file system permissions remain as they were. If FAT file systems are converted to NTFS, the normal default file system permissions are not applied. New file system DACLs are not applied in these cases to prevent the situation where changing permissions prevent user access or system operation. You should evaluate the requirements of applications and data access that is required and then apply appropriate system and file system permissions.

An option, after evaluation, may be to apply default permissions using security templates. Table 10-3 lists the default security templates that provide file system permission settings. The templates can be applied using Security Configuration and Analysis, scripts, or Group Policy.

Harden File System Shares

File system shares are access points to drives on a system. This mechanism is used to provide remote administration and to provide easy access to data across the network. By default, several access points are provided:

- **The root of each drive**   The C$, D$, and so on
- **The system root**   By default, WINNT or WINDOWS shared as ADMIN$
- **Interprocess communications**   Used for sharing information between applications by providing support for pipes, mail slots, RPC, windows sockets, and so on; shared as IPC$

- **Netlogon**   Used for authentication and for Windows 2000 and Windows Server 2003 domain controllers; shared as NETLOGON

- **The system volume**   Stores the server copy of the domain's public files, including the NELOGON share, logon scripts, and File Replication Service (FRS) staging folders and files that must be replicated (SYSVOL)

- **Additional shares that may be present**   The FAX clients share (FAX$) and the printer share (PRINT$)

NOTE   Root shares are set for access by members of the local administrators group only, and permissions cannot be changed. The permissions on these shares should be maintained.

Administrative shares are those shares that cannot be identified by viewing the file system. An Administrative share is created by appending a dollar sign ($) to the end of the share name. Administrative shares on a specific computer can be viewed by using administrative tools. To view shares on a Windows NT 4.0 server, open Server Manager and select the Computer menu Shared Directories as shown in Figure 10-2. To view shares on a Windows 2000, Windows XP, or Windows Server 2003 computer, use the Computer Management console Shared Folders | Shares node as shown in Figure 10-3. All shares will be shown, not just administrative shares.

OS	Template	Description
Windows Server 2003/XP	Rootsec	The permissions on the %System% folder are provided.
Windows Server 2003/XP	DC security	File and folder permissions are listed.
Windows Server 2003/XP	Compatws	Folder permissions that will provide compatibility for legacy applications.
Windows Server 2003/XP	Setup security	File and folder permissions as applied during setup. (Copy from a systems setup on a new install on NTFS.)
Windows 2000	Hisecws	File and folder permission to harden Windows 2000 Professional.
Windows 2000	Ocfiless and ocfilesw	Folder permissions for additional applications such as NetMeeting, Outlook Express, FrontPage, etc.
Windows 2000	Basicsv and basicwk	Basic folder and file permissions installed for default servers and workstations.

Table 10-3.   Default Security Templates with File Permission Settings

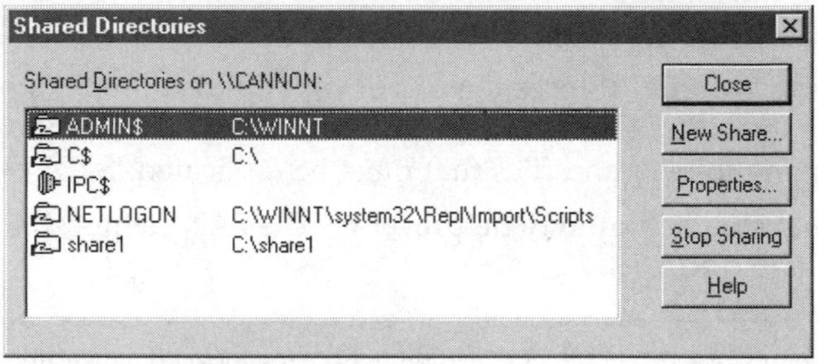

Figure 10-2. Viewing administrative shares on Windows NT 4.0

Turn Off File and Printer Sharing When It Is Not Required

Regardless of the configuration of shares on a Windows computer, the Server service must be started, and for Windows 2000, Windows XP, and Windows Server 2003, the

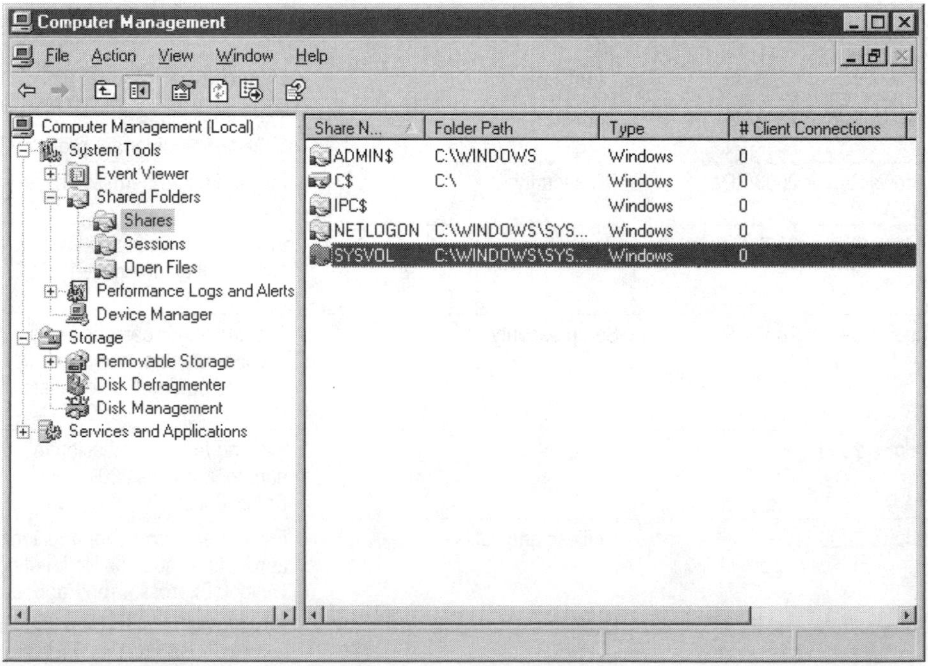

Figure 10-3. Viewing administrative shares on Windows Server 2003

File and Printer Sharing networking option must be running. For Windows 9x and Windows ME, the File and Printer Sharing networking option must be installed and selected. To turn off file and printer sharing in Windows NT 4.0, disable the Server service:

1. Open the Server Manager console through Start | Administrative Tools.
2. From the Computer menu, select Services.
3. Select the Server service and click Startup as shown here:

4. Click Disabled under Startup Type as shown here:

5. Click OK to close, and then click Stop to stop the service.
6. Click Close and then Exit the Server Manager console.

To stop File and Printer Sharing:

1. Open the network connector for the local area connection or other network interface (Start | Control Panel | Network Connections).

2. Click Properties.

3. Click to deselect File and Printer Sharing for Microsoft Networks as shown here:

4. Click OK and then click Close.

However, there are many reasons to enable this service:

- Microsoft Baseline Security Analyzer, a free vulnerability assessment tool, requires that File and Printer Sharing be enabled in order to remotely scan Windows computers.

- Windows domain controllers must run File and Printer Sharing in order for users to authenticate to the domain and for other essential domain services such as Active Directory to function.

- File and Print Servers must run this service in order for remote computers to access their file system and printer.

For domain controllers and file and print servers, the choice is obvious: sharing must be enabled. Likewise, edge servers, those that may have multiple network connections that include connections to untrusted networks, should not have sharing enabled on the external or untrusted interface. The trouble lies with the rest of the computers. For many years, sound security advice included preventing shares on workstation computers and on servers that were not file servers or domain controllers. However, if you need to remotely run vulnerability scanning software against these computers, you may need to enable sharing. Alternatively, terminal services, or local vulnerability scanning, may be the answer for more sensitive systems.

Remove Shares on Drive Roots

If a Windows computer will not be remotely administered, the decision may be made to remove the shares on drive roots. All shares, including administrative shares, can be removed by using options in the consoles where they can be viewed. Administrative shares, however, will return if the system is rebooted. To disable shares on drive roots and on the system root folder (ADMIN$), add the AutoShareWks DWORD value to the registry key

```
HKEY_LOCAL_MACHINE\SYSTEM\CurrentControlSet\Services\LanmanServer\Parameters
```

Set the AutoShareWks value to 0. Should you need to restore these default administrative shares, simply delete the AutoShareWks DWORD value and reboot the computer.

Prevent Nonadministrators from Creating Shares

Set the permissions of the following key and all of its subkeys to Everyone Read:

```
HKEY_LOCAL_MACHINE\CurrentControlSet\Services\LanManServer\Shares
```

Harden Share Permissions

When a new share is created, the default permissions on Windows 2000 and Windows NT 4.0 is Everyone Full Control. Change this immediately to Everyone Read, or to the appropriate share permissions for the specific folder. Windows XP and Windows Server 2003 shares default to Everyone Read.

Secure Printers

By default, printers are shared, giving Administrators Full Control, Everyone permission to print, document owners permission to manage the documents, and Printer Operators and Server Operators the ability to manage documents and printers. To harden printers, reduce the permissions on all printers. The following permissions should be adjusted:

- Provide only Print Operators with the Manage Printer and Manage Documents permissions. Remove Administrators and Server Operators.
- Only authenticated users should have print permission.
- For sensitive printers, such as check printers, create Windows groups for managing and printing and assign these groups management and print permissions respectively. Remove the default groups and their permissions.
- Create a subgroup of Administrators that can manage printers by providing them membership in the Print Operators group.

Secure Registry Keys

Registry keys, like files and folders, have permissions assigned to protect key system information. In addition, protection from remote access and from anonymous access should be provided. To protect the registry from remote administrative access, disable the remote registry service. Unfortunately, unless you need to administer very few servers, a better solution is to manage remote access to the registry.

Restrict Remote Registry Access

Remote access to the registry is set by setting permissions on the winreg key located at

```
HKEY_LOCAL_MACHINE\SYSTEM\Control\CurrentControlSet\SecurePipeServers
```

Permissions are set in Windows Server 2003 by right-clicking the key and selecting Permissions, and then adjusting the permissions using the object picker. Note in Figure 10-4 that by default, only the local Administrators group has full control here, while Backup Operators and the LOCAL SERVICE have read access.

Windows NT 4.0 does not, by default, set permissions on Winreg; however, this is done by application of service pack 6, as shown in Figure 10-5. To set permissions in Windows NT 4.0, use the regedt32.exe tool's Security menu and select Permissions.

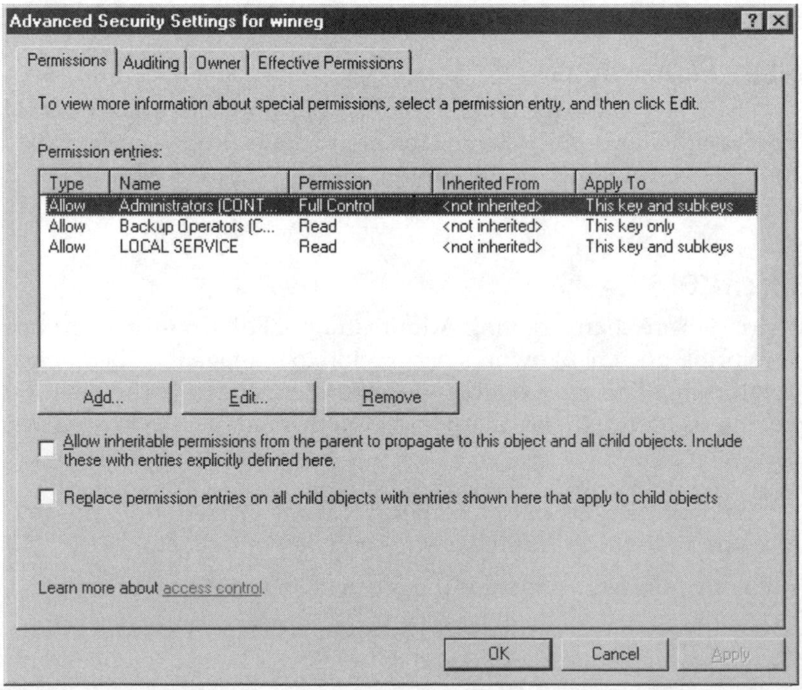

Figure 10-4.   Permissions set on the Winreg key control remote access to the registry.

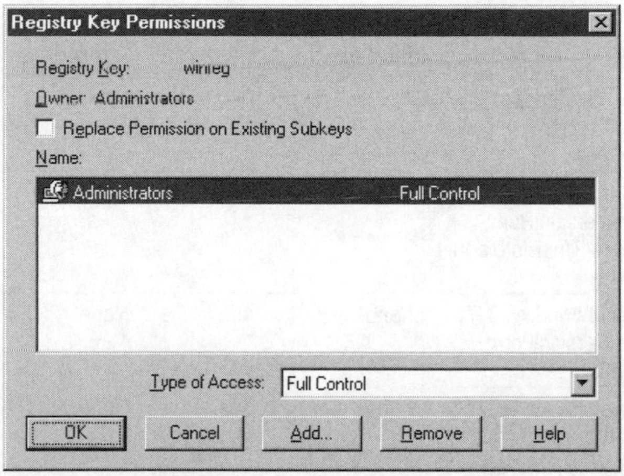

Figure 10-5. Windows NT 4.0 permissions on WinReg

In both cases, reduce risk by establishing a special administrators group that is authorized to remotely administer computers and assign that group Full Control.

Harden Permissions on Registry Keys

Table 10-4 lists sensitive Windows NT 4.0 registry keys in the HKEY_LOCAL_ MACHINE hive that need permission changes to protect them. (Unless noted, do not apply permissions to the entire tree, but only the path listed.) Table 10-5 lists several registry keys that to which access should be restricted for all Windows versions that contain them.

Subkey	Path	Installers	Everyone	Interactive	Apply to Entire Path
Software		Change	Read	None	No
Software	\classes	Add	Read	None	No
Software	\Microsoft\Windows\ CurrentVersion\App Paths	Change	Read	None	Yes
Software	\Microsoft\Windows\ CurrentVersion\Explorer	None	Read	None	Yes

Table 10-4. Registry Permissions Recommendations for Windows NT 4.0

Subkey	Path	Installers	Everyone	Interactive	Apply to Entire Path
Software	\Microsoft\Windows\ CurrentVersion\ Embedding	Change	Read	None	Yes
Software	\Microsoft\Windows\ CurrentVersion\Run, RunOnce, Uninstall, and AEDebug	None	Read	None	N/A
Software	\Microsoft\Windows NT\ CurrentVersion\Font*, GRE_Initialize	Change	Add	None	Do not change Font Drivers
Software	\Microsoft\Windows NT \ CurrentVersion\ Type 1 Installer\Type 1 Fonts	Change	Add	None	No
Software	\Microsoft\Windows NT \ CurrentVersion\Drivers, Drivers.desc	None	Read	None	Yes
Software	\Microsoft\Windows NT \ CurrentVersion\MCI\MCI Extensions	Change	None	None	Yes
Software	\Microsoft\Windows NT \ CurrentVersion\Ports	None	Read	Read	Yes
Software	\Microsoft\Windows NT \ CurrentVersion\WOW	None	Read	None	Yes
Software	\Microsoft\Windows 3,1 Migration Status	None	Read	None	Yes
System	CurrentControlSet\ Services\LanmanServer\ Shares	None	Read	None	Yes
System	CurrentControlSet\ Services\	None	Read	None	Yes

Table 10-4. Registry Permissions Recommendations for Windows NT 4.0 *(continued)*

NOTE Permissions on the Run Registry Keys may have to be modified in order to allow the installation of some software. Be sure to return the permission sets of these keys to the reduced permissions indicated in Table 10-5 after the software is installed.

Path	Keys	Permissions
HKEY_LOCAL_MACHINE\SOFTWARE\ Microsoft\ Windows\CurrentVersion	Run	Everyone: Read
HKEY_LOCAL_MACHINE\SOFTWARE\ Microsoft\ Windows\CurrentVersion	Run Once	Everyone: Read
HKEY_LOCAL_MACHINE\SOFTWARE\ Microsoft\ Windows\CurrentVersion	RunOnceEx	Everyone: Read
HKEY_LOCAL_MACHINE\SOFTWARE\ Microsoft\ Windows\CurrentVersion	AeDebug	Everyone: Read

Table 10-5.   Recommended Permissions on Run Registry Keys

Secure Directory Objects

Directory objects also have permission settings. Often these settings do more than grant access to objects. Permission settings on Active Directory objects also provide the ability to manage the object, objects in a path, or properties of objects. Directory object permissions are discussed in Chapter 6.

Secure Services

Only administrators should have the ability to modify the startup status of system services. You can control this right in Windows NT 4.0 by setting the permission to Everyone Read on the registry key

```
HKEY_LOCAL_MACHINE\System\CurrentControlSet\Services
```

Read permission for Users is set by default on Windows 2000. Windows XP and Windows Server 2003 provide more granular control. Each individual service can be controlled by using security templates or Group Policy.

1. Expand the Services node in Security Settings | System Service and select the service to manage.
2. Right-click the service and select properties.
3. Select Define This Policy Setting.
4. Select the service's startup mode: Automatic, Manual, or Disabled.

5. Click the Edit Security button as shown here:

6. Set permissions using the object picker. Note that the default setting in the next illustration is INTERACTIVE Read (Administrators and SYSTEM have Full Control.)

Use EFS to Secure Data

Correctly set file permissions can keep users out of files when the operating system is running. However, if the computer can be booted to an alternative OS, or if files can be copied to a different computer, then permissions cease to be an effective security tool. Encryption can protect files regardless of the operating system used to attempt access to the files. The Encrypting File System is available in Windows 2000, Windows XP Professional, and Windows Server 2003. It can be used to encrypt a single file or, if applied to a folder, will encrypt all files placed in the folder. It can be used to encrypt local files, or used to encrypt files stored on a file server or web server. While Windows 2000 EFS-encrypted files cannot be shared, Windows XP and Windows Server 2003 EFS-encrypted files can. In order to effectively and securely use EFS, special attention must be paid, and training, backup, and recovery procedures developed. The first step in hardening EFS is to disable it.

NOTE   Windows NT 4.0, Windows 98, and Windows ME do not include EFS. These operating systems will not be discussed in this section.

Disable EFS Until You Can Securely Implement It

Like any security tool, encryption can be misused and provide a false sense of security. If EFS is not properly managed, its protection can be voided, and worse, users may lose access to critical or sensitive files. These are the reasons for these problems:

- EFS encryption keys are protected by keys bound to the user account. If an attacker can crack, deduce, or otherwise obtain a user's password, the attacker can log on as the user and read the encrypted files. Users with weak passwords are at the greatest risk.

- Windows 2000 EFS stand-alone computers establish the local Administrators account as the EFS recovery agent. The administrator can read every encrypted file. Alternatively, an attacker who obtains the Administrator password can log on as the administrator and read the files.

- If the Administrator EFS private key (required to read encrypted files) is removed from the computer, the Administrator can still, on Windows 2000, reset the users account, log on as the user, and read the files.

- In a domain, the first domain administrator to log on to the DC will become the EFS recovery agent and be able to read all EFS-encrypted files in the domain.

- Domain administrators can reset user passwords and thus log on as users and gain access to their files.

- The user profiles store the EFS certificate and private key. If the profile is damaged, the user will lose access to his files. If the profile of the local Administrator (on a stand-alone computer) or of the domain recovery agent is damaged, then file recovery will not be possible. This actually happens a lot, as problems with profiles are frequently solved by deleting profiles, and problems with computers are often solved by reinstalling the operating system.

- Windows XP stand-alone computers do not make the local Administrator a recovery agent. This is good, since the Administrator cannot read the files, but bad, since there is no recovery.

- Statements in documentation that indicate keys should be archived are not emphasized, and users frequently don't read documentation anyway. Keys are not backed up. If EFS encryption keys were backed up, then users could recover files. But users don't, and backing up a large number of EFS keys is an impossible task. There is no default remote administration available for EFS keys. Windows Server 2003 does offer key archival, but this requires quite a bit of setup.

- EFS files can be shared. Unfortunately, once an EFS-encrypted file is shared with another user, the original owner loses control of the file. The new user can turn around and share the EFS-encrypted file with others.

- If EFS files are to be stored on a file server, they are first decrypted, sent across the network in the clear, and then encrypted on the file server. During transport, if captured, the file can be read.

For these reasons, best practices suggest that you disable EFS until you can establish a sound management policy that includes some form of key backup or archival and recovery management. To disable EFS in Windows 2000 requires only that you remove the recovery agent. Without a recovery agent, Windows 2000 EFS will not work. To prevent EFS across an entire domain, the EFS policy must also be removed. XP and Windows Server 2003 do not require a recovery agent. To disable EFS in these environments requires a registry setting.

To disable EFS in Windows 2000:

1. Add the local Group Policy Object to an MMC console.

2. Expand the Public Key Policies node through Computer Configuration | Windows Settings | Security Settings.

3. Select the Encrypting Data Recovery Agents folder as shown here:

4. In the details pane, right-click the certificate designated for File Recover and select Delete.

5. Right-click the Encrypting Data Recovery Agents folder and select Delete Policy.

To disable EFS in a Windows 2000 Domain, open the GPO for the domain and navigate to Public Key Policies node via Computer Configuration | Windows Settings | Security Settings and then follow steps 1 to 5.

To disable EFS in a stand-alone Windows XP Professional or Windows Server 2003 computer:

1. Open the local Group Policy in an MMC.

2. Expand the Public Key Policies node through Computer Configuration | Windows Settings | Security Settings.

3. Right-click the Encrypting File System folder and select Properties.

4. Uncheck Allow Users to Encrypt Files Using Encrypting File System (EFS).

5. Click OK.

To disable EFS in a Windows 2003 domain:

1. Open the domain GPO and navigate to the Public Key Policies node through Computer Configuration | Windows Settings | Security Settings.

2. Right-click the Encrypting File System folder and select Properties.

3. Uncheck Allow Users to Encrypt Files Using Encrypting File System (EFS) as shown here:

4. Click OK.

5. Right-click the Encrypting File System folder and select All Tasks, and then select Delete Policy.

Windows XP and Windows Server 2003 EFS can also be disabled by directly editing the registry. Add the DWORD value EFSConfiguration (and give the value of 1) to the registry key

```
HKEY_LOCAL_MACHINE\SOFTWARE\Microsoft\Windows NT\CurrentVersion\EFS
```

Harden EFS Practices

In order to implement solid, secure, and scalable EFS, many items must be considered. The following EFS practices should be considered as part of your EFS policy and practice.

Encrypt Folders, Not Files

If the folder encryption bit is set, each file saved to the folder will be encrypted. When files are opened by those whose keys have encrypted the EFS encryption keys, the files are transparently decrypted. This is a very convenient way of operating, as the process is transparent to the user. It is also a more secure way of operating if files are always created within the folder.

When files are first created and then encrypted, it is possible that data shreds, or clear text data from the original file, may be left the disk. The Microsoft cipher.exe tool can be used to remove any potential data shreds; however, this is a time-consuming process.

Restrict Permissions on Encrypted Files

Encrypted files cannot be opened by users who do not possess the proper keys. However, encryption does not remove a user's ability to delete a file. If a user has the delete permission, it does not matter that the file is encrypted; the file can be deleted. Likewise, a user may be able to back up an encrypted file, moving it to another folder. Be sure to use file permissions to restrict access to encrypted files.

Require Strong Password Policies and Enforce Them

If a user's password can be cracked, an attacker can log on as the user and open the user's encrypted files. A strong password policy will reduce the risk that passwords will be cracked.

Protect EFS Files in Transport

EFS is a file encryption driver that is available as part of NTFS. Normal file transfer from the local computer to a share on a network server does not transfer the encrypted file; instead, it decrypts the file, copies it across the network in clear text, and then re-encrypts it. Use IPSec to establish protected communications between client and file server. Alternatively, any encrypted transport could be used. SSL or VPNs can be used to protect the transfer of files. IPSec, SSL, and VPNs are described in Chapter 11.

Windows XP and Windows Server 2003 EFS-encrypted files can also be transported to a web server using WebDAV. When WebDAV is used, the EFS files will remain encrypted during transport.

Backup Keys

When a user encrypts her first file, a self-signed certificate and matching private key are automatically created. The certificate binds the user's account to the public/private key pair. The public key is used to encrypt the secret key created by the OS to encrypt a file. The private key is necessary in order to decrypt the secret key, which then can be used to decrypt the file. If the private key is missing or damaged, the file cannot be decrypted. To ensure that the key is available, the certificate and key should be exported, or backed up. This is a simple process:

1. Add the certificates template to an MMC console.

2. Expand the Certificates file via Certificates | Current User | Personal as shown here:

3. In the details pane, right-click the Encrypting File System certificate and select All Tasks and then Export.

4. Click Next on the welcome screen.

5. Click Yes, Export the Private Key, and then click Next.

6. Leave the settings at Personal Information Exchange –PKCS #12 (.PFX) and Enable Strong Protection (Requires IE 5.0, NT 4.0 SP4 or Above) as shown here, then click Next:

7. Enter and confirm a password and then click Next.

8. Browse to a location (a floppy disk is good) and name the file; then click Next.

9. Click Finish.

If the certificate and key are available, and if Encrypted Files are backed up, files can be recovered from a different computer using a different user account by importing the keys into the Certificates store of the new account. Backing up the keys is the first step. (However, the password should be strong and kept separately from the floppy.) Anyone who knows the password and possesses the floppy disk can import the keys and open the EFS-encrypted files the keys were used to protect.

Manage EFS by Implementing PKI

EFS certificates and associated private keys are self-signed. That is, they are not issued by a certification authority (CA). There is no way to manage them, certificates cannot be revoked, and recovery is based on certificates autogenerated for administrators. The best and most secure way to implement EFS is to implement PKI. In a domain, certificates are bound to user accounts in the Active Directory. Certificates can be revoked. Recovery agent certificates can be issued to nonadministrative users, and a carefully designed recovery program established. With Windows Server 2003, another benefit is key archival. If a PKI is established, a key archival database can be configured and key recovery agents established. With key archival, if a user's keys are lost or damaged, a backup copy of the keys can be recovered by the recovery agent. In this scenario, the recovery agent has no access to the EFS-encrypted files. PKI is discussed in Chapter 12.

Train Users and Administrators

The most important aspect of a secure and sound EFS implementation is user and administrator training. When proper EFS procedures are implemented and users trained, EFS encryption can become a premier methodology for protecting sensitive information. Without training, EFS may prove to be false security.

Provide Protection for Mobile Users of EFS

Laptop user data is especially at risk. EFS can provide solid protection if precautions are taken. Users must understand the risks. If laptops are stolen, a successful password cracking attack will provide the attacker with access to EFS-encrypted files if the user's EFS private key is located on the laptop. Best practices require the user to export the certificate and private key before traveling with the laptop. When exporting the certificate and private key, the user should click Delete the Private Key if the Export Is Successful as shown in Figure 10-6. If the keys are exported to a floppy disk, the user should make a copy to leave behind in a safe place and travel with the floppy. However, the floppy should be kept separately from the laptop so that if the laptop is stolen, the keys are not lost as well. By traveling with the keys, the user can open encrypted files by importing the keys. Care should be taken to export and remove the private keys when the user is done with them.

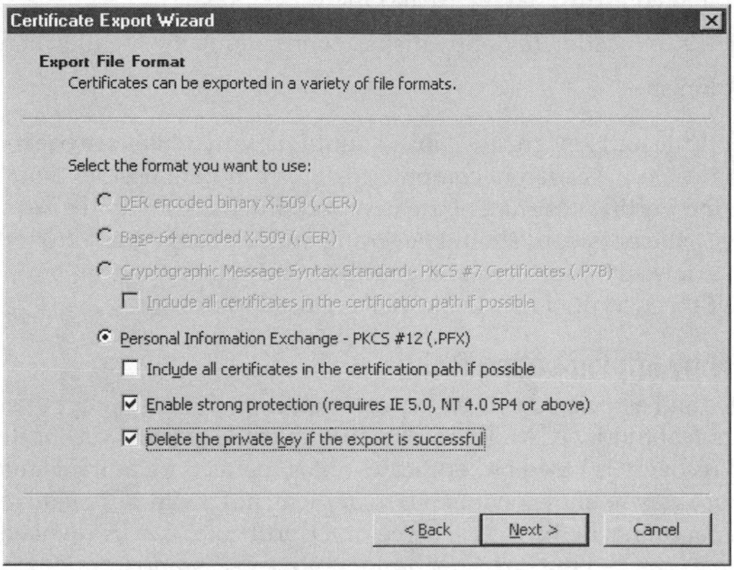

Certificate Export Wizard

Export File Format
Certificates can be exported in a variety of file formats.

Select the format you want to use:

○ DER encoded binary X.509 (.CER)

○ Base-64 encoded X.509 (.CER)

○ Cryptographic Message Syntax Standard - PKCS #7 Certificates (.P7B)

☐ Include all certificates in the certification path if possible

● Personal Information Exchange - PKCS #12 (.PFX)

☐ Include all certificates in the certification path if possible

☑ Enable strong protection (requires IE 5.0, NT 4.0 SP4 or above)

☑ Delete the private key if the export is successful

[< Back]　[Next >]　[Cancel]

Figure 10-6.　Remember to delete the private key.

Manage EFS Encryption Algorithms

Table 10-6 lists the default and possible EFS encryption algorithms for Windows OSs. If a file is encrypted with one algorithm, it must be decrypted using the same algorithm. Care should be taken to not attempt decryption with a different algorithm, as might be attempted if files are moved to different OSs. This many damage the file and will never result in file decryption. If users must move from system to system, a registry key may be used to force EFS on Windows Server 2003 or Windows XP SP1 to use a specific algorithm. To do so, add the REG_DWORD value Algorithm_ID to the registry key.

```
HKEY_LOCAL_MACHINE\SOFTWARE\Microsoft\Windows NT\CurrentVersion\EFS
```

Use the values for Algorithm_ID shown in Table 10-6.

Algorithm	Algorithm_ID Value	Compatible With
3DES	ox6603	Windows XP and Windows Server 2003
DESX	ox6604	Windows 2000, Windows XP, and Windows Server 2003
AES_256	ox6610	Windows XP SP1 and above and Windows Server 2003

Table 10-6.　EFS Encryption Algorithms per OS

Chapter 11

Harden Communications

- Protect LAN Communications
- Protect WAN Communications
- Protect Web Communications with SSL

Three basic security processes can be used to harden network communications: authentication, integrity, and encryption. Computer *authentication* is essential in order to ensure that data is actually coming from and going to appropriate computers. If a communication can spoof its origination, or if a destination can be spoofed, then there is no way to know if the information is correct, and no way to avoid sending confidential information where it should not go. *Integrity* ensures that the data has not changed during transport. If integrity is not guaranteed, then an attacker might successfully change data. *Encryption* protects data by making the message useless to any but those possessing the key. While not every protocol designed for communications security does all three, the best protection for data communications will.

An additional security mechanism, *message signing,* can guarantee that a specific message came from the computer identified as the source of the message. As part of the negotiation process, the client and server are authenticated. If authentication fails, the communication does not proceed. If authentication is successful, each packet sent is signed by the source. Without message signing, session hijacking can occur. Session hijacking is an attack where communications are intercepted and modified en route.

Protect LAN Communications

Communications between computers on the LAN can be secured using either SMB message signing or IPSec. While IPSec is a more secure protocol, it is not as easily implemented, nor available for all versions of Windows. SMB message signing can be configured for Windows NT 4.0 (post service pack 3) as well as Windows XP, Windows Server 2003, and Windows 2000. Windows 95/98 computers running the Directory Services client can also be configured to do SMB message signing. Windows 9*x*, Windows ME, and Windows NT 4.0 cannot use IPSec in transport mode.

NOTE An update for Windows 9*x*, Windows ME, and Windows NT 4.0 allows these OSs to participate in L2TP/IPSec VPNs. This is different, however, than IPSec in transport mode.

Use SMB Message Signing and Session Security for NTLM

Server Message Block (SMB) is the protocol used for file sharing and other communications between Windows computers. It is the basis for NetBIOS communications. SMB signing guarantees the origination of the communication. It is enabled by default on Windows Server 2003 computers but must be configured on the other Windows OSs. Once configured, SMB signing is negotiated during the connection request and systems that cannot use SMB signing may not be able to communicate with those that can. Two different types of configuration can be configured. First, and most effective, is to configure both server and client to always require SMB signing. Alternatively, signing can be established by mutual agreement.

NTLM Session security allows encryption (confidentiality) and integrity to be configured.

HEADS UP!

When SMB signing is required, legacy operating systems and some legacy programs will not be able to communicate. There may also be compatibility issues between later versions of Windows. For example, the KB article 823659 indicates that the secure channel of a trust between Windows NT 4.0 and Windows Server 2003 cannot be reset, that copying files between Windows XP and Windows Server 2003 will be much slower, and that you will not be able to map a network drive from the client.

Configure Message Signing Using Group Policy

To configure SMB message signing in Windows Server 2003, Windows XP, and Windows 2000, use the following Group Policy options:

- Microsoft Network client: Digitally sign communications (always)
- Microsoft Network client: Digitally sign communications (if server agrees)
- Microsoft Network server: Digitally sign communications (always)
- Microsoft Network server: Digitally sign communications (if client agrees)

Configure Message Signing Using Registry Entries

To configure client-side SMB message signing in Windows NT 4.0 post service pack 3, and in Windows 95/98 computers running the Directory Services client, add the REG_DWORD registry value RequireSecuritySignature or EnableSecuritySignature and set the value to 1. To disable SMB signing, set the value to 0. The value location is the registry path

```
HKEY_LOCAL_MACHINE\SYSTEM\ CurrentControlSet\Services\
LanmanWorkstation\Parameters\RequireSecuritySignature
```

To configure server-side SMB message signing for Windows NT 4.0 post service pack 3, configure the value at the registry path

```
HKEY_LOCAL_MACHINE\SYSTEM\CurrentControlSet\Services\LanmanServer\
Parameters\RequireSecuritySignature
```

Windows NT 4.0 must be restarted for the configuration to be enabled.

Configure NTLM Session Security

Two Group Policy Security Options control NTLM Session security settings:

- Network Security: Minimum session Security for NTLM SSP-based (including secure RPC) clients
- Network Security: Minimum session Security for NTLM SSP-based (including secure RPC) servers

For each, four options are available:

- Require message integrity
- Require message confidentiality
- Require NTLMv2 session security
- Require 128-bit encryption

Use IPSec Policies

IPSec is a security protocol built in to the Windows TCP/IP stack of Windows XP, Windows Server 2003, and Windows 2000. An IPSec policy can be configured and assigned that will protect communications by providing mutual computer authentication, encryption, integrity, protection from replay attacks, and message origination authentication. It is also widely used as a security protocol in VPNs. Its use in Windows-based VPNs is discussed in the later section "Use L2TP/IPSec VPNs."

Here are three major uses for IPSec in Windows LANs:

- To provide encryption of communications between two computers
- To manage connections on the basis of IP address and protocol used
- To prevent connections to network resources from rogue computers

IPSec policies are created using Group Policy. A policy can be developed and assigned to a single computer at a time using the local group policy, or configured in a GPO linked to an OU or entire domain and thus implemented on any number of computers.

IPSec is a complex protocol, and to thoroughly understand and troubleshoot IPSec is beyond the scope of this book. A few simple facts, however, will allow you to write and use the simple policies outlined here. These facts are easier to understand by following the policy steps, but these are their basics:

- A policy is composed of rules, filters, and filter actions.
- Rules are composed of settings and a list of filters.
- Filters specify source and destination IP addresses and protocols.
- Filter actions determine what happens if a rule's filter is matched.

- Possible filter actions are: Block, Permit, and Negotiate. Rules are often referred to by their filter action.

- Each rule can have only one filter action; however, a policy may be composed of one or more rules.

- In order for Allow and Negotiate policies to work, each computer involved must have an IPSec policy assigned.

- IPSec policies are not in effect until the policy is assigned.

- Policies may be scripted, or the IPSec Policy Wizard can be used.

- Three methods of authentication are available. Kerberos (only in Windows domains), certificates (all computers must have certificates and must be able to validate them), preshared key (the weakest, but good for testing).

HEADS UP!

It is possible to create an IPSec policy that can so successfully shut down communications that recovery of the computer system may be a difficult chore. To prevent complications, always test an IPSec policy in a test environment and always start by implementing the policy on one test computer at a time, then moving to a test domain.

Use IPSec for Confidentiality

To protect communications between two computers, use an IPSec negotiation policy. The following steps outline how to build a policy that encrypts communication between computer A with an IP address of 192.168.7.55 and computer B, which has an IP address of 192.168.7.155.

1. Add the IP Security Policy Management snap-in to an MMC console on computer A.

2. Right-click the IP Security Policies on Local Computer container, as shown here, and select Create an IP Security Policy.

3. Click Next on the Welcome page.

4. Enter the name **Encrypt1** for the policy and click Next.

5. Uncheck Activate the Default Response Rule.

6. Click Next; then click Finish.

7. On the Encrypt1 Rules page, click Add, as shown here, to add a new rule:

8. On the New Rule Properties IP Filter List page, click Add to create the filter list.

9. Enter **Encrypt** to name the filter list.

10. Uncheck the Use Add Wizard box and click Add to add a filter.

11. In the Source address drop-down list box, select A Specific IP Address.

12. Enter the IP address of computer B, **192.168.7.155**.

13. In the Destination address drop-down list box, select My IP address, as shown here:

IP Filter Properties   ? X

Addresses | Protocol | Description

Source address:

A specific IP Address ▾

IP Address: 192 . 168 . 7 . 155

Subnet mask: 255 . 255 . 255 . 255

Destination address:

My IP Address ▾

☑ Mirrored. Match packets with the exact opposite source and destination addresses.

OK   Cancel

14. Click OK to close the IP Filter Properties list page and click OK to close the IP Filter List page.

15. In the IP Filter List tab, select the Encrypt entry (the list you just created), as shown in the following illustration, and then click the Filter Action tab.

16. Click to deselect the Use Add Wizard button and click Add to add a filter action.

17. On the New Filter Action Properties page, select Negotiate Security.

18. Click Add to add a security method. The default selection, Integrity and Encryption, is acceptable. By default, 3DES and SHA1 are selected. Click OK.

19. Click Accept Unsecured Communication, But Always Respond Using IPSec, as shown here:

20. Select the General page and enter **Negotiate** for the Filter Action name; then click OK.

21. Select Negotiate on the Filter Action page.

22. Select the Authentication Methods page and click Add.

23. Select Use This String (Preshared Key). Enter a long, complex key and then click OK.

24. Select Kerberos in the Authentication Method Preference Order box and click Remove. Click OK to respond to the pop-up. Note in the following illustration that the shared key is partially visible in the interface.

25. Click Close twice to exit the policy.

26. Export the policy and import it on computer B, or re-create the policy on computer B and in both cases change the Source address to that of computer A.

27. On computer A, in the IPSec console, right-click the policy, and select Assign to assign the policy. Until you assign the policy, it is not in effect.

28. Repeat on computer B. (Don't forget to change the IP address you entered in step 11.)

Use IPSec to Manage Connections

In the preceding example, a policy was created that requires all communications between computer A and computer B to be encrypted. It also is a policy that manages connections. Although communications with other computers are unaffected, the policy does restrict communications between computer A and computer B.

IPSec policies can do more than control whether or not two computers must encrypt information sent between them. Polices can manage connections in other ways:

- Block all communications from a specific IP address, or range of IP addresses.

- Block all communications over a specific protocol/port.

- Permit communications from a specific IP address or a range of IP addresses.

- Permit communications over a specific protocol/port.

- Negotiate communication in terms of these items as well as in terms of the ability of a computer to use specified encryption, authentication, and integrity choices.

To use IPSec policies for these features, create a policy using the preceding steps but use the following adjustments.

When adding filters (see step 7) instead of using the IP address information described, use the destination and source IP address information required. In Windows Server 2003, in addition to naming a specific IP address or a specific IP subnet, you may select DNS, DHCP, WINS, or default gateway information. (The computer's TCP/IP configuration information will be used to supply the IP address of the servers from which IP addresses will be used.) Choices in Windows 2000 are more limited.

When adding filters, after managing IP address information, select the Protocol tab on the IP Filter Properties page. Use the Select a Protocol Type drop-down box to select a protocol. Use the Set the IP Protocol Port buttons and text box to set specific boxes. Figure 11-1 shows the configuration to filter on the Telnet protocol.

- Make as many filters as you want, but remember that only one filter action can be selected per rule. If you need to write a policy that blocks all telnet communications to a server but allows an encrypted telnet session from a specific computer, you will need two rules.

- Use the Filter Action page to select the filter action for the rule, or to add a filter action. The Permit filter action is present, for example, but the Block filter action is not.

Use IPSec to Prevent Connections from Rogue Computers

If an IPSec policy requires certificate authentication, and certificate distribution is controlled, then rogue computers can be prevented from connecting to network resources. This type of policy does not specify encryption or integrity. Instead, it simply requires that each computer authenticate using a certificate. If you implement

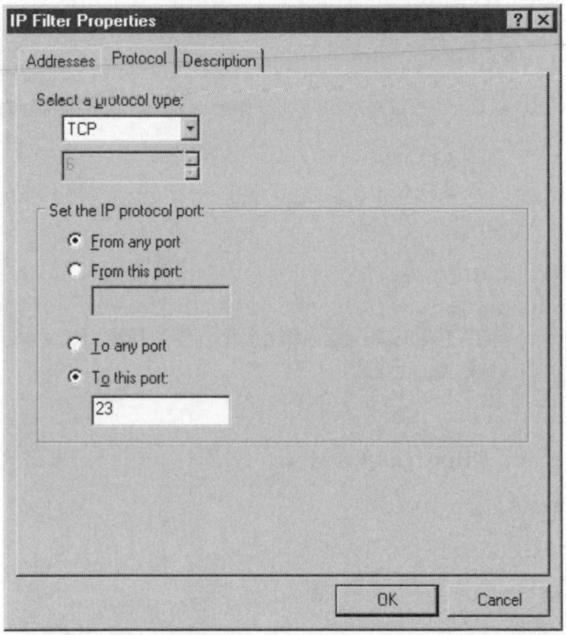

Figure 11-1. Use the IP Filter property pages to identify specific protocols.

a Windows Enterprise Certification Authority and configure automatic certificate enrollment for computers, all computers joined in the domain will have the certificate. Rogue computers, those computers brought from home by employees or brought along by contractors, vendors, and visitors, will not be able to authenticate to protected resource computers on your network.

To protect computers, create a domain IPSec policy that requires certificates for authentication but does not require anything else.

1. Right-click the IP Security Policies on Local Computer container and select Create an IP Security Policy.

2. Click Next on the Welcome page.

3. Enter a name for the policy and click Next.

4. Uncheck Activate the Default Response Rule.

5. Click Next; then click Finish.

6. Click Add to add a filter, and then select the Protocol page. Select All IP Traffic. Examine this filter list by clicking the Edit button. Note that it matches all

traffic with the exception of broadcast, multicast, Kerberos, RSVP, and ISAKMP. You can write a more specific rule to block all traffic if you wish. Click Close to close the page.

7. On the New Rule Properties, select Authentication Methods.

8. Click Add.

9. On the Authentication Method page, select Use a Certificate from This Certification Authority (CA).

10. Use the Browse button to select a copy of the CA certificate. (The Browse button defaults to the Enterprise Trust certificate store of the local computer; you must make sure that a copy of the appropriate CA certificate is in the store of each computer.) Click OK.

11. Select the Filter Action page.

12. Click Add to add a new filter action.

13. Select Negotiate Security.

14. Click Add to create a Security Method.

15. Select Custom, and then select Settings.

16. Click to deselect Data Integrity and Encryption (ESP) and select Data and Address Integrity Without Encryption (AH) as shown in the following illustration. Then click OK.

17. Select the General page and enter a name, **Authentication for the new Filter action**. Then click OK.

18. Select Authentication and click Close; then click OK to close the policy.

19. Assign the policy to all domain computers after testing.

Protect IPSec-Protected Computers During Startup

When IPSec is used to protect communications, there is a brief period of time during computer startup when network connections are possible and yet IPSec is not enforced. This is the point after which the TCP/IP driver and the IPSec driver have started, but the IPSec Policy Agent service has not yet started and applied the local- or domain-configured IPSec policy. To protect computers during this critical time, you can set the computer startup mode to block and set a persistent IPSec policy. Persistent policies are in effect whether or not IPSec policies managed by the IPSec Policy Agent are.

Set Computer Startup State   To set the computer startup state to block, use the following **netsh** command:

```
netsh ipsec dynamic set config bootexemptions value=tcp:0:3389:inbound
```

In some cases, you may want to be able to manage the computer (for recovery, for example) by using the Remote Desktop for Administration. You can set this capability by using this command. You must then create a persistent policy that will negotiate the connection between the computer and the administration station.

Set Persistent Policy   To set a persistent policy, you must use the **netsh** command. It is not possible to do so using the GUI. A persistent policy is in effect as soon as the IPSec driver starts. You can use such a policy to block all communications, then, in your IPSec policy, Allow the communications required for the specific computer. Creating a persistent policy consists of two steps. First, create an IPSec policy using **netsh** and assign it. Next, set the policy to be persistent.

A full discussion and tutorial on using **netsh** to create IPSec policies is beyond the scope of this book. Commands for assigning and making the policy persistent follow.

NOTE   Information on using the **netsh ipsec** command can be found in "Netsh Commands for Internet Protocol Security" at www.microsoft.com/resources/documentation/WindowsServ/2003/ standard/proddocs/en-us/Default.asp?url=/resources/documentation/WindowsServ/2003/standard/ proddocs/en-us/netsh_ipsec.asp.

To assign a policy named blockall:

```
set policy name=blockall assign=yes
```

Make the policy persistent:

```
set store location=persistent
```

Protect WAN Communications

In addition to local area communications, secure remote communications from other networks. Connections with other networks can be secured in a number of ways, but to secure the data as it travels between networks requires additional devices and protocols. Four technologies are currently in use:

- Dial-up access servers have a long history. Many of the legacy systems provide weak authentication and do not encrypt data in flight; however, reliable, securable dial-up access can be implemented using Microsoft tools.

- Virtual private networks (VPNs) are designed to provide tunneled, encrypted, and authenticated communication channels either client-to-server or gateway-to-gateway. Two protocols, PPTP and L2TP/IPSec, are used in Microsoft VPNs.

- The Secure Sockets Layer (SSL) has long been a methodology for authentication and securing communications between client computers and web servers; it is now commonly used as a portal to entire networks.

- Remote access rules can be applied to secure wireless networks. Even though wireless networks are often established as additional internal networks, an intruder could access them from outside the building because no physical access is required to connect to the network. Therefore, wireless networks should be thought about and secured according to remote access rules.

Hardening remote communications consists of hardening servers, clients, devices, and communications streams.

Harden the Remote Access Server

In addition to configuring secure remote access, harden the remote access server.

Harden Installation

Follow standard precautions during installation, including performing the installation offline and applying all service packs and hotfixes before adding the server to the network. Provide two network interfaces and provide secure configuration before connecting to the network.

Harden External Network Interface

The external network interface of the remote access server should provide only the basic connectivity required for the service. Two basic areas need configuration.

First, the external network interface should be configured to

- Remove File and Printer Sharing for Microsoft Networks by clicking to deselect it from the General Properties page of the connection.

- Disable NetBIOS over TCP/IP from the TCP/IP Advanced Properties, WINS tab as shown in Figure 11-2.

- Prevent attempts to dynamically register the network IP address in DNS from the TCP/IP Advanced Properties, DNS tab as shown in Figure 11-3. Attempts to dynamically register the network IP of this interface in an ISP's DNS may not be welcome. In addition, connections from external hosts should be configured on these clients. There is no reason to be resolving the Internet address of the remote access server.

Second, the network interface should be firewalled, and as an extra precaution, the Windows 2000 and Windows Server 2003 RRAS server can be configured to filter all packets on the external interface that are not necessary for remote access. See the later section "Harden Windows Server 2000 and Windows Server 2003 RRAS Configuration."

Restrict Services

Never run additional services on the RRAS server. If the Windows security baseline templates (see Chapter 8) are in use, place RRAS servers in their own OU and configure a GPO and link it to the OU. Enable the RRAS service and/or IAS service as appropriate for servers in the OU.

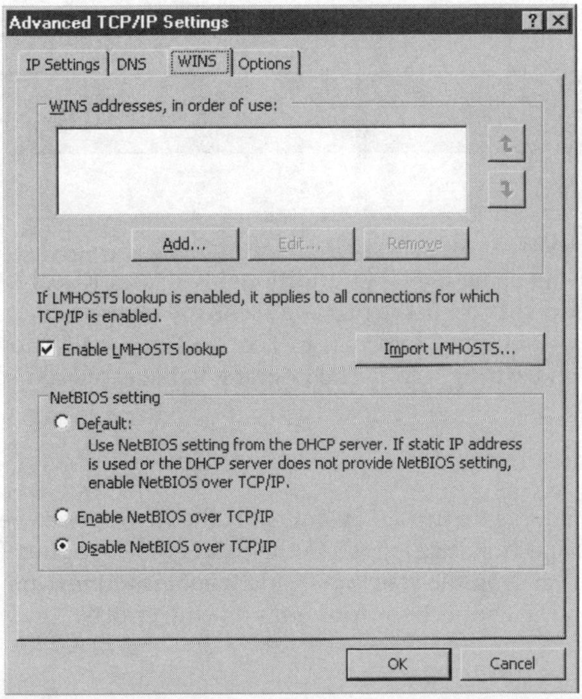

Figure 11-2. Disable NetBIOS over TCP/IP on the external network interface.

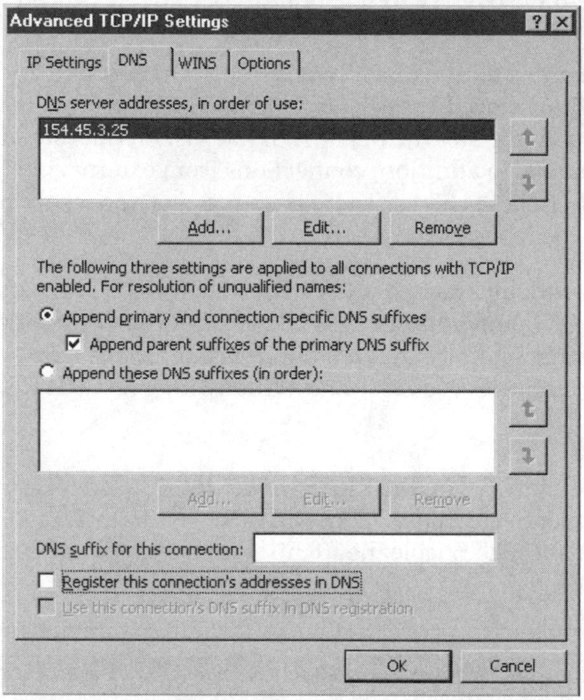

Figure 11-3.   Prevent dynamic DNS registration.

Configure Auditing

In addition to auditing using the GPO, additional RAS and RRAS logs should be configured. In Windows NT 4.0, the ppp.log file is not created by default. This log can be created, and Point-to-Point Protocol (PPP) connections will be logged, by adding the Logging value and setting it to 1. The Logging value is of type REG_DWORD and should be added at

```
HKEY_LOCAL_MACHINE\SYSTEM\CurrentControlSet\Services\RasMan\PPP
```

After the value is set, you must stop and start the RAS service before the file will be created and PPP connections are logged in the SYSTEM32\ppp.log file. Although the original intention of this log file was to provide troubleshooting information, it can serve as a record of PPP connections for your auditing efforts.

Harden NT 4.0 Remote Access Server Configuration

Windows NT 4.0 provides a basic dial-up Remote Access Service (RAS), and as an add-on, the Routing and Remote Access Service (RRAS). Dial-up access can be secured using MS_CHAPv2 authentication and data encryption, but these choices must be configured. Weaker authentication protocols and lack of encrypted communications were originally provided to ensure the ability to service connections from legacy clients.

Harden Access Port Usage

Use only the required COM port access. In many cases, this means that the RAS server should be configured only to receive calls. If the RAS server is configured for dial-back, however, configure the server for both incoming and outgoing calls.

1. Open the Network interface by right-clicking Network Neighborhood and selecting Properties.

2. Select the Services tab, select Remote Access Service, and then click Properties.

3. From the Remote Access Setup dialog box, click Configure.

4. Select the Dial Out and Receive Calls radio button as shown here:

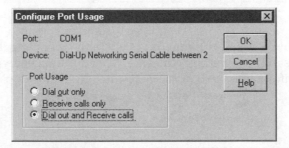

Harden Network Configuration

RAS network configuration can be secured by limiting the protocols to those used, and by requiring encryption.

1. From the Remote Access Setup dialog box, click Network.

2. Set the dial-out protocols.

3. Set the Server settings to restrict access from clients. If clients must be running IPX, for example, select only this protocol. Clients attempting to connect using another protocol will be unsuccessful. Select only those protocols your network requires. In this example, only TCP/IP has been selected.

4. Click the Configure button next to the protocol.

5. If clients need access only to specific data and that data can be available on the RAS server, then click This Computer Only in the Allow Remote TCP/IP Clients to Access box as shown in the following illustration. This will prevent

clients from accessing other network resources. The RAS server will not act as a portal to the rest of the network.

6. Click OK.

7. Select Require Data Encryption, as shown in the following illustration. MS-CHAP must be used for authentication to enable data encryption. Table 11-1 provides information on how to select other authentication protocols.

8. Click OK, and then click Continue.

Network Configuration Selection	Authentication Protocols Accepted	Discussion
Allow Any Authentication Including Clear Text	MS-CHAP, SPAP, PAP	Not an acceptable selection.
Require Encrypted Authentication	MS-CHAP, SPAP	Passwords must be encrypted.
Require Microsoft Encrypted Authentication	MS-CHAP, MS-CHAPv2	If you require data encryption, you must use MS-CHAP, or MS-CHAPv2. You cannot use SPAP or PAP. Configure clients to use MS-CHAPv2 for the most secure connection.

Table 11-1. Authentication Choices for Windows NT 4.0 RAS

Harden Client Access

The first step in hardening client access is to provide permission to only those users who should have remote access. The second is by requiring callback where possible. When callback is configured, the server terminates the successful client initial connection and dials the specified phone number. This ensures that the connection can be made only with a designated location. When users always work from the same location, callback can be an effective security measure as long as physical access to the phone line is restricted to the authorized user. When users travel and must use dial-up remote access, callback cannot provide this. Remote access is configured by visiting the user account property pages in User Manager or by using the Remote Access Admin tool.

1. Open Remote Access Admin via Start | Programs | Administrative Tool.

2. From the Users menu, select Permissions.

3. Select the user account from the Users box.

4. Select Grant Dialin Permission to User.

5. If users work from an established phone line (the same phone number all of the time), select Preset To and enter the phone number, as shown here:

6. Configure additional users.

7. Click OK to close the dialog box and then click Exit from the Server menu.

Harden Windows Server 2000 and Windows Server 2003 RRAS Configuration

While Routing and Remote Access Services can be installed on Windows NT 4.0, I recommend avoiding the use of RRAS on Windows NT 4.0. Instead, use Windows 2000 or Windows Server 2003, which provide additional security and manageability. If you must use RRAS on Windows NT, adapt the recommendations given for Windows 2000 and Windows Server 2003 RRAS to Window NT 4.0.

RRAS provides dial-up and VPN remote access. In addition to client-to-server VPNs, RRAS provides gateway-to-gateway VPN services. Network Address Translation (NAT), packet filters, and Remote Access Policies add additional configuration features. Since the versions are so similar, Windows Server 2003 is used for the examples in the following configuration settings. Differences with Windows 2000 will be noted.

Secure External Network Configuration with Packet Filters

Windows Server 2003 packet filters can be configured to secure the external network interface, permitting only VPN traffic access. To do so during RRAS setup, select the external network interface on the VPN Connection page and then select Enable Security On the Selected Interface By. . . as shown here:

To manage connections after setup, use Remote Access Policies and set Input Filters as discussed in the later section "Use Remote Access Policies."

Harden Authentication

Authentication is configured from the Server Security property page. Currently the best solution is to require smart card authentication. If that is not immediately possible, then restrict the authentication methods possible.

1. Right-click the server in the Routing and Remote Access console and select Properties.

2. Select the Security tab.

3. Click the Authentication Methods button.

4. Deselect Microsoft encrypted authentication (MS-CHAP), as shown in the following illustration. All Microsoft clients from Windows 95 onward can be configured to use MS-CHAPv2, which has many improvements over MS-CHAP. (Do not select legacy remote access communication protocols.)

5. Click EAP Methods. The Extensible Authentication Protocol can be used to configure advanced authentication methods, including Protected EAP (PEAP) and smart card or certificate authentication. They are configured in Remote Access Policies, but this property page defines the EAP methods installed on the Remote Access Server.

If IAS should be used for authentication and/or auditing, this is configured on the Security page.

Configure Logging

Additional logging should be configured in order to provide a record of remote access connections. Logging is configured from the Logging page of the remote access server's property pages. Select Log All Events as shown here:

```
COFFEE (local) Properties                              ? X

 General | Security | IP    | PPP   Logging |

   Select the event types you want logged:

    ○  Log errors only
    ○  Log errors and warnings
    ⊙  Log all events
    ○  Do not log any events

    ☐  Log additional Routing and Remote Access information (used for
       debugging)

        To view the information contained in these logs, open the
        %windir%\tracing directory.


                              OK        Cancel       Apply
```

In addition, in Windows Server 2003, a Remote Access logging node in the Routing and Remote Access Console enables configuration of logging. Use the Settings page to limit logging to select logging for authentication, accounting, and status. (If IAS is used, and authentication and accounting tasks are split between different servers, configure authentication and accounting on the respective servers.)

If log files are moved to a SQL Server database, protect communications between the SQL server and the RRAS servers by using IPSec.

You may locate the log files to a different location, but if you do, secure the log files by setting the DACL to access by SYSTEM and Administrators groups only. Audit who accesses the log files.

Use a Firewall

Use a firewall to protect the RRAS and IAS servers. If RADIUS messages must traverse a firewall, create a rule to allow communications for the RADIUS ports listed in Table 11-2.

RADIUS Ports	Authentication Messages	Accounting Messages
Standard	UDP 1812	UDP 1813
Alternative	UDP 1645	UDP 1646

Table 11-2.   RADIUS Ports

Configure Client Access

As in Windows NT 4.0, accounts in Windows 2000 and Windows Server 2003 are denied remote access by default. Users must be configured for remote access. If Windows 2000 domains are in native mode, or Windows Server 2003 domains are at least at Windows 2000 functional level, access permission may be configured using Remote Access Policies. Otherwise, access is configured similar to that for Windows NT 4.0 domains.

HEADS UP!

Each user account is configured to Deny access, Allow access, or rely on Remote Access policies. When Remote Access policies are used, connections and attempts to connect are a result of a combination of account dial-in properties and remote access policy constraints. However, if an IAS profile constraint is configured to ignore user dial-in properties, then account dial-in properties are not considered. A user may be configured in account properties to Deny remote access, and yet it may be possible for that account to connect. To evaluate remote access, you must evaluate each remote access policy in addition to user settings.

For each user account, remote access is configured from the Dial-in tab of the user account properties as shown in Figure 11-4.

Use L2TP/IPSec VPNs

Where dial-up access is required, require the use of VPNs and do not allow plain dial-up connections. VPNs are a better choice for security. Two VPN types can be configured. Where possible, use L2TP/IPSec. PPTP is considered to be a less secure VPN protocol than L2TP/IPSec; however, it can provide secure communications if correctly configured. In general, though, L2TP/IPSec is simply a better choice. Important differences in these technologies are listed in Table 11-3.

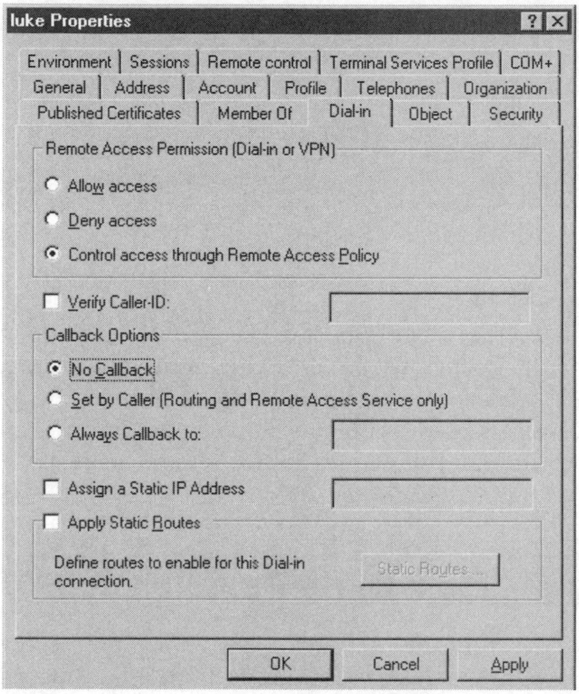

Figure 11-4. Remote access can be controlled via Remote Access Policies.

Technology	PPTP	L2TP/IPSec
Encryption	Microsoft Point-to-Point Encryption (MPPE). Only the data payload is encrypted.	IPSec. Encrypts most parts of the packet.
Tunnel	PPTP	L2TP
Authentication	User based. May be mutual, for example with MS-CHAPv2.	Requires mutual machine authentication via certificates. (Can be configured for shared secret. Do not do so.)
NAT	Typically no problems.	Can cause problems as NAT-T-compliant clients and servers enable the use of IPSec over NAT.

Table 11-3. Differences in PPTP and L2TP/IPSec VPNs

When VPN access is configured during setup, both PPTP and L2TP/IPSec ports are configured on the RRAS server. No configuration is possible directly on the ports. Settings on clients determine which protocol is used; however, if you can restrict VPN access to one or the other, you may delete the other type of communication port.

NOTE The L2TP/IPSec standard as originally written is incompatible with NAT because IPSec-encrypted packets including a checksum calculated over the IPSec source address. Since NAT modifies the source address, packets are considered to be corrupt or modified and dropped when received. NAT-Traversal, or NAT-T, uses UDP to encapsulate the IPSec packet, and therefore the packet can pass through the NAT server without a modification that will cause problems for IPSec. The NAT server must implement NAT-T. The Windows Server 2003 implementation of Internet Key Exchange (IKE), a component of IPSec, can detect NAT-T and use UDP-ESP encapsulation.

Use Remote Access Policies

When remote access policies are used, user accounts in Windows Server 2003 and/or Windows 2000 domains are configured to Control Access Through Remote Access Policy. However, the default remote access policy is configured to deny all remote access requests. Do not delete the default remote access policy.

Remote access policies are used to provide remote access configuration. The beauty of remote access policies is that many policies can be created, each specifically designed for a group of clients, a time of day, or some physical device requirement. This allows for many models of remote access control. While it is not the most desirable response, you can create a weak policy for use with legacy clients, while retaining more secure authentication and encryption for others. The weakest connections do not have to dictate security for the entire organization. Hardening remote access connections can be accomplished by setting up proper remote access policies. The following list of hardening steps is presented during a walkthrough of remote access policy creation for connections by the custom-created Auditors group. When IAS is used to centralize RRAS, additional settings can be configured. Techniques for hardening connections according to policy conditions are listed in Table 11-4. A policy condition is checked when a connection attempt is made. If the properties of a connection match the policy condition in a remote access policy, then the remote access policy is applied.

Condition	Recommendation
Authentication Type	Create policies that deny connections based on the use of legacy authentication types.
Called Station-ID	Combine with user groups and/or times of day and deny access to specific numbers. Identify restraints for allowed connections to a specific number.
Calling Station–ID	Create policy profile restrictions according to the specific location.

Table 11-4.   Policy Conditions

Condition	Recommendation
Day and Time restrictions	Deny or allow access according to the time of day.
Tunnel type	Deny or allow access depending on the protocol; specifically, prevent access via PPTP to force use of L2TP/IPSec.
Windows Groups	Deny or allow access by Windows user group.
Service Type	Deny connections according to the service requested; for example, prevent the use of telnet through this remote access server.

Table 11-4.   Policy Conditions *(continued)*

To use remote access policies:

1. Right-click the Remote Access Policy node of the Routing and Remote Access console and select New Remote Access Policy. Then click Next.

2. Select Set Up a Custom Policy, enter a name for the new policy, and then click Next.

3. Click Add to add a policy condition. Select Windows-Groups and click Add.

4. Click Add and enter or browse to and select the Auditors group.

5. Click Grant Remote Access Permissions; then click Next.

6. Click the Edit Profile button to open the Dial-in Profile property pages, as shown here:

7. Restrict connection type to VPN by selecting Allow Access Only Through These Media (NAS Port Type) and then selecting Virtual, as shown here:

8. Harden authentication. Click the Authentication tab; then click EAP Methods.

9. Click Add and select Smart Card or Other Certificate, and then click OK.

10. Click all other checked authentication methods to deselect them.

11. Require Strong Encryption. Select the Authentication tab.

12. Click to deselect Basic Encryption, click to deselect Strong Encryption, and click to deselect No Encryption.

13. Click OK. Then click Next and then Finish.

Harden Remote Access Clients

Client hardening should be done as a matter of installation and upkeep. Of critical importance on remote access clients is the use of a personal firewall and updated antiviral product. In addition, harden authentication, policy use, and encryption on the client. Client configuration can be centralized using Group Policy and for Windows NT 4.0, by creating profiles using the Connection Manager Administration Kit (CMAK). Like IEAK, CMAK is simply a way to create a standard user remote access profile and distribute it from a central location. The profile can be installed as part of an IEAK Package. A version is available for Windows 2000, Windows XP, and Windows Server 2003.

Use IAS to Centralize Authentication, Accounting, and Authorization

The Internet Authentication Service is the Microsoft implementation of RADIUS. When IAS is added to a network, it can provide centralized authentication, authorization, and auditing for remote access. Remote access policies are configured on the IAS server and manage policy for all RRAS servers configured to use the IAS server. (If remote access policies exist on the RRAS server, only the IAS remote access policies will be used.)

Harden the IAS server as you would the RRAS server. In addition, harden authentication and communications between RRAS and IAS servers.

Harden RADIUS/RRAS Authentication

When IAS is used for authentication, a shared secret must be configured on the RRAS and IAS servers and is used to authenticate connections between them. Use a long shared secret (22 characters or more) composed of a random sequence of letters, numbers, and punctuation and change it often. Use a different shared secret for each RADIUS client and RADIUS server pair, and for each RADIUS proxy and RADIUS server pair. (This will not be possible if you specify RRAS servers by IP address range.)

Provide RADIUS Message Authentication and Integrity

Use the Message Authenticator Attribute to protect IAS from spoofed IP addresses. RRAS servers are identified in the IAS properties and used to determine which RRAS servers can connect to IAS. When the Message Authenticator Attribute is used, an MD5 hash of the RADIUS message is made using the shared secret as a key. The IAS server can therefore determine that the message came from an RRAS server with knowledge of the shared secret, not just a server with one of the approved IP addresses. This also guarantees the integrity of the message.

The RADIUS Message Authenticator Attribute is configured on the property page of the RADIUS client in the RADIUS Clients node of the Internet Authentication Services console, as shown in Figure 11-5.

Use IPSec to Secure RADIUS Messages

Use IPSec to secure the entire RADIUS message. Create an IPSec policy that secures all communication between the RRAS and IAS servers.

Secure Wireless Access

Wireless access points (WAPs, or sometimes simply APs) should be considered the equivalent of remote access servers when a policy for their use is designed. While many steps can be taken to make wireless networks more secure without these advanced techniques, these techniques can markedly improve wireless security. A general discussion of hardening the normal wireless network is described in *Hardening Network Infrastructure* by Wes Noonan (McGraw-Hill/Osborne, 2004), a companion book in this series.

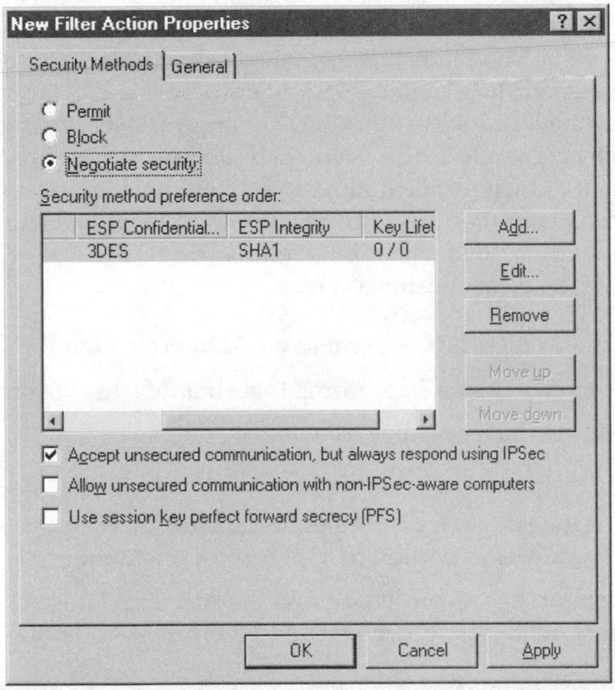

Figure 11-5.   Insist on the use of the Message Authenticator Attribute.

The measures described in the sections that follow should be used to secure wireless access using Windows RRAS.

Require APs to Be Sanctioned by IT

A wireless security policy should dictate that APs are to be implemented only by IT and should specify enforcement consequences for setting up a rogue AP. Rogue APs should be disabled, and where security policy dictates, the employee who installs them should be terminated.

Require WPA and/or 802.1x Authentication

The initial wireless APs did not provide for real authentication. Instead, the network identification of the network is typically all that is required. The identification, or SSID, can easily be discovered and provides no security at all. An alternative to this "open system" authentication mode, a *shared key* can be provided to clients and required for connection. To provide real authentication, and to resolve other security protocol issues, the new Wi-Fi Protected Access (WPA) standard, based on the upcoming 802.11i standard, is available. Unfortunately, device and software modifications are required to use WPA. You can implement 802.1x authentication, Protected EAP (PEAP) authentication, Temporal Key Integrity (TKIP) for key exchange methodologies, and Michael for integrity, all of which are parts of the standard, using IAS. You must add an upgrade to Windows XP Professional in order to use the new protocols. Windows 2000 IAS will also require an upgrade. You can find 802.1x client software for Windows 2000 and, with a support agreement, for Windows 98, Windows ME, and Windows NT 4.0.

When 802.1x authentication is added, a client requests a connection to the wireless access point, which acts as a RADIUS client. IAS can use Active Directory or its own account database for authentication and remote access policies to allow, deny, and restrict connections. Encryption keys can be automatically issued to authorized clients and changed frequently without client intervention.

To configure 802.1x authentication on IAS:

1. Establish the wireless access point as a RADIUS client in the IAS interface.

2. Configure the wireless AP according to its manufacturer's instructions.

3. Create a Remote Access Policy for wireless clients.

4. Use the Wireless-Other or Wireless 802.11 NAS-Port type Policy condition.

5. Select the Wireless-Other or Wireless 802.11 media in the Allow Access Only Through These Media portion of the Dial-in Constraints.

6. Edit the Remote Access profile, and on the Advanced page click Add, select Termination-Action, as shown here, and then click Add.

7. On the Enumerate Attribute Information dialog, change the Attribute Value to RADIUS-Request as shown in the following illustration. Then click OK. This prevents disconnection when XP clients re-authenticate.

8. Create a Connection Request Policy. Remote Access Policies restrict and manage connections from clients. Connection Request Policies manage RADIUS client. Use the policy to restrict wireless AP to time of day, days of week. Connection Request Policies are created by right-clicking the Connection Request Policies node in IAS. The policy is similar to a Remote Access Policy.

Configure 802.1x client authentication using Group Policy:

1. Open the GPO for editing and right-click Computer Configuration. Then choose Windows Settings | Security Settings | Wireless Network (IEEE 802.11) Policies.

2. Select Create Wireless Network Policy, and then click Next.

3. On the General tab, in the Networks to Access, select Access Point (Infrastructure) Networks only. This will prevent connections to ad hoc networks, or to client-to-client wireless networks.

4. Select Use Windows to Configure Wireless Networks Settings for Clients. This sets a preference for Windows configuration over a third-party wireless connection that may be installed on the client computer.

5. Leave cleared: Automatically Connect to Non-Preferred Networks, as shown in the following illustration. (You do not want clients to connect to unknown and unapproved networks without user knowledge.)

6. Select the Preferred Networks tab and select Add to define and configure 802.1xconfiguration. Restricting accessible networks protects clients from inadvertent connections to rogue networks.

7. Enter the SSID of the network.

8. Select the IEEE 802.1x tab.

9. Select and configure the EAP type. Choices are Smart Card or Other Certificate, or Protected EAP (PEAP).

10. Click the Settings button.

11. Select the trusted root certificate for the server in the Trusted Root Certification Authority box.

12. Select the authentication method in the Select Authentication drop-down box. In this example, as shown in the following illustration, Secured Password (EAP-MSCHAP v2) is selected. This method encrypts the authentication credentials, thus protecting them from a network-based attack. By default, Windows credentials of the logged-on user are used; however, the Configure

button can be used to prevent that, and a dialog for entering a different user ID and password is provided.

Protected EAP Properties

When connecting:

☑ Validate server certificate

☐ Connect to these servers:

Trusted Root Certification Authorities:

☐ Saunalahden Serveri CA
☑ Secure Server Certification Authority
☐ SecureNet CA Class A
☐ SecureNet CA Class B
☐ SecureNet CA Root
☐ SecureNet CA SGC Root
☐ SecureSign RootCA1
☐ SecureSign RootCA2

Select Authentication Method:

Secured password (EAP-MSCHAP v2) ▾   [Configure...]

☐ Enable Fast Reconnect

[OK]   [Cancel]

13. Click OK to return and review settings as shown here:

New Preferred Setting Properties

Network Properties | IEEE 802.1x

☑ Enable network access control using IEEE 802.1x

EAPOL-Start message: [Transmit ▾]

Parameters (seconds)

Max start: [3]   Start period: [60]

Held period: [60]   Authentication period: [30]

EAP type: [Protected EAP (PEAP) ▾]

[Settings...]

☐ Authenticate as guest when user or computer information is unavailable

☑ Authenticate as computer when computer information is available

Computer authentication: [With user re-authentication ▾]

[OK]   [Cancel]

Use VPNs

A VPN can be established with the remote access server placed on the network between the AP and the network. Clients connect to the AP in the normal manner, but access to the rest of the network must be established through a VPN connection. This provides authentication, authorization, and confidentiality between the wireless client and the rest of the network.

Protect Web Communications with SSL

Using SSL to protect web-based communications requires the use of certificates. Certificates are used to provide server authentication, proving the web server's identity to the client browser or application. They are also used for secure exchange of secure keys to be used for encrypting communications between client and server. This is the basis for the secure exchange of data for e-commerce and other sensitive web communications.

Client authentication can also be required and is discussed in Chapter 12. Server-side use of SSL is configured in this way:

1. Use the IIS Administration tools to create a certificate request.

2. Forward the request to a public or private certification authority (CA)

3. Install the returned certificate on the web server.

4. Configure site requirements for SSL authentication.

Chapter 12

Harden Windows Using PKI and Harden PKI

- Harden Windows Using PKI
- Harden PKI

A network's public key infrastructure (PKI) is the sum of the components it uses to implement the use of certificates. In most environments, this means the physical certification authority (CA), a software and hardware combination that issues and manages the certificates, a policy that details how PKI will be administered, the procedures that detail how the policy will be fulfilled, and the certificates themselves. Additional elements may be a registration authority (RA) that accepts requests for certificates but does not issue them, various interfaces for certificate request, and in the Windows world, certificate templates. The entire purpose of a PKI is to provide advanced security capabilities to aide in the protection of network resources including data and communications. PKI itself, therefore, must be secured.

Harden Windows Using PKI

Default mechanisms for information systems are no longer impediments to attacks. The common password is a poor barrier. When correctly managed and designed password policies are implemented and enforced, passwords can be the beginning of good access control. However, this is often not the case: users create weak passwords and share them freely; systems remain accessible via blank passwords or weak ones that are easily cracked. Likewise, permission settings can protect access to data but are subject to physical attacks—they pose no problem for the intruder who can access data drives with another operating system. It is also true that sensitive, critical information is most likely to be transmitted using clear text and therefore is vulnerable to sniffing attacks.

These processes can be made more secure by the implementation and use of Public Key Infrastructure. Windows systems have built-in capability to use various PKI methodologies. The Encrypting File System (EFS) is available for Windows 2000, Windows XP Professional, and Windows Server 2003, as is IPSec protection for LAN communications. L2TP/IPSec VPN servers can be provided by Windows 2000 Server and Windows Server 2003, while client systems have native or updatable VPN client support. IIS 4.0, 5.0, and 6.0 web servers support SSL, and certificate authentication is a built-in default for post–Windows NT 4.0 systems built on NT technology.

Harden Authentication Using PKI

Authentication can be hardened via the use of certificates. This is because knowledge of the associated private key (the one that pairs with the public key embedded in the certificate) can be restricted to the assigned account. In most implementations, after a user or computer account name is used to request authentication, the private key is used to encrypt a copy of some data known to the authentication server. The authentication server can use the public key bound to the account name by the certificate to decrypt the data and compare the result with the original string. If the data matches, then the account is authenticated.

HEADS UP!

Simply implementing PKI won't improve security at all unless the organization changes its attitude and security practices. It is possible to implement PKI and still not have good security. However, it is possible to implement sound PKI practices and harden PKI implementations so that it is easier to obtain and maintain security. The use of smart cards or other two-factor-based authentication devices is an example. If smart cards are used, two things are necessary for authentication, the card and the card PIN. It is much harder for an intruder to obtain both of these than it is for him to obtain a password. However, if it is easy to request and obtain a smart card, if users tape a copy of their PIN to the back of the smart card, and if privileges associated with user accounts are not correctly managed, the overall impact of smart card usage is a false sense of security. It is also possible that the complexity of the technology will mean improper implementation. No PKI implementation should be approached without training, study, planning, and testing.

Use Certificates for IPSec Policy Authentication

IPSec policy implementation in Windows 2000, Windows XP, and Windows Server 2003 allows a choice of authentication methods. One of them is certificates. Certificates are required for L2TP/IPSec VPNs and optional for IPSec use between two Windows computers or between Windows computers and devices such as Cisco routers.

The authentication choice is made from the Security Methods dialog box and can be done during policy creation or afterward. To change the authentication method to use certificates:

1. Obtain a computer certificate for each computer that will use the policy. If an Enterprise CA is part of the computer's domain, automatic issuance can be configured. If not, use the manual request method documented in "Train Users in Certificate Request Procedures," later in this chapter.

2. Ensure that a copy of the CA certificate from the CA that supplied the certificate for the authenticating computer is located in the computer store of the IPSec peer. Where both computers have certificates from the same CA, only one certificate is required. However, because each computer's certificate is from a different CA, a copy of each CA certificate must be available in the certificates stores of both computers.

3. Open the IPSec Security Policy Management console and double-click the IPSec policy.

4. Select the rule and click Edit.

5. Select the Authentication Methods page.

6. Click Add.

7. Select Use a Certificate from This Certification Authority (CA) and then click Browse.

8. Select the CA certificate for the CA that issued the certificate for the computer that will authenticate to this local computer.

9. Click OK. View the result to ensure you have selected the correct certificate as shown next, and then click OK.

10. Select any other authentication methods and click Remove; then click OK twice to close the policy.

Use Server Certificates for SSL

SSL can provide computer authentication (server or server and client) and protection for data during transport by securing the transmission of encryption keys. The first step to SSL is obtaining the SSL certificate. For internal use, a certificate from the Windows CA is fine. If you wish to secure communications with external customers, employees at remote locations, contractors, and partners, obtain a certificate from a public CA.

TIP   When a public CA is required, use the procedure that follows but at step 5, leave the default Prepare the Request Now, But Send it Later. This will produce a certificate request file. Follow the instructions of the public CA on submitting this file to them. When you receive the certificate, you must import it by following the same wizard, but selecting Import a Certificate from a PFX file. You can also follow these procedures if your Windows CA is not online. In essence, prepare a request file, transport it to the CA and request a certificate, and then return to the IIS server with the PFX file and use it.

To implement SSL in IIS 6.0:

1. Open the Internet Information Services Manager.

2. Right-click the server and select Properties.

3. Select the Directory Security tab and click the Server Certificate box in the Secure Communications portion of the page as shown here. Then click Next.

4. Select Create a New Certificate and then click Next.

5. If the certificate will be requested from your online CA, select Send the Request Immediately to an Online Certification Authority and then click Next.

6. Enter a name for the certificate.

7. Change the bit length of the encryption to a higher number if required, and then click Next. The larger the encryption key, the stronger the encryption, but the slower the processing will be.

8. Enter the legal name for your organization and the name of the department as shown here, and then click Next.

```
IIS Certificate Wizard                                           [×]
 Organization Information
    Your certificate must include information about your organization that
    distinguishes it from other organizations.

    Select or type your organization's name and your organizational unit. This is typically the
    legal name of your organization and the name of your division or department.

    For further information, consult certification authority's Web site.

    Organization:
    [Coffeehouse                                              ▾]

    Organizational unit:
    [Human Resources                                          ▾]



                                    < Back      Next >        Cancel
```

9. Enter a common name. This is the valid DNS name, in this case, coffee.contoso.com. Then click next.

10. Enter the country, state, and city; then click Next.

11. Change the SSL port if you want to use a nonstandard port, and then click Next. (Note, however, that if a nonstandard SSL port is used, you must make modifications to client URLs.)

12. Select a CA and then click Next. CAs that are online will be listed.

13. Review the request; then click Next and then Finish.

14. View the certificate by clicking he View Certificate button. This confirms that the certificate has been installed on the web server.

15. Click the Edit button to require SSL.

16. On the Secure Communications page, as shown next, click Require Secure Channel (SSL) and select Require 128-bit encryption; then click OK.

When an SSL certificate is present but SSL is not required, SSL can be used if https is used instead of http in the URL. On the other hand, if SSL is required, as configured in the preceding steps, then the http entered in a URL will change to https. If SSL use is not required, communications won't be secure unless the user or client app explicitly requests SSL.

Use Client Certificates for Client Authentication to IIS

Client certificates can also be required for authentication to IIS web sites. This is a good choice when you wish to ensure that only authorized client computers are used.

1. Open the Internet Information Services Manager.

2. Right-click the server and select Properties.

3. Select the Directory Security tab and click Edit in the Secure Communications box.

4. Select Require Client Certificates. (If you select Accept, client certificates clients without certificates will still be able to use the site.)

5. Select client certificate mapping if desired. Use Table 12-1 to determine the best strategy to use.

Client Certificate Origin	Usage
DS Mapping (available only when the web server and clients are members of a Windows 2000 or Windows Server 2003 domain)	Client certificate must be mapped to user accounts in the Active Directory.
One-to-One Mapping	IIS is used to map certificates to local accounts. When a user authenticates, the certificate is sent to the server. The server compares its copy to the copy received. They must match exactly.
Many-to-One Mapping	IIS is used to map a certificate to many accounts according to wildcard rules. All client certificates that include the criteria (such as issuer, or subject) are accepted.

Table 12-1. Select Certificate Mapping

Most mapping choices are available from the Edit button on the Secure Communication page of the web site after SSL is implemented. However, to use DS mapping, it must be selected in the master properties. This page can be located by right-clicking the web server, selecting Properties, selecting the Directory Security tab, and selecting Enable the Windows Directory Service Mapper, as shown in Figure 12-1.

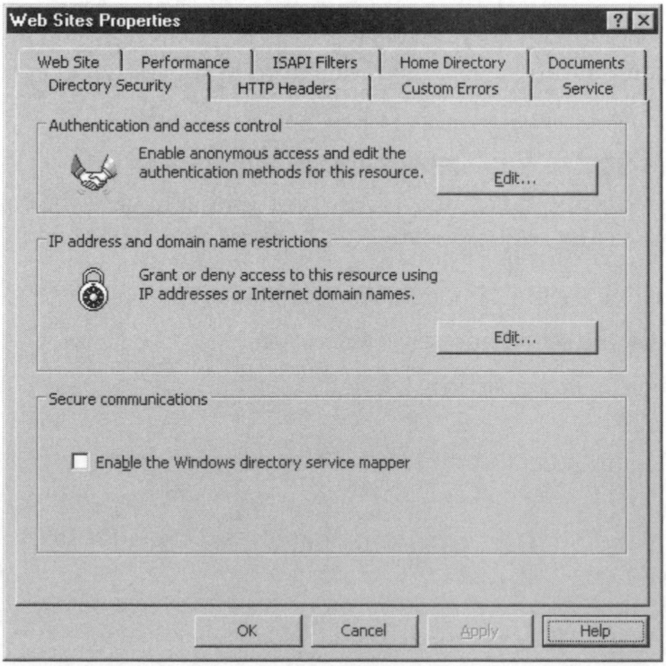

Figure 12-1. Enable DS Client certificate mapping.

Use Smart Cards and Other Hardware Devices for Authentication

Passwords are difficult to manage and control. While a strong password policy improves security, it must be vigorously enforced. Users must be trained in how to create strong passwords, and to resist sharing or revealing their password. More advanced techniques that incorporate two-factor authentication are more secure. Two-factor authentication, the requirement to use something you have, such as a smart card, and something you know, such as the related PIN number, are much harder to attack.

The first step in smart card implementation is to add a vendor-specific *cryptographic service provider (CSP)* to the CA. A CSP contains the code for the cryptographic processes. Only enterprise CAs may issue smart card certificates. Two default CSPs for smart cards, one for Gemplus and one for Schlumberger, are provided. Windows Server 2003 also includes the Infineon SICRYTP CSP. Additional CSPs can be installed and are typically provided along with the initial purchase of smart cards from a specific vendor.

Next, the smart card certificate template should be configured to allow those individuals who will be required to use smart cards, to request them. A typical smart card usage policy requires all users to employ them, in which case the Domain Users group can be selected. In some installations, however, only unique groups such as Administrators are required to use smart cards. In this case, that group can be granted permission. Instructions for granting template permissions can be found in the section "Apply Template Permissions" later in this chapter.

Finally, smart card certificate enrollment can be accomplished via client request and issuance, via a smart card enrollment station (smart cards are requested on behalf of users by an authorized smart card enrollment agent), or with Windows Server 2003 and Windows XP clients, automatically.

Protect Data with Certificates

The Encrypting File System is enabled by default, and when it is first used, a certificate is created for the user. If an enterprise CA is available and users have permission to enroll EFS certificates, the CA will generate a certificate. However, if certificate services are not available, an EFS certificate will be generated by the operating system. There are many advantages to providing CA-issued EFS certificates:

- Certificates can be revoked.
- Certificates for file recovery agents can be managed. Approved accounts can be granted permission to request file recovery agent certificates. Instead of relying on automatically generated recovery agent certificates for the first domain administrator, dedicated accounts can be required and agents selected. Granular application, including different recovery agents for different OUs, is also possible.
- A more robust and secure process can be designed for file recovery.

Other types of data protection that relate to communications can also be configured. Specifically:

- The use of SMTP for replication of AD data requires computer certificates for domain controllers.
- IPSec policies can elect to use computer certificates for authentication.
- L2TP/IPSec VPNs require certificates for authentication.

Harden PKI

Implementing PKI in a Windows environment is very simple. Implementing it correctly and securely requires planning and knowledge beyond the steps that are required to get it up and running. If you choose to use PKI to secure Windows networks, your first obligation is to understand the steps necessary to do so in a way that will secure the public key infrastructure itself. Without this, you will only obtain a false sense of security. You must invest time in planning the correct infrastructure for your organization, and you must use the information that follows to ensure that the infrastructure itself is secure.

Harden Certificate Authority Computers

The first step in securing the CA infrastructure is to ensure that computers that will be used as CAs are hardened. Follow standard procedures for installing Windows, including doing so without connectivity to the production network or Internet, applying the most current service pack and security hotfixes, and using security baseline templates. In addition:

- CA computers should not run other services.
- The local Administrators group of the CA should have limited membership, and elevated privileges of any kind should be severely limited.
- While it is possible to install certificate services on a Windows NT 4.0 server, many improvements and security advances have been made to Windows 2000 and Windows Server 2003. Always use the most recent version of the OS as the basis for certificate services.

Implement a CA Hierarchy

Windows CAs may be stand-alone or Enterprise CAs. Enterprise CAs are integrated into the Windows Active Directory domain. While it is possible to install and use a single stand-alone Windows CA, for all but the most minimal uses of certificate services, this is probably not the best choice. Instead, a combination of stand-alone and Enterprise CAs should be implemented in a CA hierarchy in order to provide the most secure, reliable, scalable, and flexible infrastructure.

A CA hierarchy is implemented by installing the first CA as a root CA and implementing additional subordinate CAs by using CA certificates issued by the root CA, or by another CA in the hierarchy. The root CA does not obtain its CA certificate from another CA; instead, it creates its own self-signed CA certificate during installation. Figure 12-2 shows an example of a CA hierarchy.

Protect the Root CA

The root CA is the root of your PKI. Since it issues the CA certificates for the other CAs in your hierarchy, compromise of the root CA means compromise of the entire hierarchy. You will not be able to rely on any of the security implemented via certificates issued by your PKI.

Keep the Root CA Offline

Implement a stand-alone root CA. The root CA can be installed on a computer that has no connections to any network and should never be connected to a network. Special preparation and installation procedures must be undertaken in order to fulfill this requirement.

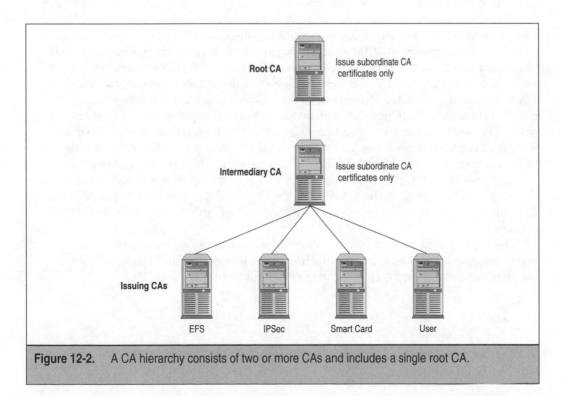

Figure 12-2.   A CA hierarchy consists of two or more CAs and includes a single root CA.

Prepare the Server for CA Installation   To prepare for root CA installation, synchronize the data and time on the hardened Windows 2000 or Windows Server 2003 server and prepare a capolicy.inf file. Time and date should be synchronized by manually adjusting them on the server to match the time and date of the Active Directory root domain PDC emulator. Remember, the server will never be online. Time and date should be synchronized because many CA processes are time dependent. The root CA will be used to issue CA certificates, and all certificates have a validity period. The *validity period* is the interval between the time the certificate becomes valid and the time at which it is no longer valid. If the time is not synchronized with the Active Directory time, certificate usage may be impaired. For example, when subordinate CA certificates are issued by the root CA, removable storage must be used to transport the certificate file to the subordinate CA. If the issued certificates have a time that is sometime in the future for the subordinate CA, the certificates will not be valid and you will not be able to install the subordinate CA.

A capolicy.inf file must be prepared and present on the computer that will become the root CA. The capolicy.inf file contains information necessary to the configuration of the root CA. More specifically, it can prevent the root CA certificate from including locations for the root CA Authority Information Access (AIA) and the Certificate Revocation List (CRL) distribution point (CDP). If no capolicy.inf file is available, the CA installation will assign a location on the local computer for these files. The AIA and the CDP are published in the CA's certificates and are critical for the proper functioning of PKI. The AIA location indicates where a copy of the CA certificate can be downloaded. This is needed for clients to check the validity of the CA's signature. Clients need the CDP to check to make sure that a certificate presented for use has not been revoked. Since the root CA will not be online, an alternative location must be provided; this can be done by configuring the CA's properties. However, default locations are created during CA installation and added to the root CA certificate, which is itself created during installation. The default locations will be located on the stand-alone CA computer's drive. The best solution is to issue a root certificate that has no AIA or CDP. To make this happen, a capolicy.inf file must be created and placed at the system root %systemroot% of the computer on which the root CA will be installed. The capolicy file will have no entries in the [CRLDistributionPoint] and [AuthorityInformationAccess] sections. If a capolicy.inf file is present, the CA obtains the CDP and the AIA from the capolicy.inf file during installation; if those sections of the file are blank, the CA will also leave its configuration blank.

The capolicy.inf file can contain other information; examples are provided at www.microsoft.com/technet/prodtechnol/windowsserver2003/technologies/security/ws3pkibp.mspx. Here is an example file listing:

```
[version]
Signature="WindowsNT$"
[Certsrv_Server]
RenalKeyLength=4096
```

```
RenewalValidityPeriod=Years
[CRLDistributionPoint]
[AuthorityInformationAccess]
```

Install the CA

To install the CA is simple:

1. Open Add/Remove Windows Components via Start | Settings | Control Panel | Add/Remove Programs.

2. Select Windows Certificate Services.

3. At the warning, click OK; then click Next.

4. Click Stand-Alone Root CA.

5. Select the Use Custom Settings to Generate the Key Pair and CA Certificate check box; then click Next.

6. Leave the default Cryptographic Service Provider (CSP) as Microsoft Strong Cryptographic Provider.

7. Leave the default integrity algorithm as SHA-1 but select a 4096-bit key. Then click Next. (A stronger key for the root CA is justified and will have little effect on performance, since the root CA will be used only to issue CA certificates.)

8. Enter a common name for the CA.

9. Enter the distinguished name suffix.

10. Enter **20 years** for the validity period. While the default period is 5 years, make the validity period longer for your convenience. If there is a reason to renew the root CA certificate before that time period ends, you can do so.

11. Accept the default storage location and click Next.

12. Once the system has completed its work in configuring the CA components, click OK at the IIS warning message. IIS should not be installed on the stand-alone root CA.

13. If required, browse to a location for the Windows server installation disk.

14. When the installation is complete, click Finish.

15. Open the Certification Authority console from the Administrative Tools menu and check to ensure the CA started.

16. Close the console.

Provide Physical Protection

The CA should be kept in a vault or other isolated, protected enclosure, and access to the location should be limited. Do not allow access to employees other than those authorized to administer and maintain the server.

Further protection can be obtained by providing a secure hardware-based location for CA key storage. A hardware security module (HSM) interfaces with the root CA (or any CA) and can be used to store the root CA certificate keys. An example of an HSM is nCipher's nShield. This hardware encryption device affords greater protection for the root CA by providing hardware-based encryption and storage of the private key. The keys are accessible only with appropriate smart cards and PINs.

Backup Keys

Immediately after installation, a backup of the root CA keys should be made and placed in a safe place. The Certutil tool can be used by issuing the following command:

```
certutil –backupkey –config computer_name\ca_name –p password A:
```

In the command, replace *computer_name* with the name of the root CA computer, replace *ca_name* with the name of the CA, and replace *password* with a password that will be used to protect the keys. To restore the keys, the password must be known. The password can be a maximum of 32 characters.

Alternatively, the Certificates console can be used. Add the local computer certificates console to an MMC, and then follow these steps:

1. Expand Certificates | Local Computer | personal Folder | Certificates.

2. Right-click the CA certificate in the details pane and select All Tasks, then Export, and then Next.

3. Select Yes, Export the Private Key and then click Next twice.

4. Enter and confirm a password, and then click Next followed by Finish.

5. Store the certificate file in a safe place.

Configure an AIA and a CDP for the Root CA

The capolicy.inf file, if used properly, creates a root CA with a blank AIA and CDP entry. You must add these locations before issuing any CA certificates, and before generating a CRL.

To add these locations:

1. Open the Certification Authority console and select the CA.

2. Select Properties from the Action menu.

3. Click the Extension tab, click the Select Extension drop-down box, and then click Authority Information Access (AIA).

4. If a web location will be provided, use the Select Extension drop-down box to select AIA and use the Add button to add the location for the AIA. An example

web location is given next. (Use the Insert button to insert variables such as CaName.)

```
http:<ServerDNSName>/CertEnroll/
<ServerDNSName><CaName><CertificateName>.crt
```

5. Add additional locations.

6. Use the drop-down box and click CRL Distribution Point (CDP).

7. Use the Add button to add locations.

8. Click OK.

Publish the CDP and AIA to Active Directory

The CDP must be present in the Active Directory if an Active Directory location is added to the root CA certificates. A copy of the AIA must be placed in Active Directory so that it can be made available to clients. To publish the first CRL and provide online copies of the CDP and AIA:

1. Right-click the Revoked Certificates node and select Properties.

2. In the CRL Publication Interval box, enter **6**, and then use the drop-down box to select Months. Click OK. The CRL must be manually copied to online location(s). Since the root CA will be used only to issue CA certificates, there should rarely by any certificates revoked; hence, a longer time for CA CRL revocation list publication is okay.

3. Click OK to close the property pages.

4. Stop and start the CA.

5. Once the initial CRL has been published, use Windows Explorer and browse to the <windir>\system32\CertEnroll directory. Copy the CRL file (*caname*.crl) and the root CA certificate file (*computername_rootCAname*.crt) to removable media and transfer them to the online locations.

To publish the root CA certificate and CDP to Active Directory:

1. Log on to the DC.

2. Publish the root CA certificate by using this command:

```
certutil -dspublish -f nameofrootfile.crt nameofrootca
```

3. Publish the CDP by using the command

```
certutil -dspublish -f caname.crl
```

Distribute the Root CA Certificate using Group Policy

The Root CA certificate must be available to clients. In order for a client to trust certificates issued by the hierarchy, the root CA certificate must available in its Trusted Root Certification Authorities certificate store. Publishing the root CA certificate to Active Directory makes it available; however, to place it in the client's local certificate store, use Group Policy:

1. Open a GPO linked to the domain.

2. Select Computer Configuration | Windows Settings | Security Settings | Public Key Policies.

3. In the details Pane, right-click the Trusted Root Certification Authorities policy and click Import.

4. Browse to and select a copy of the root CA certificate file.

5. Click Open.

6. Click Place All Certificates in the Following Store and then select Trusted Root Certification Authorities Store. Click Next and then Finish.

Configure Auditing

CA errors are recorded to the Application Event Log. Additional logging can be configured.

1. Enable auditing for the local computer by using the Local Security Policy. Include Success and Failure for Account Management, Audit Logon Events, Account Logon Events, Audit Object Access, Audit Policy Change, Audit Privilege Use, and Audit Systems Events.

2. Configure the Security Events log by increasing the default log size and selecting the Do Not Overwrite Events (Clear Log Manually) button.

3. Configure CA Auditing by opening the Certification Authority properties page and selecting the Auditing page. Select all audit events as shown next. Then click OK.

Use Intermediate CAs to Increase Reliability

Intermediate CAs are CAs that are subordinate to the root CA (obtain their CA certificate from the root CA) and only issue CA certificates. The certificates they issue are for CAs that either will themselves be intermediate CAs or for CAs that will issue end use certificates (issuing CAs). Intermediate CAs increase reliability by providing redundancy, and they increase scalability by providing a CA hierarchy for a geographical or divisional part of the organization that is tied to the same root CA.

Intermediate CAs can be installed as stand-alone subordinate CAs and be protected much as the root CA is. They will require similar preparation and configuration. Intermediate CAs can also be installed as Enterprise CAs and brought online as member servers in a domain.

The installation process is similar to that of the root CA, except you will choose subordinate instead of root CA during installation and will have to provide a CA certificate issued by the root CA to complete the installation. To do so, you will create a manual CA certificate request and transport it to the root CA. Certificate services will not start until the CA certificate is obtained and imported. If the CA will be an Enterprise CA, the appropriate AIA and CDP locations will be generated automatically. Additionally, you may install IIS on the subordinate CA to make further interaction with it easier.

Configure IIS

If IIS is installed, harden IIS. If IIS 6.0 is used, be aware that IIS is installed in a locked-down state and you must enable the use of ASP in order for the CA certificate pages to work. To do so:

1. Open the Internet Information Services Manager console.

2. Select the Web Services Extensions folder.

3. Right-click the ASP Pages button and select Enable.

4. Confirm that the ASP extensions are "Allowed" as shown here:

Obtain a CA Certificate from the Stand-Alone Root CA

Since the root CA is not online, during the installation of the subordinate CA, a certificate request file is created with the .req extension. It can be used to obtain a CA certificate.

1. Copy the request file to a floppy disk.

2. Transport the file to the root CA.

3. Open the root CA Certification Authority console.

4. Right-click the CA and click All Tasks; then select Submit New Request.

5. Enter the path or browse to the request file and click Open.

6. Select the Pending Requests folder in the Certification Authority console.

7. Note the Request ID. The Request ID will also be visible in the Issued Certificates node after the certificate is issued. It must be used to request a copy of the certificate.

8. Right-click the request and click All Tasks. Then click Issue.

9. Locate the issued certificate in the Issued Certificates node.

10. View the certificate to make sure the correct CDP and AIA are indicated; then close the certificate file.

11. From the command line, request a copy of the certificate by using the following command:

```
certreq -retrieve -config nameofcomputer\nameofCA requestnumber
A:\nametherequestfile.p7b
```

Import the Subordinate Certificate

The new certificate must be installed on the subordinate CA. To do so:

1. Transport the certificate file to the subordinate CA.

2. Open the Certification Authority console on the subordinate CA.

3. Right-click the CA node. Select All Tasks and then Install Certificate.

4. Browse to the floppy disk holding the file, select the file, and click Open. The CA node should turn green to indicate that the service has been started. The certificate will automatically be published to the Active Directory.

Configure the Subordinate CA

After the subordinate CA is installed, but before it is used:

Back up the CA keys.

Establish CRL and delta CRL publishing schedules.

Configure auditing.

Split Certificate Purposes Between Multiple Issuing CAs

Enterprise CAs should be established and used as issuing CAs. These CAs should not issue CA certificates, only end-use certificates. For example, one CA might be delegated to issue all smart-card certificates and another to issue all IPSec certificates. Your arrangement, location, and purpose for each issuing CA will be dictated by the requirements of your PKI.

Installation will be similar to installing the intermediary CAs except that if intermediary CAs are online, the issuing CAs can obtain their CA certificates during installation. After installation, perform configuration steps as described for intermediary CAs.

Provide Physical Protection for Subordinate CAs

If intermediary CAs are installed as stand-alone CAs, protect them by providing secure locked locations and limit physical access. Online subordinate CAs should be provided protection beyond that applied to ordinary servers. Locked racks, hardware-based key storage, requirements for smart card or other hardware-based logon, and limited physical access should be standard operating procedures.

Require Certificate Approval

In Windows 2000, stand-alone CAs cannot automatically issue certificates. Instead, each request must be approved. Enterprise CAs, on the other hand, automatically issue requested certificates. The assumption is that users have been authenticated by Active Directory, and certificates are restricted using certificate template permissions. Your policy and practice should reflect the needs of your organization. It may be just fine to automatically issue certificates for some purposes but not others.

Require Certificate Approval for Stand-Alone CAs

Windows Server 2003 CAs use these same defaults, but the defaults can be modified. A stand-alone CA can issue certificates automatically. This modification should not be made. An Enterprise CA can require approval, but this is probably not a practical way to operate an issuing CA that must issue thousands of certificates. To make this choice for the entire CA:

1. Open the CA Properties pages.
2. Select the Policy Module page.
3. Click the Properties button.
4. On the Request Handling page, click the Set the Certificate Request Status to Pending check box, as shown next, to require approval of every certificate request.

Require Certificate Approval for Some Certificate Types

A Windows Server 2003 Enterprise CA installed in a Windows Server 2003 functional level domain can create custom templates. One of the items that can be configured is the requirement that the certificate be manually approved. This means that the CA can be configured to automatically issue some certificates and yet require approval for others. An example of a certificate that should require approval is the Key Recovery Agent certificate. It is configured this way by default. To require certificate approval:

1. Right-click the Certificate Templates node in the Certification Authority console and select Manage.

2. In the Certificate Templates console, right-click the template and select duplicate template.

3. Enter a name for the new template.

4. Select the Issuance Requirements page.

5. Select CA Certificate Manager Approval as shown here:

Limit Certificate Issuance

Just as servers should be limited to running on the services that they actually need, CAs can be limited to issuing on the types of certificates that they are authorized to issue, and certificates can be managed by restricting who may obtain them.

Reduce Certificate Types Issued

Limit CAs to issue only the types of certificates they need to issue. This can be done for Windows 2000 Enterprise CAs by deleting the templates that are not required in the CA Policy node. Windows Server 2003 CAs can be limited by deleting such templates from the CA Certificate Templates node. For intermediate Enterprise CAs, eliminate all certificates except the Subordinate Certification Authority certificate. For Issuing CAs, delete that template, and all templates for certificates that the CA will not issue. By default, the CA cannot issue all types of certificates. Additional certificates can be added to the CA by right-clicking the Certificates Templates node, selecting New and then Certificate Template to Issue, and selecting the templates from the Enable Certificate Templates dialog box as shown in Figure 12-3.

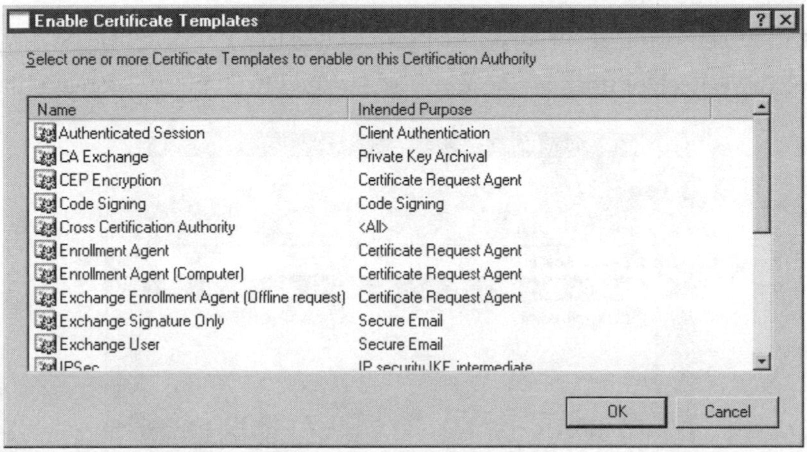

Figure 12-3.   Select additional certificate templates to issue.

Apply Template Permissions

Template permissions specify who may obtain a certificate. Always set template permissions to limit access to templates to only those users who have the need and approval to use that type of template. For example, if EFS Recovery Agents are going to be created, best practices indicate the following:

- Create a group to hold accounts that can be used for EFS Recovery.
- Open the EFS Recovery Agent template properties.
- Use the Security page and add the new group.
- Select this group and give them the Read and Enroll Permissions.
- Select Domain Admins and deselect the Enroll permission.
- Select Enterprise Admins and deselect the Enroll permission.

In Windows 2000, certificate templates can be managed by Adding the services node to the Active Directory Sites and Services console and opening the Certificate Templates node, and then setting security for each template. To restrict template enrollment in Windows Server 2003 CAs:

1. Right-click the Certificates Template node in the Certification Authority console.
2. Double-click the template.

3. Select the Security page.

4. Add or select the group to apply permissions to.

5. Select to check or uncheck, as appropriate, the Enroll permission as shown here:

6. Click OK.

Establish Role Separation

A sound security practice is to establish role separation wherever possible. This means that you restrict user actions and access to only those duties and resources that users should have access to. One example is presented in Chapter 10 in a discussion of file permissions for Accounts Receivable and Accounts Payable Clerks. Windows Server 2003 allows role separation of CA administration and certificate management. To accomplish this:

1. Create separate custom Windows groups for each role, for example, CA Admins and CA Managers.

2. Add appropriate user accounts to each group. No user should have an account in both groups.

3. Open the Certification Authority properties pages and select the Security tab.

4. Add the new groups using the object picker.

5. Select the CA Admins group and give them the Manage CA permission.

6. Select the Certificate Manager group and give them the Issue and Manage Certificates permission as shown here:

7. Select Domain Admins and Enterprise Admins groups and remove their permissions for administering the CA and certificates.

Enforce Role Separation

Giving different groups different responsibilities promotes role separation. However, nothing prevents a user from obtaining membership in each group and thus voiding the advantages of role separation. In addition, if administrator groups' permissions are not correctly configured and administrators monitored, role separation is also not accomplished.

Windows Server 2003 CAs, however, are subject to enforced role separation. That is, if separate groups are given distinct roles, you can enforce role separation. If an account should be placed in both management groups, they will not be able to perform either administrative role. Likewise, members of the operating system administrative groups no longer have permissions to administer the CA.

HEADS UP!

An administrator can remove role separation and regain the ability to administer the CA. If you want to keep roles separate, and you should, you must also train administrators, prohibit them from removing role separation unless approved, and audit administrative actions.

To enforce role separation:

1. Configure the groups and make sure no account has access to both.
2. From the command prompt, issue the following command:

   ```
   certutil -getreg ca\RoleSeparationEnabled
   ```

3. Stop and start certificate services.

TIP To remove role separation, use the following command:

```
certutil -delreq ca\RoleSeparationEnabled
```

Configure Autoenrollment

Autoenrollment of certificates can contribute to security, since users do not have to figure out how to enroll. By making the activity transparent, or by requiring minimal steps, you make security happen without user resistance.

In Windows 2000, enrollment for most certificates consists of a manual request for a certificate followed by certificate issuance. In some cases, where administrator approval is required, enrollment is not completed until the administrator issues the certificate and the user returns to the request console to download the approved and issued certificate. The exception is that computer certificates can be configured using Group Policy to be automatically issued to domain member computers.

Windows Server 2003 provides three places where autoenrollment can be configured:

1. By using the certificate template
2. By using group policy
3. By modifying enrollment security permissions

A user must have both enrollment and autoenrollment permissions on a template in order to autoenroll a certificate. The autoenrollment permission is new to version 2 certificates in Windows Server 2003. Version 1 certificates in Windows 2000 or Windows Server 2003 will not have this permission. To configure autoenrollment using certificate templates:

1. Open the templates property pages by using the Certificate Templates console.

2. Double-click the certificate.

3. Select the Request Handling page.

Use one of the options explained in Table 12-2 and illustrated here:

Setting	Description
Enroll Subject Without Requiring Any User Input	Users won't know that a certificate is being installed.
Prompt the User During Enrollment	User will be notified and may need to respond. An example is the installation of smart cards.
Prompt the User During Enrollment and Require User Input When the Private Key Is Used	During enrollment and during key usage, the user will need to provide input.
CSP Selection	The available CSPs are listed and the user must select the one to be used.
Supply in the Request	Disable autoenrollment.

Table 12-2. Use the Request Handling Page to Configure Autoenrollment Possibilities

There are two ways to prevent autoenrollment of certificates. One is that you can require the user to enter a subject name:

1. Select the Subject Name page.

2. Click Supply in the Request as shown here:

Alternatively, you can require signatures for certificate issuance:

1. Select the Issuance Requirements page.

2. Click This Number of Authorized Signatures.

3. Enter a number greater than 1, as shown here:

Properties of New Template

| General | Request Handling | Subject Name |

Issuance Requirements | Superseded Templates | Extensions | Security

Require the following for enrollment:

☐ CA certificate manager approval

☑ This number of authorized signatures: `2`

If you require more than one signature, autoenrollment is not allowed.

Policy type required in signature:

Application policy

Application policy:

Certificate Request Agent

Issuance policies:

Add...

Remove

Require the following for reenrollment:

◉ Same criteria as for enrollment

○ Valid existing certificate

OK   Cancel   Apply

4. Click OK to close the property pages.

Train Users In Certificate Request Procedures

With automated certificate procedures and restrictions on certificate requests, many users will not need to know how to manually request certificates. Those who do should be trained in how to obtain certificates. Those administrators who will be responsible for the management of computer certificates should also be trained in how to obtain certificates for computers. The process is similar but may vary slightly, depending on the type of certificate required. There are two distinct ways to request a certificate manually, either using web enrollment or using the Certificates snap-in. The following procedures detail requests for a user and computer certificate. More information on requesting specific types of certificates is detailed in the help files that are available through the Certification Authority interface.

To obtain a computer certificate using the Certificates snap-in:

1. Open an mm.

2. Right-click the File menu and select Add/Remove Snap-in.

3. In the Add/Remove Snap-in dialog box, Click Add.

4. In the Add Standalone Snap-in dialog box, select the Certificates snap-in and click Add.

5. In the Certificates snap-in, select Computer Account.

6. In the Select Computer dialog box, select the local computer or use the Browse button and select a different computer; then click Finish.

7. Click Close, and then click OK.

8. Expand the Certificates container, right-click on The Personal Certificates folder; then select All Tasks and click Request New Certificate.

9. Click Next, and then select the type of computer certificate desired.

10. If required, click Advanced in order to select a cryptographic service provider (CSP) and CA.

11. Click Next, enter a friendly name, click Next, and then click Finish.

To obtain a user certificate using web enrollment:

1. Open Internet Explorer.

2. Enter the URL **http://** *CA_server_name***/certsrv**.

3. Click Request a Certificate.

4. Click User Certificate.

5. If additional information is necessary, provide it; but in many cases the information necessary is provided from Active Directory for you.

6. If additional options are required, such as the selection of a CSP, then click More Options and complete the information necessary.

7. Click Submit.

8. If the web page returned indicates Certificate Pending, the administrator will need to approve the certificate and you will need to return to the certsrv web site later to obtain the certificate.

9. If the web page indicates Certificate Issued, click Install this Certificate.

10. When the process is complete, close Internet Explorer.

Harden PKI Policies, Procedures, and Practices

Despite the best intentions of administrators and the closest adherence to hardening recommendations, good security cannot be obtained unless security policy and procedures are compiled with hardening recommendations in mind. Finally, if users and administrators are not required to follow these procedures, security can and will be weakened in practice. Examples of good policies to follow have been described above. In addition, observe the following guidelines:

- Develop and follow sound backup procedures for CAs and certificates.
- Develop disaster recovery and business continuity plans for PKI.
- Practice CA recovery.
- Train employees in proper certificate usage, for example, sharing of EFS-encrypted files, smart card usage.
- Train IT staff in their specific responsibilities and duties in regard to PKI.
- Develop file or key recovery plans for EFS. Key archival is available in Windows Server 2003, and file recovery can be implemented using either Windows 2000 or Windows Server 2003.
- Implement Delta CRLs in Windows Server 2003.
- Establish a policy that spells out reasons for certificate revocation and attendant practices.

Part III

Once Is Never Enough!

Chapter 13

Harden the Security Lifecycle

- Create a Business Continuity Plan
- Generate a Security Policy
- Perform Hardened Operating System Installation
- Harden Operating System, Application, and Data Protection
- Manage Changes with a Formal Change Management Program
- Be Prepared for Disaster Recovery
- Monitor and Audit

The process of hardening systems is not a one-time job. In order to maintain a high level of information security in your organization, you must not only configure systems according to hardening recommendations, you must apply and monitor security throughout the security lifecycle. The security lifecycle of Windows operating systems is composed of the following iterative steps:

1. Business continuity planning
2. Security policy generation
3. Hardened operating system installation
4. Hardened application and data protection configuration
5. Change management
6. Disaster recovery
7. Monitoring and auditing

Create a Business Continuity Plan

Business continuity planning is, quite simply, a plan that seeks to ensure business operation in spite of any event that may disrupt the business. Events can be natural disasters such as floods and tornadoes. Events can be fire, lack of electricity, equipment malfunction, and accidents. Events can even be digital attacks or misconfiguration. In short, any event that might interrupt business operation is something that a good business continuity plan will cover. The plan will estimate risk, recommend steps to mitigate the risk, provide disaster recovery instructions, and include a plan for bringing the business back to normal operation.

TIP   The disaster recovery plan is part of the business continuity plan. Traditionally, disaster recovery planning grew out of a need to ensure that data processing could continue even if the data center was not available. In the hearts and minds of IT, disaster recovery is business continuity. To the organization, however, disaster recovery is only the immediate steps that keep the business in operation, while business continuity includes steps that bring operation back to normal and comprehends all business operations, not just IT. One example of such a distinction is that disaster recovery might include moving operations to an alternative IT site after a fire, while business continuity would go further and include the building of a new data center.

These are the steps in involved in business continuity planning:

1. Determine the plan scope.
2. Perform business impact assessment.
3. Develop plans for continuance of each business process.

4. Test the plans.

5. Implement the plans.

6. Maintain the plans.

Determine Plan Scope

While the goal of business continuity planning is to provide plans for all business operations, this is not always possible if no plan has ever been developed. In this case it is more likely that the organization will develop a plan based around some critical aspects of the organization. IT operations is a good candidate, but it is even more appropriate to single out specific operations such as order entry, shipping, invoicing, or other critical services and write a plan that encompasses manual operations as well as the flow of information through the network and data storage and processing.

You should determine if your organization has a business continuity plan. Next, obtain a copy to determine what has already been developed that covers IT operations. You should also research the status of disaster recovery planning at your organization. While disaster recovery is only one part of business continuity planning, you may find that disaster recovery planning exists, while business continuity planning does not, or that different groups are working at cross-purposes on these plans. From your research, you should be able to determine the scope of the current plan (or that there is no plan).

Next, determine what your role in the planning process should be. If a plan is already established, your role may be to participate in the testing and maintenance of the plan. If no plan is in operation, start by setting a scope for the plan. Pick an area that is critical and for which a plan can be developed. For example, you might start with planning for operations after a natural disaster, or of recovery after a security compromise.

ONE STEP FURTHER

The development of intrusion detection and response activity can be considered as part of the business continuity plan. You may find management support and budget for this activity by approaching your business continuity planning team.

Perform Business Impact Assessment

Business impact assessment (BIA) is the process of determining the impact of an event on a business process. These are the steps necessary for the assessment:

1. **Compile a list of all possible events that might have an impact on operations.** Don't forget to list every event, even if it is unlikely. Events should include not just hurricanes for coastal business and tornadoes for those in the Midwest;

each location should list all possible weather-related events. List tragedies such as fire and chemical spills. In addition, list acts of stupidity and malfeasance as well as terrorism.

2. **Identify critical services.** Critical services are those that a business cannot live without even for a short time. Examples are many of the data center operations but might not include the installation of new desktop computers. Production, order entry, shipping, and customer support of some items are critical, but vacations, renegotiation of employee benefit contracts, and the company picnic are not. You will have your own list of critical services, and you should recognize that after some time, the other operations will have to be returned to normal operation. Their replacement is also a part of business continuity planning, just not a immediately critical one in the event of a business interruption.

3. **Determine the maximum tolerable downtime (MTD) for each critical service.** The MTD is the time that is available between the cessation of operation of some critical service and the point at which the business cannot recover. The time will vary, depending on the services, the industry, the organization, and the size of the operation. Examples of MTD might be the purported two hours of downtime often quoted by major insurance companies after which they cannot survive, or the three days another company might be able to get by without shipping product. The MTD is not a number that can be pulled out of a hat; it must be arrived at by those that truly know the impact of the operation. You will have to obtain these numbers from management in the specific area. Many times, the MTD is arrived at by calculating the monetary loss that interruption of service will cause, but monetary loss is not the only factor. MTDs for IT are often determined by the operations that are performed for others. Internal IT MTDs are also important.

4. **Prepare a full report that lists all information and orders critical services by their MTDs.** Those operations that can cause the business to fail in the least amount of time are important to identify and to protect. A report on the BIA serves several purposes. Because it identifies the most critical operations over time, it is essential in the business continuity planning process. It also provides support for planning and expenses that will prevent or mitigate the impact of some disasters.

5. **Return the report to business units for validation before using in any planning.** It is important that numbers are validated, and that all parties have had the opportunity to review the information.

6. **Provide the report with recommendations for further work to senior management.** Senior management support is necessary in order to fully plan for business continuity and to implement operations that will either mitigate the impact of business interruption events or deal appropriately with them.

Reasons for Business Failure

Many things contribute to business failure. Loss of revenue is not the only factor that should be taken into consideration during the calculation of MTD. Other items include impact on other operations, loss of sales, lost clients, increased expenses, expenses necessary to restore normal operations, fines and penalties, and additional monies expended for legal and civil obligations.

Perform Risk Analysis

Where BIA seeks to identify how quickly operations must be operational after an interruption, risk analysis seeks to identify how likely a specific threat is to cause an interruption, and it seeks to place a cost for mitigating the risk. Risk analysis is often performed in order to develop a threat model for information systems. The rationale is that you should delegate scarce resources to develop mitigation for those threats that are most likely to occur or that may cause the most problems should they occur. Both BIA and risk analysis should be part of the preplanning phase of business continuity planning; that is why risk analysis is discussed in this section. However, risk analysis should be a part of any security evaluation of IT. Risk analysis can help you determine where to place your efforts. As in many other things, if you effectively deal with the areas that bring the most risk, you will have the most impact on security. While an organization-wide risk analysis should be undertaken as part of business continuity planning, you can perform risk analysis for the ongoing operations of IT. Risk analysis should also be a part of the planning for the implementation of new systems, and of the proposed changes to others.

Risk analysis can be broken down into several steps:

1. **Identify assets.** Some threats are specific to a type of asset. If you do not have that asset, you are not going to experience loss as a result of a threat to that asset.

2. **Assign value to assets.** Knowing what is at risk is important, as it influences what you might spend to protect it.

3. **Identify risks.** All risks should be listed with no attempt to filter for probability. Probability is important, but it is only one thing to consider when preparing a response to potential threats.

4. **Identify single loss equivalency (SLE).** For each risk and each asset, determine the loss possible if the risk became reality. This is different than determining the asset value. For example, if a sprinkler system breaks and destroys an e-commerce server, the server's replacement may be a few thousand dollars, but the loss potential should also include the money lost because orders cannot be placed at the server. This loss can be calculated by examining the amount of revenue gained during a similar time period.

5. **Identify annual loss equivalency (ALE).** This calculation multiples the SLE by the number of times the incident might be expected to occur in a year. Determining the probability that a specific incident will happen at all, let alone how many times a year it might happen, is not easy. However, insurance companies may be able to provide some information based on history. Experienced employees and consultants can also help. For example, if no antiviral products are in use, and patches are not kept up to date, many would argue that there is a 100 percent chance that a virus or worm will infect systems within an organization of any size.

6. **Recommend countermeasures.** Countermeasures can prevent or mitigate the extent of loss. The entire reason for performing risk analysis is to determine on which assets money and efforts should be spent. This entire book has provided recommendations for hardening efforts that are countermeasures for known and unknown risks.

Develop Plans

After information about critical operations has been compiled, proceed with the development of business continuity plans. The following actions should be considered.

- **Prevention**   Preventive plans consider what can be done to prevent events such as fire or compromise of the computer system. These plans will include items such as fire and safety inspection, insurance review, equipment maintenance, and information security hardening.

- **Mitigation**   Mitigation seeks to lessen the impact of events. Items include training, backups, offsite storage of backups and software, evacuation drills, and intrusion detection and response.

- **Emergency response**   Emergency response includes those actions taken immediately to avoid injury and loss of life, as well as to alert authorities, notify management, prevent additional damage, and rescue critical data and equipment. It's important to establish procedures and make assignments and always emphasize that people are the most important assets to save by emergency response.

- **Recovery**   Recovery is the activity that brings critical operations fully back online.

- **Normal operations**   Steps taken when business operations return to normal, in addition to providing replacement facilities and equipment, can also include the return of less critical operations such as employee benefits.

Test

Before a plan is implemented, test parts of the plan. Tests can include discussion about operations with those who will have to perform the actions designated in the plans, training on procedures, simulated walkthroughs, and full tests of recovery operations. If a plan, for example, calls for rebuilding the root CA at the offsite location, a test would encompass first rebuilding the root CA on location, and then doing the same thing at the offsite location. If recovery plans include operations that are managed by third-party organizations, then tests for contact lists should be performed at all hours. Interruption events don't always happen during business hours.

Implement Plans

Plan implementation includes more than providing each department with a copy of the plan. In many cases, plan implementation may include obtaining contracts for offsite storage and possible temporary location or other recovery efforts; increase in or different insurance; replacement of failure-prone equipment; and improvement of operations, data centers, and equipment. Also necessary may be data systems hardening steps and implementation of incident response teams or other new operations.

Employees will have to be trained, and periodic testing and maintenance planning dates established.

Maintain Plans

Businesses change and grow over time. The critical operations of today may not even be part of the business tomorrow. Phone number change, as do personnel. Change management processes at your organization should be followed to include updates to plans, and full reviews, including annual BIA, should be accomplished.

Generate a Security Policy

It should come as no surprise that you must have official recognition of what constitutes a secure system. Many of these policies may exist in your organization already. Many of them need adjustments, and many may not be written yet. Information on where security policy fits into the security lifecycle can be found in Chapter 13.

Perform Hardened Operating System Installation

Many of the recommendations made in this book can be implemented during operating system installation. For example, registry configuration and security policy items that are managed by Group Policy can be applied during system installation, as can the installation of the current service pack and all known post–service pack security patches. Doing these things during or shortly after installation but before adding the computer to the network can go a long way to protect the system from compromise. Several operations will assist you in doing so.

Prepare Default Security Templates

Many of the hardening steps recommended in this book involve changes to security policy either via Group Policy or by applying custom security templates using Security Configuration and Analysis. These methods should not be abandoned. However, the default security configuration of the operating system is created during installation by the application of default security templates. To ensure that systems are installed in the best security configuration, modify these security templates to fit your security policy, before installation. If, for example, you install the operating system from a network share, you will be adding the contents of the i386 directory from the installation CD-ROM to the share. You can then easily replace the default templates with those designed to fulfill your policy.

The default templates are for workstations, defltwk.inf; for servers, defltsv.inf; and for domain controllers, defltdc.inf. Take care to thoroughly test this process before implementing it in production.

Use Slipstreaming

Slipstreaming is the process of incorporating service pack files with the installation files at a network share. When a computer is installed from the share, the service pack code is incorporated and the newly installed computer is at the service pack level. To slipstream service packs for Windows NT 4.0, Windows XP, Windows 2000, or Windows Server 2003:

1. Put a copy of the I386 folder on a server. For this example, our path is C:\I386.

2. Assuming a service pack CD-ROM is in the D drive and the path to the update.exe file is D:\i386\update\update.exe, use the following command to slipstream the service pack:

```
D:\i386\update\update.exe –S:C:\i386
```

Use RIS to Add Service Packs During Installation

Alternatively, you can use RIS to add service packs during installation. RIS, the Remote Installation Service, was introduced with Windows 2000. Hardware-compatible PCs can boot, locate a DHCP server to obtain an IP address, connect to the network, and contact a boot RIS server to install Windows. You must create a RIS server by installing the RIS service and configuring it. For complete information on installing and configuring RIS, see "How to Use Remote Installation Service to Install Windows Server 2003 on Remote Computers" at http://support.microsoft.com/default.aspx?scid=kb;en-us;325862.

When RIS is installed, it creates many folders and files for creating RIS installations, including templates for the files that you must build to support specific installations. One template, ristndrd.sif, is the sample RIS template for creating an unattended installation file. You can rename the file, but you must use the correct syntax and keep the .sif extension. To include service packs:

1. Copy update.exe from the service pack to the sp subfolder of a network share.

2. Call update.exe by placing two commands in the [GuiRunOnce] section of the ristndrd.sif file. (After a reboot, RIS performs an administrative logon, and these commands will run.)

   ```
   net use n: \\server\share password /USER;username /peristent:no

   N: \sp\update.exe -u
   ```

3. Save the file.

Install Hotfixes During Installation

In addition to installing service packs during installation, install hotfixes. To do so, use the cmdlines.txt file approach, the srvpack.inf approach, or RIS.

Use Cmdlines.txt

To install hotfixes during installation, set up an automated installation using Setup Manager. Setup Manager (setupmgr.exe) can be found in the deploy cab file of the \support\tools folder of the Windows Server 2003 installation CD-ROM. This file can be used for both Windows Server 2003 and Windows XP. Windows 2000– and Windows NT 4.0–specific Setup Manager files must be used to prepare automated installations.

1. Create a folder to be used for distribution.

2. Use the Setup Manager tool to create the answer file, and name it unattend.txt. This file can be used to contain computer-specific information that might be needed by commands in the cmdlines.txt file. Instructions for creating the answer file are located at www.microsoft.com/resources/documentation/ WindowsServ/2003/all/deployguide/en-us/Default.asp?url=/resources/ documentation/windowsserv/2003/all/deployguide/en-us/acicb_ui_ dmof.asp.

3. Use the Setup Manager tool to create cmdlines.txt. Command lines placed in this file will run during the GUI part of Windows installation. This is where you will place commands to install hotfixes. Help in using cmdlines.txt can be found at www.microsoft.com/resources/documentation/WindowsServ/2003/all/deployguide/en-us/Default.asp?url=/resources/documentation/windowsserv/2003/all/deployguide/en-us/acicb_ui_yext.asp.

4. Add hotfix command lines to the [commands] section of the cmdlines.txt file. An example hotfix command line that would install the Q123456 hotfix is

   ```
   "Q123456 /q"
   ```

5. Add the I386 folder from the installation CD-ROM to the folder.

6. Add cmdlines.txt and unattend.txt to the i386\OEM subfolder

7. Add hotfix executable files to the \i386\oem subfolder.

Use svcpack.inf

Another way to install Windows and include current hotfixes is to use the svcpack.inf file. You must have a service pack- integrated Windows version.

TIP   The **/Q** switch, when used with the **update** command, does not provide information during file extraction. The **/N** switch prevents backup of older files, and therefore the hotfix cannot be uninstalled. The **/Z** switch prevents a reboot after the install.

---

1. Prepare a distribution share.

2. Create an I386 folder within the share.

3. Xcopy files and folders from the installation CD-ROM to the i386 folder.

4. Open i386\dosnet.inf in Notepad.

5. Find the uniproc line in the [OptionalSRCDirs] section of the file.

6. Add a line right after this that contains the word **svcpack**. The section will look like

   ```
   [OptionalSRCDirs]
   uniproc
   svcpack
   ```

7. Save the file and close it.

8. Create the i386\svcpack folder.

9. Copy hotfix executables to the i386\svcpack folder.

10. Rename the files using the 8.3 naming format. The files should have the form Q*xxxxxx*.exe.

11. Use the *filename* **–x** command to expand each hotfix to a unique temporary location.

12. Hotfixes provide new files and replacement files. For each replacement file, delete the original file from the I386 folder.

13. Copy the sp3.cat catalog file to the distribution folder if the sp3.cat file is later than the one in the distribution folder. (Use the catver.exe tool to determine the versions of the sp3.cat files.)

14. For each hotfix, copy hotfix files from the temporary folders to the distribution folder. If any of the hotfix files are in a subfolder, copy the folder and its contents to the distribution folder. (Do not copy symbols subfolders or the hotfix.exe, hotfix.inf, update.exe, update.inf, spcustom.dll, spuninst.exe, update.ver, or spmsg.dll files.)

15. Delete the i386\svcpack.inf file.

16. Create a new svcpack.inf file with Notepad and include these lines:

```
[version]
signature="Windows NT$"
MajorVersion=5
MinorVersion=0
BuildNumber=2195
[SetupData]
CatalogSubDir="I386\svcpack"
[ProductCatalogsToInstall]
Qxxxxxx.cat
[SetupHotfilesToRun]
```

17. Note the Q*xxxxxx*.cat entry under ProductCatalogsToInstall. Add a line for each catalog file provided with a hotfix.

18. Add a line in the [SetupHotfixesToRun] section of the file using the following format:

```
Qxxxxxx /q /n /z
```

19. If hotfixes include replacement drivers, edit dosnet.inf and add the following lines:

```
[OptionalSrcDirs]
svcpack
```

20. Force the use of new drivers by adding the driver name to the ForceCopyDriverCabFiles section as shown here for the usbhub.sys driver:

```
[ForceCopyDriverCabFiles]
usbhub.sys
```

21. Run Windows (2000, Server 2003, XP) setup.

22. Verify that hotfixes install by looking for them in the Add/Remove Programs tool in the Control Panel, as well as in the uninstallation folders for each hotfix in the %systemroot% folder.

Use RIS

To use RIS to install hotfixes:

1. Put patches on an accessible network share.

2. Configure RIS to install the most current service pack.

3. Add script lines to the [GuiRunOnce] section of the unattended installation file.

Harden Operating System, Application, and Data Protection

The first 12 chapters of this book outline the steps to harden Windows networks. In addition to these steps, you should learn and use appropriate steps to harden the other operating systems that you use, your network infrastructure, and the other components of your information systems. You will find a wealth of information in other books in this series, including these:

- *Hardening Network Infrastructure* by Wesley Noonan (McGraw-Hill/Osborne, 2004)

- *Hardening Linux* by Paul Love, Ronald P. Reck, John Terpstra (McGraw-Hill/Osborne, 2004)

- *Hardening Enterprise Security* by the Kansas City Five (McGraw-Hill/Osborne, 2004)

Manage Changes with a Formal Change Management Program

You will never secure your Windows network. Never. There are three reasons for this:

- **There is no such thing as perfect security.** There will always be a way that a determined attacker can compromise a system. We can only harden systems against known vulnerabilities and use standard security practices that *may* protect systems from as-yet unknown vulnerabilities.

- **New applications, new hardware, new systems, new infrastructure, and new people are constantly being added.** Each one of these brings the potential of introducing a new vulnerability.

- **The best security plans are worthless if they are not enforced.** Security policy may be disregarded, or temporary changes may be made that weaken security.

But there is hope. Everything that you do to increase the security of your Windows systems sets speed bumps and roadblocks in the way of those who would attack your systems. To keep these stumbling blocks enforced, you must implement a formal change management program. A *change management program* forces a review and approval process whenever changes are made to any aspect of information systems. These changes include software updates, hardware replacement and repairs, configuration changes, and anything that means something will be different.

Windows configuration changes (including scripts and Group Policy changes) and patching are two small parts of the program and represent two types of changes that must and can be handled by change management. Upgrades, migration, new installations, and change management programs are usually handled by committees composed of representatives from different areas of the organization, not just IT, and that may have a temporary membership when a specific area is being addressed. Typically, the change management program moves slowly and deliberately to weigh the impact and cost of proposed changes. If changes are approved, the exact procedures used for making them may be detailed along with the testing process and an audit of their correct installation and the actual impact.

Many Group Policy configuration changes will not suffer from an exhaustive review; in fact, a comprehensive examination of what they mean, how they relate to other settings already in place, and what their impact will be is a good thing. As you may have discovered, improper or untested changes to Group Policy can destroy the operation of your network just as surely as any directed attack. On the other hand, some changes to systems must be made quickly. A good change management program will have a separate procedure for things such as patching and emergency security configuration changes.

Change management offers the following benefits for security:

- Proposed changes are studied for their impact on existing systems. Current hardware, software, and wetware (people) systems are studied.

- A discussion of proposed security changes presents an opportunity for educating management about the need for security and for specific security initiatives.

- Changes that would weaken security are also subject to intensive review and may be thwarted.

Upgrades, Migration, Replacements, and New Installations

The earlier section "Perform Hardened Operating System Installation" details the steps to be used to ensure that new installations join the network already secured. An established plan for providing replacement systems and new installations of currently approved versions of Windows is not part of the change management program except as change management approves service packs and hotfixes, and installation practices must be in sync with this process.

Upgrades and/or migration to newer versions of the operating system, should, however, be considered by the change management process.

Security Configuration Change

As you attempt to institute changes to the security practices of your organization, you may feel frustrated by formal change management processes. You should, instead, champion the process. Yes, change management can delay the implementation of practices that you and I deem imperative for good security. But this same careful consideration and lumbering progress can also mean that once implemented, good security will not be lightly tossed aside.

Still, there will be times when a security configuration change must be made immediately in order to secure the network. You may find that a service pack has re-enabled a service deemed risky for your organization, or implemented a default action that now must be turned on if you are to maintain your current security status. The trick is to understand the change management process and obtain a procedure that pre-approves changes that perform maintenance, and fast-tracks emergency changes.

An important thing that should be established is the "how" of security configuration change. The approval of the actual change should be a different decision. For example, if Group Policy is used to apply security configuration changes, then once a change is approved, no discussion is required on how the change will be made.

Patch

It was not that long ago that common wisdom was "If it's not broke, don't fix it." In other words, even if Microsoft produced a patch or a service pack, no one got excited about implementing it. It is hard to realize that the patching process has become a major part of network administration in only the last couple of years. Any network administrator who does not understand that she must implement a sound patching program condemns her network to at least massive worm and virus attacks on a periodic basis and at worst gives up systems to attackers for the asking. You must patch, what's the best way?

Patching is a process that is best served by developing a procedure in concert with change management that gives systems administrators the responsibility for testing and approving each patch in concert with areas of the organization that may be impacted by the patch or lack of a patch. The patching process procedure should include the following steps:

1. Filter.
2. Order.
3. Obtain.

4. Test.

5. Apply.

Filter

First consider, which patches may impact which computers? Some patches are issued for products that are not used in your organization. They do not have to be considered, but all patches should be reviewed.

Order

Putting the current patches in order means determining which are the most critical to apply, which are next most important, and so on. Microsoft's rating can assist you in this determination, but other resources should be used as well. If you subscribe to security lists, the discussions in these lists can help you determine how to rate the vulnerabilities that the patches fix. If, for example, there is discussion or evidence attack code that seeks to leverage the flaw, then you might rate the patch as more important. Two types of security lists can help. The first lists are primarily notices of vulnerability and patch availability. These are lists such as

Microsoft's Security Bulletin Notification Service (www.microsoft.com/technet/security/bulletin/notify.mspx)

Microsoft's Security Newsletter (www.microsoft.com/technet/security/secnews/default.mspx)

CERT Coordination Center (www.cert.org/)

You can also read Microsoft's security bulletins online at www.microsoft.com/technet/security/default.mspx. Security discussion lists are a second type of list. Many of these also copy the Microsoft security bulletins, or provide pointers to them. In addition, you will find other, nonofficial vulnerability notices, discussion of problems installing patches and service packs, and other security topics.

- For a Windows-specific security list, sign up for ntbugtrac at www.ntbugtraq.com/.

- A moderated list for security information, bugtrac can be read or subscribed to at www.securityfocus.com/archive/1.

- Subscribe to an unmoderated vulnerability list, full-disclosure at http://lists.netsys.com/mailman/listinfo/full-disclosure.

You will also need to determine your own network's needs. The requirements for isolated environments will be very different from mobile systems and those directly exposed to the Internet. Deciding which systems to apply patches to in what order may also be part of your planning.

Obtain Patches Directly

Service packs and patches should be obtained only by downloading directly from Microsoft. Several methods are available, including using the Windows Update catalog, direct downloading from the Microsoft download site, or taking advantage of the automatic downloads made possible by Windows Software Update Services (SUS).

To obtain patches using the Windows Update Catalog:

1. Browse to Windows Update (http://v4.windowsupdate.microsoft.com/en/default.asp) or select Windows Update from the Tools menu of Internet Explorer.

2. In the Other Options section, click Personalize Windows Update.

3. Under the Personalize Your Windows Update Experience section, check Display the Link to the Windows Update Catalog under See Also as shown here:

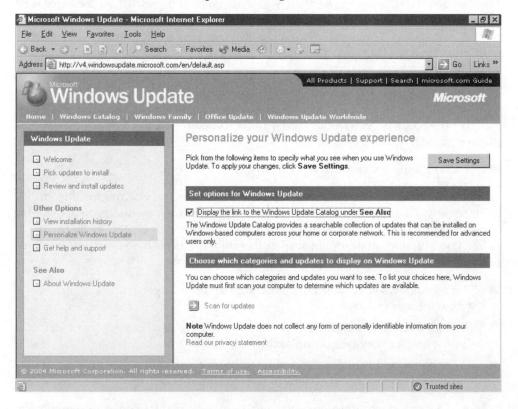

4. In the upper right-hand corner of the window, click Save Settings.

5. Click the Windows Update Catalog listing now displayed under the heading See Also in the left pane as shown here:

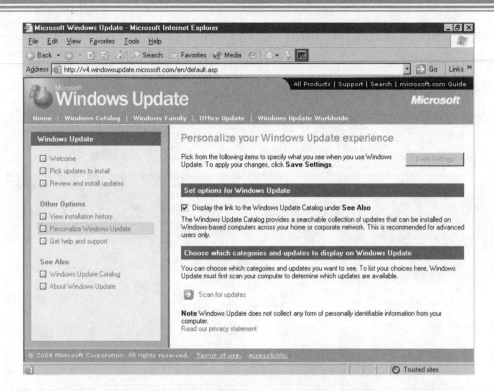

6. Select Find Updates for Microsoft Windows Operating Systems as shown here:

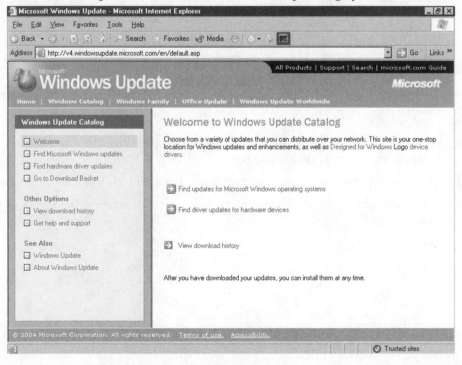

7. Select the operating system from the Operating System drop-down list. (Note that you can find updates for Windows 98 as well as for more recent versions of the OS.)

8. Click the Advanced Search options and set as necessary as shown here:

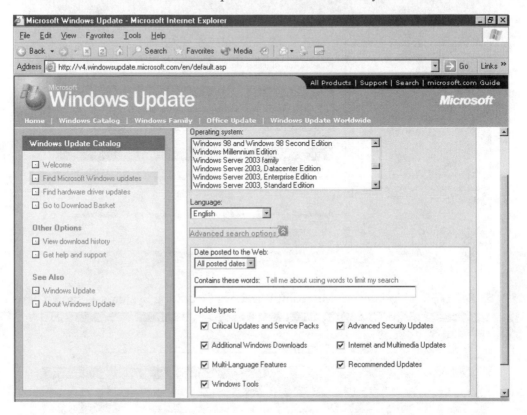

9. Click Search.

10. When the search is complete, select from the list presented to display brief descriptions of the available patches.

11. Click the Add button adjacent to each patch in order to select it for download.

12. When you have selected all updates, click Go to Download Basket as shown here:

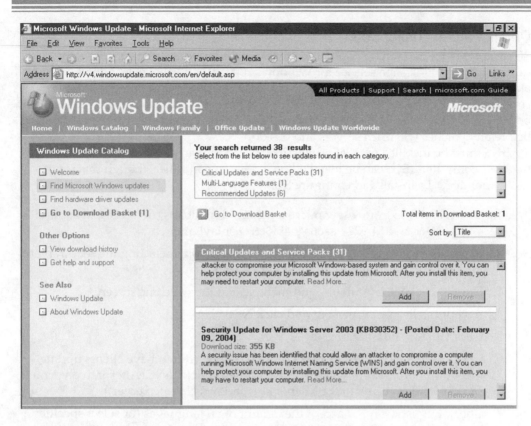

13. Enter or browse to the location where you want to store updates.

14. Click Download Now.

HEADS UP!

Other methods for downloading patches exist. The Windows Update site can be used to scan a local computer and recommend necessary patches as well as provide a way to download and install them. Automatic Update can be configured to notify users that patches are available for download and then provide the means to carry out the downloads. However, these methods do not allow testing of the patch, nor are they reasonable methods in an enterprise environment, since it would be difficult to get users to use Windows Update and Automatic Update would unnecessarily consume bandwidth. These methods may be okay in smaller environments or as emergency measures for mobile systems. A list of recommended and tested patches could be prepared by administrators, and mobile users could be taught how to use other means to select, download, and apply patches.

Obtain Patches Using SUS

SUS is a free tool that can be used to create the backbone of an automated patch download and application service for Windows 2000 SP3 and above, Windows XP SP1 and above, and Windows Server 2003. While downloading is automated, it can be configured to require an administrator request. What's more, downloaded patches must be approved before they can be distributed and applied, and clients must be configured before any patches will reach servers and desktops.

SUS must be installed on a Windows 2000 or Windows Server 2003 domain member computer. (SUS can be installed on a domain controller, though this is not recommended.) To install and configure SUS:

1. Download SUS from www.microsoft.com/downloads/details.aspx?FamilyID= a7aa96e4-6e41-4f54-972c-ae66a4e4bf6c&DisplayLang=en.

2. Make sure to read the requirements for installation, including the requirement for IIS. (You must allow Active Server Pages.)

3. Double-click the executable, and then Next at the welcome screen.

4. Accept the license agreement and click Next.

5. Click Custom Installation.

6. Select Save the Updates to This Local Folder in order to have clients update from the computer on which SUS is installed. Click Next. (Alternatively, you can direct SUS clients to the Microsoft Windows Update Server.)

7. Check English Only, or accept the default of all languages (or select specific languages), and then click Next. (This is an important step, as the time for downloading patches in a language you don't need, and the disk space for storing them, is a waste.)

8. Leave the default I Will Manually Approve New Versions of Approved Updates and click Next.

9. Click Install.

10. When installation is complete, it will attempt to take you to the http:// localhost/susadmin site so that you can configure the system. You can, of course, administer SUS from your administrative workstation.

11. Use the susadmin pages to configure SUS.

NOTE   Internet Explorer on Windows Server 2003 is configured by default in a restricted mode, and you may not be able to immediately access the SUS administration site.

To configure SUS:

1. Open the SUS administration page at http://*server_name*/susadmin.

2. In the left pane, click Synchronize Server.

3. Configure synchronization. Click Synchronization Schedule. The server can be set to automatically synchronize with Windows Update (download new patches and service packs), or you can choose to synchronize manually. If you choose this option, make sure to sign up to be notified when new software has been added for download.

4. Click OK.

5. In the left pane, click Set Options as shown next. Options are to configure the proxy server, choose the server name used by clients to access the server, point the SUS server to another server for updates, decide which language updates should be downloaded, and so forth.

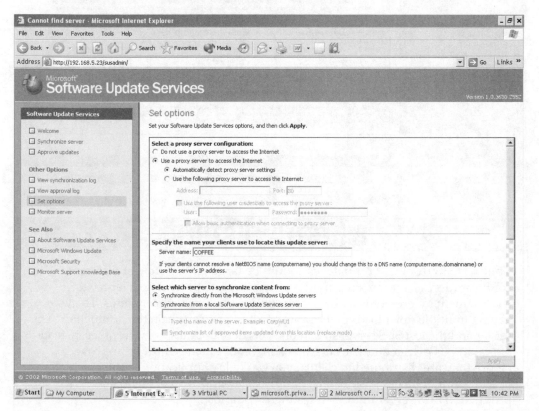

6. Synchronize the server. Click Synchronize Now to download the most recent service pack and hotfixes.

7. Once you have tested updates, use the View Approval Log option to approve service packs and hotfixes for distribution as shown here:

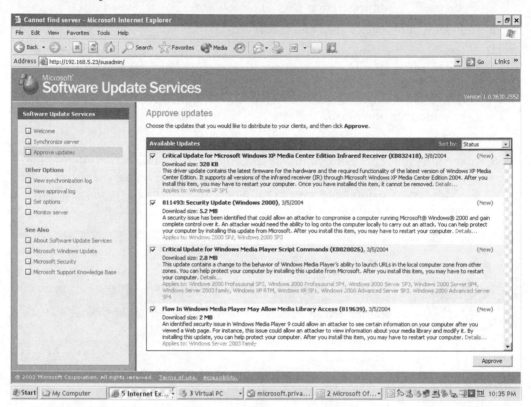

ONE STEP FURTHER

Your test environment for patches should be large enough to test different configurations. You can simplify the distribution of patches to a large test environment by providing a SUS server specifically for the test systems. To avoid having multiple downloads of the same patches, you can chain the production SUS server and the test SUS server so that one gets new updates from the other instead of making its own requests from Microsoft. Since patches must be approved before they are distributed to clients, you can delay application to the production network until patches pass testing. Simply delay approval of any patch on the production SUS server until your testing is complete.

Test

You can find anecdotal evidence that supports whatever you want to believe about the problems that hotfixes can cause. Horror stories about machines that crashed and required operating system installation abound, as do testimonials that in five years only one hotfix caused a problem and that was with one machine with special hardware.

The reality, of course, is that both situations can occur, and the proper response is to test all hotfixes before adding them to production machines. Ideally, tests should be run on systems as close to those in production as possible, though even this is no guarantee. After testing, automated installation to most desktops and less critical servers should be scheduled. For critical servers, updating should be approached with caution and you should be prepared to deal with the unexpected.

Apply Updates Using Group Policy

If your organization has more than a few seats, you will need some automated way to apply approved patches. Many third-party solutions are available. Two easy ways to automate updating of approved patches using native tools are to use a logon or startup script or to use SUS.

To use Group Policy, create a script that checks for file versions and installs patches if they have not been installed.

1. Determine which OUs contain computers on which the update should be applied.

2. Create a GPO and link it to these OUs.

3. Open the GPO in the editor and navigate to Computer Configuration, Windows Settings, Scripts.

4. Double-click Scripts and then Startup.

5. Use the Add button on the Scripts page as shown in the illustration.

6. Browse to the script file, add any parameters in the Script Parameters box, and click OK twice.

7. Allow Group Policy to replicate.

8. Reboot computers. The patch is applied on reboot.

Apply Updates Using a Script

Using Group Policy is not the only way to use a script to apply patches. You may wish to provide an IP address file of computers to update, a network patch location, and a script that uses both to apply patches to multiple computers. A detailed explanation and example script can be found in the article "How to Use a Visual Basic Script to Install the 824146 (MS-03-039) or 823980 (MS03-026) Security Patch on Remote Host" at http://support.microsoft.com/default.aspx?scid=kb;en-us;827227.

Apply Updates Using SUS

SUS can be used to apply updates if SUS clients are configured. (Windows XP SP1 and above, Windows 2000 SP3 and above, and Windows Server 2003 can be SUS clients.) SUS clients are configured through Group Policy. For Windows 2000 domains, add the wuau.adm template to the Computer Configuration, Administrative Templates node. The wuau.adm template is provided with the SUS download. The template is already installed in Windows Server 2003.

1. Expand the Computer Configuration, Administrative Templates, Windows Components node and select Windows Update.

2. Double-click Configure Automatic Update Properties.

3. Click Enabled.

4. Select number 4, Auto Download and Schedule the Install. (Under Configure Automatic Updating. Notify for Download and Notify for Install will prompt users to request updates and to install updates at their leisure. Auto Download and Notify for Install requires the user to request the install.)

5. Use the scheduling day and time boxes to select the time for installation as shown in the illustration.

6. Click Next Setting to move to the Specify Intranet Microsoft Update Service Location.

7. Click Enabled.

8. Enter URLs for the update server and intranet statistics server as shown next. (If you have one SUS server, these will be the same.)

```
Specify intranet Microsoft update service location Properties    [?][X]

 Setting | Explain |

   [icon] Specify intranet Microsoft update service location

   ( Not Configured
   (•) Enabled
   ( Disabled

   Set the intranet update service for detecting updates:
   [http://coffee                              ]

   Set the intranet statistics server:
   [http://coffee                              ]

   (example: http://IntranetUpd01)



 Supported on:   Windows Server 2003 family, XP SP1, 2000 SP3
   [ Previous Setting ]   [ Next Setting ]

            [ OK ]    [ Cancel ]    [ Apply ]
```

9. Click Next Setting to move to the Reschedule Automatic Updates Scheduled Installations page.

10. Click Enabled.

11. Enter a number in the box for Wait After System Startup (minutes) as shown next. This number is the number of minutes after computer startup that the system will wait before installing a missed scheduled install. A missed scheduled install could happen if, for example, the schedule to install updates is set for 5 P.M., an update is awaiting installation, and the user turns off their computer at 4 P.M. If the Reschedule Automatic Updates Scheduled Installation

setting is enabled, once the system is rebooted, the system will wait the set number of minutes and then install the update.

```
┌─────────────────────────────────────────────────────────┐
│ Reschedule Automatic Updates scheduled installations Prope... [?][X] │
├─────────────────────────────────────────────────────────┤
│ Setting │ Explain │                                       │
│                                                           │
│  ▣ Reschedule Automatic Updates scheduled installations  │
│  ─────────────────────────────────────────────────────   │
│                                                           │
│   ○ Not Configured                                        │
│   ● Enabled                                               │
│   ○ Disabled                                              │
│  ┌─────────────────────────────────────────────────────┐ │
│  │ Wait after system startup(minutes):   [10]  [▲▼]    │ │
│  │                                                     │ │
│  │                                                     │ │
│  │                                                     │ │
│  │                                                     │ │
│  │                                                     │ │
│  └─────────────────────────────────────────────────────┘ │
│  Supported on:  Windows Server 2003 family, XP SP1, 2000 SP3 │
│  [ Previous Setting ]    [ Next Setting ]                 │
│                                                           │
│            [  OK  ]    [ Cancel ]    [ Apply ]            │
└─────────────────────────────────────────────────────────┘
```

12. Click Next Setting to move to the No Auto-Restart for Scheduled Automatic Updates Installations.

13. Click Enabled. This setting prevents the system from restarting automatically even though the update requires it. Those patches that require a restart will not be fully installed until the system is rebooted.

HEADS UP!

Automatic restart after patch application is a problematic option. If desktops are left on all the time and patches are never applied except when no user will be using them, then you've solved one problem by introducing another. When desktops are left on all the time, they may be more easily targeted for attack. However, if desktops are rebooted at an arbitrary time, when users may be working, there may be loss of data or other problems. Yet to allow users to be in control of when and whether updates are installed is unacceptable. It seems the best solution is to schedule updates but prevent automated reboots and ensure that reboots do occur. Similar issues affect servers; however, the problem is that many servers today must be operational 24 × 7, so reboots must be planned and administrators will have to understand which patches require reboots and which ones don't so that they can schedule reboots to ensure patch application.

Be Prepared for Disaster Recovery

All systems will eventually fail. Whether the failure is due to hardware, software, malicious attack, improper configuration, user mistake, or any other reason, the most important thing is to restore service. You cannot do so if you are not properly prepared.

TIP KB article 287061, "Windows NT 4.0 and Windows 2000 Disaster Recovery and Backup and Restore Procedures," contains links to articles on disaster recovery. Go to http://support.microsoft.com/default.aspx?scid=kb;en-us;287061.

Use Fault-Tolerant Configurations

Many fault-tolerant devices are available that can prevent hardware meltdown from becoming network meltdown. Use RAID drives to prevent drive failure from requiring a restore. Investigate, test, and use other hardware devices that work in tandem—when one fails, the other takes over or continues on. Use clustering to provide fault tolerance for database and other cluster-aware applications. Use load balancing to link multiple servers such as firewalls. When one server fails, the load is automatically redirected to other servers. Use duplicate servers and configure network devices or software applications to use either. DNS is a good example of this; client TCP/IP protocol configuration provides the ability to list two DNS servers. If one is not available, the system will automatically attempt to use the other.

Schedule and Perform Backups

In order to properly prepare for recovery, you must back up data and system configurations. The procedures for actually performing backups are simple. However, the creation of a complete backup plan and its management is not.

Create Backup Data Plans

Some data may be disposable, such as documents downloaded from web sites for browsing, statistics downloaded from a central server on a daily basis, temporary files, and other information. However, to ensure the recovery of data that is not, you must have a plan for backing up data that includes

- When to back up
- When to do full backups vs. system configuration backups vs. data backups
- What media are used
- Whether backups will be automated
- How long backups are kept

- How many times backup media will be reused
- What type of backup media will be used
- Where will offsite storage be and how often will backups be moved offsite
- Who will have access to backups
- Where will backups be stored locally
- Who can restore systems
- Which data will be backed up

NOTE In many organizations, users must store all data on network drives. It is easier to back up this data, and it is easier to restore desktop systems. When data is stored on the network, recovering a user system is usually accomplished by simply doing a reinstall. Since the standard desktop systems can be imaged, quick recovery is possible once any necessary hardware repairs or replacements are complete.

Do Full System Backups

Windows provides a native tool for performing backups. While the capabilities of the tool vary depending on the operating system, the basics of its operation are very similar from version to version.

TIP System State backup can be performed only locally. You cannot back up system state to the network using the built-in tool. System state backup is not available for Windows NT 4.0.

To do a full system backup for Windows NT 4.0, you will need to install and configure a tape drive. Windows Server 2003, Windows 2000, and Windows XP can back up to additional media types. A member of the Backup Operators group, or a user granted the backup files and directories user right, can back up data. The local Administrators group can back up system state. To back up:

1. Open the Backup program via Start | Program Files | Accessories | System Tools.
2. Select the Backup tab.
3. Select the Drives in the left pane.
4. Select System State. (System State backup backs up boot files, the COM+ Class Registration Database, and the Registry. If the server is a domain controller, Active Directory is also backed up. If IIS is installed, the metabase will be backed up. If certificate services are installed, then their configuration is backed up.)
5. Select the backup destination (file, tape).

6. Select the backup media or filename (if a file will be used, enter the path).

7. Click Start Backup.

Schedule Backups

Backups must be done on a regular basis. There are no set rules for frequency, but many organizations follow a daily backup plan. When the amount of data to back up prohibits backing up all data every day, a weekly full backup is supplemented by a daily partial backup that either backs up those files that have changed since the full backup (differential) or those that have changed since the last partial backup (incremental). Another type of backup that can be used backs up only those files that were created or modified on the current day. This, however, does not ensure complete recovery.

These are the important things to remember about partial backups:

■ Using a differential backup will increase the amount of time needed to back up each day a differential backup is performed, as all new and changed files since the full backup will need to be backed up.

■ If differential backups are made, and a computer must be restored, you will need only two backups, the full backup and the last differential created.

■ Using a incremental backup will reduce the amount of time needed to back up.

■ If incremental backups are made and a computer must be restored, you must use the full backup and all of the incremental backups made since the full backup.

To perform an immediate backup:

1. Open the Backup program via Start | Program Files | Accessories | System Tools.

2. Select the Backup tab.

3. Select the Scheduled Jobs tab.

4. Click Add Job.

5. Follow the wizard to configure what to back up and create a schedule.

Regularly Back Up Configurations

In addition to performing full backups, regularly back up system state data. For Windows XP, Windows Server 2003, and Windows 2000, back up the system state and any configuration files not backed up with system state. For Windows NT 4.0, back up the registry and any configuration files and create a Windows NT 4.0 boot disk. Create an emergency repair disk for Windows NT 4.0; this process gives you the opportunity to back up the registry. (Creating an emergency repair disk does not back up the registry for Windows XP, Windows Server 2003, and Windows 2000.)

HEADS UP!

In order to restore system state on a Windows 2000 or Windows Server 2003 domain controller, the backup must not be older than the Active Directory tombstone lifetime. The *tombstone lifetime* is the amount of time for which deleted objects remain as deleted objects in the Active Directory. (When you delete an Active Directory object, the deletion event must somehow be transmitted to all copies of the AD so that it can be deleted there as well. The tombstone is the record of a deletion event, as it is the object "marked" for deletion.) When the time is up, the tombstone is deleted. If a backup of system state older than the tombstone lifetime (by default, 60 days) is restored, all data will be rejected as out-of-date. It is simple to avoid this issue—make regular backups.

Keep a Log of Backup Activity

When backups are made, a log is created. Print and keep backup logs. They are records of backups and may also be helpful during restore operations in locating files.

Create a manual log to record when different systems were backed up and the backup media removed. Keep details of how the media are labeled, who removed them for storage, and where they were stored. When tapes are reused, record that as well.

Make Emergency Repair Disks

Windows 2000, Windows XP, and Windows Server 2003 emergency repair disks can be created by using the native backup tool. Making the disk also places current setting information in the systemroot\repair folder. This information may be necessary when attempting to restore the system; it might also be used to compromise the system. Manage the permissions on this folder and provide full access to only the system and Administrators.

To create an emergency repair disk for Windows NT 4.0:

1. Open a command prompt and enter **rdisk /r**.

2. In the Repair Disk Utility dialog, select Create Repair Disk as shown here:

The **/r** switch copies the information to the repair folder as well. If the data becomes too large for a single floppy, you can use the Update Repair Info button and then copy the contents of the repair folder to other backup media.

Use Restore Points

Windows XP automatically takes snapshots of the system configuration and provides the ability to return the system to a state prior to the installation of a new driver, or a configuration change. Restore points can also be manually requested and are a good practice before making major system changes. To make a restore point:

1. Click Start | Accessories | System Tools | System Restore.
2. Click Create a Restore Point and then click Next.
3. Enter a descriptive name for the restore point and click Create.
4. Click the Home button to return to the System restore page, or close the window.

To restore the system to the restore point:

1. Click Start | Accessories | System Tools | System Restore and then click Next.
2. Use the Select a Restore Point page to select a date and then select the desired restore point.

Plan and Perform Special Backup Operations

If you completely back up entire servers and their data, you can do a complete system restore, but what if it's simply some component of the server that fails? Or what if you simply need to move some service from a crashed server to one that is already operational?

An example of such operations would be recovery of DNS. Of course, if you have followed best practices, you have more than one DNS server. In Windows NT 4.0, you've configured a secondary DNS server. If zone transfers are a frequent part of your maintenance, then the loss of a single DNS server is not the end of networking as you know it. But what if you have only two DNS servers and both fail? Can you quickly get up and running on an existing Windows NT 4.0 server? Sure, if you've a backup of the winnt\system32\dns folder's file, and you have prepared a boot file or backed up the DNS registry keys.

In addition to making full backups and system state backups, you must consider the special needs of various services and applications running in your environment. Areas to consider are

- Active Directory
- DNS

- DHCP
- RIS
- Certificate services
- EFS
- Exchange Server
- SQL Server

Practice Recovery Operations

How do you know that your backups are good? How do you know if you'll be able to recover from a disk crash or other failure? Practice. While you cannot take every backup and attempt to use it to restore every computer, you can do periodic restores and you can keep ready the information necessary to perform restores. Test this list by doing practice restores.

Practice Restoring Active Directory

Restoring Active Directory can be a complex process. To understand the process and to be able to determine the exact steps for each situation requires detailed knowledge. The information that follows should not be used without such understanding. Many of the steps and much of the knowledge required to perform Active Directory restores is in the white paper "Active Directory Disaster Recovery" at www.microsoft.com/technet/ prodtechnol/windows2000serv/technologies/activedirectory/support/ adrecov.mspx#XSLTsection126121120120.

Do a nonauthoritative restore to provide a basis from which to update the newly restored operating system via replication. This approach also reduces the amount of time necessary to restore the system and prevents unnecessary replication traffic. If the Active Directory is not large, this process may be forgone and the replication process will update the local copy.

1. Boot into Directory Services Restore Mode to take AD offline.

2. Select the Windows AD operating system and log on using the local administrator account and Directory Services Restore password you created during dcpromo. Then click OK.

3. Start the backup utility.

4. Click Restore Wizard and then click Next.

5. Check the System State Entry and click Next.

6. Click Finish.

7. Reboot.

Do an authoritative restore if the backup copy contains the correct Active Directory data, in other words, if you need to restore Active Directory to a state prior to that currently on the network. The authoritative restore process designates the restored AD as the copy all other domain controllers should synchronize their database with.

1. Nonauthoritatively restore AD.

2. Open a command prompt.

3. Enter **ntdsutil**.

4. Enter **authoritative restore**.

5. At the prompt, enter **restore database**.

6. Enter Quit as many times as necessary to exit ntdsutil.

7. Reboot.

Do a primary restore if you must rebuild the domain from scratch using a backup. The first DC will need a primary restore; all other DCs should be nonauthoritatively restored.

1. Use the backup utility.

2. Select System State.

3. Click the Advanced option.

4. From the Advanced Restore Options dialog box, select When Restoring Replication Data Sets, Mark the Restored Data as the Primary Data for All Replicas.

Practice Restore Operations for Services

System state backup data, once restored, may not complete the restoration process for all services. Several services need additional steps in the restore process.

- The WINS database is restored but may be out of date. If WINS data is supported by multiple WINS databases, update WINS by performing a WINS replication; otherwise, WINS will update itself over time.

- The DHCP database is restored but may be out of date. Reconcile the restored database by selecting the scope in the DHCP snap-in, and then using the Action menu and selecting Reconcile. DHCP will operate in safe mode, querying the network to see if an address it is about to assign already exists. Quit this mode after one-half of the lease duration has expired.

Establish and Practice Using Emergency Management Services

Windows Server 2003 introduces the ability to use Emergency Management Services (EMS) to restore a server that cannot be restored by any other means. EMS can be used via out-of-band connections such as a null modem cable, a modem, or a service processor. EMS might also be used to disrupt server operation. Limit the ability of users to access out-of-band services by physically protecting the server and any out-of-band connections, and by selecting equipment with and using secure access mechanisms. Consider a separate management interface for out-of-band connections.

Practice Using the Recovery Console

The recovery console is a tool provided for Windows 2000, Windows Server 2003, and Windows XP computers to assist in the recovery. You can use the recovery console to view files, change drivers, and use powerful commands to do such operations as fixing the boot sector.

Evaluate the need for and practicality of installing the recovery console. The recovery console can be used to compromise a system if its security configuration is not used. You can use the recovery console by booting from the installation CD-ROM.

To install the recovery console, you will need the Windows installation CD-ROM. If the CD-ROM is placed in the D drive, the command to install the recovery console is

```
D:\i386\winnt32.exe /cmdcons
```

Monitor and Audit

Information systems do not escape the natural process of decay. We recognize that and monitor hardware for signs of wear. But the hardening process and its product can also decay over time. Security can also be accidentally or maliciously adjusted. The purpose of monitoring and auditing is to find those areas where this has or is occurring, prompt action to recover from any harm, and return systems to their hardened state.

HEADS UP!

It has become common to identify the words "Perform an audit" with doing a pentest. Even more disturbing, there are those who think the first thing that should be done when building a security program is to have internal and external penetration tests performed. This is *not* the way to audit the security status of your organization. Just as security is much, much more than understanding the latest hack attack, auditing is much more than simulating attacks in order to test defenses. The proper way to establish and maintain security is to harden the network according to security principles, best practices, and the use of tested solutions to known attack vectors, and then, to test these defenses.

Monitoring encompasses periodic checking of configuration settings and regular activity review and action when something exceeds the norm. Auditing is the process of formal review of policy compliance, forensic review of collected data, and penetration testing (pentesting) of controls. Many of the same tools can be used during both activities. This book describes how to use commonly available native Windows tools, but there are many third-party tools that you may find valuable.

Configure System Auditing

You must record activity in order to have it for review or to use in intrusion detection. To configure auditing, you must set audit processes at the system level, and to audit object level activity, you must set audit requirements on the object. In both the following examples, most, if not all, auditing choices are selected. You determine the settings to match your requirements. It is imperative to set system auditing; however, you probably will not want to set object auditing for every object. Instead, use object auditing to monitor critical or sensitive data, or to track the activity of suspects.

Windows NT 4.0 auditing settings can be set for domain controllers using User Manager for Domains and for domain members or stand-alone computers using User Manager. For other post–Windows NT 4.0 systems based on Windows NT technologies, use Group Policy. The local Group Policy may be used for stand-alone computers and to set auditing for domain members if auditing is not set at the domain level. Best practices are to set auditing for domain members by setting it in a GPO linked to the OU within which the computer account resides.

Configure Auditing for Windows NT 4.0

Table 13-1 lists and describes audit categories for Windows NT 4.0. To configure system auditing for Windows NT 4.0:

1. Select Programs | Administrative Tools | User Manager | Policies and then click Audit.

2. Select all events except Process Tracking as shown here:

3. Click OK.

Audit Selection	Description	Success	Failure
Logon and Logoff	Records user logon and logoff at the computer whose console the user is using.	Y	Y
File and Object Access	Turns on the ability to set auditing at the object level. Does *not* begin recording information until object auditing is configured on objects.	Y	Y
Use of User Rights	Records use of a right.	Y	Y
User and Group Management	Records changes to users and groups.	Y	Y
Security Policy Changes	Records changes to audit settings.	Y	Y
Restart, Shutdown, and System	Records typical system events.	Y	Y
Process Tracking	Creates an event for every action a process takes. Does not provide useful information except where software is being tested. Set on test systems only.	N	N

Table 13-1. Audit Policy for Window NT 4.0

To set object auditing on files:

1. Right-click the file in Windows Explorer and select Properties.

2. Click the Security tab.

3. Click Auditing.

4. Click Add to add user groups you want to monitor.

5. Select Events to audit as shown in the illustration.

6. Click OK to close.

Configure Auditing for Windows XP and Windows 2000

Auditing is set for Windows XP and Windows 2000 using group policy. On stand-alone computers, the Audit policy can be set either in the local group policy or by configuring Local Security Policy. For computers joined in a domain, audit settings can vary according the policy configured in the GPO linked to the OU in which the computer account exists.

TIP When a domain account is used from a workstation, the account logon events are recorded on the domain controller, but the logon events are recorded on the workstation. The use of two types of logon events solves the problem often cause by Windows NT 4.0 logon/logoff audit events, which were recorded only where the interactive event occurred. Logon and logoff records were present only on the computer used by the user interactively. In order to audit these events, audit logs from all workstations need to be collected and filtered. By using two different types of events, the records on the domain controller can provide domain logon records.

The Audit Policy is part of the Windows Settings, Security Settings, Local Policies node. To set or modify audit policy, select the Audit Policy container and then change policy settings by double-clicking the settings in the details pane. Table 13-2 lists the Audit Policy choices for Windows XP, Windows 2000, and Windows Server 2003.

Review Windows Server 2003 Audit Settings

Windows Server 2003 audit settings are set by default. This is a major departure from previous Windows system defaults. Review these settings and modify to meet the preceding recommendations. Windows Server 2003 default audit settings are displayed in Figure 13-1.

Audit Policy	Description	Success	Failure
Audit Account Logon Events	Records logon and logoff records where accounts reside.	Y	Y
Audit Account Management	Records changes to accounts.	Y	Y
Audit Directory Service Access	Enables the recording of configured directory object audit settings.	Y	Y
Audit Logon Events	Records activity where the user logs on interactively.	Y	Y
Audit Object Access	Enables the recording of configured audit settings on file, folder, printer, and registry objects.	Y	Y
Audit Policy Change	Records policy changes.	Y	Y
Audit Privilege Use	Records use of user rights.	Y	Y
Audit Process Tracking	Records every action a process takes.	N	N
Audit System Events	Records system events such as shutdown and startup.	Y	Y

Table 13-2. Audit Categories for Windows Server 2003, Windows XP, and Windows 2000

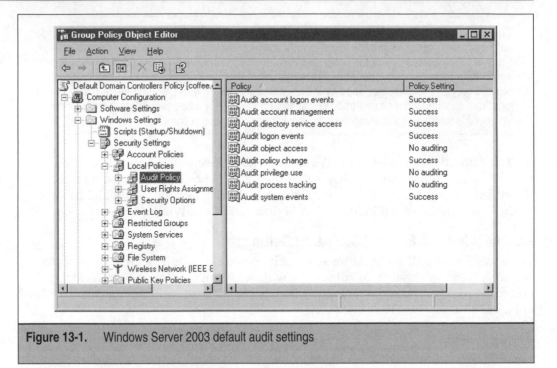

Figure 13-1. Windows Server 2003 default audit settings

Configure Audit Logs

Audit logs must be configured both to provide enough room to record events and to dictate the retention policy of audit events.

Configure Logs for Windows NT 4.0

To configure logs in Windows NT 4.0, use the Event Viewer Administration tool and select Log Settings from the Log menu as shown in Figure 13-2. The defaults are displayed in the figure; the following changes should be made.

- **Expand the log size.** Unlike normal Windows files, the security log cannot expand ad infinitum or until the disk is full. All Windows event log files are restricted and may only reach the limit set for them. The size required will depend on the amount of activity on the computer, which may also be a function of the role it plays on the network. Set the file size large and monitor its growth. Size is also a function of how frequently you archive the logs.

- **Set Event Log Wrapping to Overwrite Events as Needed.** If you allow events to be overwritten after some number of days, you risk losing events. If you prevent any event overwrites and the log becomes full, the log will simply stop recording events. By setting as needed, at least the most current events will still be in the log. You should, however, audit the log growth to prevent any overwrites. If the log will reach its limits before your normal archival time, either change the archive frequency or make the log file size larger.

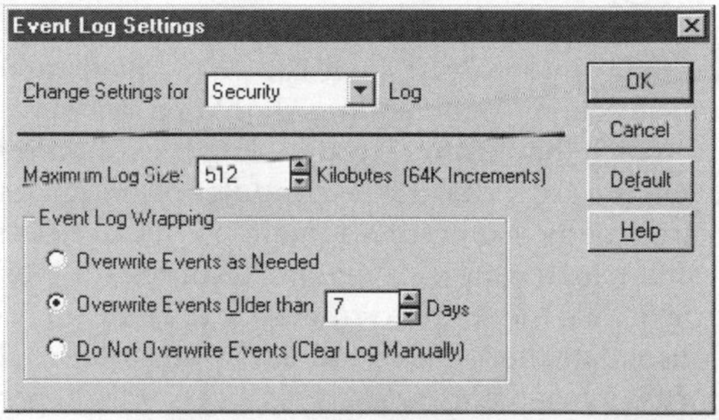

Figure 13-2. Modify log file settings from this default.

Configure Logs for Windows 2000, Windows XP, and Windows Server 2003

Event log settings in Windows 2000, Windows XP, and Windows Server 2003 are configured in Group Policy in the Security Settings, Event Log section. Make the following adjustments:

- Change the Maximum Security Log Size to meet the requirements of your systems.

- Enable Prevent Local Guests Group from Accessing the Application Log, the Security Log, and the System Log (three settings).

- Set the Retention Method for Security Log to Overwrite Events as Needed.

ONE STEP FURTHER

Three additional audit settings are available in the Windows Server 2003 Security Options and via registry entries for other Windows systems based on NT technologies. Configure these settings for critical systems, but be aware what they mean. Shut Down System Immediately if Unable to Log Security Audits will prevent remote access to the computer if the event log is full. This setting should be set only on systems for which you supply real-time monitoring. The event log must be manually cleared and the setting reset in order to regain remote access to the computer.

Audit the Access of Global System Objects records of the use of semaphores (locking objects), mutexes (mutually exclusive controls), and DOS devices. This setting enables powerful audit resources for the review of software but simply records too much information in a production environment.

Audit the Use of Backup and Restore Privileges records each file accessed during a backup and probably provides more information than is needed for most production computers.

Archive Audit Logs

Log files should be periodically archived. Logs can be manually archived by using the Save Log File As menu selection. Archived logs should be stored at a location other than the computer on which they were recorded. Log files should be consolidated for review. Each entry in the log includes the computer on which the log entry was recorded, so identification of the log entry origination is always possible.

A script can be written, for example, using the Resource Kit tool dumpel, to dump log data to a text file. Schedule the script to run using the built-in Scheduler program or the **AT** command. Consolidate the log files and use appropriate tools for filtering. The text file is easily imported into a database such as Access or SQL Server. Queries and reports can then be written to filter events.

Use Security Events for Intrusion Detection and Forensics

Audit policy is configured so that security events will be collected. Then what? The events can be used to discover what happened after a security breech. They can also be used to aid in the detection of intrusions. To do either of these things, you must find a way to filter event logs. Again, two types of filters are needed. To forensically examine a specific event, you will need to be intimately familiar with the normal events recorded for security, system, and applications. This knowledge can help you understand which events to look for when tracking activity. To detect intrusions, you filter on events that are likely to indicate abnormal activity. Keep in mind, however, that some normal events, if recorded in unusual circumstances, may indicate intrusion, and some abnormal events may simply be the result of something other than intrusion. Often, it is a combination of events that provides a clearer picture. Table 13-3 lists authentication events that should be monitored. All security events should be monitored; for a comprehensive list, see the Knowledge Base articles 299475 (http://support.microsoft.com/?id=299475) and 301677 (http://support.microsoft.com/default.aspx?scid=kb;EN-US;301677).

Event ID	Description
529	Unknown username or known username with bad password.
530	Account logon time restriction violation.
531	Account currently disabled.
532	Account expired.
533	User not allowed to log on this computer.
534	Logon type restricted; user has not been granted requested logon type at this machine.

Table 13-3.   Track Security Log Authentication Events

Event ID	Description
535	Specified account password has expired.
537	Unsuccessful logon.
539	Account locked out.
544	IPSec association establishment failed because peer could not authenticate.
545	IPSec peer authentication failed.
614	IPSec policy agent disabled.
615	IPSec policy agent changed.
616	IPSEc policy agent encountered a potentially serious flaw.
617	Kerberos policy changed.
643	Domain policy changed.
675	Account logon preauthentication failed.
676	Authentication ticket failed.
677	Service ticket request failed.
681	The logon to account *<client name>* by *<source>* from *<workstation>* failed; the error code was *<error>*.
682	A user reconnected to a disconnected Terminal Services session.
683	A user disconnected a Terminal Services session without logging off.

Table 13-3. Track Security Log Authentication Events *(continued)*

To examine and filter events, you can create queries to use with an Access or SQL database developed from archived logs. To perform more current examinations, the tool EventCombMT can be used to consolidate current security log information and filter by specific events. EventCombMT can be downloaded from the Security Guide Scripts Download page www.microsoft.com/downloads/details.aspx?FamilyID= 9989d151-5c55-4bd3-a9d2-b95a15c73e92&DisplayLang=en.

After downloading the EventCombMT tool:

1. Double-click the executable to open the tool; then click OK.
2. Set the domain box entry to the domain to review.
3. Right-click the box Select to Search/Right Click to Add.
4. Add servers to search. All server can be added, or all DCs.
5. Select the Security Log file.

6. Select the Event type (either Success Audit or Failure Audit, or both).

7. Enter the event IDs to search for as shown here:

8. Click Search to start the search.

9. A temporary file, eventcombmt.txt, is created in the temp folder to record the search process. The results of the search are recorded in a text file named for the server and type of event log and are displayed in the window.

Audit Security Configuration

To ensure that security configuration remains in force, the settings should be audited. This means that both Group Policies should be checked for compliance and computers should be checked to determine if settings are being applied. Two free tools can be used for this purpose, Security Configuration and Analysis, and Resultant Set of Policy.

Audit Configuration Compliance with Security Configuration and Analysis

The Security Configuration and Analysis snap-in can be used to audit Security settings on a single computer. To use the tool:

1. Have available a security template that is composed of the settings that are correct for this computer.

2. Add the Security Configuration and Analysis tool to an MMC console.

3. Open a new database by selecting Open Database, typing a filename, and then pressing ENTER.

4. Browse to and select the security template in step 1 and click Open.

5. Right-click the Security Configuration and Analysis node and select Analyze Computer Now.

6. Click OK to approve the log file path.

7. When the process completes, review each policy, looking for red and white *x*s. The *x*s indicate variances from the approved policy as shown here:

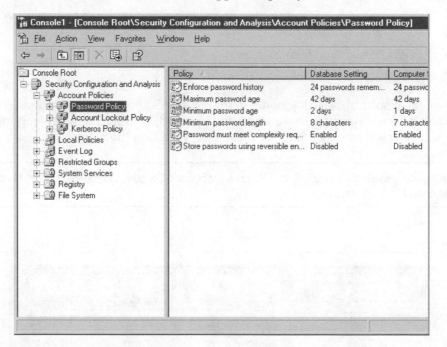

ONE STEP FURTHER

The command-line tool secedit.exe can be used in a script to perform an analysis. A script could be written to perform an analysis of multiple computers. You can review the results using the Security Configuration and Analysis tool.

Audit Configuration Compliance with Resultant Set of Policy

Windows XP and Windows Server 2003 offer a new tool, Resultant Set of Policy, that can be used to validate security settings for a specific purpose. To use the tool:

1. Add the snap-in to an MMC console.

2. Right-click the Resultant Set of Policy node and select Generate RSoP Data. Then click Next.

3. Select Logging Mode and click Next. Logging mode will perform a test by connecting to a specific computer and checking the results of Group Policy application for a specific user on that computer. Planning mode can be used to see the results of different combinations of GPOs. It does not connect to a specific computer to complete the test.

4. Select a specific computer to test and click Next. The local computer may be used. You may also restrict the scan to user settings only.

5. Select a specific user account to test and click Next. You can restrict the scan to computer settings only.

6. Review choices and then click Next.

7. When the scan is complete, click Finish.

View the results by selecting nodes in the console as shown in Figure 13-3. Note that RSoP does not compare the settings with those set by policy; it merely reports what is. It does indicate the source of the settings by listing the Source GPO.

TIP A downloadable tool, the Group Policy Management Console, can be used to run these tests and show more information.

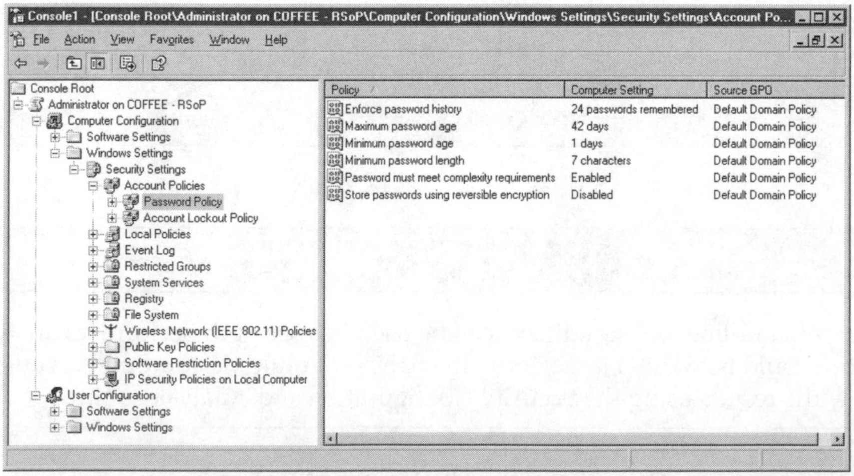

Figure 13-3. Resultant Set of Policy shows the actual applied policy.

Audit Patch Status

It's not enough to schedule and apply patches; you must determine if patches are actually being applied. A tool that can assist you in these efforts is the Microsoft Baseline Security Analyzer. Download the tool from www.microsoft.com/downloads/details.aspx?FamilyID=8b7a580d-0c91-45b7-91ba-fc47f7c3d6ad&DisplayLang=en. To use the tool:

1. Run the tool from the Programs menu.

2. Click Scan a Computer.

3. Configure the scanner as shown next. You can prevent it from scanning specific types of vulnerabilities and point it to a SUS server. (Using your SUS server requires the tool to indicate only patches missing that you have approved for installation.)

4. Click Start Scan.

5. When the scan is complete, a number of security vulnerabilities may be indicated along with the patch status of this system as shown here:

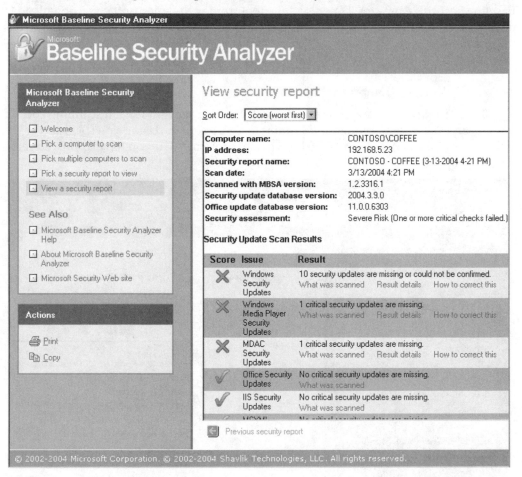

ONE STEP FURTHER

You can use a command-line version of MBSA, mbsacli.exe, to script scans. The results can be placed in a database for analysis. An article that provides simple instructions for doing so can be found in my article "Auditing Patch Management" at http://mcpmag.com/columns/article.asp?EditorialsID=531&whichpage=2&pagesize=10.

Part IV

How to Succeed at Hardening Your Windows Systems

Chapter 14

Harden WetWare

WetWare is an expression commonly used to describe the people part of an information system. It's the successful combination of software, hardware, and WetWare that makes or breaks any IT project. Information security does not escape this truism. To harden Windows systems, you must harden WetWare. Specifically, here are three reasons for hardening WetWare.

First, while it is possible to construct technology controls that do not give people any choice but to use them, it is impossible to implement a technology control that will always be impervious to directed attack. Furthermore, the more technology users resent the security controls or find them difficult, the more they will attempt to avoid using them, or to subvert them.

- If passwords are required for authentication and users must use one in order to access resources important to their job, the users will use as simple a password as they can. If they are forced to use complex passwords, they will write them down. If you remove all copies of their password, they will "borrow" someone else's account and password if that will work, and so on.

- If you create the strongest defenses that are known to peoplekind, you can bet that some enterprising individual will eventual subvert them, or social-engineer their way around them.

Next, before you can make many of the changes recommended in this book, you will need management approval. You will need approval to purchase firewalls, gateway filters, intrusion detection systems, and additional servers. You will also need management approval to attend security-related conferences and seminars and to develop security awareness campaigns for the rest of your staff, for management, and for all users. Management in many companies traditionally has not recognized the value of information security. Even if they do, you may find yourself at odds with the organization's implementation.

Finally, you have only to discuss information security with your own peers and with IT management to discern the lack of security activity and to see the disparity between what people say and what they themselves do, along with the huge differences of opinion among rational, intelligent, experienced IT personnel over issues of information security.

To harden Windows systems, we must harden the people who use them, and that includes management, the user population, and IT pros. You can be successful at doing this, but there are great obstacles in your way. Here are some tools that will assist you.

Vet and Improve Security Policy

Without an information security policy, your organization's security status will always be subject to the will of those who can dictate security, because they control access to resources, or to the lowest common denominator. This is in stark contrast to the way things were when information systems first became a part of business.

Long before PCs and networks, data processing resources were primarily located in the data center and strictly controlled. Management, in many cases, bowed to the will of those in control of the data center for many reasons, but one of them was the lack of choice. Mini-computers, sometimes referred to as mid-range computers, empowered departments and divisions to break off and control access to their own data and data processing. Think of this as you would a kingdom spread across much territory. The lord of some distant land, though still paying tribute to the king, controls his own area. Still, the control over information systems was under the control of those who owned and managed them. Information security could be dictated as well.

Today, however, this is quite often not the case. Few organizations maintain control and enforce security by ownership alone. Instead, every desktop computer can become the processing center for critical operations. Every user can control the flow of information and destroy it by clicking an attachment.

This book, and others in the series, sets forth strategies and illustrates technical controls that can improve the security posture of your information systems. In most cases, however, implementation of these controls requires something other than technical knowledge. Information security policy is the wedge that can be used to leverage your technical knowledge into actual controls.

Determine Current Information System Security Policy

Do you have a current policy? Many organizations do. In fact, many times when participating in an IT audit, I've found that a policy does exist, but IT pros may be unaware of it. The first step in creating good information system security policy is to find out what already exists. If you look, you may find that there may be three policies: the written policy, the rules that everyone believes constitute the policy, and the way things are actually done. All of these must be identified before any changes can be made.

While codifying the current policy, determine how policy changes are made, and how the information is distributed. In many organizations there is a committee that meets periodically to review policy. If this is so in your organization, get the names of the members of this committee, and when and where it meets. Don't forget to find out what these people do. What are their titles? Where do they fall in the power structure of the organization? What do they know about technology, and what is their stance on information security? This information will be useful to you later if you seek to make changes, or even if you just want to see current policy enforced.

Evaluate Policy

Once you have determined the security policy, written or otherwise, you must evaluate it against the security process that you believe is correct. You may find that policy supports your opinion, is close to it, or is totally opposed. If policy supports your opinion but is not followed, your approach to policy will be different than if you find that it's totally opposed. Can you, for example, simply draw attention to the lack of policy enforcement and work toward change, or will that simply get you fired? At this point, in the evaluation stage, the best action is no action. You have a lot more studying to do.

Note, too, the good things in the policy. In addition to support for your security beliefs, you will find many items that speak to information security that you have not even thought about. Information security is a very old profession (in every culture, ancient stories talk about secrets and how they were revealed), and people have had a long time to experiment and learn from mistakes. The people who wrote the policy may not agree entirely with you, may not know networks or Windows, but they probably know the principles of information security.

Once you have a broad understanding of the entire policy, look for an area that both needs to be changed and falls within your area of expertise. You will have far more success if you are perceived as the technology expert, and if you start with a specific area. Proclaiming the entire policy in need of immediate rewriting is a good way to end your career as a policy writer.

Participate in Security Policy Creation and Maintenance

For many organizations, there are formal procedures to be followed when proposing policy changes. In others, change proposal is less formal. Alternatively, there may be a formal procedure to be followed, but real change is accomplished by using the less-formal approach. Find out what works in yours.

If a formal policy and procedure exists, how can you have an impact? That will depend on the procedure. Can any individual make recommendations directly to the committee? Do you need to be sponsored? Find out and start by following procedure.

If policy creation and change is less formal, how is it done? Again, even though it may not be written down, there is a process. Find it and start by following it.

If no written policy exists, your job may be harder or easier. The climate today supports formal information security policy and programs. New laws dictate requirements for privacy and security and even for the reporting of incidents. Analysts predict that the enforcement of laws will intensify and major law suits over information security breaches are just around the corner. Viruses and worms have crippled the networks of companies that have little security and even those that have some. For these reasons and more, you may find receptiveness to new information security initiatives such as policy writing that require little in the way of expenditure.

If you are successful at generating interest in a written policy, you may find yourself in charge of writing it. Is this something you want? Or would you rather simply be one of many who contributed to the process?

Policies, Standards, Guidelines, and Procedures

Before you attempt to write a policy, you should understand what a policy really is. Though there is some difference of opinion, and certainly many organizations use different approaches, the following definitions are generally accepted by information security professionals:

- Policies describe how management feels information assets should be protected. Policies do not dictate which type of VPN to use to protect remote communications; instead, policies state that remote communications will be protected.

- Standards set mandatory rules for policy implementation. The standard, for example, might state that all remote communications will be authenticated and encrypted. Standards are often included as part of the policy document.

- Guidelines suggest, or recommend, how the standards can be met. If VPNs are used, remote communications can be both authenticated and encrypted. Alternatively, dial-up communications can be authenticated and encrypted even if they are not tunneled. The guidelines might make the use of VPNs optional, or even specify when each recommendation might be used. The actual decision on which products to use may be based on research that compares products for their ability to securely fulfill the guidelines and meet other requirements such as performance, ease of use, reliability, compatibility, or cost.

- Procedures are written to specifically dictate how the policy, including its standards and guidelines, will be implemented, used, and maintained. They are, of course, dependent on the products and processes selected. While policies are an upper management decision, and guidelines and standards are set by management, many procedures are process intensive and also require technical expertise. Someone who understands technology, information security, and the policy, however, should review procedures. An inadvertent omission or modification or even malicious perversion can change the actual implementation.

How to Write a Policy

If you are called on to write a policy, the process is really quite simple. Write simple, forceful statements. Leave out technical details. Remember that in addition to the policy, you will need to recommend standards and guidelines, and that procedures will be written as a separate process, after the decision on which products and activities will be needed to implement and comply with the policy. If you find it difficult to get started, use the Prairie Home Companion method.

The Prairie Home Companion method is named after the stories told during a popular public radio show by the same name. The stories are told as if they are little snippets of life as it is in a small rural town in Minnesota. Each story appears to wander and twist across the lives of interesting people, and every story ends with a simple statement that is the lesson. As you listen to the story, you may be totally unaware of how it will end, or what the lesson is, but there always is one. If you can't seem to get your policy statement, your message, down, try the same approach: simply write down everything you think is necessary, and then try to break out the standards, guidelines, and procedures. You will be left with the policy or perhaps be better able to state, in a sentence or two, the broad summation of what you have written.

TIP   A good tutorial on writing policies is Scott Barman's book *Writing Information Security Policies* (New Riders, 2001).

Many organizations develop security policies by developing a single comprehensive document. This is probably the most difficult way to do so. Instead, consider framing your security policy as a collection of policies that when organized and published represents the current security policy. This modular approach allows you to get a policy in place without the tedious and frustrating process of getting everyone to agree on everything. You can actually make your first security policy the one that describes how security policy will be developed and modified. This can start with a simple line such as this:

"The information systems security policy will consist of many smaller policies that specifically address security issues, or define how policies are developed, approved, enforced, modified, and retired."

Note that this policy does not state who develops the policies, or exactly how.

When writing a policy, make it simple, formal, and commanding. Use simple sentences that convey only the important message. When I say formal, what do I mean? Most people think here about legal statements, constitutions, legal code, that nasty little licensing agreement, the EULA, on a Microsoft software product. That's not it at all. Instead, simply say what you mean. You can give the words the power or formality by using forceful, commandment-style words such as "shall" and "shall not." Yep, I did say "commandment." If you think of the words that are used in the ten commandments, you'll get the idea. "Thou shall not kill." No question there. Formal, commanding, a rule that must be followed. You can learn to write this way with practice. Here are some more examples:

- "The data center shall be located in the center of the building away from windows."

- "A user ID shall consist of the first initial and last name of the employee. Duplications shall be resolved by appending a number."

- "An employee remotely accessing ABC's network shall follow ABC's established security policies and procedures."

- "The Information Security Committee shall define acceptable services accessible through the Internet. This committee will periodically review business needs and adjust the policy accordingly."

- "No user will access the Internet without first attending a training session that explains company Internet usage policy, and the user's responsibility while online."

- "All incoming and outgoing e-mail shall be scanned for viruses and other malicious content and for executable attachments. Executable attachments shall be removed."

- "All software development shall include data entry validation."

- "Software developers shall not write their own encryption algorithms, nor code well-known encryption algorithms where prewritten and tested work is available."

Learn to Speak Business

You'll have to learn to speak business because management is not going to learn to speak Geek. To speak business simply means to express security concerns in the context of business value. Instead of complaining that passwords are weak and therefore you need to implement smart cards, learn to identify the impact such a change will have on business and state it showing net business value. If you have trouble thinking what the business value is, just think money.

Will the change cost money? Will it save money over time? Will it prevent the expenditure of money? Does it keep employees and equipment in full operation and therefore not waste the money paid to them and for them? Does it prevent fines? Will the company's stock market price increase?

This does not mean that reasons such as fair treatment, civic duty, and legislative imperatives are not considered during business decision making. It simply means that you cannot invoke these as the prime reason for making changes. Unless, of course, you can show how failing to follow these "good" initiatives can cost the company money—see the later section "Understand Current Laws."

If your organization is governmental, or nonprofit, money still plays a role, but there may be other factors that appear to be more important. Learn what those factors are, and you will find selling security much easier. The more that you learn about how a business or other organization operates, the easier it will be for you to present your security initiatives with emphasis on the things that will make management see their value. The following items are examples of how to show the business value for security products and processes. Be sure to fully develop both the costs and benefits of any security initiative.

- Getting dollars for purchasing and implementing gateway filters for e-mail may be an easier sell if you can show how much was lost due to business interruption and cleanup during the last worm attack.

- Providing licenses for antiviral and antispyware products to employees for use at home can be demonstrated to be of good value because connections from home can introduce malware into the organization's network.

- Following generally accepted security principles, including the implementation of information security policies, procedures, and products, is generally believed to be evidence of compliance with some of the new legislation, such as the Sarbanes-Oxley Act. This legislation carries stiff fines and jail time for C-level officers of a noncomplaint organization.

- Purchasing and implementing wireless infrastructure that can authenticate and encrypt communications can be shown to be necessary to prevent confidential information leakage. Leakage of specific sensitive information may result in theft of trade secrets, stock market plunges, and other business-crippling responses.

Take the First Step

IT and the rest of the organization have often been at odds. Management sees IT as a service that costs money but does not make any. Users see IT as those snobbish, geeky technical people who can't speak like normal people and constantly frustrate them and otherwise make it difficult for them to do their job. IT pros have often worshiped technology for technology's sake, with little regard to the reason that technology exists within a business. They have often felt misunderstood and often can't understand why technology is so difficult for the rest of the world.

I apologize to those of you who do not see yourself in this picture. These may be stereotypes, but they do represent common ideas, ideas that you are going to have to surmount if you wish to secure your networks. Just as management won't buy in to security technology just because you are passionate about information security, most people won't follow new ways of doing things because it's the way you are supposed to or because someone dictates it.

In order to develop a culture of security within your organization, you will have to take the first step. You will have to learn to discuss technology so that others can understand it, or at least you must not adopt a condescending attitude.

Understand Current Laws

Laws can support your security programs, and laws can hamper their development. To understand how to use them to improve security and how to avoid finding yourself arrested for breaking them, you will need to learn what they are, and how they impact you. The information provided here should not be considered legal advice; you will want to consult your organization's legal staff, read the laws and public discussion of them, and perhaps consult your own legal advisors.

Rules to Live By

The first legal issue you must deal with is your authority for the activity that you perform when using your organization's IT resources and its information. Use the following points as guidelines.

Do Not Abuse Your Authority

Just because you have the ability to do something does not give you the right to do it. As an administrator, programmer, or privileged user, you may be granted specific rights on the network. They may be explicitly tailored to your duties, may inadvertently give you more privileges than you need, or may give you the ability to perform some activity if, and only if, it is required and approved.

You may have the ability, for example, if you gave no permissions on a document, to take ownership of a document, give yourself read permission, and read the document. This doesn't mean you should. In many organizations, data is organized into classifications that dictate who can access it and how it should be handled. Sensitive documents about the financial status of a corporation, for example, are not typically made available to all employees. Even publicly traded companies do not make data available before the public release of quarterly statements. If that information is present on computers and in databases that you have access to, that access does not provide you with the right to read it.

You can easily obtain powerful password-cracking software and have the necessary access to password databases to use them. You may even feel—and many would agree— that using such a tool to audit compliance with security policy is something that should be periodically done. However, without management approval, you should not perform such an audit. Even with management approval, you need to set up stringent controls over the procedure and its results.

You may want to test the defenses of your network, or determine if a specific patch really closes a vulnerability. However, your penetration test may be perceived as an attack and therefore get you fired or even arrested, or it may crash critical systems and cause business interruption and even loss of life.

There are many similar activities; activities that you have the ability to do but shouldn't, and activities that may even be considered good security practice but might also be considered as attacks. Your job is not to blindly assume that technical capability = authority.

Get Written Authority

What, then, should you do? Can you trust your instincts, do what others do, assume oral approval will suffice? The best practice, when it comes to understanding what you should or shouldn't do, and what might get you fired or arrested, is to have your administrative duties clearly defined in writing. This is where policy and all its standards and guidelines can come into play. This is where written procedure, not just the "how to" but the "when to," provides a solid path. This is where job descriptions that spell out your duties are priceless. If you don't have these things, you need to work toward getting them.

Meanwhile, before engaging in some activity that might be considered an attack on your systems, or that might appear to be legally wrong, but that is, you believe, part of your job, obtain written authority. For example, obtain written authority to perform periodic password audits, pentests, or other intrusive activity.

Current Legislation Snapshots

Knowledge of current legislation that affects IT is important for three reasons. First, you should know what is a computer crime in order to plan your response. You will want to know what intrusions you should document and keep evidence on and what not to do—an overly aggressive response to perceived criminal action, or the use of intrusive security applications, can land you, the IT administrator, in trouble with the law. Your knowledge of the law can also help in referring to law enforcement. It might also help in determining if the event should be approached as a civil or a criminal offense. Second, you should be aware of your organization's legal responsibilities, as they may impact how your job is done, what information is archived, and where your organization may need to adapt to comply with the law. Finally, an understanding of the law can help you in obtaining a more comprehensive security policy; the purchase of products, software, and training related to security; and the recognition of the importance of security. The following snapshots present information on laws in the United States. If you work in a different country, other laws will apply. Regardless of your residence, or the location of your organization, international laws may affect the way you do business, including the way you secure that businesses data.

The Gramm-Leach-Bliley Act

The Gramm-Leach-Bliley Act (GLB) requires financial institutions to implement a security program that safeguards customer information. Several federal agencies have authority over financial institutions, and each has its own standards. For example, the Federal Trade Commission Safeguard Rule requires that a financial institution

- Designate employee(s) to coordinate information security to ensure accountability.

- Perform an assessment of risks to customer information, which must include risks posed in all operational areas, such as employee training, management, and information systems in addition to threats from attack and as the result of intrusion response.

- Design and implement safeguards to control the risks and monitor the effectiveness of these safeguards.

- Select service providers that maintain appropriate safeguards and include safeguard requirements in the service provider contract.

- Evaluate and adjust information security programs on the basis of the results of monitoring.

The Health Insurance Portability and Accountability Act

The Health Insurance Portability and Accountability Act (HIPAA) extends provisions similar to those of the GLB to the health care industry and requires the protection of health-related personal information that is maintained electronically by health plans, health care clearing houses, and health care providers. Specifically, they must

- Implement "appropriate administrative, technical, and physical safeguards."
- Perform risk assessment and adopt security measures to mitigate risks.
- Ensure confidentiality, integrity, and availability of electronic personal information.
- Protect against reasonably anticipated threats or hazards to information systems.
- Protect against information disclosure.
- Ensure the organization's workforce complies with the rule.
- Have written policies and procedure to prevent, detect, contain, and correct security violations. Policies must include employee sanctions.
- Institute emergency contingency plan and security awareness training.
- Provide physical safeguards, including workstation security, access control, and authentication.
- Use written contracts with business associates that specify protection of transmitted information.

The Sarbanes-Oxley Act

The Sarbanes-Oxley Act requires that the annual reports of publicly traded companies contain an internal control report that indicates management's responsibility for establishing and maintaining adequate internal controls, for financial reporting, and for assessing how effective these controls are. Criminal penalties for inaccurate reporting can be given to officers of the company. Internal controls include risk assessment and monitoring and are further defined as those controls that safeguard assets, allow reliable financial reports, and allow compliance with laws and regulations.

California Section 1798.82

This act requires that all who do business in California disclose to California residents information security breeches that affect their nonpublic information. It does not require the entity to actually have a physical presence in California.

The Computer Fraud and Abuse Act

The Computer Fraud and Abuse Act (CFAA, Title 18 U.S.C. Section 1030) is designed to protect data and systems. It seeks to punish people whose unauthorized access to computers causes harm. In addition to direct intrusion, the act also covers harm as the result of denial of service attacks, viruses, worms, and so on. Specifically, it defines prohibited acts as

- Unauthorized access to information protected for national security reasons
- Unauthorized access to confidential information on the Internet
- Unauthorized access to nonpublic government computers
- Unauthorized access of a protected computer to commit or further the commission of fraud
- Intentional acts that cause damage to computers
- Trafficking in passwords that affect interstate commerce or government computers
- Threats to cause damage to a protected computer for purposes of extortion

A protected computer was once narrowly defined as one used by a financial institution, by the United States Government, or in interstate or foreign commerce or communication. In 1996, this definition was broadened to include any computer used in interstate commerce, and in 2001, the Patriot Act included computers that might be located outside the United States but that affect U.S. interstate commerce. In essence, it now represents just about every computer.

Two key concepts are necessary to invoke prosecution under the law: damage and unauthorized access. Unauthorized access is defined not only as trespass (that is, you go where you have no authority) but also excess of authorization. Excess of authorization includes elevation of privileges, for example, an ordinary user with authority to access your network is able to obtain administrative privileges. It also includes cases where the administrator of a system or network exceeds her designated administrative authority on that system. Damage is any impairment to the integrity or availability of data, programs, or systems. Some parts of the act define evidence of damage as the loss of at least $5,000, while other parts of the act exclude any monetary requirement. Monetary amounts are not required as evidence of damage if any of these things occur:

- Modification or potential modification to the medical diagnosis, treatment, or care of one or more individuals
- Physical injury
- A threat to public health or safety
- Damage to computer systems used by government for administration of justice, national defense, or national security

---

TIP   To calculate loss, include the cost of incident response, damage assessment, restoration of data or systems, and loss of revenue due to interruption of service.

Penalties for violation of the act depend on whether the provision is a misdemeanor or a felony, and whether or not this is a first offense. A misdemeanor, for example, is punishable by a maximum sentence of one year in prison, while a felony is punishable by a five-year maximum sentence and $250,000 fine. Civil action may also be taken if the damage is at least $5,000.

NOTE   One interpretation of the act does not see hacks for access, such as the unauthorized use of a wireless network, as a violation unless loss of $5,000 can be demonstrated. However, the act does cover things such as the intentional release of viruses and worms, denial of service attacks, and damage to systems.

Two important modifications to the law by the Patriot Act are that the law can now punish an attempt to commit any of the prohibited acts and that the act cannot be invoked for negligent design of hardware or software.

Federal Wiretap Law

Federal wiretap law punishes unauthorized interception of electronic communication in transport, including interception of e-mail while in transport.

Economic Espionage Act

The Economic Espionage Act punishes criminal theft of trade secrets, copyright and trademark infringement, of a product involved in interstate commerce with knowledge or intent that the owner of the secret would suffer injury.

Possession of child pornography is also punishable, if you knowingly receive it, or if you hold it for a long period of time without deleting it; to avoid breaking the law, an organization must take prompt action to delete or report to authorities any child pornography found on their computer systems.

The Electronic Communications Privacy Act

The Electronic Communications Privacy Act (ECPA) forbids unauthorized people from accessing or damaging electronic messages in transit and in storage. Electronic messages are defined as e-mail, instant messaging, and even keystrokes. The act specifies that such access is criminal if it is intentional and involves unauthorized interception or disclosure. It also covers the act of attempting to intercept or disclose such information and knowingly using or endeavoring to use the information. Unauthorized use of packet sniffers and keystroke loggers is covered under this law.

HEADS UP!

IT is often required to monitor electronic communication; you should understand when you are authorized to do so and when you are not.

Exceptions to the law are, of course, law enforcement, self-defense, and consent. As a provider, self-defense is defined as actions, during the normal course of employment, necessary for the protection of rights or property of the provider of service. An acceptable use banner, an acceptable use policy, or employee handbook documentation may indicate consent. Banners, for example, can warn that a legal boundary is crossed by proceeding beyond that point. If this kind of advanced notice is given and an unauthorized person attempts to and succeeds in gaining access, it is easier to show that the intrusion was with wrongful intent.

The Homeland Security Act modifies this act to include the provision that if the breech is committed for purpose of commercial advantage or gain, results in malicious destruction, or is a criminal act, then the violation is a felony.

Understand Vulnerabilities of Windows and Other OSs

In order to properly secure your systems, you must continue to seek out knowledge of Windows vulnerabilities and how to mitigate them. You must also, however, become knowledgeable about the vulnerabilities of other OSs. You will often find that you need to be able to intelligently and without passion discuss this information. You may find that many would seek to prevent the use of Windows systems, for security reasons. You might, for example, wish to implement a Windows-based VPN or install a firewall on a Windows server and find many arguments against this based on the opinion that Windows cannot be secured. You will find that many of these same people have no real knowledge, or you may find them extremely knowledgeable.

In order to best promote security, you will need to be able to provide honest and accurate information in response to questions or accusations of security problems. For example, someone may voice the opinion that Windows systems lack authentication. If you are knowledgeable about the ins and outs of authentication on all Windows systems, you will be able to present correct information. Many such accusations are the result of the individual's only Windows experience being with Windows 98. You may find that rational discussion explaining authentication in Windows systems based on NT technologies may help the individual to change her opinion, but even more benefit may be obtained because others listening may be stimulated to seek knowledge instead of repeating the accusations of others.

If you understand that there are vulnerabilities in other operating systems, you will also be better equipped to approach information security as an all-encompassing necessity, and not just from the perspective of the Windows network. This mature response does much to advance your standing in management's eyes.

Know and Incorporate Voluntary Standards

There is no single law or standard that sets down the rights and wrongs of information security in a way that everyone can agree upon. However, there are voluntary standards that seek to express best practices, and much work is proceeding in an attempt to codify information security.

ISO 17799

ISO 17799, or the "Code of Practice for Information Security Management," is an international standard that recommends practices for information security management. It evolved from the British national standard BS 7799. The standard provides information on ten areas:

- **Policy**   There must be one and it should have the approval and support of management.

- **Organizational security**   Infosec should be managed according to a formal management framework that establishes how policy is approved, how roles are defined, and how security is implemented.

- **Asset classification and control**   Information should be classified and access controlled on the basis of that classification.

- **Personnel security**   Protect against user error, fraud, intentional abuse. Security issues should be addressed starting at recruitment and continuing past termination.

- **Physical and environmental security**   Protect from chemical spill, natural disaster such as storms and earthquake, unauthorized physical access.

- **Communications and operations management**   Provide documentation, incident response, planning, logging, network controls, e-mail security.

- **Access control**   Provide requirements for authentication, define authorization.

- **System development**   Secure the development lifecycle, including secure coding, protection of software code, management of the process, maintenance, use of test data.

- **Business continuity management**   Provide plans for dealing with any threat.

- **Compliance**   Document how compliance will be monitored, how enforcement will be obtained, and the penalty for noncompliance.

TIP   Read more about ISO 17799 at www.iso17799-web.com and purchase a copy of the standard at www.iso17799.net.

The National Strategy to Secure Cyberspace

The U.S. National Strategy to Secure Cyberspace is a collection of best practices and a call to develop a culture of security. It asks that all those who are responsible for electronically stored information ensure that it is properly protected. This is not legislation, just a call for voluntary compliance.

Start or Participate in Security Awareness Education

You cannot make security babes out of ordinary users. However, you can improve the status of security within your organization and within the world by developing and participating in security awareness education. Organizations that have spent time educating users in how to identify unusual activity, how to avoid being socially engineered, and not to open attachments have benefited from fewer successful intrusions and less damage due to virus and worm attacks.

Security awareness and user involvement cannot, by themselves, secure information networks and the data they store and transmit. However, security awareness can make major improvements—security awareness that explains why, as well as how, to secure information and computer systems, that improves compliance, and that begins the establishment of an organizational culture of security.

Security Awareness Objectives

The foremost objective of a security awareness program must be to raise the level of information security awareness of every individual in the company to the point where their actions bear witness. Just as advertisers sell a product and count their success in sales, you are selling a set of behavioral modifications and can count success when you see it happening.

It is good practice to state your goals for the program and provide measurable objectives. In addition, categorize your audience, specify the information you will include in the program, and describe how employees will benefit. These are goals to include:

- Participation by all employees, contractors, and business partners
- Programs for new employees and refresher programs

- Management support as evidenced by providing time for employees to participate

- Evidence of participation and understanding, including a signed statement from employees that they understand policies, the information provided, and what their responsibilities are

- Assignments to individuals to provide security awareness programs and/or contractual arrangements with outside providers

- Increased compliance with security policy, for example, the use of more complex passwords that can be tested by documenting average time to crack them and how this changes over time

Operations

Many different types of activities can make up a security awareness program. These include meetings; online information; videos and other instructional media; posters; imprints on notepads, pens, and the like; contests; and demonstrations. There is an endless stream of subject matter that can be presented in numerous ways. Topics for discussion may include items such as

- Privacy of customer and personnel information

- Impact of DoS attacks

- What malware is and how to prevent it from doing damage

- Software vulnerabilities and how the organization is mitigating them

- Social engineering

- How the risk one employee takes can impact the function of the entire network

- Incidents and their cost, including financial data and impact on job security

- How to recognize and report security incidents

- How to securely use current information systems, including desktop systems and remote connections

- How to protect data on laptops

- How to manage wireless networks

- How to create strong passwords and how to manage them

Appendix

Resources

- Required Reading
- Tool Downloads
- Security Bulletins and Discussion Lists

Where should you go from here? What else do you need to know? How can you learn more? It's tempting to provide you with a thousand links to information on the Internet, suggest you read a hundred good books, get to know a dozen top experts. But what good would that really do? Some of the links might change, books be out of print, experts be unavailable. Instead, here are my lists of the most essential articles, tools, and security lists.

Required Reading

You must be thoroughly familiar with the concepts and ideas discussed in these articles. Some are long, and some are short, and some come with helpful templates and tools. Get them, print them out, study them.

- **Certificate authorities**   The capolicy.inf file can be used to define the CA policy. Examples are provided at the following site:

  www.microsoft.com/technet/prodtechnol/windowsserver2003/technologies/ security/ws3pkibp.mspx

- **Desktop roles**   One example of predefined desktop roles is outlined in a Microsoft white paper, accompanied by sample GPOs and a script that can be used to implement a test environment. Microsoft calls its desktop roles "common desktop scenarios." Download this documentation and the GPOs from this site:

  www.microsoft.com/downloads/details.aspx?FamilyID=354b9f45-8aa6-4775- 9208-c681a7043292&DisplayLang=en

- **Disaster recovery**   The "Active Directory Disaster Recovery" paper found at this site contains information about recovering Active Directory:

  www.microsoft.com/technet/prodtechnol/windows2000serv/technologies/ activedirectory/support/adrecov.mspx#XSLTsection126121120120

- **Internet Explorer (IE) management policy**   For an example of a good server IE management policy, examine the paper on Windows Server 2003 Enhanced Security Configuration at the following site, which is accompanied by VB scripts and sample IE .adm files:

  www.microsoft.com/downloads/details.aspx?FamilyID=d41b036c-e2e1-4960- 99bb-9757f7e9e31b&DisplayLang=en

- **Security checklists**   Checklists for baseline security are available here:

  www.microsoft.com/technet/security

- **Security settings** The paper "Threats and Countermeasures: Security Settings in Windows Server 2003 and Windows XP," located at this site, details every security setting":

  www.microsoft.com/downloads/details.aspx?displaylang=en&familyid=1b6acf93-147a-4481-9346-f93a4081eea8

- **Windows forests** When defining administrative roles for Windows forests for Windows 2000 and Windows Server 2003, use the document "Best Practices for Delegating Active Directory Administration," located at this site:

  www.microsoft.com/downloads/details.aspx?FamilyID=29dbae88-a216-45f9-9739-cb1fb22a0642&displaylang=en

- **Window Server 2003 security** The "Windows Server 2003 Security Guide," located at this site, provides templates and instructions for securing Windows Server 2003:

  www.microsoft.com/downloads/details.aspx?displaylang=en&familyid=8a2643c1-0685-4d89-b655-521ea6c7b4db

- **Windows Time Service (Windows Server 2003)** Information about Windows Time Service in Windows Server 2003 can be found at this site:

  www.microsoft.com/technet/prodtechnol/windowsserver2003/technologies/security/ws03mngd/26_s3wts.mspx

- **Windows Time Service (Windows 2000 Service Pack 4)** Information about Windows Time Service post Windows 2000 Service Pack 4 can be found at this site:

  www.microsoft.com/technet/prodtechnol/windows2000pro/maintain/w2kmngd/16_2kwts.mspx

- **Windows 2000 security** The "Windows 2000 Security Operations Guide," located here, provides security settings and templates for Windows 2000:

  www.microsoft.com/downloads/details.aspx?displaylang=en&familyid=f0b7b4ee-201a-4b40-a0d2-cdd9775aeff8

- **Windows XP security** The "Windows XP Security Guide," located at this site, provides instructions and templates that can be used to secure Windows XP:

  www.microsoft.com/downloads/details.aspx?displaylang=en&familyid=2d3e25bc-f434-4cc6-a5a7-09a8a229f118

TIP Read more about ISO 17799 at www.iso17799-web.com, and purchase a copy of the standard at www.iso17799.net.

Tool Downloads

Microsoft provides many security tools. The most important ones are listed here:

- **Dsrevoke tool**   You can download this tool and instructions for using it (dsrevoke.doc) here:

  www.microsoft.com/downloads/details.aspx?FamilyID=77744807-c403-4bda-b0e4-c2093b8d6383&displaylang=en

- **Group Policy Management Console (GPMC)**   You can download this tool for simplifying Group Policy management here:

  www.microsoft.com/downloads/details.aspx?FamilyId=C355B04F-50CE-42C7-A401-30BE1EF647EA&displaylang=en

- **Internet Explorer Administration Kit (IEAK)**   This product, a set of tools that can be used to deploy and administer IE, is free and can be obtained by ordering the CD-ROM or downloading the product from this site:

  www.microsoft.com/windows/ieak/downloads/default.asp

NOTE   IEAK and its license are free, but you must be licensed to use the product to distribute IE.

- **Microsoft Baseline Security Analyzer**   You can download this tool here:

  www.microsoft.com/downloads/details.aspx?FamilyID=8b7a580d-0c91-45b7-91ba-fc47f7c3d6ad&DisplayLang=en

- **Software Update Services (SUS)**   Download SUS from this site:

  www.microsoft.com/downloads/details.aspx?FamilyID=a7aa96e4-6e41-4f54-972c-ae66a4e4bf6c&DisplayLang=en

Security Bulletins and Discussion Lists

You can read Microsoft's security bulletins online at www.microsoft.com/technet/security/default.mspx. Other online resources are security discussion lists. Many of these also include the Microsoft security bulletins or provide links to them. In addition, you will find other, unofficial vulnerability notices, discussions of problems installing patches and service packs, and other security topics on these sites:

- **bugtrac** A moderated list for security information, bugtrac can be read or subscribed to at www.securityfocus.com/archive/1.

- **Full-Disclosure** Subscribe to this nonmoderated vulnerability list at lists.netsys.com/mailman/listinfo/full-disclosure.

- **ntbugtrac** A Windows-specific Security list, sign up for ntbugtrac at www.ntbugtraq.com/.

- **Security Watch** Subscribe to my weekly security column at www.mcpmag.com.

Index

M

Q

S

INTERNATIONAL CONTACT INFORMATION

AUSTRALIA
McGraw-Hill Book Company
Australia Pty. Ltd.
TEL +61-2-9900-1800
FAX +61-2-9878-8881
http://www.mcgraw-hill.com.au
books-it_sydney@mcgraw-hill.com

CANADA
McGraw-Hill Ryerson Ltd.
TEL +905-430-5000
FAX +905-430-5020
http://www.mcgraw-hill.ca

**GREECE, MIDDLE EAST, & AFRICA
(Excluding South Africa)**
McGraw-Hill Hellas
TEL +30-210-6560-990
TEL +30-210-6560-993
TEL +30-210-6560-994
FAX +30-210-6545-525

MEXICO (Also serving Latin America)
McGraw-Hill Interamericana Editores
S.A. de C.V.
TEL +525-1500-5108
FAX +525-117-1589
http://www.mcgraw-hill.com.mx
carlos_ruiz@mcgraw-hill.com

SINGAPORE (Serving Asia)
McGraw-Hill Book Company
TEL +65-6863-1580
FAX +65-6862-3354
http://www.mcgraw-hill.com.sg
mghasia@mcgraw-hill.com

SOUTII AFRICA
McGraw-Hill South Africa
TEL +27-11-622-7512
FAX +27-11-622-9045
robyn_swanepoel@mcgraw-hill.com

SPAIN
McGraw-Hill/
Interamericana de España, S.A.U.
TEL +34-91-180-3000
FAX +34-91-372-8513
http://www.mcgraw-hill.es
professional@mcgraw-hill.es

**UNITED KINGDOM, NORTHERN,
EASTERN, & CENTRAL EUROPE**
McGraw-Hill Education Europe
TEL +44-1-628-502500
FAX +44-1-628-770224
http://www.mcgraw-hill.co.uk
emea_queries@mcgraw-hill.com

ALL OTHER INQUIRIES Contact:
McGraw-Hill/Osborne
TEL +1-510-420-7700
FAX +1-510-420-7703
http://www.osborne.com
omg_international@mcgraw-hill.com

Bulletproof your systems before you are hacked

The Hardening series shows you how

Hardening Windows® Systems
Roberta Bragg
0-07-225354-1
$39.99

Hardening Linux
John H. Terpstra, Paul Love, Ron Reck,
Geoff Silver, Tim Scanlon
0-07-225497-1
$39.99

Hardening Network Infrastructure
Wesley J. Noonan
0-07-225502-1
$39.99

Hardening Code
Nishchal Bhalla & Kartik Trivedi
0-07-225651-6
$39.99